the
Jammu
fox

A Biography of
Maharaja Gulab Singh
of Kashmir
1792-1857

by Bawa Satinder Singh

SOUTHERN ILLINOIS UNIVERSITY PRESS
Carbondale and Edwardsville

Feffer & Simons, Inc.
London and Amsterdam

Library of Congress Cataloging in Publication Data

Bawa Satinder Singh, 1932–
 The Jammu Fox; a biography of Maharaja Gulab Singh
of Kashmir, 1792–1857

 Bibliography: p.
 1. Gulab Singh, Maharaja of Kashmir, 1792–1857.
 Title
DS475.2.G8S56   954′.6′0310924 [B]   73–23023
ISBN 0–8093–0652–2

To Karrie

Contents

Maps

Illustrations [between pages 144–145]

Preface

BEFORE the first quarter of the nineteenth century drew to a close, the British East India Company had emerged as the single most important political power in India. The Mughal empire had long since been in the process of disintegration and India's body politic was in a general state of decay. Most of the Indian rulers had either lost their states to the British or had accepted the Company's suzerainty. There was, however, one notable exception. Ranjit Singh, the versatile Sikh ruler, had succeeded in establishing a vast and powerful kingdom in the northwest at the very time other Indian princes had relinquished or were in the process of relinquishing their sovereignty to the British. But Ranjit Singh's death in 1839 marked the beginning of the end of the Sikh kingdom as well, and one of the late ruler's chief lieutenants, Gulab Singh, a Dogra from Jammu, exploited the situation to advance his own career. Gulab Singh, through ability and foresight on the one hand and intrigue and treachery on the other, helped dismember the Sikh state and, with the blessing of the British, became the Maharaja of Kashmir. This book is a study of this complex, interesting, and doubtlessly controversial man.

In a fictional narrative bearing upon the politics of the Sikh state which appeared during the 1840s, Sir Henry M. Lawrence, a prominent Company official, wrote that "Gulab Singh's history would itself fill a volume," and then added, somewhat wistfully, that "if the public give encouragement, some portions of it may appear."[1] Although Lawrence was never able to fulfil this ambition, some attempts have since been made to write the life story of the Dogra ruler. Unfortunately, most of these biographies seem to have been either officially authorized or politically motivated. As a result the authors of these studies have tended to produce largely partisan and superficial works which fail to satisfy the serious student of history. The first among these is an official chronicle entitled "Gulab Nama," compiled in 1865 by Dewan Kirpa Ram who was then the Prime Minister of Kashmir.[2] It was composed on the orders of Maharaja Ranbir Singh, the son and successor of Gulab Singh. The memoir is written in the typically ornate style of the nineteenth-century Persian writers, and its main purpose was apparently to extol the virtues of Gulab Singh. A second work entitled *The Biography of Maharaja Gulab Singh* was written in 1923 by Pandit Salig Ram Koul, a Kashmir lawyer. Koul wrote the book by consulting merely a handful of sources, including the "Gulab Nama," and penned a very complimentary account of the life of the Dogra leader. However, the most widely known work on the subject was written in 1930 by Sardar K. M. Panikkar under the title *Gulab Singh*.[3] The biography by Sardar Panikkar, a distinguished Indian diplomat and educator who once served as an official in the Kashmir government,[4] is also largely based on a limited number of sources. But Panikkar, though a brilliant writer, deliberately and systematically attempted to distort the true image of the Dogra chief. His book is plainly biased in favor of Gulab Singh, and he seldom takes into consideration both sides of the picture, whether he is dealing with the Dogra leader's service under the Sikhs, his relations with the British, or his reign as the Maharaja. One other biography entitled *The Building of the Jammu and Kashmir State—Being the Achievement of Maharaja Gulab Singh* by Arjun Nath Sapru appeared in the form of a short monograph in 1931. Sapru's narrative differs from those of his predecessors in that it is an independent study and must be considered more scholarly than the biographies by Koul and Panikkar. But his bibliography reveals that he, too, did not have access to many important sources, which perhaps explains the reason for the limited scope of his work. For instance, Sapru makes little or no mention of Gulab Singh's dealings with the Sikhs and the British during the crucial years between 1839 and 1845. Moreover, his examination of the Dogra ruler's career ends essentially in 1846.

Not all accounts of Gulab Singh, however, can be considered adulatory. As a matter of fact, most of the writers outside the state of Kashmir have tended to be quite critical of the Dogra chief. Though no full-fledged anti–Gulab Singh biography has appeared to date, several recent Panjabi authors, while dwelling upon nineteenth-century Sikh history, have described him in very harsh terms.[5] In addition, Gulab Singh's European detractors, many of whom were his contemporaries, also denounced him in the most unflattering language.[6] These critics, whether consciously or otherwise, have failed to provide either a detached or an impartial appraisal of the Dogra ruler.

Gulab Singh has thus been painted by various authors either as an illustrious hero or as a despicable villain. It has, therefore, been my objective to write not only a comprehensive but also a dispassionate account of the life of the Dogra leader who indeed played a significant role in the history of northwestern India during the past century. I have tried to bring into clear focus Gulab Singh's role as a fiefholder, Raja, and Maharaja on the one hand, and as a man, soldier, and politician on the other. This biography is the result of an effort extending over ten years, during which time I have made two extensive trips to India and three to England to broaden my knowledge of the Dogra leader. I have done my best to collect everything pertaining to Gulab Singh, and this study is based largely on the primary sources that I gathered, both unpublished and published. As the bibliography will indicate, I have also been able to utilize hitherto unused original material such as the secret dispatches of Mirza Saif-ud-Din, the private papers in the possession of Mirza Kemal-ud-Din, and the private papers of Lord Henry Hardinge. I have, however, purposely made very cautious use of two nineteenth-century works—the *Memoirs of Alexander Gardner* edited by Hugh Pearse, and *A History of the Reigning Family of Lahore*[7] edited by G. Carmichael Smyth—which have been relied upon rather too readily by various scholars of Sikh history. Serious doubts have been raised as to the reliability of these books.[8] Consequently, I have quoted rarely from them and only when I thought it essential to do so.

I would like to place on record my sincere thanks to the University of Wisconsin, which made it possible for me to go to England and India to collect research data for this book. It is impossible for me to express my deep sense of gratitude to Dr. Cuthbert Collin Davies of Oxford under whom I wrote part of this book as my doctoral dissertation at the University of Wisconsin. Dr. Davies gave me invaluable guidance not only while I was working on the dissertation but also when I was revising and expanding it into its present form. It is also not easy for me to give an adequate expression of my gratitude to my teachers at the University of Wisconsin, Professors Fred H. Harrington and Robert E. Frykenberg, and my good friend, Professor Richard Lowitt of the University of Kentucky, for their constant interest in my work. For counsel and assistance I also feel deeply indebted to Mr. V. S. Suri, former Director of the Panjab State Archives, Patiala; Mr. Hassan Shah, former Principal of Ranbir Singh College, Srinagar; Mr. Mahmud Ahmed, former Director of the Research and Publication Department of the Jammu and Kashmir Government, Srinagar; and Mr. Stanley Sutton, Librarian of the India Office Library, London. I also owe thanks to Mr. Khushwant Singh, Dr. Barkat Rai Chopra, Mr. F. M. Hassnain, Mufti Jalal-ud-Din, and Mr. G. A. Mir for their time and help. In addition, I want to express my heartfelt thanks to Dr. Karan Singh, the great-great-grandson of Gulab Singh, and

Lady Helen Hardinge of Penshurst, for their assistance in securing me access to hitherto unused material. To His Holiness the Dalai Lama, I am grateful for providing me with some insight on Zorawar Singh's invasion of Ladakh and Tibet from the Tibetan point of view. I wish to thank my colleague, Dr. James P. Jones, and my friends, Dr. Stephen Bertman and Mr. Paul George, who read this manuscript and made some valuable suggestions. My warm thanks are due also to my colleagues, Professors William W. Rogers, Donald D. Horward, and Richard A. Bartlett, for their counsel. I also want to thank Mr. James Reese, who made the maps, and Mr. Raymond Frost, who helped prepare the illustrations. Finally, I wish to express my deep debt to my wife, Karrie, to whom this book is affectionately dedicated. Although it is customary for writers to thank their spouses, I must confess that without her abiding enthusiasm in my research and without her sometimes merciless but always valuable criticism, this work could not have been completed. I want, however, to add that for all the evaluations made or errors committed none of those who have assisted me or whose advice I have sought are responsible.

Bawa Satinder Singh

Tallahassee, Florida
February 1973

The Jammu Fox

Genealogical Table of Gulab Singh's Family*

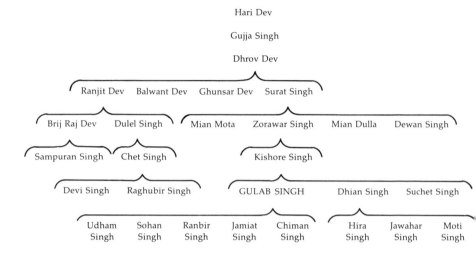

Hari Dev

Gujja Singh

Dhrov Dev

Ranjit Dev   Balwant Dev   Ghunsar Dev   Surat Singh

Brij Raj Dev   Dulel Singh   Mian Mota   Zorawar Singh   Mian Dulla   Dewan Singh

Sampuran Singh   Chet Singh   Kishore Singh

Devi Singh   Raghubir Singh   GULAB SINGH   Dhian Singh   Suchet Singh

Udham Singh   Sohan Singh   Ranbir Singh   Jamiat Singh   Chiman Singh   Hira Singh   Jawahar Singh   Moti Singh

Genealogical Table of Ranjit Singh's Family†

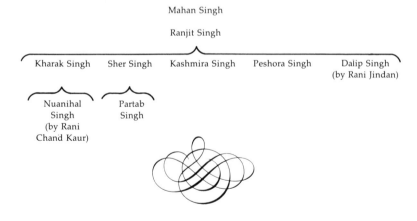

Mahan Singh

Ranjit Singh

Kharak Singh   Sher Singh   Kashmira Singh   Peshora Singh   Dalip Singh (by Rani Jindan)

Nuanihal Singh (by Rani Chand Kaur)   Partab Singh

*This family tree has been prepared with the help of genealogies in "A Journey to Cashmeer," p. 9; Badhrah, "Raj-Darshani," fols. 311/2–312/1; "Gulab Nama," p. 110; J. D. Cunningham, appendix 25; Panikkar, p. 13; Sapru, p. 7; Kahan Singh, p. 197.
†J. D. Cunningham, appendix 24; K. Singh, "Ranjit Singh" (London, 1962), table 1.

1 The Years Under Ranjit Singh

[Gulab Singh] is a man of . . . middle height and
extreme beauty: a superb head, with long, curly black
hair, an aquiline nose of extreme delicacy, great oval
black eyes and a small mouth with perfectly cut
lips.—Victor Jacquemont

"Sometimes when I wished *to frighten a man*," [Gulab
Singh] says, "I had him scalped, *all but a little piece*,
and just as he thought he was *really* going to be killed,
I put his scalp on again, and let him go!" This he
tells with a bland smile, as if talking of peeling
apples.—Herbert Edwardes

GULAB SINGH[1] was born on October 18, 1792.[2] A Hindu,[3] he was descended from one of the numerous Dogra[4] families who had inhabited the Jammu hills for centuries. Although there is no agreement on the actual origin of the Dogras or when they first came to Jammu,[5] it was probably during the decline of the Mughal Empire in the eighteenth century that this region passed under the control of several petty and warring Dogra chieftains. Out of this conflict Gulab Singh's forefathers ultimately emerged victorious.

Raja Hari Dev, a confirmed ancestor of Gulab Singh, held a considerable tract of land in the hills during the seventeenth century.[6] Early in the ensuing century his grandson, Raja Dhrov Dev, occupied the town of Jammu and the surrounding hill territories.[7] Dhrov Dev was succeeded by his son, Ranjit Dev, a brother of Gulab Singh's great-grandfather, Surat Singh (see the genealogical table of the Jammu family). While the fortunes of the collateral branch of his family declined, Ranjit Dev continued to grow more powerful. He ruled as the Raja of Jammu from 1750 to 1781,[8] bringing additional lands under his control and winning the allegiance of the neighboring rulers of Basohli, Bhadarwah, and Kishtwar. Ranjit Dev astutely consolidated his position and enhanced his prestige by aligning himself with Ahmad Shah Abdali,[9] who invaded India several times during the middle of the eighteenth century and established Afghan hegemony over most of northwestern India.

However, with Abdali's death in 1773, Afghan power began to dissipate. By 1790, while Kashmir and Peshawar were still under Afghan control, Sind became independent under the Talpur Amirs and Panjab was carved up among Sikh *misls* (military confederacies). The ambitious chief of one of these *misls*, Mahan Singh, who counted among his supporters the less fortunate branch of the Jammu ruling family led by Surat Singh's son, Mian[10] Mota, raided the hills during the reign of Ranjit Dev.[11] He again attacked during the rule of Ranjit's son, Brij Raj Dev, occupied Jammu, and pillaged the neighboring territories. But the Sikh leader decided not to annex the Dogra kingdom[12] and finally withdrew to Panjab after Brij Raj promised to pay him a yearly tribute.[13]

However, Jammu failed to recover from the pounding delivered by Mahan Singh, and toward the end of the century the Dogra kingdom crumbled into various miniscule states. It was during this period that Gulab Singh's immediate ancestors regained some of their family's lost prestige. His grandfather, Zorawar Singh, and his father, Kishore Singh, managed to acquire the small estates of Dyman and Andarwah, respectively. It was probably at Andarwah that Gulab Singh and his two younger brothers, Dhian Singh and Suchet Singh, were born.[14]

Some doubt has been cast on the true relationship of the three brothers to Ranjit Dev. According to an anonymous nineteenth century historian, the brothers were merely "means, squires or dependants, of the Raja of Jummoo."[15] Godfrey Thomas Vigne, a British traveler, claimed that they were "despised by the lovers of legitimacy."[16] Joseph Davey Cunningham, a captain in the British East India Company's army and author of the highly acclaimed *A History of the Sikhs*,[17] also felt that Gulab Singh's family "was perhaps illegitimate."[18] But none of them cites any evidence which might lend credence to their point of view. In fact, Cunningham's own genealogical table of the Jammu family lists Ranjit Dev as a brother of Surat Singh, and Gulab Singh and his brothers as the latter's direct descendants.[19] Other genealogies also include the three brothers among the bona fide members of Jammu's ruling house.[20]

Gulab Singh, nicknamed Goolanloo,[21] spent most of his childhood on the estates of his father and grandfather. He received no formal education, and a European visitor, who came into close contact with him during 1831, affirmed that Gulab Singh "can neither read nor write."[22] He was raised instead as a warrior, becoming at an early age an accomplished horseman and proficient in the use of sword and gun.[23] His elders also inculcated upon him a yearning to reassert the power of his branch of the Dogra family and to create a new kingdom in the hills under its hegemony.

While Gulab Singh was still a youth the political scene in Panjab underwent a radical change which was to profoundly affect the entire northwest. The end of the eighteenth century witnessed the emergence of Mahan Singh's son, Ranjit, as the most prominent leader among the Sikhs. During the early nineteenth century he systematically destroyed the Sikh *misls* and soon made himself the Maharaja of Panjab. Contemplating further territorial expansion Ranjit Singh looked to Jammu and, encouraged both by his father's example and the continued political divisions among the Dogras, he sent a large force into the hills during 1808. This time, however, the invasion briefly united the feuding Dogras and they jointly

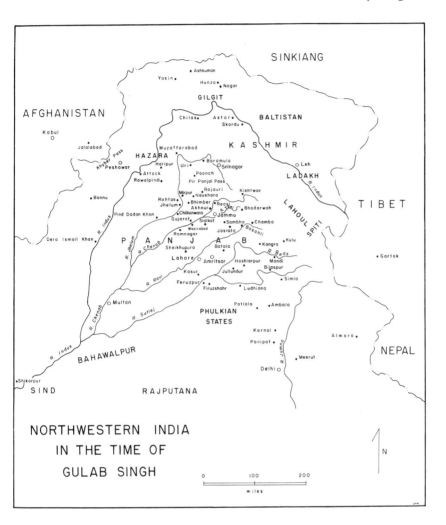

NORTHWESTERN INDIA
IN THE TIME OF
GULAB SINGH

fought against the Sikhs. Gulab Singh himself, though only fifteen, brandished his sword with fiery zeal and leaped into the fray, although he often had to jump from the ground to engage the foe.[24] But such individual gallantry was not enough, and the Dogras were decisively beaten. Jammu thus became a part of the Sikh kingdom.

The Sikh conquest of Jammu shattered Gulab Singh's aspirations and he left home in search of a new life. For months he drifted from place to place looking for employment. He went to Peshawar where Shah Shuja, the deposed Amir of Afghanistan, was collecting an army in an attempt to regain his throne. But instead of enlisting, Gulab Singh returned to the hills and briefly served under the Raja of Kishtwar. In 1809, he determined that his best opportunity now lay in seeking service with the Sikhs. He therefore obtained employment at the Samaj jagir (fief) of Nihal Singh Attariwala, a courtier of Ranjit Singh, where he played a prominent role in quelling an uprising by the local zamindars (landowners). Attariwala was so impressed that he sent him to Lahore for induction into the Sikh army.[25] Soon after Gulab Singh enrolled he came to the attention of Ranjit Singh during an inspection. Herbert Edwardes, a Company employee, describes how the young Dogra's physique and poise made a deep impression on the Maharaja's mind: "[Gulab Singh] was a remarkably fine and powerfully made man, with a handsome face, and a head of hair and beard like a lion, and as black as the plumage of the raven. He could sit like a Centaur on an unbroken colt. . . . Runjeet contemplated him with delight. He was just the stuff of which a conqueror makes up his army."[26] It is generally believed that Gulab Singh eventually assisted his two brothers to enter the service of the Sikhs,[27] though one writer suggests that it was Dhian Singh, not his elder brother, who first secured employment at Lahore.[28] There is also a difference of opinion regarding the starting rank and salary of the three Dogras.[29]

But whatever the nature and circumstances of their initial employment, there is no doubt that the newcomers rapidly rose to prominence. A few English writers attributed this phenomenon to the Maharaja's uncurbed profligate desires, and thinly veiled references have been made that Ranjit Singh was a homosexual. For example, Charles Masson, a versatile but somewhat querulous traveler,[30] wrote that Dhian Singh's "personal attractions pleased the Maharaja; and his subservience to his impure desires has effected his promotion . . . and the advancement of all his family. He has not proved deficient in talent although much so in moral excellence . . . Suchit Singh, it is asserted, was once as much a favourite of the Maharaja as his brother, Dhaiyan Singh."[31] The controversial George Carmichael Smyth also made similar charges: "Suchet Sing was, from his early youth, remarkable for his debaucheries. Like his brother, Dehan, he had risen to favour and station in the court of Runjeet by the most infamous means. They had both attracted the eye of the old monarch by their beauty of person, and secured his patronage by the most criminal compliance with his desires."[32] Lastly, Henry Montgomery Lawrence, the Company official who was destined to play an important role in the affairs of the Sikh state, wrote in his rhapsodized *Adventures*[33] that Dhian Singh rose to power by participating in "Runjit Singh's debaucheries."[34] But such allegations are not substantiated by the other sources of that period, both European and Indian, complimentary to the Maharaja or otherwise. Although they allude to Ranjit Singh's love of wine and women, they do not brand the Maharaja a sexual pervert. Thus the swift ascendancy of the Jammu brothers cannot be ascribed to a licentious relationship with the Maharaja. It is far more probable that the brothers acquired influential positions through their innate ability and high ambitions combined with a calculated use of intrigue and ruthlessness.

These latter traits were abundantly exhibited by Gulab Singh on several expeditions dispatched by the Maharaja to extend his northern boundaries. During 1813 Ranjit Singh was particularly impressed by his performance in an otherwise disastrous campaign against Afghan-occupied Kashmir,[35] and rewarded him with the command of two hundred horsemen[36] in addition to a few small jagirs near Jammu.[37] In 1815 Gulab Singh persuaded the Sikh ruler to allow him to remove the administrator of Reasi, Mian Bhup Dev, whom Ranjit Singh had only recently put in charge of the hill state. Bhup Dev's ancestors had once held Reasi and he was considered by many of its inhabitants to be their legitimate ruler. This had aroused the jealousy of the Jammu brothers, who considered him both an enemy and a rival and were therefore anxious to remove him. When Gulab Singh entered Reasi a revolt broke out, but he firmly suppressed it. Bhup Dev fled and, as the following account reveals, the Dogra commander proceeded to smother any lingering sparks of rebellion with harsh measures:

After the Reasi revolt had been put down, some *zamindars* came to Gulab Singh bearing gifts. Gulab Singh accused one of the *zamindars*, named Surata Bhagial, of aiding Bhup Dev and refused to accept his gift. Surata, who idolized Bhup Dev, summoned up the courage to say, "Of course Bhup Dev is our real ruler and jagirdar [fiefholder]. Our fathers and grandfathers obeyed him and his ancestors. Today you have usurped this land by force." Gulab Singh was so enraged that he took his sword and cut him to pieces. The limbs of his body were hung on a *shisham* tree as a lesson to others.[38]

In 1818 Gulab Singh participated in the invasion of Multan. During the siege of the Multan fort he volunteered to rescue a Sikh soldier who had fallen at the foot of the walls and, despite incessant enemy fire, brought him to safety. The Maharaja lauded this brave act in his darbar (court).[39]

Deception rather than courage singularized Gulab Singh's next exploit. In 1819 he sought and received the Sikh ruler's permission to crush another uprising in the Jammu hills.[40] As in the case of

Bhup Dev, Gulab Singh had personal reasons for obtaining this assignment. The rebellion had been incited by Mian Dido, who claimed to be a direct descendant of Ranjit Dev and therefore was considered a foe by the Jammu brothers. Dido roamed "the country with a large gang of followers, bidding open defiance to [the Sikh] measures,"[41] and gained much popularity by robbing the wealthy and giving to the destitute.[42] Aware that order could be restored only by eliminating this Robin Hood of the Jammu hills, Gulab Singh, immediately upon his arrival, set out to locate the elusive Dido.[43] He discovered that wherever Dido went hillfolk offered him food and shelter. Therefore, the wily Dogra commander impersonated the rebel leader and appeared in several villages. Those who unsuspectingly came forward to welcome him were severely punished. Soon people refused to welcome Dido,[44] either because they feared that he was an impostor or because they dreaded the consequences of assisting him. Bereft of support, the rebel leader was compelled to return to his estate at Chukti. When this news reached Gulab Singh, he and his troops hastened to Chukti and surrounded the insurgent's home. Dido was absent but his ninety-year old father, Mian Hazari, valiantly emerged with sword in hand. The old man was brutally cut down by Attar Singh, a lieutenant of the Dogra commander. Soon afterward the Sikh force caught up with their quarry and surrounded him atop a hill. Gulab Singh seemed eager to take him alive, for he gave Dido several chances to surrender. However, the rebel not only refused but in fact, at an unguarded moment, he moved with lightning speed, and his sword struck Attar Singh's head with such impact that it bisected his entire body.[45] Then, in flaunting defiance, he calmly puffed on his hookah and hurled insulting epithets at Gulab Singh. He even challenged him to a personal duel, contemptuously taunting that "if he were a man he should come forward to fight."[46] But the Dogra leader had no intention of sharing the fate of Attar Singh. Dido's deadly sword kept Gulab Singh's entire contingent at bay until at last one of the soldiers, keeping a safe distance, shot the dauntless rebel to death.[47]

During the time that Gulab Singh was thus occupied with military expeditions, his two brothers were winning distinction at Lahore by displaying unstinting loyalty to the Sikh ruler. In 1818 the Maharaja appointed Dhian Singh to the prestigious office of *deodhiwala* (keeper of the gate),[48] and admitted Suchet Singh as a courtier to his darbar. Early in 1820, while Gulab Singh was still pursuing Dido, the Maharaja gave Jammu in jagir to the entire

Dogra family but, as the following official record indicates, the award was not entirely unconditional:

The *taluka* [district] of Jammu is granted to the Mians [Kishore Singh and his three sons], the devoted servants of the *sarkar* [Maharaja] on the condition that they offer 400 cavalrymen to the *sarkar* and hold themselves in readiness, for rendering suitable services whenever called upon to do so. They must guard the route to Kashmir[49] used by the caravans of pashmina [shawl wool] traders[50] and pilgrims. Any loss incurred by the travellers must be reimbursed by them. They must either arrest and hand over Dido, the rebel, kill him, or drive him beyond the Sutlej.[51]

When the Maharaja heard that Dido had been liquidated,[52] he rewarded Gulab Singh with an additional jagir.[53]

During the early 1820s the Sikh ruler sent Gulab Singh on new campaigns in the hills. In 1820 the Dogra commander seized Rajauri and Bhimber.[54] In 1821 he captured the strong fort of Rehlu Basohli.[55] During the same year he was also dispatched to conquer Kishtwar, a state he had formerly served. Resorting to intrigue to gain his ends, he attempted to sow seeds of dissension between its Raja, Tegh Singh, and his minister, Lakhpat Rai, by composing an incriminating note addressed to the latter, but which was deliberately allowed to fall into the hands of the ruler. Gulab Singh's communication read, "I received your letter and became acquainted with the state of affairs. I have come here to do what must be done. I hope you will keep me informed of all the developments."[56] This strategy produced the desired results. The Raja immediately attempted to seize his minister, who nevertheless managed to escape.[57] Taking advantage of the resulting chaos, Gulab Singh entered Kishtwar, arrested the Raja, and occupied the state without opposition. Tegh Singh was sent to Lahore where Gulab Singh reputedly had him poisoned.[58] Lakhpat Rai later joined the service of the Dogra leader.

The Maharaja was so elated with the latest territorial acquisitions in the hills that he decided to place Jammu solely under the charge of Gulab Singh. The Sikh ruler personally traveled to Akhnur where, on May 4, 1822, he conferred upon Gulab Singh the title of Raja of Jammu in a colorful ceremony on the banks of the Chenab.[59] At the same time he also bestowed on Suchet Singh the title of Raja and the hill jagirs of Sambha and Ramnagar.[60] In return, the Dogra brothers reaffirmed their allegiance to the Maharaja "for the ever increasing favors conferred upon them and promised to render services whenever or wherever called upon."[61] Gulab Singh's control over Jammu was further strengthened when during the same year his distant cousin, Chet Singh, a grandson of Ranjit Dev, formally renounced all claims to the hill territories in favor of the Jammu brothers.[62]

Oddly enough Dhian Singh did not share in the rewards granted to his brothers in 1822. But during the coming years it was Dhian Singh who emerged as the Maharaja's closest adviser, and in April, 1828, the Sikh ruler installed him, amidst pomp and show, as his wazir (minister) and gave him the unique title of *Raja-e-Rajgan* (the Raja of Rajas).[63] Shahamat Ali, a Persian secretary to the Company's agent, described the occasion in these words:

> The ceremony was performed with great state; and to mark the estimation in which Ranjeet Singh held him, he [gave Dhian Singh] the title of Raja of Rajas, directed the officers of his court to present Nazars [gifts] to him, and to regard the newly created Raja as his principal minister; while a proclamation was issued, that if any one in future called him Mian he should be fined 1000 rupees, and that if not a public servant, he should lose his nose and ears.[64]

In addition, Dhian Singh received several hill territories, including the principality of Poonch, in jagir. During the autumn of 1828 the Maharaja also gave the title of Raja to Dhian Singh's young son, Hira Singh, and in 1834 granted him Jasrota in jagir. Ranjit Singh became very fond of this lad and assigned him a special position in his darbar. Lepel Henry Griffin, the author of several books on Panjab, writes that Hira Singh "was allowed a chair in [the Maharaja's] presence when all others, except two or three of the most holy Bhais [saints] were compelled to stand; without him he never went out to take the air."[65]

Such ostentatious demonstrations of the Maharaja's preference for these four members of the Dogra family tremendously enhanced their prestige. The Jammu, or the Dogra Rajas, as they began to be called, were soon recognized as Ranjit Singh's favorites and became a power to be reckoned with throughout the Sikh kingdom.

In addition to Hira Singh, Dhian Singh had two other sons, Jawahar and Moti. Gulab Singh fathered three legitimate sons, Udham, Sohan, and Ranbir. He also had two illegitimate sons, Jamiat and Chiman, by "a slave girl."[66] Suchet Singh, who married often and was involved in numerous affairs, had no male offspring. Women did not enjoy a high position in the family and, since there is no reference to female progeny of any of the three brothers, it is conceivable that they, like many other Rajputs, practised female infanticide.[67]

Though his brothers and Hira Singh remained at Lahore, Gulab Singh was now permitted to spend most of his time at Jammu[68] governing the jagirs of his family and organizing new expeditions into the adjoining mountains. Acting in the name of the Sikh government, he gradually brought under his control most of the region lying between Jammu and Kashmir, and launched a series of invasions into Ladakh which ultimately led to its conquest (see Chapter 2).

In the 1830s Gulab Singh was given the responsibility of administering Gujarat[69] and the salt mines of Pind Dadan Khan near Jhelum. The two districts, which bordered on the territories of Dewan Sawan Mal, the Sikh governor of Multan, led to bitter altercations between the two men. When these disputes were referred to Lahore for arbitration, the Maharaja repeatedly manifested his partiality for Gulab Singh. For instance, during April of 1834, after the troops of Gulab Singh and Sawan Mal had engaged in a bloody fracas over the possession of a border village, the Sikh ruler ordered the Multan governor to renounce his claim in favor of the Jammu Raja.[70] Another clash between the two men in June aroused the indignation of Ranjit Singh, who ominously warned Sawan Mal that if he wished "to spend [the rest of] his days in joy and health he was to withdraw his hand from mischief."[71] Nevertheless, their feud persisted and in August, 1836, the Maharaja once more intervened, revealing his partisanship in a somewhat quizzical decision:

A letter from Raja Gulab Singh intimated that on account of the excessive rains the river Jhelum had overflowed into Pind Dadan Khan and that salt up to the value of six lakhs[72] of rupees had been washed away. The Maharaja said the *nazim* [governor] of Kashmir had sent the water through the Jhelum and that the salt had gone to the territory of Dewan Sawan Mal, so those two must pay for the loss equally.[73]

Ranjit Singh also continued to award additional tracts of territory to the four Jammu Rajas, and by 1837 they held a total of eighty-five jagirs in the mountains.[74] During that year the Jammu family drew up a forty-two-clause compact by which its internal affairs and expanding possessions were to be managed. Vowing to maintain unity in its ranks, the family agreed that the expenses and profits of its holdings were to be shared jointly. Gulab Singh was to continue to administer all the hill jagirs during the absence of the other three Rajas and, in the event of a dispute among themselves, was to act as mediator.[75] Although there are a few inferences to the contrary,[76] a study of the period indicates that there were no serious rifts among the members of the Jammu family until Dhian Singh's death in 1843. Despite his privileged position in both his family and the kingdom, Gulab Singh still had to fulfill all his obligations to the Sikh government. This included paying his share of the revenues and tributes.[77] In 1836 alone he transmitted to Lahore fourteen lakhs of rupees and 125 camels.[78] Moreover, he presented himself at the Sikh capital on important occasions and was required to be on hand during foreign dignitaries' visits such as the one paid by Lord William Bentinck in 1831.[79]

Ranjit Singh also continued to dispatch the Jammu chief on military campaigns. During 1836, he put down a rebellion of the Yusafzai tribesmen near Hazara but, as the following account of the expedition shows, he now achieved his ends by an increasing use of cunning and brutality:

> The Maharaja despatched Raja Gulab Singh with a force consisting of three battalions of infantry, a thousand horse and twelve pieces of artillery. On the approach of the Sikhs the Yusafzais fled into the mountains. Raja Gulab Singh continued his operations leisurely. Hunger soon forced the Yusafzais to return to the plains to find their hearths and homes reduced to ashes. Hundreds pressed by hunger sought the camp of the Sikhs and putting a piece of straw in their mouths as is their custom fell at the feet of the passive Hindu crying, "we are your cows". They were blown off from the guns a dozen at a time.[80]

In 1837 Gulab Singh marched on Poonch where Shams-ud-Din Khan, the man he had nominated to administer Dhian Singh's jagir, had rebelled against the Dogra authority. Shams, a member of the former ruling family, was supported by the chiefs of several adjoining states. But when the Jammu Raja arrived in Poonch, the allies fled. Shams was forced to take shelter with Nur Khan Terola, a neighboring prince, and the revolt collapsed. However, Gulab Singh, determined to prevent the possibility of another rebellion, proceeded to launch a barbaric reign of terror in Poonch. Scores of Shams' followers, thousands according to some, were mercilessly killed.[81] Vigne describes how the Jammu Raja personally supervised the sadistic murders of certain rebels:

Some of his prisoners were flayed alive under his own eye. The executioner hesitated, and Gulab Sing asked him if he were about to operate upon his father or mother, and berated him for being so chicken-hearted. He then ordered one or two of the skins to be stuffed with straw; the hands were stiffened, and tied in an attitude of supplication; the corpse was then placed erect; and the head, which had been severed from the body, was reverted as it rested on the neck. The figure was then planted on the wayside, that passers-by might see it . . .[82]

Khuihami, a nineteenth-century Kashmiri historian, writes that on one occasion, when his victims were being slowly skinned to death inch by inch, Gulab Singh turned a deaf ear to their piteous appeals for a drink of water.[83] On another occasion, as two young comrades of Shams named Malli and Sabzalli were being tortured to death in public, even Udham Singh was so overcome by the ghastly sight that he turned his face away. His eldest son's behavior so mortified Gulab Singh that he slapped him and remonstrated that "if such penalties were not imposed in administering a kingdom, it would be impossible to protect the poor."[84] The news of such atrocities so unnerved the Terola chief that, to save his own life, he treacherously decapitated Shams and meekly sent the dead man's head to Gulab Singh.[85] Later, the Poonch leader's wife and children were also killed. When word reached Lahore that the rebellion in Poonch had been suppressed, the exultant wazir informed the Maharaja that Shams-ud-Din "had been made to leave this mortal abode along with his wife and children by the good efforts of Raja Gulab Singh."[86] However, Sham's martyrdom made him a legend among his people and he, along with Malli and Sabzalli, became the subject of a folk song (see Appendix A) which reportedly is sung by minstrels in the villages of Poonch till this day.

Some of Gulab Singh's British contemporaries in India alluded to the inhuman punishments inflicted by him during this period. Herbert Edwardes relates examples of his harsh sense of justice from stories narrated to him by the Raja himself:

when sent by Runjeet to subdue a turbulent province, he seized "a few" of the chiefs, flayed them alive, stuffed their skins with chaff, and hung them up pour encourager les autres. "Sometimes when I wished only to frighten a man," he says, "I had him scalped, all but a little piece, and just as he thought he was really going to be killed, I put his scalp on again, and let him go!" This he tells with a bland smile, as if talking of peeling apples. On another occasion, when the men of a district ran away, he set a price upon their heads and had them hunted down. And when the wives of the murdered men, now left destitute, came to beg for mercy in a body, he sold them to his soldiers, and so recovered the money which he had paid for their husbands' heads.[87]

In another reference to Gulab Singh's cruelties Edwardes wrote: "There is hardly a noble family in the hills into which he has not carried, at one time or another, death by poison, assassination, or intolerable imprisonment."[88] Charles Napier, a Company general, dwelt on the same subject and claimed that in his hill campaigns the Raja "took 5000 prisoners, skinned all the chiefs alive, half skinned the others, that is so far as not to kill outright, and sent them to die at their villages!"[89] The outrages committed by the Jammu chief also moved Emily Eden, the sister of Lord George Auckland, the Governor-General, to indignantly remark, albeit in rather exaggerated fashion: "Half of [Gulab Singh's] subjects are deprived of their noses and ears."[90] However, an anonymous Englishman, although fully aware of the Raja's faults, also took note of many other personal traits and thus perhaps provides a more balanced picture of the man:

Goolab Sing is avaricious and cruel by nature, deliberately committing the most horrible atrocities for the purpose of investing his name with a terror that shall keep down all thoughts of resistance to his sway. With all this he is courteous and polite in demeanour,[91] and exhibits a suavity of manner and language that contrasts fearfully with the real disposition to which it forms an artfully designed but still transparent covering. He is an eater of opium, he tells long stories, keeps irregular hours, sleeps little, has a mind unsettled, of good memory, free, humorous and intimate even with the lowest and poorest classes of his subjects. The partaker and often the companion of their toils and labour, their free, jocose, and humorous neighbour, their king and continual visitor—yet in reality a leech, sucking their life's blood. Still he must be accounted the very best of soldiers, and, for an Asiatic and an unlettered, uneducated man, he is an able, active, bold, energetic, but wise and prudent commander. He looks more to the future, its wants and requisites, than either to the present or past—slowly goes on and feels his way as he goes—always ensuring supplies and resources—quick in taking opportunities—fond of the defensive though ready to assume the offensive when opportunity offers or requires—but always considering arms as his last resource.[92]

Between 1831 and 1839 the Dogra chief, on the orders of Ranjit Singh, welcomed several European visitors to his territories, and a few of them throw valuable light on the personal character and political power of the Jammu Raja. One such traveler, Victor Jacquemont, a distinguished French naturalist, was received at Pind Dadan Khan by Gulab Singh during April of 1831 "in the midst of all the pomp of his little court."[93] According to Jacquemont's own interesting account, he was overwhelmed by the reception: "We embraced each other for about a quarter of an hour, enough literally to stifle each other, till we raised each other from the ground, by turns."[94] The two men took an instant liking to each other and spent hours discussing a variety of subjects ranging from the geology of salt mines to the organization of European armies.[95] From Pind Dadan Khan the Frenchman proceeded northward alone,[96] but on his way back in October, he again met Gulab Singh at Jammu. The Raja treated him to such diversions as elephant rides and wild hog hunts, and heaped upon him gifts, including shawls, robes, and a handsome white horse.[97] They also spent time in further conversation. On October 8 Jacquemont recorded in a letter to his father the gist of these long conferences and spoke of their mutual admiration:

We talked about his mountains, Cashmere, the immortality of the soul, steam-engines, then the soul again, the universe, &c. &c. Gulab Sing was so pleased with these physics and metaphysics, that we kept it up pretty late in the night by the light of . . . torches and candles, which furnished my Rajpoot philosopher with more than one comparison and idea. I decidedly like that man; and my reason for it is that he seems to like me.[98]

During his two visits the French traveler did not fail to notice the political strength of the Jammu Raja. He described him "as the greatest lord in the Punjab"[99] after the Maharaja, but felt that the Dogra chief was even "better obeyed at a distance than Runjeet Sing."[100] Jacquemont also penned a fascinating portrait of Gulab Singh's appearance and dress:

He is a man of some forty years of age at most, of middle height[101] and extreme beauty: a superb head, with long, curly black hair, an aquiline nose of extreme delicacy, great oval black eyes and a small mouth with perfectly cut lips. His proportions combine grace with adroitness and strength. His costume was most elegant, though at the same time very simple and soldierly: a small white turban of the finest muslin, tastefully rolled and raised over the left ear; a close-fitting tunic of the same stuff and the enormously full Sikh breeches, falling in a profusion of folds on the thigh and fitting closely round the knee, which they half-conceal. He wore no jewels save earrings and a necklace of magnificent pearls, but the handle of his sabre was covered with emeralds, rubies, and diamonds. On his back was a great shield of glazed rhinocerous hide of a glossy black.[102]

However, Jacquemont's favorable impressions were not shared by Vigne, who also traveled extensively through Jammu, Kashmir, and Ladakh during the latter part of the decade and developed an intense dislike of the Raja. Before his departure for the mountains, Vigne was granted several audiences by Ranjit Singh[103] who, believing him to be a Company official, ordered the Jammu authorities to extend every courtesy to the visitor.[104] But Vigne was an egotistical snob who looked with contempt upon almost everyone he encountered in the Sikh state, including the Maharaja.[105] Upon his approach to Jammu he took offense at the jampan (portable sedan) sent by Gulab Singh to carry him to the city, because he felt it "was not, on account of its shabby appearance, such as he ought to have sent me, as his own and his master's guest."[106] He also scoffed at a courtesy call paid by Udham Singh and complained that "an assumed and stupid air of indifference was upon him during our interview,"[107] an estimate at variance with that of Jacquemont, who wrote that the young man in question impressed him "with his charming countenance and his modesty."[108] But even Vigne must have been impressed by the official reception accorded him by Gulab Singh at Jammu, for he wrote: "The courtyard of the palace was alive with the crowds of officers and attendants, gorgeously apparelled in red and yellow shawls and silks, and armed with spears, swords, shields, and matchlocks. Two guns were discharged close to me just as I entered, by way of salute; and Gulab Singh received me in the open pillard hall of the palace."[109] The visitor also found Jammu to be a flourishing town with "a good bazaar, numerous streets, and perhaps, 7000 or 8000 people."[110] He was particularly struck by the freedom of worship enjoyed by all of Gulab Singh's subjects, and wrote that Jammu was "the only place in the Panjab where the Mullahs [priests] may call the Musulmans to prayers."[111] Nonetheless, his basic hostility toward the Raja persisted, and he rebuffed various attempts by his host to befriend him. On one occasion the Raja tried to engage Vigne in conversation, asking "whether it was true that the King of France paid tribute to the King of England,"[112] but the visitor remained indifferent and uncommunicative. At another time Gulab Singh made a futile attempt to interest him in his weaponry, but Vigne, as he himself recorded, continued to be inflexibly perverse: "He exhibited his arms and discussed their various merits. Amongst them were some bell-mouthed blunder-busses, one of which he loaded and fired in the usual manner . . . and thinking that he had astonished me, looked at me for applause, spoke of the number of men that such a weapon could wound at the same time, and seemed a little disconcerted at my not expressing great wonder."[113] His aversion to Gulab Singh deepened into intense hatred as he passed through several mountain principalities under Dogra control, met some of their dethroned chiefs, and listened to tales of their woeful experiences with the Jammu Raja.[114]

Another traveler, Baron Charles Hugel, a colonel in the Prussian army, visited the hills in 1836 and expressed astonishment at the extent of the territory controlled by the Jammu chief and his brothers.[115] He noted that Gulab Singh resided regally at a palace and described it as "a pretty white edifice, built like the whole of Jamu, about 150 feet above river Tohi [Tawi]."[116]

During the 1830s the East India Company also became well aware of the Jammu Rajas' existence, but its officials made conflicting estimates of their standing in the Sikh kingdom. For instance, Alexander Burnes, a special Company emissary who made a short trip to Lahore during 1831, discounted the importance of the Dogras by remarking, "It is not to be supposed that such men have any great influence with [Ranjit Singh]; yet they had managed to instil that belief into the minds of the people; and make every use of their supposed influence, to fill their coffers, and nourish the arts of corruption."[117] But during the same year Captain Claude Wade, the Company's political agent stationed on the Sikh frontier at Ludhiana, was much impressed by the Rajas when he visited Panjab. Describing the Jammu chief as "a very clever man,"[118] he expressed a desire to meet him and had his wish fulfilled later in the year.[119] Thereafter Wade carefully observed Gulab Singh's activities, and assessed not only the Sikh-Dogra connection but also the actual strength and prestige of the Jammu family. By January, 1838, Wade concluded that the Jammu Rajas

owe their present commanding position in the councils of their master to the personal favour and protection of His Majesty [Ranjit Singh] and have lost no opportunity of using it to augment and strengthen their power. . . . They hold immense tracts of territory also in the plains, besides the monopoly of the salt mines, and by means of arming the transit duties, from the Satlej to Peshawar have their offices in all the principal towns and exercise more or less of influence or interference in every department of the government.[120]

Later that year the agent had occasion to refer to the soaring ambitions of the Rajas. Obviously mindful of Ranjit Singh's failing health, he expressed the fear that after the Maharaja's death the powerful Dogras might attempt to seize not only Kashmir, which the Sikhs had finally occupied in 1819, but the entire Panjab kingdom.[121]

Others took cognizance of the extraordinary influence of Dhian Singh and the role he might play upon Ranjit Singh's death. Henry Edward Fane, the commander-in-chief of the Company's forces, visited Lahore in 1837 and called the Sikh wazir the "most powerful person in the Punjab."[122] William Barr, an assistant to Wade who toured Panjab during 1839, characterized the wazir as "the most influential person in the state" and predicted that even Kanwar Kharak Singh, the heir apparent, would need his blessings for a smooth succession to the Sikh throne.[123] William Lewis M'Gregor, a Company surgeon and the author of a two-volume work on the Sikhs, wrote: "Dhyan Singh's influence is great, and he uses his power with a moderation and judgment which never fail to elicit the admiration of all who know him."[124] He added that the wazir's "personal followers are numerous, and in the event of a war of succession, the three brothers would be formidable rivals to the adverse party."[125] Henry Lawrence wrote that Dhian Singh "decidedly is, next to his master, the ablest man in the Punjab."[126] William Godolphin Osborne, military secretary to the Governor-General, who joined Auckland on a trip to Lahore in late 1838, even believed that the Sikh minister "in all probability will be one, and not the least powerful or deserving candidate for the throne of the Punjab on Runjeet's decease."[127] Emily Eden, who also accompanied Auckland, wrote that in the event of the Maharaja's death Dhian Singh "will probably take Cashmere, and the hill provinces, and they say is strong enough to take all the rest."[128]

The two non-Company travelers in the mountainous region also appraised the political situation in the Sikh state. Hugel believed that the "money, troops, cannon and fortresses" in the hands of the Jammu Rajas threatened the future of the state created by Ranjit Singh, whose heirs were too debilitated to challenge the Dogra family's authority.[129] Vigne considered Gulab Singh to be practically independent of Lahore and suspected, like Wade and Emily Eden, that the Rajas eventually planned to take over Kashmir.[130] He argued that the Jammu chief was eager to acquire Ladakh "for the purpose of completing a military circle around Kashmir, and of being able to pour his troops into the valley from every side, immediately upon the death of Runjit."[131] On the basis of his own experiences in the Himalayas and his belief that the Dogra Rajas "cordially hate" the British,[132] Vigne recommended to the Company a course of action he felt would ultimately curb the power of Gulab Singh:

I think that the best line of policy that the Indian Government . . . can adopt, when it has the opportunity, is to follow up that display of its love of legitimacy . . . by reinstating the rightful Rajahs upon their Ghuddis [thrones]. . . . In several instances I have been asked, indirectly, rather than openly, for my intercession with the British Government; and it was every where evident, that nothing but the presence of Rajah Gulab Sing's people, who were always with me, prevented a similar application at every place I came to.[133]

Some Europeans in India suggested that during his twilight years Ranjit Singh was painfully conscious of the threat posed to his

kingdom by the Jammu Rajas. Cunningham stated that "the grasping ambitions of the favorites . . . caused Runjeet Singh some misgivings amid all their protestations of devotion and loyalty."[134] If
Lawrence's *Adventures* are to be relied upon, the Maharaja agonized
over his predicament but accepted it philosophically. " 'Why,' said
the King, 'it is my fate—I threw myself on them—it is my des-
tiny.' "[135] Herbert Edwardes, too, referred to the predominance of
the Dogra brothers in the Sikh state: "Runjeet Sing in his later years
felt that more than one of his servants had grown too strong for the
interests of the throne; but he wisely forbore to show distrust when
it was too late."[136] Masson felt that the Sikh ruler would arrest the
Rajas if he could ever be certain of laying his hands on all of them
at once, but concluded that they were much too shrewd to fall into
such a trap.[137] Hugel believed that the Maharaja could insure the
continuation of the dynasty he had founded only by "an alliance
with the Company, which his pride and the policy of the latter have
hitherto precluded."[138]

Although such theories might not be entirely untenable, there is
no unequivocal evidence to corroborate them. Ranjit Singh neither
publicly condemned the Rajas nor expressed any serious fear of
their strength. Nor did he appeal to the British for assistance to cur-
tail their power. Moreover, the "Umdat-ut-Tawarikh" explodes
Masson's hypothesis, for it reveals that all four Jammu Rajas were
with the Sikh ruler more than once during 1838, but there is no hint
of an attempt to seize or purge them.[139] Vigne comes closest to
proving that Ranjit Singh might have entertained some temporary
doubts. When the English traveler privately complained to the
Maharaja about the transgressive activities of Gulab Singh, the
Sikh ruler politely rebuffed him.[140] But his criticism obviously
prompted Ranjit Singh to make a personal check in the hills during
March, 1838.[141] The Rajas extended to him a rousing welcome.
Among other festivities held during his visit, the Dogra chief escorted Ranjit Singh on an elephant through Jammu's streets and
showered the welcoming crowds with thousands of rupees.[142] But at
one point during this triumphant tour the Maharaja, in Gulab
Singh's presence, purposely asked an aide: "Why, what was it that
the English Sahib [Vigne] . . . was telling me about the disloyal proceedings of my Rajahs?"[143] The question evoked an emotional response from the Dogra chief, and his impassioned reassertion of his
subservience apparently dissipated any apprehensions the Maharaja might have had. According to Vigne, Gulab Singh "knelt at
his master's feet, and said that he was once only a poor soldier, and
was ready at the Maharajah's bidding to become so again—that all

he possessed was owing to the bounty and kindness of his master, who had raised him from the low station he once held, and that he would gladly give up all again for his sake if it were necessary."[144] Ranjit Singh is said to have been so overcome by such eloquence that tears filled his eyes[145] and he returned to Lahore convinced of the Jammu chief's faithfulness.

The Maharaja continued to display confidence in Gulab Singh to the end. During Auckland's visit the Raja was introduced to the Governor-General as "an administrator of civil and military affairs and a brave man,"[146] and later selected as one of the officials to escort the distinguished visitor to various parts of Panjab.[147] The Sikh ruler's enthusiasm and affection for the other Jammu Rajas, notably Hira Singh, also underwent no change. Emily Eden records that the Rajas were very much in evidence during Auckland's tour. She found Hira Singh, "loaded with emeralds and pearls," still seated next to the Maharaja at the darbar.[148] To his English visitors Ranjit Singh described the youthful Raja as "his best-beloved son," and when Emily Eden expressed a desire to sketch Hira Singh, the Maharaja had him escorted to her camp "with quantities of elephants, and two regiments."[149] Osborne was also struck by Hira Singh's prestige and wrote that he "is a greater favourite with Runjeet Sing than any other of his chiefs."[150]

Early in 1839 the Maharaja dispatched Gulab Singh to Peshawar to assist his British allies to cross the Khyber on the eve of the First Anglo-Afghan War. He was still at Peshawar with Kanwar Naunihal, Kharak Singh's son, when word arrived from Lahore that the Maharaja was near death. Upon hearing the news, the young but ambitious Kanwar at once attempted to build a party of his own and demanded that the officials present at Peshawar pledge loyalty to him. The Jammu chief, however, tactfully refused by declaring that he was faithful to Ranjit Singh's whole family.[151]

In the mourning that followed the Maharaja's demise on June 27 no one demonstrated more grief than Dhian Singh, who stunned the darbar by announcing that he intended to be cremated with his benefactor. Attempts were made to dissuade him, and Kharak Singh even went to the extent of putting "his head upon [Dhian Singh's] feet, and assuring him that he . . . would always look upon him as a substitute for the *sarkar*."[152] Finally, the wazir yielded to these importunities, but expressed his determination to retire from public life after a year.[153] At the funeral Dhian Singh "wept and cried"[154] and "attempted four times to jump into the burning pile, but was withheld by the multitude."[155] But such hysterical sorrow gradually subsided and the kingdom seemed to return to normal.

Kharak Singh was inaugurated as the new Maharaja, Dhian Singh retained the wazarat (ministry), and the Jammu family's possessions were confirmed. On the surface at least everything appeared harmonious, but underneath lurked serious portents for trouble which were to shake the Sikh state to its very foundations.

Gulab Singh's rise to prominence in the Sikh state is marked by four salient features. First, he was able, assiduous, handsome, and robust—qualities which earned him the admiration of Ranjit Singh. Secondly, he possessed a character which could both charm and repel. Although generally soft-spoken, gracious, and affable, he could, if the occasion demanded, transform himself into a cold-blooded schemer or a savage tormentor. It may be argued that he ought to be judged by the ethical standards of his time, but there are few in the Sikh state who can be accused of committing the kind of cruelties perpetrated by Gulab Singh. Thirdly, in his phenomenal rise to power the Raja obviously received the firm backing of his brother, Dhian Singh, who, through his administrative skill and political acumen, had acquired remarkable strength and patronage at Lahore. Finally, the Jammu chief and his brothers were lavishly rewarded by Ranjit Singh for their services. The Sikh ruler did not necessarily condone the abominable methods employed by Gulab Singh, but he was doubtless gratified by the degree to which he extended the borders of the Sikh realm. The Maharaja's grandfatherly infatuation with Hira Singh further elevated the Dogras' fortunes. But such flagrant favoritism weakened the position of the Sikh ruler's legal heirs. Ranjit Singh exhibited deplorable judgment and an utter lack of political sagacity in neither recognizing the possibility of an eventual threat from the Jammu Rajas nor providing safeguards for the future security of the kingdom he had so arduously created.

2 Triumph in Ladakh and Baltistan; Disaster in Tibet

The Maharaja said that the King of China had 12 lakhs of soldiers. How could possession over that country be established? [Zorawar Singh] replied, "By the grace of ever triumphant glory of the Maharaja he would take possession of it."—"Umdat-ut-Tawarikh"

Although we conquered your country with only 10,000 men, we did not place a single man of our own over your districts; and this is the way you show your gratitude.
—Zorawar Singh to Tshe-pal

L ADAKH is surrounded by Himachal Pradesh, Jammu, Kashmir, Sinkiang, and Tibet. It covers nearly 46,000 square miles at an average elevation of over 12,000 feet. Its terrain, filled with high mountains, brackish lakes, large rocks, and considerable dust, is frequently swept by windstorms and snowdrifts.[1] The conquest of such a rugged and forbidding land during the nineteenth century was one of the most striking accomplishments of Gulab Singh.

Ladakh, which adopted Buddhism at an early date, was under the political domination of Tibet until the tenth century. Even after Ladakh emerged as an autonomous kingdom it continued to recognize the ecclesiastical supremacy of Tibet and paid occasional homage to its former masters. During the succeeding centuries Ladakh, although attacked by neighboring Kashgarh and Baltistan, managed to retain its separate identity. However, during the last quarter of the seventeenth century Ladakh's sovereignty was gravely imperiled by the Skopa, a Mongol tribe from central Asia. In utter desperation De-lek Nam-gyal, then the *gyalpo* (ruler) of Ladakh, turned to Aurangzeb's governor of Kashmir for aid against the aggressors.[2] The Mughals helped expel the Skopa, and De-lek, in turn, was obliged to pay an annual tribute to Kashmir.[3] Ladakh continued to send this tribute to the Afghans after they occupied Kashmir in 1751 and, after some temporization, to the Sikhs from 1819.[4]

Nonetheless, the Ladakhis feared that Ranjit Singh's annexation of Kashmir was merely the prelude to a Sikh conquest of their homeland. The troubles of the Buddhist kingdom were further compounded by the domestic squabbles which then plagued it. According to one source Ladakh was at that time "administered by the Khalum [kahlon], or prime minister of the Rajah, who was himself but a mere pageant: at all times the sovereign was liable to be deposed by the intrigues of the influential lamas [Buddhist monks], and his place supplied by the next in hereditary succession."[5] To counter the purported Sikh menace, therefore, the Ladakhi authorities began to entertain hopes of obtaining protection from the British East India Company. They found a sympathetic listener in William Moorcroft, a Company agent who lived at Leh, Ladakh's capital, from 1820 to 1822. During their informal discussions the

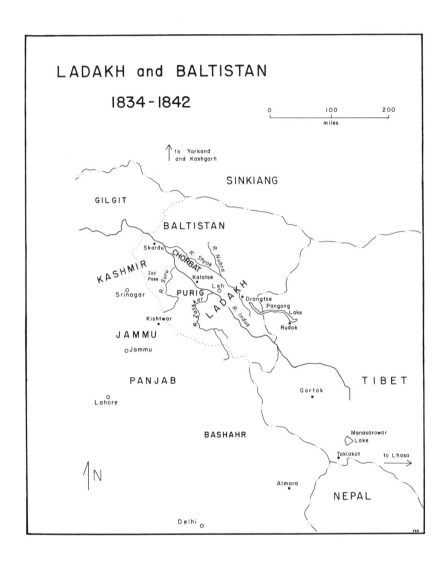

LADAKH and BALTISTAN

1834-1842

0   100   200
              miles

to Yarkand
and Kashgarh

SINKIANG

GILGIT

BALTISTAN

Skardu

CHORBAT
R. Shyok
R. Nubra

KASHMIR

Zoji
Pass
R. Suru

Kalatse

Leh
PURIG

LADAKH

Srinagar

Drangtse
Pangong
Lake

R. Zanskar

R. Indus

Rudok

Kishtwar

JAMMU

oJammu

PANJAB

Gartok

Lahore

TIBET

BASHAHR

Manasarowar
Lake

Taklakot

to Lhasa

N

Almora

NEPAL

Delhi o

Ladakhi minister "showed a disposition to tender a proffer of allegiance to the government of British India."[6] Moorcroft, who anticipated a Sikh, and possibly a Russian, advance into Ladakh, felt that the kingdom ought to be brought within the British sphere of influence. He was so carried away by his zeal to preserve Ladakh from the "oppressive weight of Sikh exaction and insolence," and to secure it for the British "as a strong outwork against . . . the autocrat of the Russias,"[7] that he, without his superiors' consent, proceeded to negotiate a treaty with the Leh officials and sent its draft to the Company's headquarters at Calcutta for ratification. The Company, however, declined to share Moorcroft's enthusiasm, perhaps because of a genuine lack of interest in this remote and difficult region, or perhaps because it felt that the extension of British protection to Ladakh might be construed as a violation of the Anglo-Sikh treaty of 1809.[8] The Company upbraided Moorcroft for his role in the framing of the treaty, refused to ratify it, and informed Ranjit Singh that its agent "had acted without the sanction of the government."[9]

While this rebuff by the British apparently left Ladakh at Ranjit Singh's mercy, there is no evidence to indicate that the Maharaja really contemplated an invasion of the Buddhist kingdom. Thus the assumption that he harbored belligerent designs on Ladakh seems to be a myth born from the suspicions of the Ladakhis and the overzealousness of Moorcroft. The attack on Ladakh originated not in Lahore, but in Jammu. Although Ranjit Singh did not try to stop the Dogras, there is nothing to suggest that the Maharaja actually ordered Gulab Singh to embark on such a venture. Also, as will be noted, while the Sikh ruler once intervened on Gulab Singh's behalf with the Company early during the invasion, he extended to the Dogra leader no military or financial help for the Ladakhi operations.

The ambition to acquire new territory was certainly one of the major factors behind the Jammu chief's decision to conquer Ladakh. However, he was also tempted by the considerable economic benefits to be derived from Ladakh. The occupation of the Himalayan kingdom promised to give him not only a monopoly over Leh's flourishing entrepôt frequented by merchants from Tibet, Sinkiang, and Kashmir,[10] but also control of the important route between Tibet and Kashmir over which passed the lucrative pashmina trade.[11] The Company, too, was interested in acquiring a share of the pashmina traffic, but it believed that Dogra intervention in Ladakh would so disrupt the regular trade route that the Tibetans would be forced to channel their wool into British India.[12] Therefore, when Gulab Singh, on the eve of the invasion, "made a confidential inquiry, whether the Company would have any objection to such a campaign," the British authorities did nothing to dissuade him.[13]

The Jammu Raja was undoubtedly encouraged by the attitude of both the Company and the Sikh government. Several exploratory Dogra expeditions into Ladakh which met with little or no resistance also convinced him of the kingdom's military impotence.[14] Ladakh's army was in wretched condition, its morale was "incredibly cowardly"[15] and its weapons "several centuries behind."[16] The army was also quite limited in number and, according to a contemporary's estimate, composed mainly of "horsemen, armed with a few matchlocks, bows and arrows, and swords, and may amount in all to 2,000 men; [and an] infantry [of] about 1,200 men armed with matchlocks, bows and arrows, and swords."[17]

During the summer of 1834 the Jammu chief mustered an army of ten thousand men, and ordered his able commander, Zorawar Singh,[18] to lead it into Ladakh.[19] Zorawar Singh entered the Buddhist kingdom through Kishtwar, readily defeated a Ladakhi force under one General Mangal, and established Dogra control over the western province of Purig by the middle of August. After a brief pause to refurbish his troops, the Jammu commander marched toward Leh.[20] Though in deep trouble, Tshe-pal Namgyal,[21] the *gyalpo*, clung naïvely to the hope that his kingdom might yet be rescued by the intervention of the Company. When by sheer coincidence a Scottish adventurer, Dr. George Henderson, appeared in Leh at this crucial juncture, Tshe-pal immediately concluded that "he had come to ratify the treaty which poor Moorcroft had entered into with him, in the name of the Company."[22] Repeated disclaimers by Henderson eventually convinced the Leh authorities that he was not an official British emissary,[23] but Tshe-pal, nonetheless, proceeded to detain him for three months, "hoping thereby to make the invading general, Zerawar Singh, believe that he was an envoy, sent from the East India Company, with proffers of assistance."[24] The Ladakhis succeeded in deceiving the Dogras who, fearful of British intrusion into the conflict, halted their advance. Baron Hugel describes the hectic diplomatic activity that followed in the wake of the *gyalpo*'s ingenious bluff, which led the British to once again disavow any interest in Ladakh:

During this interval, Zerawar Singh's military operations were suspended, and he advised Gulab Singh of the supposed envoy's arrival, requesting fresh instructions. Gulab Singh, on his part, applied to the Maha Raja, who, without a moment's delay, addressed the political resident [Wade] at Ludiana, to ascertain the meaning of such proceeding.

The resident satisfied Ranjit Singh with an assurance, that Dr. Henderson, the traveller, had passed the Setlej in direct violation of the orders of his Government; and that there was not the slightest idea of interfering with Ranjit's plans of extending his conquests northwards.[25]

With its hoax exposed, the Ladakhi government resolved to make direct contact with Zorawar Singh. The *gyalpo* gathered an army of twenty-two thousand men, most of whom were obviously recruited in haste,[26] and dispatched it under Banka,[27] the *kahlon*, to face the Dogra forces. Banka initially tried to induce the enemy to withdraw by sending a Ladakhi delegation to negotiate with Zorawar Singh. The envoys "at first talked boldly, and tried to frighten the Dogras, but they afterwards declared their readiness to agree to honourable terms."[28] No accord, however, could be reached. With the approach of winter, Banka surprised the Jammu troops by assuming the offensive. He took "a circuitous route, attacked the Dogras in their rear, and made many prisoners, who were thrown bound into the river in sight of their comrades."[29] Zorawar Singh was forced to retreat into the Suru valley but Banka, perhaps under the erroneous assumption that the enemy's back had been broken, waited for months before pursuing the Dogras. This unexpected respite gave Zorawar Singh time to regroup and reinforce his troops. It also permitted him to adopt a new course of action which he used effectively after the Ladakhi troops finally arrived in the Suru valley. Alexander Cunningham, a major in the Company's service and author of a monumental work on Ladakh, describes how the Dogra commander's well-devised stratagem succeeded:

[Zorawar Singh] having received intelligence of [Ladakhi] movements, despatched a party of 100 men to oppose them, when they were within one kos (one mile and a half) of the place. Now the straggling manner in which the Dogras were obliged to wade through the snow, and the unsoldier-like way in which their tents were scattered over the open country completely deceived the Ladakis as to the real number of their enemies. They were, besides, quite exhausted with their long and fatiguing march through the snow; and therefore, instead of attacking the Dogras at once, they halted for a consultation, which ended in the whole body sitting down to prepare their evening meal of tea and wheaten flour. On seeing this the Dogras attacked them with their swords, and after five or six were killed on each side, and several were wounded, Banka Kahlon and the other Ladaki leaders became alarmed, and fled with numbers of their men. The remainder of the Dogras, who had hitherto held aloof, now rushed to the attack, and completed the rout.[30]

Thereafter, Zorawar Singh promptly recovered the territory he had recently lost, and during the spring of 1835 resumed his march on

Leh. A panic-stricken Tshe-pal sued for peace, and personally negotiated with the Jammu commander for almost four months before a final settlement was reached. By the terms of the agreement Tshe-pal was retained as the *gyalpo* but Ladakh was "to be considered a vassal-state of the Dogra kingdom of Jammu."[31] Ladakh was also to pay a war indemnity of fifty thousand rupees to the Dogras,[32] and send an annual tribute of twenty thousand rupees to Jammu.[33]

No sooner had the two sides come to terms than the chief of Sod rose in arms against the Dogras. Zorawar Singh quickly curbed the outbreak and, adopting Gulab Singh's *modus operandi*, seized several rebels who were "hanged upon trees; while by a promise of fifty rupees for every head the Dogras obtained 200 prisoners, who were at once beheaded."[34] Having restored order in Sod, Zorawar Singh triumphantly returned to Jammu at the end of 1835, leaving behind a Dogra agent with the *gyálpo* at Leh.[35]

Although Jammu had carried out the Ladakhi campaign in the name of Lahore, the impressive victory of the Dogras aroused a certain uneasiness among the Sikhs. It made Kharak Singh "especially apprehensive of the designs of the Jummoo family."[36] Ranjit Singh himself might have felt slighted because not until the Henderson episode was he informed of Zorawar Singh's progress.[37] The Maharaja later expressed irritation upon being informed by his governor in Kashmir, Mahan Singh, that the Dogras were obstructing the normal flow of pashmina from Tibet, and ordered Gulab Singh to rectify the situation.[38] Aware of Lahore's misgivings over the Ladakhi campaign, the Jammu chief attempted to placate his overlords by reiterating that his expedition had actually helped expand the Sikh kingdom's boundaries, and by dispatching Zorawar Singh to make a personal report of his success to the Maharaja. The Jammu commander met the Sikh ruler on March 16, 1836, when he boasted to a rather startled Ranjit Singh of his intention to carry the Sikh standard into Tibet and even China. The "Umdat-ut-Tawarikh" records the interesting exchange between the two men:

[Zorawar Singh] said that the country of Tibet extended over a distance of 500 *kos* and its boundary was contiguous with that of China, where the King of China had his sway, and told the Maharaja that if he wished to give an order for the conquest of the country of China he was ready to kindle the fires of battle and challenge the King of China. The Maharaja said that the King of China had 12 lakhs of soldiers. How could possession over that country be established? [Zorawar Singh] replied, "By the grace of the ever triumphant glory of the Maharaja he would take possession of it."[39]

But despite his obvious skepticism and possible apprehension, the Maharaja once again did nothing to limit the extent of Dogra activities in the Himalayas.

In 1837 Zorawar Singh was forced to return to Ladakh when Tshe-pal, at Mahan Singh's instigation, rebelled against Jammu's authority. He refused to pay the balance of the indemnity, arrested the Dogra agent, and closed several trade routes passing through Ladakh. Nonetheless, when Zorawar Singh speedily approached Leh, Tshe-pal again changed his tune and begged for forgiveness. The Dogra commander, however, rejected his pleas and retorted, "Although we conquered your country with only 10,000 men, we did not place a single man of our own over your districts; and this is the way you show your gratitude!"[40] Zorawar Singh's first act of retribution was to impose additional indemnities. But as Tshe-pal was unable to meet the demands, the Dogra recompensed himself partly by confiscating the personal valuables of the royal princesses and partly by accepting "tea and wool, gold and silver utensils, and other goods" from a Ladakhi chief.[41] Zorawar Singh then exploited Ladakh's internal feuds to his advantage by forcing Tshe-pal to abdicate and installing a noble, Ngorub Standzin,[42] as the new *gyalpo*. Having once more exhibited the superiority of Dogra arms, the Jammu commander again returned home. This time, however, he left behind distinct reminders of the Dogra pre-eminence by stationing Jammu troops in forts throughout Ladakh. As an added precautionary measure, he took with him several prominent Ladakhis, including a son of Ngorub, "as hostages for the good behaviour of the new king."[43]

Nevertheless, during the winter of 1838, Ngorub also attempted to throw off the Dogra yoke, and besieged the forts occupied by the Jammu troops.[44] Zorawar Singh marched back into Ladakh and, en route to Leh, stopped at Chatrgarh to suppress a local uprising. After seizing several of the rebels, he deprived them of their noses and ears, "which frightened the people so much that they immediately tendered their submission."[45] Then the Dogras, treading through heavy snow, advanced to Leh via Zanskar. The Ladakhi capital was reoccupied and, in a move which bore striking similarity to the juggling of Mir Jafar and Mir Kasim by the British in post-Plassey Bengal, Ngorub was deposed, and Tshe-pal was reinstated as the *gyalpo*. Tshe-pal again pledged his loyalty to the Dogras. Ladakh's annual tribute was increased to twenty-three thousand rupees, and the *gyalpo* was now also required to pay for the maintenance of the Jammu troops stationed in his kingdom. But in 1839

Zorawar Singh returned to Ladakh to face yet another challenge from the ousted Ngorub and some other disgruntled Ladakhi nobles. The Dogra promptly suppressed the rebellion, arrested the leading insurgents, and went back to Jammu.[46]

The resentment against the Dogras, however, persisted, and during the winter of 1840 one Sukamir of Purig raised the banner of rebellion against Jammu. Zorawar Singh reappeared, caught Sukamir, and ordered his right hand and tongue to be severed. A. H. Francke, a Moravian missionary who worked in Ladakh for several years at the end of the nineteenth century, describes the barbaric punishment and the tragicomical events that followed:

Zorawar ordered the executioner to come with his sword, and to place a pot filled with butter over a fire. Then, whilst Zorawar was abusing his victim, the executioner was ordered to cut off Sukamir's right hand and to dip the stump at once into the boiling butter. (This is the Dogra way of stopping excessive bleeding.) Then the executioner had also to cut off Sukamir's tongue. To warn the Ladakhis against following other evil advisers, Zorawar ordered Sukamir's hand to be exhibited in public on a pole at the Kalatse bridge. The hand arrived there alright, and was placed during the night in the rest house. But a cat stole it, and the peasants of Kalatse greatly feared that all their hands might be cut off, as a punishment for their neglect. Fortunately an old Lama had died only a few days before. His hand was cut off and fastened on the top of the pole at the bridge, where it served its purpose as well as the other would have done.[47]

With Ladakh firmly under their control, the Dogras turned to the conquest of the predominantly Muslim principality of Baltistan. This decision was influenced by several favorable developments. One, the Dogras had been well aware of the serious estrangement between Ahmed Shah, the Balti *gyalpo*, and his eldest son, Muhammad Shah. As early as 1835 Muhammad Shah had sought Zorawar Singh's aid to usurp his father's throne, but the Jammu commander, because of his preoccupation with Ladakh, "contented himself with giving promises of future assistance to the Balti prince."[48] Perturbed by the Dogra threat to his kingdom, Ahmed Shah indicated to Vigne, during his visit in 1835, a desire to accept British suzerainty.[49] But the Company obviously remained as cool to Baltistan's overture as it had been to that of Ladakh. Two, the Dogras probably believed that, not only because of their lack of interest in Baltistan but also because of their own deep involvement in Afghanistan, the British were unlikely to challenge Jammu's latest plan of conquest. Three, Ranjit Singh's death gave the Jammu chief almost a free rein in the Himalayas, since Kharak Singh, despite his earlier misgivings, adhered strictly to a policy of noninterference "in respect to [the Dogra's] conquests on the North Eastern Frontier of Kashmir, from fear of defection of his family if too suddenly controlled."[50] And four, Jammu procured the tacit acquiescence of Mahan Singh, who might otherwise have opposed the Dogra subjugation of Baltistan, by giving him undisputed control over Jussorah, a district sandwiched between Ladakh and Kashmir.[51] The Kashmir governor's tergiversation "left Iskardo [Baltistan], and the whole valley of the Upper Indus, a free field for the aggressions of [the Dogra Rajas'] lieutenants."[52]

Encouraged by the prevailing conditions, the Jammu chief ordered Zorawar Singh to occupy Baltistan. Accompanied by an army of fifteen thousand Dogras and a Ladakhi contingent, the Jammu commander marched toward Baltistan at the end of 1840. He found the Indus crossing extremely hazardous because the Baltis, in anticipation of the invasion, had destroyed the only bridge in the vicinity. When he dispatched a lieutenant, Nidham Singh, with five thousand men to search for a new passage across the Indus, they were surrounded by thousands of Baltis, and Nidham Singh "was cut off with nearly the whole of his detachment."[53] The news of this disaster, combined with the shortage of food and the advent of cold weather, so demoralized Zorawar Singh's army that many soldiers became "utterly indifferent whether they should be cut off by the sword of the enemy, or be frozen to death by the cold."[54]

The Jammu commander, however, refused to give up and, after weeks of desperate reconnoitering, the Dogras discovered a sizable segment of the Indus which had frozen, and crossed it into Baltistan.[55] The Balti troops were caught off guard and decisively beaten. As they fled in confusion the Dogras "pursued, and slaughtered" them.[56] Finally, Zorawar Singh reached the Balti capital of Skardu, and besieged its strategically located fort[57] where Ahmed Shah had taken refuge. The gyalpo soon surrendered "for want of water,"[58] was deposed, and imprisoned. The Dogra commander replaced him with Muhammad Shah who, as a puppet ruler, agreed to pay an annual tribute of seven thousand rupees to Jammu.[59] To deter the Baltis from future insubordination Zorawar Singh decided to instil fear in their hearts by ordering two of Sukamir's former comrades, Rahim Khan and Hussein, to be brought to Skardo from Ladakh for public punishment. Francke narrates details of the horrifying scene that ensued:

When both [the accused] were secured, Zorawar issued an order to all the Dogras, Ladakhis, and Baltis who were assembled at Skardo, to come together in a lucerne field, in the middle of the town. Everybody had to appear, even the women, the old, the lame, and the blind. . . .

Then Rahim Khan was escorted into the middle of the assembly. . . .
There he was told to eat a quantity of hemp, because he was assured it
would save him much pain. Butter was again boiled, which made people
anticipate what was to happen. Then the executioner appeared and cut
off Rahim Khan's right hand, his tongue, his nose, his ears, all the time
making ample use of the hot butter, and, having finished, threw his victim
in the middle of the crowd. After Rahim Khan, Hussein was treated in a
similar way, but he was deprived only of his hand and tongue. He remained alive, whilst Rahim Khan died after two days.[60]

His objective attained, Zorawar Singh stationed a garrison of Dogra
troops at Skardu and returned to Leh.

Jammu's latest victory caused much consternation to George
Clerk, Wade's successor, who felt that it could be the beginning of
Dogra incursions into other Himalayan territories. In communications to his superiors he expressed the fear that Gulab Singh would
next advance into Gilgit and in such a venture might receive assistance from Sheikh Ghulam Mohi-ud-Din, the new governor of
Kashmir.[61] He also believed that the Dogras would try to subdue
Yarkand in southwest Sinkiang, and warned that such a course of
action might further impair Anglo-Chinese relations,[62] since the two
countries were then engaged in the Opium War near Canton. But
the Company brushed aside the agent's apprehensions with the
response that "it is a question which the British Government is not
called upon to arbitrate."[63] Even one of Clerk's assistants, Mackeson, took issue with his judgment by remarking that it was physically impossible for the Dogras to annex Yarkand.[64]

However, Gulab Singh made no hostile move toward Gilgit or
Yarkand but turned his attention instead to the east. He revived
an ancient Ladakhi claim to Tibet's western districts,[65] and in May,
1841, Zorawar Singh entered Tibet with a force of five thousand
men[66] comprised of soldiers from Jammu, Ladakh, and Baltistan. At
first the Dogra commander encountered no opposition and he
swiftly occupied the cities of Rudok and Gartok. Elated by such
effortless gains, Zorawar Singh continued to advance and by early
September succeeded in occupying the strategic city of Taklakot,
thus cutting off the trade route between Tibet and the British
protectorate of Bashahr, and placed a Dogra contingent at a site
opposite the Company-held district of Almora.[67] While the Dogras
plundered gold and silver from the Tibetan monasteries, the rabid
Muslim troops from Baltistan gleefully demolished the Buddhist
idols.[68]

The British authorities, who had remained indifferent to the
plight of Ladakh and Baltistan, expressed grave concern over

Zorawar Singh's intrusion into Tibet. In the first place, they feared that, because of the lingering Opium War, the Chinese might suspect the Dogra invasion to have been encouraged by the Company.[69] Secondly, the Tibetan campaign threatened British economic interests. As anticipated by the Company at the outset, the Ladakhi conflict had indeed disrupted the traditional flow of Tibetan goods to Kashmir and diverted them to the British-dominated areas of Bashahr and Almora. But upon occupying western Tibet, Zorawar Singh, to the Company's distress, attempted to block this new and profitable avenue of trade. The Raja of Bashahr bitterly complained both of his commercial losses and of the threat posed by the presence of Dogra troops on his Tibetan frontier.[70] This prompted the British to ask Sher Singh, the new Maharaja at Lahore, not only to restrain Zorawar Singh from menacing Bashahr but to order his total withdrawal from Tibet. However, Sher Singh, too, hesitated to challenge the Jammu Rajas and merely instructed the Dogra commander, through Dhian Singh, not to molest the British protectorate.[71] Zorawar Singh responded by denying that he had any interest in Bashahr, but vehemently defended his right to block the flow of Tibetan wool and tea into British India, since it was causing havoc to the long-established Tibetan-Ladakh-Kashmir trade.[72]

The Dogra rebuff infuriated the Company, and some of its political agents bitterly complained of the positions taken by Lahore and Jammu. Perturbed by the absence of any Sikh control over Zorawar Singh's proceedings, Clerk lamented that Sher Singh was "quite powerless to restrain the Jummooes in that direction,"[73] and caustically remarked: "The Govt. at Lahore, in Runjeet Singh's time, knew little enough of Ladakh affairs, and knows less now."[74] Lushington, the agent at Bashahr, charged that the Dogra encroachment in Tibet was also adversely affecting Almora's trade, and declared that "no one has a right to molest the established interests of the British Government or of those who are under its protection. Least of all can the upstart Raja of Jummoo possess such a right."[75] Such complaints, however, failed to deter the Dogras, and Zorawar Singh threatened that if Ladakh's trade monopoly was not fully restored he would march on the Tibetan capital of Lhasa itself.[76]

The British authorities, who at first had sought to attain a Dogra withdrawal from Tibet through diplomatic pressure on Lahore, now determined to take a tougher stand. This resulted from a deep anxiety that the Dogra presence on the Nepalese frontier might lead to an alliance between Jammu and Nepal.[77] The Company feared that such a coalition might endanger the Kumaon hills which the British had acquired from Nepal after a bloody conflict in 1816.

Clerk reflected the typical British viewpoint when he wrote: "There would be a degree of insecurity to British interest in the connection of Nepal with any Hill state to the west of it, and that insecurity would be . . . imminent in a union of the abundant resources of the Jummoo Rajas with the malevolence and bravery of the Goorkha army."[78] By October British trepidation reached such a feverish pitch that Clerk, apparently acting on Auckland's orders, demanded that Sher Singh order the Dogras to evacuate Tibet by December 10, 1841. Characterizing Zorawar Singh's operation as illegal the agent added indignantly that "it is to the British Government intolerable."[79] Clerk followed up his threat by dispatching Cunningham to Tibet "to see that the ambitious Rajas of Jummoo surrendered certain territories which they had seized from the Chinese of Lassa, and that the British trade with Ludakh, &c. was restored to its old footing."[80] Confronted by the British ultimatum, the Sikh ruler finally summoned up the courage to command Gulab Singh to withdraw from Tibet. Advocating prudence, he told the Raja: "You ought to observe this very strictly, for times are critical, and precaution necessary."[81] Sher Singh then informed Clerk of his action.[82]

Gulab Singh, without doubt impressed more by the British indignation than by the Maharaja's directive, agreed to yield, but before he could make contact with Zorawar Singh,[83] the military situation in Tibet underwent a drastic change. Early in November Lhasa sent an army of about ten thousand men to drive the Dogras from Tibet. After a few skirmishes the adversaries met on December 10, ironically the date set by the British for the Dogra withdrawal, and began a fierce three-day battle on the shores of Lake Manasarowar, northeast of Taklakot.[84] The Dogras, benumbed by the grisly winter, proved no match for the "force from Lassa enured to frost and snow."[85] On December 12, Zorawar Singh was wounded in the shoulder "and as he fell from his horse the Chinese [Tibetans] made a rush, and he was surrounded and slain."[86] The Jammu commander's death determined the outcome of the battle. The weather had chilled the bodies of the Dogra soldiers; their leader's loss now froze their spirits. Bereft of the will to fight, they hurriedly dispersed in a frantic, but largely futile, effort to save their lives. Alexander Cunningham describes the cataclysmic conditions under which the Dogras fought, and the circumstances of their ultimate destruction:

> The Indian soldiers of Zorawar Sing fought under very great disadvantages. The battlefield was upwards of 15,000 feet above the sea, and the time mid-winter, when even the day temperature never rises above the freezingpoint, and the intense cold of night can only be borne by people

well covered with sheepskins and surrounded by fires. For several nights the Indian troops had been exposed to all the bitterness of the climate. Many had lost the use of their fingers and toes; and all were more or less frost-bitten. The only fuel procurable was the Tibetan furze, which yields much more smoke than fire; and the more reckless soldiers had actually burned the stocks of their muskets to obtain a little temporary warmth. On the last fatal day not one-half of the men could handle their arms; and when a few fled, the rush became general. But death was waiting for them all; and the Chinese gave up the pursuit to secure their prisoners and plunder the dead, well knowing that the unrelenting frost would spare no one.[87]

Cunningham also records that out of the sizable Dogra force "not more than 1,000 escaped alive, and of these some 700 were [made] prisoners of war."[88] The Tibetans treated some of their prisoners humanely, but dealt out frightful penalties to others. Those who had desecrated the Buddhist monasteries especially bore the brunt of their wrath. One such culprit, Ghulam Khan, "was tortured with hot irons. His flesh was picked off in small pieces with pincers; and mangled and bleeding, he was left to learn how slow is the approach of death to a wretch lingering in agony."[89]

Further adversity awaited the Dogras. Ladakh, never fully reconciled to Jammu's overlordship, found in this Dogra debacle an opportunity to regain its independence. Jigmet Nam-gyal,[90] who had become the *gyalpo* upon Tshe-pal's death early in 1841, rose against the Dogras. About twenty-five hundred Ladakhi rebels surrounded the two Leh forts which were held by a few hundred Jammu troops. Even some Balti malcontents arrived at Leh to make common cause with the Ladakhis.[91] The Dogra position became even more precarious when the Tibetans, inspired by their recent success, began to dream of bringing Leh back into Lhasa's orbit and decided to advance into Ladakh. Thus the very presence of the Dogras in Ladakh was at stake and another showdown seemed imminent.

The British reaction to these latest developments was mixed. Ellenborough, the new Governor-General, took delight in the Dogra misfortunes. Claiming that he had endeavored in vain to discourage Dhian Singh and Gulab Singh "from their wild views of conquest beyond the Himalayas," he declared rather vindictively that their defeat "will teach them reason better than I could."[92] His agents, however, were not so jubilant. J. D. Cunningham feared that the event might lead to the formation of a Nepalese-Tibetan entente.[93] Clerk believed that, despite the Dogra ejection from Tibet, British trade would continue to suffer. He predicted that Gulab

Singh would move to reassert his power in Ladakh[94] and establish his relations with Tibet "on such a footing as to place the wool and the tea trade of Cashmere beyond all risk of deterioration."[95]

During the spring of 1842 a Lhasa force under Pishi, a Tibetan commander, arrived at Leh and allied itself with the rebels besieging the Dogra-held forts.[96] The exuberant Tibetans even boasted of attacking Kashmir.[97] But such overconfidence was short-lived as the Jammu Raja took measures to meet the challenge issued by the Ladakhis and the Tibetans. It was not until February that the news of Zorawar Singh's death reached Gulab Singh at Peshawar where Lahore had once again dispatched him, this time to assist the new advance of British troops into Afghanistan.[98] On leaving Peshawar the Jammu chief proceeded to Srinagar, the Kashmiri capital, where with Governor Mohi-ud-Din's assistance he "organized a new force of 7,000 men under Hari Chand and Wazir Ratnu for the conquest of Ladakh."[99] This force entered Ladakh directly from Kashmir,[100] probably via the caravan route which winds through the high Zoji Pass.[101] As it approached Leh, the Tibetans and Ladakhis raised the siege of the Dogra forts and dispersed. The Tibetans beat a hasty retreat eastward. They camped at Drangtse near Pangong Lake on the Tibetan-Ladakhi border where another Lhasa force of three thousand men under the joint command of Ragasha and Zurkang arrived to strengthen their ranks.[102] In September the Dogra-led army arrived near Drangtse and confronted the enemy. Taking advantage of the deep and narrow valley where the Tibetan army lay, Hari Chand and Ratnu inundated the enemy's camp by diverting nearby streams, and the Lhasa troops fled in disarray. Many Tibetans, including the commanders, were taken prisoner. Ragasha was beheaded, "for he was a welcome subject to the Dogras to revenge the death of Zorawar on the Tibetans."[103] Zurkang and the other prisoners were taken to Leh.

However, both the Dogras and the Tibetans were so exhausted by their protracted conflict that a mutual desire for conciliation soon became evident, and Gulab Singh, as a gesture of his good faith, ordered Zurkang's release.[104] Negotiations were opened, and a peace settlement was reached during late September by which 1) the Tibetans recognized Dogra supremacy over Ladakh, 2) the Dogras renounced any claim to western Tibet, 3) both parties accepted the old boundaries between Ladakh and Tibet, and 4) Tibet agreed to resume its traditional trade with Ladakh.[105] Shortly thereafter the prisoners of war were exchanged.[106] Once harmonious relations with Tibet were re-established, Gulab Singh ended the rule of the *gyalpos* in Ladakh, retired Jigmet Nam-gyal to a small estate, and installed a Dogra governor to administer the former Buddhist kingdom.[107] Henceforth Ladakh was to be ruled by a governor appointed directly by Jammu.

Though officially Ladakh and Baltistan now became a part of the Sikh kingdom, Lahore's control over them was, at best, nominal. For all practical purposes the Dogras emerged as the real rulers of the new acquisitions and, as Lahore became progressively engulfed in political turmoil, even the pretense of its sovereignty over that area began to disappear.

Two men can justly claim most of the credit for the conquests of Ladakh and Baltistan and their incorporation into the Indian body politic. First, of course, is Gulab Singh, whose foresight, drive, and ambition impelled him to seek such a goal. But if the Jammu chief planned and financed the actual invasions, there is no indication that he personally participated in any of these campaigns. In fact, this scholar came across no evidence that Gulab Singh ever set foot in Ladakh. The man who intrepidly transformed the Dogra Raja's dreams into reality was Zorawar Singh. Like his master he was competent, shrewd, and ruthless, but in physical daring, military achievements, and unmitigated loyalty he far surpassed Gulab Singh. Although it is a little farfetched to compare him to Alexander and Napoleon, as one adoring Dogra writer does,[108] Zorawar Singh could, nonetheless, be described as one of the most gallant and triumphant soldiers India produced in the first half of the nineteenth century. He won singular laurels during a period of Indian history not particularly noted for its military exploits and heroics. It is therefore surprising that, although Zorawar Singh is now almost a legend among the Dogras, he has received little recognition for his achievements beyond the confines of Jammu.

3 The Rise and Fall of Dhian Singh

Who did the deed? *Chance! says* everybody in the
crowd. *Dhyan Singh! thought* everybody in the kingdom.
—Herbert Edwardes

To the ordinary observer, the policy of the Dogras
would appear to have been parricidal, as well as
fratricidal. . . . [But] in all their tortuous intrigue the
common Dogra intent was undeviatingly pursued.
—C. Grey

WITH the death of Ranjit Singh, Dhian Singh emerged as the most prestigious and perhaps the most powerful figure at Lahore. The wazir was well-bred, urbane, courtly, and, in spite of a slight limp,[1] carried himself with remarkable aplomb. The British contemporaries who encountered him near the end of Ranjit Singh's reign raved about his physical appearance and elegant manners. Fane reported that Dhian Singh was a "most striking figure,"[2] Emily Eden termed him "uncommonly good-looking,"[3] and Henry Lawrence wrote that he was "a fine-looking man, of a noble presence, polite and affable, of winning manners and modest speech."[4] Osborne found the wazir "a noble specimen of the human race; rather above the usual height of natives, with a quick and intelligent eye, high handsome forehead, and aquiline features."[5] M'Gregor described him not only as "remarkably handsome," but also "mild in his deportment" and "affable to strangers."[6] However, the same British who were so impressed with his looks[7] and power, at first failed to perceive that he, too, like his elder brother, was rapacious, scheming, and, on occasion, unmerciful.

Judging from the manner of the Jammu Rajas' rise, it may be safely assumed that in the wake of Ranjit Singh's death they not only intended to maintain their position of strength but to extend it. As noted earlier, several Company officials and European visitors before 1839 had alluded to the ambitions of the two elder Jammu brothers. A few other nineteenth-century writers dwelt further on the subject. Charles Gough and Arthur Innes conjectured: "It is probable that these two designed to share the rule of the whole Punjab between them, the plan being that Gholab Singh was to acquire the whole of Jammu, Kashmir, and the northeast generally; while Dhian Singh should rule at Lahore."[8] Alexander Gardner believed that the Dogra "dream was that Hira Singh, the heir of their family, or at least the most promising of its rising generation, might eventually succeed to the throne of Ranjit Singh. Those to be swept away were male members of the Maharaja's family, and all those ministers, advisers, and chiefs who would not join the Dogra party."[9] Lepel Griffin supports this theory by referring to a deeply-laid conspiracy:

Dhyan Singh had a dearer ambition. . . . His eldest son Hira Singh had been the darling of the old Maharaja . . . [and] had been brought up like the Maharaja's own child, and as such was regarded by the Khalsa army. Was it then too bold an ambition to hope that some day he might rule the Punjab as king; with Dhyan Singh, his father, as his chief adviser, holding all real power in the state; with one uncle, the gallant and debauched Raja Suchet Singh, as commander-in-chief, and the other, Gulab Singh, ruling all the hill country. Then, in firm alliance with the Kabul Amir and the court of Nepal, the Dogra family of Jammu might become the most powerful in all India, and found a dynasty for itself.[10]

Although the charges relating to Gulab Singh's aspirations in the mountains may be considered largely valid, it is impossible to determine fully the credibility of the other imputations, since the rest of the Jammu Rajas lost their lives before they could attain the goals attributed to them. However, it is difficult to believe that such canny politicians as these Dogras would have attempted to put on the Sikh throne either Dhian or Hira Singh, for the simple reason that they were Hindus. Such a move would have certainly caused a great uproar among the Sikhs in general, and the powerful khalsa[11] (Sikh army) in particular. Nevertheless, there is little doubt that Dhian Singh planned to be the real power behind the throne and hoped to control the Sikh government through puppet Maharajas.

Therefore, Dhian Singh welcomed Kharak Singh's succession to the throne. The wazir probably expected him to be only a figurehead, since the new Maharaja was generally considered to be an ailing imbecile and a languorous weakling. His European contemporaries were united in their condemnation. Osborne wrote: "He is the worst looking of the Sikhs I have yet seen. . . . His manners . . . appear to be awkward and unconciliatory, and he is but little liked or respected in the Punjab."[12] J. D. Cunningham dubbed him the "unworthy master of the Punjab."[13] Emily Eden labeled him "an idiot."[14] Honigberger, a Transylvanian physician in Lahore's service, wrote that "besides being a blockhead, [he] was a worse opium eater than his father."[15] M'Gregor declared that the new Maharaja "possessed none of his father's qualifications for rule."[16] It is, however, to the credit of Kharak Singh that he attempted to rule Panjab effectively and jealously guarded his prerogatives against the encroachments not only of the potent Dogras, but also of his own ambitious son, Kanwar Naunihal Singh. Less than three weeks after his accession the Maharaja barred Naunihal Singh "from any interference with the political business"[17] of the kingdom. Soon after he also tried to curb Dhian Singh's pre-eminence by appointing as his chief adviser and confidant a courtier named Chet Singh,[18] who was even allowed to reside in the royal quarters. At the same time the Maharaja stripped Dhian Singh and Hira Singh "of the privilege of free admission into the king's *zenana* [ladies' quarters], so that the minister was unable to make important representations on State affairs privately to the king."[19] However, when the Sikh ruler ordered the wazir to delegate some of his power to the new favorite, Dhian Singh slyly evaded a direct answer by stating: "I am the servant of the Maharaja and of the Koonwur Nownihal Singh but cannot serve Surdar Chiet Singh."[20] Nevertheless, the Sikh ruler continued his anti-Dogra campaign by publicly supporting a charge made by Missar Beli Ram, the officer in charge of the *toshekhana* (treasury), that Gulab Singh was not regularly paying his revenues to Lahore.[21]

While the Maharaja was undoubtedly justified in thus asserting himself, he had nonetheless committed the serious blunder of simultaneously alienating both his son and his wazir. The Kanwar, who had until then been considered anti-Dogra,[22] now began to drift toward the Jammu Rajas and away from his own father. He obliged the Dogras by demanding, though unsuccessfully, that his father dismiss Chet Singh.[23] In return, Gulab Singh twice attempted to persuade the Sikh ruler to accommodate Naunihal Singh by assigning him a political role in the kingdom, but the Maharaja remained adamant and declared that he would neither "give up his authority,"[24] nor "attend to the Koonwur's unreasonable displeasure."[25]

Rudely shaken by the unanticipated independence demonstrated by Kharak Singh, the Jammu Rajas reacted by hatching a scheme to slander the Maharaja in the eyes of the Sikhs. Specious reports were circulated that Kharak Singh had treasonably sold out to the British and was conspiring to dissolve the khalsa.[26] Latif, the historian, describes the malicious scandalmongering and its disastrous consequences to Kharak Singh's image as a ruler:

A rumour was set afloat that Kharak Singh had formed a league with the British Government and had consented to acknowledge their supremacy, to pay a tax of six annas per rupee, to disband the Sikh army, and to do away with the sardars [chiefs or commanders], who were to be replaced by English officers. This rumour was soon circulated through [Lahore], and became the chief topic of conversation in the markets and streets. The civil and military freely vented their indignation at this supposed treacherous compact. Kharak Singh was openly calumniated, and the soldiery began to look upon him as a traitor, unworthy of his position.[27]

The Maharaja was unable to convince the darbar of his innocence, and his unpopularity reached such a height that his own wife, Rani Chand Kaur, "the mother of Nau Nehal Singh, became his bitterest enemy, and gave her full consent and connivance to her husband's dethronement."[28] Hoping to exploit his father's troubles to his own advantage, the restless Naunihal Singh, who had gone to Peshawar, hastily returned to Lahore.[29] The Jammu Rajas entered into an alliance with the Kanwar,[30] and together they plotted to frighten and humiliate the Maharaja by murdering Chet Singh and punishing Beli Ram. At dawn on October 8, 1839,[31] the Dogra brothers, with Naunihal Singh and their partisans, stormed into the palace after Gulab Singh had shot the gatekeeper to death.[32] The conspirators then "entered the sleeping apartment of Kharak Singh with drawn swords"[33] where the Maharaja tried in vain to save Chet Singh's life by shielding him with his own arms.[34] Chet Singh threw himself at the feet of his assassins but was pitilessly put to death. Although J. D. Cunningham writes that "Golab Singh was perhaps the most resolute actor in this tragedy,"[35] Latif believes that the Maharaja's confidant was actually murdered by the wazir.[36] Chet Singh's estates were immediately confiscated and his brother arrested. At the same time, Beli Ram, too, was divested of his property, incarcerated, and starved for two days. Subsequently he was brought before the darbar, accused of embezzling from the *toshekhana*, beaten, and told by Dhian Singh that "he also would have been killed had not the Koonwar kindly interceded for him."[37] He was then returned to prison.

The triumph of his adversaries over his two chief supporters cast the Maharaja into such despondency that he went into seclusion[38] and for a time even considered abdication.[39] The Kanwar and Dhian Singh acted swiftly and, although Kharak Singh was not actually deposed, they made him a captive and assumed most of his powers. According to Shahamat Ali, the Sikh ruler "once attempted to fly from his persecutors to the British frontier, but was overtaken and carried back to his house, or more properly to his dungeon."[40] The hapless Maharaja was also forbidden, despite his expressed desire, to meet Wade, who visited Lahore during early November.[41]

But the Kanwar's expedient alliance with the Jammu Rajas soon began to crumble, which improved his relations somewhat with his father. This new development probably helped Kharak Singh regain his freedom in late November, and he promptly resumed his crusade against the Dogras. During December, although he failed to deprive Dhian Singh of the office of *deodhiwala*, he did succeed in removing from Gulab Singh's jurisdiction the Pind Dadan Khan salt mines and a few districts between the Jhelum and Indus rivers.[42] In January 1840, he decided to rescue Beli Ram, who had indicated "that if he was released he would point out lakhs of rupees which were due from Rajah Gholab Singh."[43] The Maharaja freed the treasurer, reprimanded the Jammu chief for his financial delinquency, and demanded that he promptly remit his unpaid taxes.[44] To add to the humiliation of the Dogra Rajas, Kharak Singh then launched a fiery campaign of revilement against the wazir at the darbar. Dhian Singh was very disconcerted by such tactics, and for several days he shunned the darbar. When he returned, expecting to find that the Maharaja had been mollified by his absence, Kharak Singh sarcastically inquired: "Are you still alive?"[45] During July the Sikh ruler asked Gulab Singh to relinquish his control over the Minawar district in the Jammu hills. The Dogra Rajas acquiesced, declaring with outward imperturbability "that they were the faithful servants of the Khalsah Government, and were ready to give up not only the [Minawar] district but everything they had belonging to them."[46] At heart, however, they deeply resented this latest command of the Maharaja. Dhian Singh was so distressed that he now lamented "not having burnt with the widows [of Ranjit Singh]."[47] Greatly embittered by the Maharaja's attitude, the wazir ultimately retaliated by letting Gulab Singh haul away, during the withdrawal from Minawar, valuables worth lakhs of rupees. Word of the Jammu chief's action threw Kharak Singh into a rage, and he "heaped thousands of terms of abuse on the Rajas exclaiming: 'Who are these Rajas that they should carry away property and coin from the fort of [Minawar]?' "[48]

Although the Maharaja continued to berate and persecute the Dogras, he deliberately refrained from meting out similar treatment to his impetuous son. There were two reasons for this. First of all, despite Kharak Singh's return to court, Naunihal Singh continued to enjoy some measure of authority among the Sikhs. Several factions at Lahore, including one led by the aristocratic Sandhawalia family, backed the Kanwar, and the Maharaja was anxious to avoid a collision with them. Secondly, the Sikh ruler must have welcomed the growing estrangement between Naunihal Singh and the Dogras,[49] and he did not intend to repeat his mistake of alienating both sides at once, thereby reviving their alliance. But if a certain degree of reconciliation took place between the Maharaja and his son,[50] it was marked by little mutual respect and confidence. On the other hand, although relations between Naunihal Singh and the Dogras deteriorated, they never reached the point of a total rupture. It might be argued, as Cunningham does, that the Kanwar's "great aim was to destroy, or to reduce to insignificance, the potent Rajas of Jummoo."[51] Certainly Naunihal Singh played an active role in crushing the revolt led by the Raja of Mandi during the summer of 1840, which had reportedly been inspired by Gulab Singh.[52] In addition, he must have relished the harassment of the Dogras at his father's hands. Yet the Kanwar realized only too well that neither he nor the Maharaja were in a position to eliminate the Jammu Rajas at that time. Consequently, Naunihal Singh rejected the advice of his supporters who suggested that he disband the khalsa because of its alleged attachment to Dhian Singh and substitute it with "soldiers of his own raising."[53] Besides the very real possibility that the plan might backfire, the Kanwar was also influenced by his apparent belief, despite his anti-Dogra sentiments, that Dhian Singh was almost an indispensable figure at the court, whose sudden departure might endanger the stability of the Lahore government. This is demonstrated by his action when Dhian Singh, irked by the Minawar affair, informed the Kanwar, whether truthfully or not, that he planned to relinquish the wazarat and quit Lahore. Naunihal Singh seemed rather unnerved by this and attempted to dissuade him from his proposed course of action. The *Panjab Intelligence* provides an account of the dialogue between the two men:

Raja Dhian Singh, having consulted with Raja Soocheit Singh, stated to Koonwur Nownihal Singh, "My engagement that I would continue to assist in the affairs of the *Raj* [government] for one year from the demise of the late Maharaja is now fulfilled; by the blessing of Providence the year's duty has been satisfactorily accomplished; and I, therefore, beg permission to retire to Benares, as I have always expressed my wish to do." The Koonwur said, "Your departure will throw the affairs of the *Raj* into confusion." The Raja replied, "We owe everything to the *Sircar* [Ranjit Singh], but I no longer feel inclined to interfere in the state affairs; Rajas Heera Singh, Goolaub Singh and Soocheit Singh will remain your servants." The Koonwur answered, "Wait awhile."[54]

Dhian Singh stayed on at Lahore and, though there was no discernible renewal of the Kanwar's old rapport with the Dogras, Naunihal Singh's relations with his father again took a turn for the worse. When Kharak Singh fell ill at the end of July,[55] the Kanwar once more reduced him to the status of a "virtual prisoner."[56] The unfortunate Maharaja lingered on in ill health until November 5 when he died at the age of thirty-nine, allegedly "by drugs as well as by unfilial harshness."[57]

Kharak Singh must be considered one of the most vilified figures in Sikh history. As previously observed, he was mercilessly derided by his European contemporaries. Indian writers seem to have followed their lead, and continue to describe him in most uncomplimentary terms.[58] Some of the judgments made against Kharak Singh are perhaps justified. He did not possess a magnetic personality and lacked the qualities of leadership. However, most of his critics fail to point out that Kharak Singh alone was not responsible for the political anarchy that prevailed during his reign. His famous father should share at least a part of the blame. Many historians have vied with one another in extolling Ranjit Singh's virtues, a large measure of which is well-deserved, but few have dared to admit his shortcomings. His failure to adequately train Kharak Singh for the role he was expected to play, and his elevation of the Jammu Rajas to such heights of power that the position of his own heir was undermined must be considered major blunders. On the other hand, some of the criticisms leveled against Kharak Singh are grossly exaggerated, others utterly groundless. For instance, he was reviled as a man given to sensual pleasures and addicted to drugs, but apparently his father and some other members of the darbar were equally guilty of such indulgences. His physical appearance was ridiculed, but perhaps he was no worse-looking than Ranjit Singh. He was accused of conspiring with the British, but there is no concrete evidence to substantiate such a charge. When Kharak Singh became the Maharaja, he was painfully aware of the threat to his throne. Unflinchingly he attempted to reduce the influence of the Dogras, strengthen his own position, and reign over the Sikh kingdom to the best of his ability. He tried to delegate some authority to Chet Singh in the hope that he would act as a counterforce to Dhian Singh, endorsed Beli Ram's accusations against Gulab Singh, and actually forced the Jammu chief to give up a piece of his territory. But the odds against Kharak Singh's efforts to establish his rule on a firm footing were too great. He was repeatedly frustrated by the intrigues of the powerful Dogras and the aspirations of his own unfaithful son. Even his wife all but abandoned him. The khalsa, too, seemed more loyal to the wazir than to the Maharaja. In retrospect, then, Kharak Singh's efforts to assert his power deserve some recognition, and his failures merit sympathy, not contempt.

The passing of Kharak Singh paved the way for Naunihal Singh's succession to the throne. He was then only nineteen. While not very handsome since his face, like that of Ranjit Singh, was pockmarked, he did possess "a steady, determined look."[59] Although young, he had already proved to be a good soldier, and his grandfather reportedly "anticipated that in him the Sikhs would find a successor worthy of filling the throne of Lahore, and preserving his kingdom entire."[60] Yet it can only be conjectured whether this brave but restless and conniving young man would have fulfilled the expectations of Ranjit Singh because, by a strange twist of fate, he lost his life on the very day of his father's death. While he was leading the mourners back into the capital after Kharak Singh's cremation on the banks of the Ravi, the arch of a gate collapsed, striking the Kanwar and several other members of his party, including Udham Singh who was killed instantly. Dhian Singh, though injured,[61] remained calm and ordered that Naunihal Singh, whose head was severely battered,[62] be removed to the royal quarters. He summoned Honigberger to treat the prince, but the European doctor was unable to render much assistance, since, as he himself records, the patient's "state was such that no hope of his recovery existed."[63] Naunihal Singh died a few hours later.

The peculiar circumstances surrounding the sudden and unexpected death of Naunihal Singh led some Europeans in India to speculate that the Jammu Rajas were involved in the incident. Cunningham wrote that "it is difficult to acquit them of the crime."[64] Henry Steinbach, a Prussian colonel in the Sikh army, believed that the archway's collapse had been prearranged by Dhian Singh.[65] In melodramatic style Herbert Edwardes, too, implicated the wazir: "Who did the deed? *Chance! says* everybody in the crowd. *Dhyan Singh! thought* everybody in the kingdom."[66] It cannot be denied that the Dogras were indeed capable of committing such a crime. Nor was a motive lacking, for the prince was much too ambitious and independent-minded to suit the designs of the Jammu Rajas. But the conditions under which Naunihal Singh was fatally injured tend to preclude the possibility of a deliberate plot and premeditated murder. The very fact that the falling arch killed Gulab Singh's eldest son and injured the wazir seems to eliminate the theory of foul play. It is also difficult to believe that such crafty manipulators as the Dogras would have risked certain retaliation from the Sikhs by so flagrantly assassinating Naunihal Singh in public. That no such outburst ensued seems to indicate that most Sikhs accepted the prince's death as a dreadful mischance.[67]

The deaths of Kharak Singh and his son left Panjab without a legitimate male claimant to the throne. Although Ranjit Singh was said to have had at least five more sons[68] in addition to Kharak Singh, doubts have been cast on their paternity.[69] The most prominent of these reputed sons was Kanwar Sher Singh,[70] who was in residence at his estate in Batala when he heard the news of Naunihal Singh's death. He immediately announced his intention of occupying the empty throne and hurried to Lahore. According to Fane, Sher Singh was an attractive man, "as handsome a black-bearded gentleman as one often sees."[71] The Kanwar was affable, too, and Emily Eden found him "a very jolly dog."[72] But Sher Singh was neither an able nor a vigorous leader and, in the words of Cunningham, "he possessed no commanding and few popular qualities."[73] He had befriended the Auckland entourage during 1838,[74] and was considered an Anglophile. When Ranjit Singh died the Kanwar had secretly requested the British to recognize him as the new Maharaja, but "Auckland hastily desired Sher Singh to be told Khurruk Singh was his master."[75]

The Kanwar's second attempt to become the Maharaja was challenged by Rani Chand Kaur. The Rani, said to be "as ambitious as immoral,"[76] astounded many by installing herself as regent at Lahore with the assistance of the Sandhawalia sardars[77] who, in turn, began to dream of superseding the Dogra Rajas at the darbar. Determined to thwart Sher Singh's aspirations, the Rani, on the one hand, flirted with the idea of grooming others for the throne. At one time she contemplated adopting Hira Singh as her son, at another she announced that one of Naunihal Singh's widows was expecting a posthumous child.[78] On the other hand, she entertained hopes of becoming the sovereign herself, and even declared: "Why should I not do as Queen Victoria does in England?"[79]

This unforeseen tug-of-war between Chand Kaur and Sher Singh left the Dogras scrambling for a policy which would best suit their interests. After some deliberation they resolved to pursue a cunning course of action which would give them a foot in each camp. It was decided that Dhian Singh and Suchet Singh should back the new Maharaja, while Gulab Singh and Hira Singh should espouse Chand Kaur's claims. In this way the Jammu Rajas hoped to attain a twofold goal. First, no matter which party won, it would be under obligation to them. Second, a protracted Chand Kaur–Sher Singh conflict might further diminish the power of the Maharaja and simultaneously increase their own. They performed their roles so adroitly that throughout the succession crisis few, if any, at Lahore perceived the real strategy of the Jammu Rajas. As Grey ably observes:

> To the ordinary observer, the policy of the Dogras would appear to have been parricidal, as well as fratricidal. . . . But it was only apparently so, for though on opposite sides, the Dogras were not [loyal to either rival], but only adhered the better to bend them to their interest, or betray if occasion served, and opportunity required, for in all their tortuous intrigues the common Dogra interest was undeviatingly pursued.[80]

As presumably anticipated by the Rajas, the two contenders expressed delight over the support pledged by the two respective pseudo-factions of the Dogra family. The Rani invited Gulab Singh to come to Lahore,[81] and he promptly came accompanied by "some battalions of hillmen, and ten guns."[82] As a mark of good will Chand Kaur ordered that the state of Minawar, which had been taken away from the Jammu chief by her late husband, be immediately restored to him.[83] Sher Singh, on his part, threw himself into Dhian Singh's arms. He also made a confidential appeal for assistance to Auckland, which led the Governor-General to believe that the Sikh prince "would write away half of the Punjab to the British Government to obtain interference in his favour."[84] But while the British were in sympathy with Sher Singh's claim to the throne, they once again refused to involve themselves in Sikh politics. Meanwhile, efforts were being made by several parties at Lahore to resolve the problem of succession, and an agreement was finally reached whereby the Rani and Dhian Singh were confirmed as regent and wazir respectively, and Sher Singh became head of a council of state.[85] But this was a measure born of expediency and, since the throne remained empty, bickerings between Chand Kaur and the Kanwar continued. A permanent solution to the difficulty seemed to lie in the proposal that the Rani marry Sher Singh, but Chand Kaur angrily rejected it,[86] much to the relief of the Jammu Rajas who must have seen in such a matrimonial alliance the failure of their divisive tactics. Ultimately, the Rani ordered the expulsion of Sher Singh from Lahore.[87] Although the latter was disposed to counteract, Dhian Singh persuaded him to desist and return to Batala, "promising, at the same time, that he would establish him on the throne of Lahore."[88] Simultaneously, however, Gulab Singh and Hira Singh assured the Rani that "they would not allow anybody to interfere with her affairs until the last breath of their lives."[89] Dhian Singh then publicly considered retiring to Jammu in protest against the Rani but delayed his departure, it was said, upon the advice of his elder brother. Gulab Singh was anxious that the wazir should consolidate his standing with the khalsa so that, in the event of an armed clash between the partisans of the Rani and the Kanwar, it would remain faithful to the Jammu Rajas.[90] Whether Dhian Singh was fully successful in this task is doubtful, although he did manage to convince many Sikh soldiers "that a woman should no longer be allowed to rule them, but that a man of energy and talent was required for this purpose, recommending strongly that the Prince Shere Singh should be recalled and placed on the throne."[91]

Dhian Singh, accompanied by his brother, Suchet Singh, finally left for Jammu at the beginning of January, 1841. But his absence from the Sikh capital was to be brief. Soon after his arrival at Jammu, the wazir advised Sher Singh to return to Lahore, and promised to join him there. However, the Kanwar had been taking independent action to insure his ascent to the throne. Jawala Singh, his vakil (agent), was already in Lahore advocating his master's cause with the Sikh troops. He received promises of support after bribing them with two lakhs of rupees and assuring them that their monthly salaries would be raised from seven to twelve rupees.[92] Heartened more perhaps by the report of his vakil than by the communication from Dhian Singh, the Kanwar prepared to go to the Sikh capital. To further enhance his chances for success, he once again contacted the British and informed Clerk "that whatever aid might be afforded him would be rewarded by a grant of all the Sikh Possessions on the left bank of the Sutlej."[93] When Sher Singh arrived at Lahore on January 14,[94] he immediately felt that a strong anti-Rani sentiment was in the air.[95] Assisted by seventeen thousand Sikh troops, he thereupon laid siege to the city's fort,[96] where Chand Kaur and her partisans were lodged, and ordered its occupants to surrender.

The Kanwar's action caught Gulab Singh, who was with the Rani in the citadel, completely off-guard. Although he had successfully put up a pretense of loyalty to Chand Kaur, he had not anticipated an actual clash between himself and Sher Singh, much less a contest between his Dogra troops and the khalsa. He was astounded that Sher Singh had decided to move independently of Dhian Singh, who was still at Jammu, and dismayed at the large number of Sikh troops who had defected to him. His greatest fear now lay in the possibility that the Kanwar might become the Maharaja without the help of Dhian Singh. If this occurred, the new ruler would owe no political debt to the Jammu family, a development which would spell trouble for the Dogras' privileged status in the kingdom. Realizing the gravity of the situation, Gulab Singh decided to do his utmost to hold the Kanwar at bay until his brother could return to Lahore. Therefore, he reaffirmed his loyalty to Chand Kaur and advised her not to submit to Sher Singh. The Rani was apparently so gratified by this that she assigned to Gulab Singh the responsibility of defending the fort.

The Jammu Raja promptly gathered together his own troops and those belonging to the pro-Rani chiefs, and found himself at the head of a force totalling about five thousand men.[97] He distributed considerable cash among the soldiers, who were thus persuaded to swear allegiance to the Rani's cause.[98] The Raja then made an effective barricade by "placing the soldiers all around in such a manner as to render it impossible for anybody to force entry into the fort."[99] Gulab Singh's stubborn stand[100] dashed Sher Singh's hopes of an uncontested entry into the fort. Consequently, the Kanwar sought to discuss with the Jammu chief terms for the fort's surrender, but the latter declined, suggesting in return a truce until Dhian Singh's arrival.[101] But Sher Singh rejected the Dogra's proposition and began to lose patience. When the khalsa clamored for action,[102] he threatened to take the fort by force. Gulab Singh, however, refused to be intimidated and curtly retorted that "as a Rajpoot he would defend the fort of which he had assumed the charge to the last."[103]

Sher Singh had not issued an empty warning. He ordered an assault but unwisely moved the Sikh troops into an exposed position in Hazuri Bagh,[104] an area directly in front of the fort. Gulab Singh's gunners made the most of the attackers' vulnerability, and from their fortified position launched such heavy shelling that at the end of the fighting "no less than 2,000" Sikhs lay dead.[105] The survivors were forced to retreat to a safe distance, but the adversaries continued to snipe at each other for several days and the number of casualties continued to mount. During the hostilities utter confusion prevailed in the Sikh capital. Wild rumors were afoot, including one "that the British were in Lahore."[106] The Sikh soldiers themselves turned into a pack of marauders, and Kanihya Lal provides a candid description of their lawless activities in the city: "The troops immediately set to plunder. All the shops, houses, and streets situated between the Delhi Gate and the Fort were plundered by the Sikhs. They broke open the locks of shops, and the Chatta Bazar, a shoe mart, was set on fire. . . . All the officers and the clerks of the army living in the city, in any lane or street, were robbed in daylight . . ."[107] This behavior on the part of the khalsa was an outgrowth of its failure to take the fort. It was also an indication that the Jammu chief had successfully frustrated Sher Singh's attempted coup.

Dhian Singh found Lahore in the throes of utter chaos when he arrived on January 18,[108] his return no doubt hastened by the news of the unexpected bloodshed. The dispirited Kanwar immediately turned to the wazir and begged him to intercede with his brother on his behalf. Subsequently, mock negotiations were opened during which the minister appealed to Gulab Singh and Hira Singh,[109] who was also in the fort, to consent to the Kanwar's elevation to the throne. The Jammu chief, however, succinctly maintained his pose of inflexibility by reiterating his fealty to the Rani. He then defended his actions in a simulated tirade against Dhian Singh. But the concluding part of the diatribe, as recorded in the "Tarikh Nama," reveals that he was already beginning to drift away from his rigid commitment to Chand Kaur:

Raja Gulab Singh told Raja Dhian Singh that even though the latter had been the principal functionary of the Great Maharaja [Ranjit Singh], he was his junior in years. The events that he [Gulab Singh] had witnessed or participated in had not been shared by [Dhian Singh]. He told him that he had fought against the Kanwar not for the usurpation of kingship but had done so for the protection of Rani Chand Kaur and the treasury lodged in [the fort]. Also the honor of the Rani Sahiba would have been outraged and rumors would have spread throughout the Sikh state that Rani Chand Kaur, daughter-in-law of the Great Maharaja, had been molested. He had, therefore, taken up arms against the descendants of the Great Maharaja. He was always loyal and devoted to them. Had it been someone else he would have found out how brave the inmates of the fort were, but he had taken into consideration the fact that outside the fort was the son of the Great Maharaja and inside was the daughter-in-law of the *sarkar*. He was, however, a devoted servant of both.[110]

At last, the Jammu chief apparently convinced the Rani that they were fighting against impossible odds, and the two sides agreed to make peace. By common consent Sher Singh became Maharaja, Dhian Singh was confirmed as wazir,[111] and Chand Kaur was awarded the lucrative jagir of Kudi Kuddiali.[112] Thus the Dogra strategy was crowned with success. The new ruler occupied the throne only with the Jammu Rajas' aid and, as future events would reveal, the power of the Maharajas had been significantly curtailed. The battle of succession also provided other benefits to the Dogras. The gullible Chand Kaur, despite her failure, was so moved by Gulab Singh's recent support that she placed her new jagir in his charge.[113] Attar Singh and Ajit Singh, the leaders of the anti-Dogra Sandhawalia family who had stood behind the Rani to the end, were so terrified by the new turn of events that they quit Panjab and sought shelter in British India.[114] Another Sandhawalia leader, Lehna Singh, was imprisoned.[115] Furthermore, before evacuating the fort, Gulab Singh, with the Rani's knowledge, appropriated a large portion of the Sikh treasury. Latif writes:

Raja Gulab Singh carried away all the money and valuables belonging to the Maharani Chand Kour under the pretence of keeping it safely for her . . . [and he] carried off the accumulated treasures of Ranjit Singh which were in the fort. Sixteen carts were filled with rupees and other silver coins, while 500 horsemen were each entrusted with a bag of gold mohurs [seals], and his orderlies were also entrusted with jewellery and other valuable articles.[116]

In vain did Sher Singh remonstrate with the Jammu chief, for the latter rebuffed him, arguing that "whatever expenses were incurred inside the fort or whatever had been granted to any employee had been granted with the express permission of Rani Chand Kaur."[117] However, before Gulab Singh left Lahore the khalsa turned so bitterly against him, aroused probably both by his ransacking of the treasury and his part in the infliction of heavy casualties in its ranks during the recent fighting, that the darbar was compelled to send a trustworthy Sikh force to escort the Raja and his men back to Jammu.[118] Disquieted by the khalsa's attitude and fearful that such hostility might spread to the ranks of his own army, the Dogra leader immediately upon his return dismissed "every Sikh soldier from the many forts held in jagir or farm by his family."[119]

Despite the artifices and deceptions practiced by the Dogras during the recent events, Sher Singh felt obligated to grant them new favors. In a special decree, overflowing with prodigious tributes to the Jammu Rajas, the new Maharaja confirmed to them and their progeny in perpetuity all their jagirs and allowed them to maintain their own troops. Sher Singh also vowed that he and his descendants would "from generation to generation" abide by this agreement.[120] The contents of the decree are relatively unimportant inasmuch as the favors it granted were more or less already enjoyed by the Dogras. But its issuance was an impolitic step, for the Maharaja thereby legalized the extraordinary status of the Jammu Rajas in the Sikh kingdom. The net result was the recognition of a Dogra state within the Sikh state, a Dogra army within the Sikh army. The decree, therefore, raised the prestige of Jammu and dealt another blow to the supremacy of Lahore.

Nevertheless, the Dogras as well as Sher Singh now had to reckon with a new political force in the state—the khalsa. A year before Ranjit Singh's death the Sikh army had numbered a little over forty-six thousand men.[121] Even though the Sikh soldiers earned little[122] and their salaries were often in arrears,[123] they idolized Ranjit Singh, and as long as he lived they remained a disciplined and viable force. But in the anarchy that followed his death, the khalsa gradually came to look upon its leaders with contempt and, after the bloody events of the Sher Singh–Chand Kaur dispute, it emerged as an unrestrained, riotous body. The Sikh soldiers' appetite had been whetted by their wanton activities during the siege of the Lahore fort and, even after Sher Singh's succession, they continued to ransack the capital, murder civilians, and terrorize their officers.[124] They also forced the Maharaja to raise their salaries to nine rupees per month.[125] By the middle of 1841 their contumacy had reached such a level that they no longer considered themselves responsible to the government, but regarded themselves as the true agents of the people. Thereupon, every Sikh battalion elected an executive body of its own known as the panch (council of five), which was to administer its own affairs and negotiate demands with its commanders and the government.[126] The panches, "acting in concert,"[127] became a most powerful body in the Sikh kingdom, but they often displayed a deplorable lack of judgment and, as Cunningham writes: "Their resolutions were often unstable or unwise, and the representatives of different divisions might take opposite sides from sober conviction or self-willed prejudice, or they might be bribed and cajoled."[128] Yet the khalsa considered itself patriotic, feared a British occupation of Panjab, and wished to preserve the sovereignty of the Sikh state. This conflict between purpose and method was potentially dangerous, and in it lay one of the major causes of the disintegration of the Sikh kingdom.

The lawlessness initiated by the khalsa at Lahore spread to other parts of the state, and during the spring of 1841 the Sikh troops stationed in Kashmir murdered the provincial governor, Mahan Singh. The Jammu Raja saw in this rebellion an opportunity to extend his influence into Kashmir and immediately sought Lahore's permission to crush it. In obvious collusion with his brother, Dhian Singh also pressured the Maharaja for the immediate dispatch of an expedition exclusively under the charge of the Jammu chief to restore order in the northern province.[129] But wary of Gulab Singh's reported designs on Kashmir, the Sikh ruler hesitated to make a decision, which led Clerk to remark that, "though the Maharaja is apprehensive that he might have much difficulty in restoring his authority in Cashmere without having recourse to the awe in which the Raja's name and resources are held in that direction, he is said to be very averse to delivering over its government to the Raja's exclusive superintendence."[130] Nonetheless, the Maharaja was so fearful of alienating his wazir that he finally compromised and decided to send a force under the joint command of his son, Kanwar Partab Singh, and the Jammu Raja.[131] However, it was not until August that the turmoil in Kashmir was finally brought to an end. Gulab Singh dealt out such harsh punishment to the miscreants that the Sikh troops at Lahore, already nettled by their own recent treatment at his hands, sorely complained "that he slaughtered the Khalsa as if they were Afghans."[132] Although this triumph did not actually bring Kashmir under the Jammu chief's jurisdiction, it was believed that Mahan Singh's successor, Sheikh Ghulam Mohi-ud-Din, had received his assignment on the recommendation of Gulab Singh and hence was considered his henchman.[133]

At Lahore Dhian Singh continued to pursue a policy calculated to preserve and extend his own interests and those of his family. Fearing that Jawala Singh, the Maharaja's former vakil, was entertaining ambitions to replace him as the wazir, Dhian Singh had him arrested during May of 1841. The minister succeeded in turning the Maharaja against the prisoner,[134] and Jawala Singh "died of foul means immediately afterwards."[135] Moreover, when Sher Singh, who considered Chand Kaur to be a troublemaker,[136] had her murdered in June of 1842,[137] no complaint or remonstrance was heard from the Jammu Rajas. They apparently saw in her elimination a welcome opportunity for Gulab Singh to arrogate to himself the jagir of Kudi Kuddiali already under his supervision.

However, in the aftermath of the Rani's death, it seems Dhian Singh felt that the Maharaja was attempting to free himself from his domination. He retaliated by engineering the arrival at Lahore in August 1842 of Rani Jindan, one of Ranjit Singh's wives, and her son, Dalip Singh, a four- or five-year-old boy reputed to be another son of the Great Maharaja,[138] and "threatened to supplant" Sher Singh with the young prince.[139] As relations with Dhian Singh gradually worsened, the Maharaja came increasingly under the influence of a double-dealing priest named Bhai Gurmukh Singh.[140] The Sikh ruler also moved to make peace with the Sandhawalias in hopes of using them "as some counterpoise to the Rajas of Jummoo."[141] In November he released Lehna Singh, and permitted Attar Singh and Ajit Singh to return to Lahore.[142] But the Maharaja's maneuvers had little effect on the power and attitude of the Dogras. For instance, during January 1843 the wazir successfully prevented a meeting at Feruzpur between the Maharaja and Ellenborough in the fear "that his sovereign might induce the English viceroy to accede to his ruin, or to the reduction of his exotic influence."[143] The Jammu chief, on his part, showed his displeasure with Sher Singh by refraining from paying periodic visits to the Lahore darbar as had been his custom during Ranjit Singh's reign.[144]

Dogra relations with the Maharaja finally reached the breaking point, and Dhian Singh, with the approval of his elder brother,[145] conspired to assassinate Sher Singh. But the wazir was determined not to commit the crime himself. Instead, he goaded the Sandhawalias into killing the Maharaja by convincing them "that they had been inveigled to Lahore for their more assured destruction."[146] Dhian Singh probably hoped that such a scheme would also lead to the extermination of the anti-Dogra Sandhawalias, "whom he first designed to use as tools and then put to death as traitors."[147] On September 15 the Sandhawalias treacherously murdered not only Sher Singh but also his son, Partab Singh,[148] and then occupied the Lahore fort. Later on that same day they even managed to outwit the unsuspecting Dhian Singh by inviting him to the fort, where he, too, was slain. M'Gregor provides a description of the fateful encounter:

. . . at length, Lena Singh, taking the Rajah's hand in his, enquired "Who was now to be king?" Dhyan Singh replied "There is no one but Dhuleep Singh." Lena Singh rejoined "And so he is to be made king and you become his prime minister, while we get nothing for our pains?" The Rajah became annoyed, and wanted to get away, but the Gooroo Goormukh Singh being present observed, "What is the use of words? Remove the Rajah as you have done Shere Singh and his son, and then your path will be clear." On hearing this remark, Ajeet Singh, who was standing behind the Rajah, shot him in the back, and he fell dead on the spot.[149]

Immediately thereafter Ajit Singh declared himself the wazir, and designated Dalip Singh as the next Maharaja.[150]

However, the Sandhawalias, in their haste to seize the reins of government, had neglected to dispose of Hira Singh and Suchet Singh, who were then both at Lahore. On learning of his father's death, Hira Singh approached the khalsa and pleaded with them to wreak vengeance on the assassins.[151] He promised the soldiers higher salaries[152] and exploited their fears of a British takeover by warning that the "Sikhs who now took pride in the profession of arms would be compelled to seek an ignoble living by following the plough."[153] Though suspicious of the Dogras, the khalsa was aroused, and on September 16 it successfully stormed the fort and slaughtered many of its archly anti-Dogra occupants, including Ajit Singh, Lehna Singh, Gurmukh Singh, and Missar Beli Ram.[154] Attar Singh was at that time absent from Lahore and, upon receiving the news of the defeat at the fort, once again escaped across the Sutlej.[155] Having thus avenged his father's death, Hira Singh himself succeeded to the wazarat. He also installed Dalip Singh as the new Maharaja and Rani Jindan as her son's regent.

The abrupt death of Dhian Singh ended the remarkable partnership of the two elder Jammu brothers through which they had jointly controlled the political scene in the Sikh kingdom for over four years. Gulab Singh was naturally apprehensive about what this latest development at Lahore would do to his aspirations. But since the wazarat passed to a member of his own clan, the Jammu chief was somewhat relieved to find that the Dogra domination at the Sikh capital had not fully vanished with his brother's demise. He could look forward to the future with a degree of confidence.

The period from June 1839, to September 1843, was one of great personal triumph for Gulab Singh. The crafty Raja, in league with his powerful brother, Dhian Singh, followed a calculated and treacherous policy which successfully served to attain their ends. The two brothers demonstrated their skill in the arts of intrigue and diplomacy by pitting Naunihal Singh against Kharak Singh, and Chand Kaur against Sher Singh. Nor did they hesitate to use blackmail and murder whenever it was deemed necessary. Like the Sayyid brothers in early eighteenth-century Mughal Delhi, the Jammu Rajas had become the king-makers of the Sikh state. Only once did they seriously miscalculate, and the error proved costly, for it resulted in the death of Dhian Singh. His elimination was a blow to the hopes and aspirations of the Jammu chief. Yet he recovered from the loss quite rapidly. With a weakened Sikh government at Lahore, Gulab Singh moved swiftly from autonomy toward complete independence. He continued to formulate his underhanded policies with skill and determination. But he executed them somewhat more cautiously now that his influential brother and ally was dead.

4 The Wazarat of Hira Singh

Heera Singh is strikingly handsome, though rather effeminate in appearance . . . he is intelligent and clever . . . gentlemanlike, and amusing.—W. G. Osborne

Raja Soochet Singh . . . says openly that until Raja Heera Singh is dead he can have no peace.—Richmond

[Gulab Singh] has sent a message to Pundit Julla, that on the first shot fired against Jummoo, he shall have joints of his brother served up to him.—Henry Hardinge

RAJA Hira Singh was in his mid-twenties when he succeeded to the wazarat. Varying accounts of his appearance, character, and ability have been provided by his British contemporaries. While Emily Eden described Hira Singh as "very handsome,"[1] M'Gregor wrote that he "is effeminate; and his character for energy and intellect inferior to that of his father."[2] Osborne found him "intelligent and clever . . . gentlemanlike and amusing,"[3] but Cunningham believed Hira Singh "had little more than a noble presence and conciliatory address to recommend him."[4] Whatever the accuracy of such estimates it soon became evident that Hira Singh had few qualifications for the wazarat. The ability to both command respect and inspire awe was an essential prerequisite for anyone who hoped to govern post–Dhian Singh Panjab, but the new minister possessed neither. Hira Singh had become wazir because of the sudden burst of sympathy over his father's assassination and, to some extent, because of his close association with the celebrated Ranjit Singh. The khalsa had impulsively acquiesced in his assumption of the high office, ignoring other men of distinction in the Sikh kingdom, including Dhian Singh's two surviving brothers. But if Hira Singh was young and relatively inexperienced in the fine art of running a government by intrigue and contrivance, crafts in which his puissant father and wily uncle at Jammu excelled, he nevertheless was determined to be his own wazir. He endeavored to give to the Sikh kingdom stable rule, and there were moments when he seemed to achieve this goal, but in the end his lack of skill and judgment, made even more glaring by the absence of that personal magnetism so necessary for success, resulted in failure.

No sooner had Hira Singh assumed the wazarat than he encountered the hostility of the unpredictable khalsa. The abrupt deaths of Sher Singh and Dhian Singh had "led to the virtual transfer of all power to the disorganized army."[5] Hira Singh seemd impotent, and there were rumors that, from fear of the khalsa, he intended to flee on "relays of horses [which had] been already placed for him on the road to Jummoo."[6] This new turn of events caused Ellenborough to feel that the disintegration of the Sikh state was imminent, and he informed Queen Victoria: "The tendency of these events is to produce a separation between the government of the hills and that of the plains, the Sikhs retaining the plains, and the Rajpoots, under Goolab and Heera Singh, the hills."[7] The young wazir, however, decided to remain at Lahore and, in an effort to appease and befriend the soldiers, he raised their monthly wages by two and a half rupees. But this did not fully satisfy the khalsa. As its political influence and bargaining power continued to increase, the army "felt that it had become the master of the state" and debated whether to eradicate all Dogra influence from Lahore.[8] For a while such a state of uncertainty prevailed in the Sikh capital that Ellenborough observed: "The Punjab is practically without a government, and the nominal minister, Heera Singh, will probably soon cease to live or to reside at Lahore."[9]

The authority of Hira Singh was also challenged by some influential rivals. One such man who opposed the new minister was Jowahir Singh, uncle of the youthful Maharaja and brother of Rani Jindan. Described by one source as "a man of some energy and talent"[10] but by another as "a drunken debauchee,"[11] Jowahir Singh aspired to the wazarat. Hira Singh also found a foe in his uncle, Suchet Singh, a man noted for his physical beauty[12] and many wives, who resented his nephew's ascendancy and considered himself the logical choice for wazir. Bitter and frustrated, he entertained plans to oust Hira Singh.[13]

Bewildered by his opponents, Hira Singh turned to his uncle at Jammu for counsel and requested him to visit Lahore. But Gulab Singh, aware of the khalsa's abiding animosity toward him, hesitated to go.[14] Since Dhian Singh's death he had remained "in the hills . . . engaged in securing himself there and unwilling to trust himself in the plains."[15] For a while it was even doubted whether, in the event of an anti-Dogra eruption at Lahore, the Jammu Raja would "make the effort to support his relations."[16] Nevertheless, Gulab Singh gradually realized that in order to safeguard his own interests it was imperative that the Dogras continue to maintain some influence over the Lahore government. Therefore, he decided to accept Hira Singh's invitation and arrived at Lahore on November 10, 1843. However, for his own safety, he brought with him about ten thousand Dogra troops. This unusually large force aroused considerable speculation about Gulab Singh's motives. Richmond, the successor to Clerk at Ludhiana, went so far as to conclude that "the designs of the Raja may probably be to secure the fort and city of Lahore."[17]

The Jammu chief, however, had come to the capital with an olive branch. Determined to stabilize the position of Hira Singh and improve his own relations with the khalsa, he pretended to be both a loyalist and an upholder of the Sikh state. Assuming the role of a sagacious leader, he asked the Sikh chiefs to unite and resolve their differences, asserting repeatedly the benefits of a stable government.[18] He appealed to Rani Jindan to treat Hira Singh as her own son but, at the same time, warned his nephew "to be alert and trust nobody."[19] He, of all people, rebuked the revenue dodgers and, to set an example, actually made a token contribution to the Lahore treasury. Furthermore, he assured the khalsa that he would pay all his debts to the Sikh government.[20] Gulab Singh so mesmerized the Sikh army that it decided, for the moment at any rate, to forgive his past conduct. His success became obvious when Jowahir Singh attempted to rouse the khalsa against the visiting Dogra leader "of whom he said he stood in fear."[21] The soldiery responded "by making him a prisoner and by informing Raja Golab Singh of what had happened."[22]

The visit to Lahore proved to be both politically and financially profitable to the Jammu chief. Since the Raja's activities had helped to buttress his nephew's position at Lahore, Hira Singh manifested his gratitude by granting important favors to Gulab Singh. For example, the wazir helped his uncle to further extend his influence over Kashmir by ordering that the affairs of that province were to be "managed by Raja Golab Singh alone and no orders could be given about them in Lahore."[23] Though the Dogra chief did not actually acquire possession of Kashmir at that time and Mohi-ud-Din remained its governor, Hira Singh's announcement was at least a partial renunciation of Lahore's unquestioned supremacy over Kashmir and an acknowledgment that that northern province now lay in Jammu's sphere of influence. The wazir also rewarded his uncle with several farms in Hazara.[24]

But despite the overall success of his trip, the Jammu Raja could not bring about a reconciliation between Suchet Singh and Hira Singh. Nevertheless, he tried to reduce tensions by persuading his brother to accompany him to Jammu. There the childless Suchet Singh adopted Ranbir Singh, the Dogra chief's youngest son, who thus became heir to his numerous estates in the hills and considerable financial assets.[25]

But the enmity between Suchet Singh and Hira Singh continued unabated. Soon after his arrival at Jammu, Suchet Singh announced his intention of going back to Lahore and said "openly that until Raja Heera Singh is dead he can have no peace."[26] Worried by the possible consequences of his uncle's return, the wazir tried in vain to placate him by offering him the governorship of Peshawar.[27] He also asked the Jammu Raja to dissuade his brother from returning to the Sikh capital, exhorting metaphorically that since "the lion was still in the cage—take care he get not out."[28] But the wazir proceeded to alienate Suchet Singh even further by appointing Missar Julla, an ambitious and unscrupulous Brahman from Jammu, as his chief adviser.[29] Julla succeeded in acquiring considerable influence in the Sikh kingdom, and the "Tarikh Nama" provides an estimate of his power: "A word from the Pandit's tongue was implicitly obeyed from Lahore to Peshawar and from Multan to Kashmir. There was no need to commit it in black and white. Every chief whether big or small and all the courtiers were overawed by the Pandit's fortune to such an extent that they trembled like leaves of trees before him and acted as weak and lifeless persons."[30] Suchet Singh naturally considered Julla a new rival at Lahore and seethed with anger on learning that, in order to increase his influence over Hira Singh, the Pandit was deliberately deepening the cleavage between him and his nephew. He felt compelled to retaliate and during December purportedly encouraged two princes, Kashmira Singh and Peshora Singh, who were said to have also been fathered by Ranjit Singh,[31] to denounce the new Maharaja and the wazir and lay claim to the throne of Panjab.[32] However, the rebellion of the two Kanwars, who then held Sialkot in jagir, collapsed when Gulab Singh opposed their claims, partly because the uprising was directed against his own nephew and partly because the princes were not protégés of the Dogras. He apparently not only prevented Suchet Singh from going to their assistance, but personally marched at the head of a force to neighboring Sialkot to put down the upstarts. The Dogra Raja occupied the town, arrested the Kanwars, and took them to Jammu.[33] He also seized one and a half lakhs of rupees belonging to Kashmira Singh,[34] which later led the prince to bewail that "Raja Golab Singh had taken away all he possessed save his life."[35]

But the Kanwars' revolt destroyed the recently established rapport between the Dogras and the khalsa. For instance, when word of the rebellion reached Lahore, the army irately refused Hira Singh's command to put it down, declaring "that if the troops leave Lahore the Dogruhs will put their own men into it, that no doubt such deceit is intended, but the Khalsa will not be deceived, & will destroy root & branch the Jummoo chiefs."[36] Later, they fulminated against Gulab Singh's operations at Sialkot, demanding to know how he had "dared to do so without consulting the Khalsa,"[37] and called for the release of the Kanwars.[38] The Sikh troops also questioned the real intentions of the Dogras, charging that they "are bent upon the extinction of the Khalsa"[39] and "want to become masters of the Punjaub."[40] Hira Singh was so disquieted by this belligerent attitude that he advised Gulab Singh to free the Kanwars and cautioned that, for his own safety, "he shouldn't come to Lahore [for a while]."[41]

Although the princes were released, the khalsa remained unmollified and, momentarily at least, revived the talk of removing Hira Singh.[42] During January the troops spurned the wazir's suggestion that Jowahir Singh, who was still in their custody, be removed to Jammu.[43] In March the khalsa, as a further act of defiance, freed Jowahir Singh and permitted him to live with his nephew in the royal quarters.[44] Gulab Singh supported the khalsa's action[45] in an effort to appease both the soldiery and Rani Jindan. In fact, the Jammu Raja, mindful of the Rani's displeasure over the confinement of her brother, had recommended his release as early as January.[46] Nevertheless, the manner in which Jowahir Singh was set free indicated that the Dogra power had been dealt another blow at Lahore. In a report on the latest round of events, Richmond correctly perceived that the Dogra influence "can only last so long as the troops continue to be cajoled by the art and dissimulation of Raja Golab Singh."[47]

The Jammu leader had an additional motive for keeping the Sikhs in good humor. Because of the increasing troubles of the Dogra clan since the death of his prestigious brother, Gulab Singh feared that the former rulers of the hill principalities he had forcibly brought under his sway might try to reassert their power.[48] He was "apprehensive that if one person raises opposition, there may soon be a general outbreak."[49] To prevent such an eventuality he attempted to create an image of unimpaired solidarity between the Dogras and the Sikhs, and adopted a careful policy of propitiation toward his enemies in the hills. Thus, when the brother of the late Raja of Chamba rose against his authority, Gulab Singh "instead of further irritating the rebel . . . by threats, & continued attempts at coercion . . . pacified him by the gift of a considerable jagheer."[50]

But if the Jammu Raja succeeded both in staving off any immediate threat from the khalsa and in maintaining peace in the hills, he was unable to preserve unity within his own family. The feud between Suchet Singh and Hira Singh continued undiminished. Cognizant of the dangers inherent in a violent showdown between the two men, the Jammu chief first remonstrated with his brother to settle his differences with their nephew, but "Suchet Singh paid little heed to him."[51] The Dogra leader then advised Hira Singh to compromise and "make Raja Soochet Singh Vizeer and to regard himself as Maharaja."[52] He also suggested the quiet removal of Pandit Julla, who continued to foment trouble between Lahore and Jammu. The wazir, however, rejected his uncle's counsel and instead repeated his demand that he "keep Raja Soochet Singh in the Hills."[53] In fact,

Hira Singh proceeded to antagonize Suchet Singh even further by seizing, at Julla's suggestion, his uncle's estate of Jasrota.[54] Suchet Singh was so incensed by this action that he announced "that he would never rest until he had brought Raja Heera Singh & Misser Julla to account."[55] Once again the Jammu chief intervened by warning Hira Singh that, if he refused to reconcile Suchet Singh, the latter, in utter desperation, might "go over to the English" and gravely jeopardize the Dogra standing in the Sikh state.[56] The wazir responded "that he would attend to his advice, [and that] he regarded him as his father,"[57] but in reality he did nothing to soothe Suchet Singh's ruffled feelings. Finding that his nephew had no intention of making any concessions, Suchet Singh prepared to go to Lahore and boasted that upon his arrival he would put strings in the nostrils of Julla and make him dance in the streets of the capital.[58] To demonstrate that he had not been issuing idle warnings, Suchet Singh, without his brother's knowledge, left Jammu and arrived on the outskirts of Lahore on March 26 with a band of about four hundred followers. Hira Singh, abetted by Julla, dispatched a large force to challenge the intruders. Though woefully outnumbered, Suchet Singh fought valiantly against his nephew's troops, but he and many of his comrades were finally cornered and killed.[59] During the cremation ceremonies for Suchet Singh at which the wazir himself led the mourners,[60] it is reported that as many as forty-five of the dead Raja's wives immolated themselves.[61] However, his chief Rani was then in the hills and thus escaped the ordeal of sati.

Gulab Singh mourned his brother's death, declaring that if "the death of Dhian Singh cut him as it were in two . . . the loss of Soochet Singh was as the loss of an arm."[62] He reacted by sending to the British the first of several confidential but unsuccessful overtures which he was to make before the First Anglo-Sikh War for a mutual alliance against Lahore (see Chapter 6). He also protested Hira Singh's role in the affair and warned him that all the hill chiefs would now know "that among the Rajas of Jummoo there was no unanimity and they would arise on all sides."[63] The wazir expressed remorse and reportedly sent "a confidential servant to Jummoo to intercede for him and Misser Julla with Raja Golab Singh and to try to induce him to pardon them on account of the death of Raja Soochet Singh."[64] The nephew's repentance seemed to pacify his uncle, for when Attar Singh Sandhawalia and Kanwar Kashmira Singh led their suicidal revolt against Lahore in May, the Jammu chief offered his aid to the wazir.[65]

This reconciliation, however, was short-lived, and Suchet Singh's death, in fact, marked the beginning of a crisis in the relations between Lahore and Jammu which continued till the end of Hira Singh's wazarat. First of all, Suchet Singh's chief Rani arrived at Jammu and demanded that the Dogra leader punish her husband's murderers.[66] She warned "that if Raja Golab Singh does not revenge her on the slayer of her husband, she will herself proceed to Lahore and solicit the aid of the Khalsa."[67] Secondly, serious trouble arose when Hira Singh made clear his disapproval of his uncle's attempt to take over all of Suchet Singh's jagirs and possessions in the hills, worth about two crores[68] of rupees,[69] by claiming that they now belonged to his son, Ranbir Singh, whom the late Raja had only recently adopted. The wazir also vetoed the Jammu chief's attempt to dignify Ranbir Singh by investing him with the title of Raja, declaring that "heretofore titles were conferred by the Darbar—this new practice was not good."[70] A controversy also developed over a comparatively small treasure belonging to Suchet Singh, estimated at fifteen lakhs of rupees, which had been deposited at Feruzpur, a town across the Sutlej under British jurisdiction.[71] At the end of May the wazir, encouraged once again by Julla, formally demanded that the Jammu chief divide equally with him all the possessions of Suchet Singh.[72] The underlying reasons for Hira Singh's stand seem to have been not only that he considered himself legitimately entitled to a share of Suchet Singh's estate but also that he was eager to replenish the exhausted Lahore treasury with such an inheritance. The Sikh economy was in a deplorable condition and by May of 1844 the Lahore treasury contained only thirty-five lakhs of rupees.[73]

The Jammu chief's immediate response was to express bitter resentment over his nephew's demand, and in a stinging letter to Hira Singh he wrote "that just as he had killed Raja Suchet Singh and performed his last rites, he could murder him and perform the funeral ceremonies in the same way so that he might get hold of the properties of both Suchet Singh and himself."[74] He went on to chide his nephew for not evenly dividing the properties of Dhian Singh with his two brothers, Jawahar and Moti Singh.[75] But when rumors began to circulate that Hira Singh might send the Sikh army to take forcible possession of the disputed estates,[76] the Jammu Raja began to temporize. He presented his nephew with a variety of excuses, complaints, and counterdemands. During June, the wily Dogra sent repeated assurances to the wazir that he was eager to divide the disputed estates with him but that Suchet Singh's widow "was mistress of the whole, and [he] had no power to demand the money from her."[77] However, at the same time he advised the Rani that "she should be careful not to allow Raja Heera Singh's people to get any footing in [her husband's territories]."[78] During July, Gulab Singh informed the wazir that he would divide Suchet Singh's estates if, in return, he was given control over Kashmir because, as he put it, "Sheikh Gholam Moheeoodeen, the Governor of Cashmeer, was now sick and infirm and . . . Cashmeer was bounded by many districts under him."[79] He also asked that additional farms in other parts of the kingdom be granted to him.[80] But when the wazir neither demonstrated any inclination to accede to his uncle's wishes nor betrayed any intention of relinquishing his claims to Suchet Singh's property, the Jammu chief loudly complained that Dhian Singh "had always deferred to [him] but Heera Singh's conduct towards him was the reverse."[81] Expressing his disenchantment with the new state of affairs, he threatened to renounce his position and retire to the holy Hindu city of Benares.[82] Hira Singh was momentarily beguiled by his uncle's sophistry and invited him to Lahore for negotiations,[83] promising to "respect his uncle Golab Singh in the manner he was respected by Raja Dhian Singh."[84]

The Dogra chief, however, refused either to go to Lahore or to settle his differences with the Sikh government. The wazir now retaliated not only by insisting on the division of Suchet Singh's estates but also by demanding that the Jammu Raja pay the revenue debts which he owed to Lahore.[85] An open break thus resulted between the two men, and during late July and throughout August Gulab Singh took various measures to strengthen his position against Hira Singh. In anticipation of an invasion from Lahore, he fortified his defences[86] and circulated the news that "all those in the Hills would unite to oppose Raja Heera Singh."[87] Apprehensive of a sneak attack on Suchet Singh's jagirs, the Dogra chief reinforced the forts in Reasi and Sambha.[88] When officials of Hira Singh attempted to gain control over the Reasi fort by offering bribes to its occupants, they were arrested,[89] and at Sambha Ranbir Singh repulsed some of the wazir's soldiers who had tried to take possession of the jagir.[90] Meanwhile, Gulab Singh's agents were busy sowing seeds of dissension within the ranks of the Sikhs by distributing gold medals and bracelets among the khalsa at Lahore.[91] The Jammu Raja also made overtures to the Sikh generals, Tej Singh and Kahn Singh, who were stationed at Peshawar,[92] and there were even rumors that he had "some secret correspondence" with his old enemy, Dewan Sawan Mal, the governor of Multan.[93] Another Sikh leader, Chattar Singh Attariwala, openly announced his support for Gulab Singh.[94] Even Jawahar Singh and Moti Singh took his side against their own brother. For instance, Moti Singh rejected the wazir's invitation to move to Lahore, declaring "that since his childhood he had been under Raja Golab Singh and wished to remain where he was."[95]

Jawahar Singh, in particular, enraged Hira Singh by seizing several Sikh forts near Naushara.[96]

The Jammu Raja also directed his wrath against Pandit Julla, whom he considered chiefly responsible for Suchet Singh's death and the real instigator of his own quarrel with his nephew.[97] The Dogra chief demanded that Hira Singh "make over the person of Pundit Julla" to him,[98] but was rebuffed by the wazir. Gulab Singh then turned upon several members of Julla's family who still lived at Jammu, including a brother named Charan Das. They were harassed, threatened,[99] and thrown into prison.[100] Julla was outraged by the suffering and humiliation inflicted upon his relatives and repeatedly urged Hira Singh to send the khalsa against Jammu.[101] Although the wazir agreed to the necessity of an armed attack upon his uncle's stronghold, he nonetheless demurred, fearing that the insubordinate army might refuse to go.[102] He turned down Julla's offer to personally lead an invasion, but promised to dispatch the army when it would be more favorably disposed to carry out his orders. The wazir also rejected Julla's advice to confiscate "all the farms held by Raja Golab Singh."[103] Meanwhile, the Dogra leader continued to persecute the Pandit's relatives. Feigning a change of heart, Gulab Singh ordered their release and permitted them to leave Jammu but, on the outskirts of the city, they were waylaid by a party of Dogra Mians. Thirty members of Julla's family were killed and all their baggage seized. The assailants, however, spared the life of Charan Das, who was taken back to Jammu. When news of the bloody ambush reached Lahore, a maddened Julla once more exhorted the wazir to invade Jammu, but the latter, while consoling his favorite, still took no action.[104]

As he continued his anti-Lahore campaign, the Jammu Raja for a time became so obsessed with the idea of obliterating his enemies at the Sikh capital that in August he even conspired with Kanwar Peshora Singh. The two men entered into an agreement by which the Kanwar was to occupy Lahore with an army financed by the Raja, after which Peshora Singh would sit on the Sikh throne and Gulab Singh would succeed to the wazarat. The Dogra chief actually gave all honors and insignia of royalty to the Kanwar and advanced him the sum of fifty thousand rupees with which the prince enlisted about five thousand men. But Gulab Singh thereafter lost his nerve and repudiated the compact with the Kanwar.[105] The ramifications of such a bold and hazardous move, if it had actually been carried out, can only be conjectured.

While extreme antagonism and tension prevailed between Lahore and Jammu, Hira Singh endeavored to attain a reconciliation by persuading Imam-ud-Din, the administrator of Jullundur and son of Mohi-ud-Din, to intercede on his behalf with the Dogra chief. Imam-ud-Din visited Jammu for several weeks, but finally returned to report that Gulab Singh had no intention of giving in to Lahore's demands.[106] Another attempt at mediation was made by Jawahar Singh, whom the Dogra chief reluctantly permitted to go to Lahore at the end of August.[107] At the capital he advocated the cause of the Jammu Raja and informed Hira Singh that their uncle "wished to have the river Ravee regarded as the boundary of his jagheers and possessions."[108] He tried to impress his brother with the power and prestige of his adversary, and advised him not only to seek an accommodation with Gulab Singh but also "to consider him as his father and Guide."[109] The wazir, however, summarily rejected Jawahar Singh's suggestions and instead attempted to woo him away from the Jammu chief by offering to invest him with the title of Raja and the post of commander-in-chief of the Sikh army.[110] But in return he demanded that Jawahar Singh lead a Sikh expedition against Jammu. Refusing to be a party to any move against his uncle, Jawahar Singh turned down the wazir's offer and asked his brother's permission to return to Jammu,[111] a request which was denied.[112]

During September Hira Singh finally succumbed to the pressure exerted by Julla and announced that a full-scale attack on Jammu should be launched immediately. Such a decision, however, was opposed by several dignitaries at the Lahore darbar. Bhai Ram Singh, Dewan Dina Nath, Fakir Nur-ud-Din, and Imam-ud-Din all warned the wazir "that if he were to send troops against his uncle disorders would spread throughout the country."[113] Mehtab Singh Majithia, a Sikh general, even advised Hira Singh to surrender Julla to the Jammu chief "and so remove the cause of mutual discord."[114] But the wazir refused to abandon his confidant, and rumors soon spread that Imam-ud-Din and Jawahar Singh were conspiring to murder Julla.[115] It was in the midst of this schism that Hira Singh approached the Sikh army "to make preparations for the Expedition to Jummoo."[116] The army, however, declined to move and instead advised the wazir to seek a reconciliation with Gulab Singh.[117] It also made clear its intention to remain neutral by declaring that Hira Singh and his uncle "had disputes regarding their private business and that therefore the Khalsa should not assist either party."[118]

Although encouraged by the anarchic conditions prevailing at Lahore, Gulab Singh continued to worry about Hira Singh's determination to invade Jammu and took several steps to reinforce his position and undermine that of his nephew. He reportedly asked Arsala Khan, a Yusafzai leader, to help bolster Jammu's defenses by bringing in five thousand of his troops.[119] Maddad Khan, a Hazara chief, was likewise summoned to Jammu.[120] Gulab Singh also announced that the Rajas of Kangra, Kulu, Mandi, and Chamba, as well as the jagirdars of the Jullundur doab,[121] had vowed to support him against Lahore "and would immediately join him with their forces, whenever required to do so."[122] It was rumored, too, that the Jammu Raja had personally received representatives of the warlike Chibhali tribesmen, who lived between the Jhelum and Chenab rivers, and encouraged them to plunder the Sikh territories.[123] In addition, Gulab Singh again dispatched his agents to widen the breach between the khalsa and the wazir at Lahore, promising that if the army would desist from invading Jammu and hand over Julla to him, he would fix "15 Rupees as the pay of the infantry and 30 Rupees as the pay of the cavalry and would also present such gifts to all officers."[124] Some of the Sikh troops were so taken in by this legerdemain that they expressed their intention of accepting the offer and replacing Hira Singh with Gulab Singh as the wazir.[125] About five hundred Sikh troops even deserted to Jammu "and others were ready to follow the example."[126]

The tumultuous state of affairs at Lahore and in other parts of the Sikh kingdom persuaded Hira Singh to make yet another attempt to settle his differences with his uncle by peaceful means. He sent Dina Nath to Jammu at the head of a mission which was, however, advised by Julla to warn the Dogra chief to accept Lahore's terms, "otherwise the Sikh troops should march against him without delay."[127] On the other hand, Gulab Singh, while extending a warm welcome to the Sikh delegation, expressed his intention of reaching an agreement only on the condition that Julla should either be surrendered to him or banished from Lahore.[128] In an attempt to impress the visitors with his military might, the Jammu Raja paraded before them his soldiery, apparently both regular and irregular, of "about fifty thousand Infantry and Cavalry with two hundred Guns and six hundred swivels."[129] He also bragged that in the event of a Sikh invasion "the Afghans, the English and the Khalsa themselves would assist him."[130] Hira Singh was so infuriated by his uncle's intransigence that he ordered the mission to return to Lahore, and resumed preparations to invade Jammu.

When news of Hira Singh's decision reached the Dogra chief, he once again resorted to actions calculated to browbeat and embarrass the Lahore government. He ordered the erection of fourteen gallows at Jammu and warned that he would hang the surviving members of Julla's family the moment he heard that the Sikh army had commenced to march against him.[131] He also tried to win over Rani

Jindan, who had become alienated from the wazir,[132] by informing
her "that Raja Heera Singh had nominated her son as ruler of the
Punjab but had taken to himself all authority in the country and
that if she (the Ranee) would give assurances to him, he (Raja Golab
Singh) would try to remove his nephew (Heera Singh) from the
court."[133] The Dogra's message prompted the Rani to assume a
nonpartisan stance in the Lahore-Jammu dispute and to dismiss a
request by Hira Singh and Julla that the young Maharaja accompany
the expedition against Jammu.[134] Gulab Singh also allowed word
to leak out, true or otherwise, that he was in correspondence with
Dost Muhammad Khan, the Amir of Afghanistan.[135] In addition, the
Jammu chief attempted to create disturbances in various parts of the
Sikh kingdom. He massed a Dogra force in the vicinity of Rohtas,
and his son, Ranbir Singh, ransacked some of Hira Singh's hill
jagirs.[136] Gulab Singh also helped instigate an anti-Sikh insurrection
in Kashmir.[137] Meanwhile, the Raja's friend, Chattar Singh Attariwala, coaxed the people living between the Chenab and Indus rivers
to raise the standard of rebellion against Lahore.[138] Such lawlessness
prevailed for a while that three thousand Sikh troops stationed at
Haripur defected to Jammu.[139]

This time, however, despite the intense anti-Lahore drive launched
by Jammu, Hira Singh refused to be intimidated. Early in October
the wazir succeeded in persuading a part of the Sikh army to march
upon Jammu under Jodh Singh, another Sikh general.[140] Hira Singh's
vigorous response and reports that Tibet planned again to invade
Ladakh in the event of a Dogra-Sikh war,[141] quickly dampened the
pugnacious spirit of the Jammu chief. The Raja sued for peace and
announced his willingness to accept Sikh terms.[142] Hira Singh then
ordered the advancing force to halt at Sialkot,[143] and allowed Jawahar Singh to return to Jammu in order to reopen negotiations with
Gulab Singh.[144] As Jawahar Singh parleyed with his uncle, the
Dogra chief again demanded Julla's ouster from Lahore. In order to
appease the Jammu Raja, the wazir asked Julla "to go for some
time" to Jasrota, but the latter refused, declaring that, if he left
Lahore, Gulab Singh and the Sikh chiefs "would remove Raja Heera
Singh himself from his office."[145] But in spite of the Dogra leader's
continued resentment against the wazir's friend, Jawahar Singh's
efforts bore fruit, and Gulab Singh released Charan Das and the
surviving members of Julla's family and, after one last momentary
spell of vacillation, agreed to normalize relations with Lahore.[146]
Finally, at the end of October, the Raja sent his son, Sohan Singh,
to the Sikh capital to reach a peace settlement with the wazir. After

lengthy discussions the two sides arrived at an agreement by which, first, the jagirs of Suchet Singh were to be held jointly by Gulab Singh and Hira Singh; second, the forts owned commonly by the Jammu family in the hills were to be garrisoned both by the troops of the Dogra chief and the wazir; and third, the monetary assets of Suchet Singh lying in the hills, which came to about one and a half lakhs of rupees, were to be equally divided between Gulab Singh and Jawahar Singh. No decision was made regarding Suchet Singh's treasure at Feruzpur, since it lay under British jurisdiction.[147]

The new arrangement was indeed a blow to the long and stubborn stand taken by the Jammu Raja, but he had neither wholly nor permanently been checkmated. For instance, the settlement was silent on Gulab Singh's overdue revenue payments to Lahore, which had been one of the key points of dispute. In addition, the drastic changes about to take place at Lahore were soon to permit the Dogra leader to reestablish full control over the disputed jagirs. It may also be added here that this new agreement was angrily denounced by Suchet Singh's widow,[148] not only because it took no account of her but also because it clearly indicated that Gulab Singh had reneged on his vow to avenge her husband's death. However, her protests were apparently ignored.

The rapprochement between Lahore and Jammu proved to be short-lived. Few observers believed that the Jammu Raja, who considered Julla the main stumbling block to the fulfillment of his ambitions, would reconcile himself to the Missar's continued presence at Lahore. "The belief is universal," observed George Broadfoot, Richmond's successor, "that Pandit Julla will fall before Goolab Singh from whose revenge few men in the long run have yet escaped."[149] During October the Dogra chief objected when Hira Singh and Julla conferred the title of Raja on Missar Lal Singh,[150] a handsome Hindu Brahman who had acquired a special position at the darbar because of his scandalous relationship with Rani Jindan.[151] Gulab Singh, ever apprehensive of the ascendancy of a non-Dogra party at the darbar, warned his nephew of the consequences of his new policy and prophesied, with remarkable accuracy, "that two Rajas will never survive at Lahore."[152] As the disagreement over Lal Singh continued to strain relations between uncle and nephew, Kanwar Peshora Singh led a surprise assault in November on one of Gulab Singh's battalions stationed at Gujarat. The assailants killed six hundred Jammu troops, burned the encampment, and seized the battalion's treasury and guns. Rather than await Gulab Singh's response to the attack, the wazir sent him an insolent directive "to punish the Koonwur or the Durbar will do it if he is too feeble [to do so]."[153] But before either the Jammu or the Lahore troops could reach Gujarat, the Kanwar beat a hasty retreat into British India. This persistent bickering between Lahore and Jammu was, however, suddenly overshadowed by the final split between the khalsa and Hira Singh during December. The army, which had never fully warmed up to the wazir, felt affronted by his refusal to authorize yet another pay boost.[154] When at this juncture Rani Jindan and her brother, Jowahir Singh, complained of mistreatment at the hands of the wazir and Julla, the army determined to eliminate them from power once and for all. Sensing trouble, Hira Singh and his confidant fled from Lahore on December 22, 1844, but were overtaken by Sikh troops and put to death.[155] The Sikhs also killed about one thousand of Hira Singh's followers.[156] An unexpected victim of this violence was Sohan Singh, who had not yet left Lahore and had been forced to retreat with his cousin.

Gulab Singh, who was deeply anguished by the premature death of his second son, nonetheless must have received the news of Hira Singh's death with mixed emotions. On the one hand, it was welcome to him inasmuch as his nephew had challenged his authority and publicly humiliated him. The Jammu chief had been put on the defensive and forced to bow to the wishes of Hira Singh, or so it seemed. Two issues were fundamental to their quarrel. First, was Gulab Singh to continue his undisputed control over the Jammu family's hill possessions? And secondly, how much voice was the Jammu Raja to have in the formulation of important decisions under Hira Singh's wazarat? Such disputes had never arisen while Dhian Singh was alive. The two brothers had had, in general, distinct spheres of power, the wazir confining himself to the plains, and the Jammu chief to the hills. Although after 1839 Dhian Singh often turned to his brother for counsel and assistance on important matters of state, he personally made the final decisions at Lahore. But after his death, the Jammu Raja probably wanted to be recognized and respected as the single most powerful figure in the Sikh state. Although the wazarat had fallen to Hira Singh, the Dogra chief had hoped to dictate decisions to his young and inexperienced nephew. But while Hira Singh respected his uncle, he fell under the influence of Pandit Julla and demanded that the Dogra chief adhere to the same arrangement which had governed his political relationship with Dhian Singh. He went even further. Unlike his father, he eventually declined Gulab Singh's advice on governmental affairs at Lahore. He demonstrated his independent turn of mind by refusing to oust Julla and denying Suchet Singh the right to return to the

Sikh capital. He also exhibited his deep determination to rule by purging Suchet Singh when he defied him. Moreover, Hira Singh challenged the Jammu Raja's supremacy in family affairs by demanding an equal division of his dead uncle's hill possessions. But Gulab Singh was a calculating politician. He resisted his nephew's demands with excuses and procrastination. When Hira Singh's attack on Jammu seemed imminent and all was at stake, he was even ready to conspire with Rani Jindan and Kanwar Peshora Singh. However, Gulab Singh was also a realistic man who took all people in power seriously, including his nephew. In the end, he compromised with Hira Singh because he concluded that he could lose much more if he did not.

On the other hand, Hira Singh's death was a blow to the Dogra leader because it marked the end of the Jammu family's control over the Lahore government. Although the structure of the Sikh state was beginning to crumble, Gulab Singh realized that the khalsa was still quite capable of destroying him and with him his dream of establishing an independent mountain principality. Therefore, the immediate problem facing Gulab Singh, the sole survivor of the four Jammu Rajas, heir to vast possessions but also to innumerable enmities, was how to coexist with Lahore.

5 Lahore Under Rani Jindan

The lion or rather the lioness into whose mouth Golab
Singh has put his head will bite it off unless . . .
—Lord Ellenborough

The Panchayats rebuked the Darbar and declared Gulab
Singh to be the chief personage, after the Maharaja, in
the state.—George Broadfoot

*t*HE abrupt death of Hira Singh left the Sikh kingdom without a wazir. In the aftermath of this latest upheaval, Rani Jindan emerged as the most prominent figure at Lahore and formally assumed charge of the government on behalf of Dalip Singh. Her brother, Jowahir Singh, and her lover, Lal Singh, vied with each other for the wazarat. But the office remained vacant for several months because neither contender could win the confidence of the khalsa, an element now so powerful that without its concurrence no one could any longer rule successfully at the Sikh capital.

While differences within its ranks remained, the new government nonetheless seemed to share a rabid anti-Dogra sentiment "and the cupidity of all parties in the state was excited by a renewal of the designs against Golab Singh."[1] The revival of such an attitude was not only provoked by the pertinacious hostility which prevailed at the capital toward the Jammu chief, but was further aggravated by the deplorable condition of the Sikh finances. During December the Lahore treasury contained eighty lakhs of rupees, indicating some improvement since April, but this sum was far short of what the government needed to effectively administer the kingdom. The darbar hoped to remedy the situation by sending an army against the Jammu chief to wrest from him control of his vast hill territories, on which he had paid little or no revenue in recent years, and to seize his treasury, which was rumored to contain crores of rupees. By doing so the Lahore government believed it would have "enough to pay the army for ten years leaving the whole revenue to them."[2] The darbar was further encouraged to embark upon such a course of action by its agents, who reported the Dogra Raja to be in such a state of shock at the recent events that if the troops marched against Gulab Singh promptly "he could be put under chains, but if this was postponed it might become impossible to overpower him."[3]

However, the plans to attack Jammu were interrupted by the sudden appearance of Kanwar Peshora Singh at Lahore on January 1, 1845. The Kanwar, who still entertained ambitions of sitting on the Sikh throne, had come to the capital at the invitation of the khalsa, and some of the panches even took an oath of loyalty to him. Riding on the crest of such popularity, Peshora Singh gallantly announced his intention of uniting the khalsa and waging war upon the Jammu Raja.[4] But this idolization proved transitory when Rani Jindan, sensing the threat posed to herself and her son by the Kanwar's presence at Lahore,[5] responded by inveigling the fickle-hearted army away from Peshora Singh with promises of expensive gifts. Forsaken by the khalsa, the dispirited Kanwar quit Lahore and retired to his jagir at Sialkot.

Gulab Singh, who had been keeping a close watch over the developments at Lahore, was particularly disturbed to learn of the darbar's intention to launch military operations against Jammu and took various steps to safeguard his position. On the one hand, he attempted to ingratiate himself with the new government by sending a formal acknowledgment of his allegiance and by a request that the Sikh ruler grant him his continued protection. On the other hand, employing methods reminiscent of the measures taken against Hira Singh, he tried to brace for a possible attack by asking a Barakzai chief to raise an army of ten thousand Afghans for him.[6] Furthermore, he bribed Bhai Ram Singh and a few other courtiers by pledging them many lakhs of rupees. He thus was successful in creating a small pro-Dogra party at the Sikh darbar to fill in part the void caused by the elimination of every member of the Jammu family from the ranks of the Lahore government.[7] This clique gradually gained importance and played a significant role on behalf of Gulab Singh before and during the ensuing Anglo-Sikh war.

But if the Dogra Raja was able to bribe various Sikh officials, he failed in his attempts to win over Sham Singh, a khalsa general who had been sent by the darbar to restore order in the Sikh territories adjoining those of Gulab Singh.[8] Panicked by the fear that Sham Singh might next turn upon Dogra lands, the Jammu chief requested Chattar Singh Attariwala to negotiate an agreement with Lahore which would prevent the Sikh general from embarking upon such a venture. Chattar Singh apparently succeeded in terminating the threat by reaching an understanding with the darbar on January 14 according to which Jammu was to make substantial concessions. Among other things, the Dogra leader was to pay his revenues regularly, surrender all the jagirs of Suchet Singh and Hira Singh to Lahore, and divide the estates of Dhian Singh between the late wazir's two surviving sons.[9] However, the khalsa, which had harbored ambitions of completely annihilating the Dogras and seizing all their possessions, rejected this agreement.[10] Nor did Gulab Singh seem to have any desire to voluntarily give up an inch of the territories under his control.

While controversy now arose at Lahore over the exact nature of the policy to be pursued toward Jammu, the Sikh government sent a force to capture a large treasure hidden by Gulab Singh at the Jasrota fort. Having gotten wind of Lahore's action, the Jammu chief hastily dispatched a Dogra force under Jawahar Singh to Jasrota to retrieve the hoard. But on January 20 Sikh spies reported to Lahore that Jawahar Singh had deserted to the Sikhs, professed his allegiance to the darbar, and expressed his eagerness to fight against his own uncle. Gulab Singh's foes at the Sikh court, assuming that his nephew's defection would automatically lead to the acquisition of the Jasrota treasure, were thrilled. The Dogra leader's vakil "was called, taunted, and told that his master's power was now broken."[11] In a mood of unrestrained exultation the government announced its intention of launching a rapid offensive against Jammu with the assistance of Jawahar Singh. However, the Dogra chief's antagonists had rejoiced prematurely. On the following day it was discovered that the news of Jawahar Singh's defection was fallacious and had been circulated by informers in expectation of handsome awards. Simultaneously, word reached the Sikh capital that Gulab Singh's agents were inciting the people of Hazara, Peshawar, and Kashmir to throw off Lahore's yoke. In a complete turnabout, the Sikh government abandoned its belligerent posture of the previous day. The Jammu Raja's vakil and partisans were now summoned and flattered. Bhai Ram Singh was requested to go to Jammu, seek a reconciliation, and secure the ratification of the almost-forgotten January 14 agreement, even if in doing so he had to offer the wazarat to Gulab Singh. But the Bhai declined to be a mediator, and instead tried to further detach the khalsa from the darbar by dwelling upon the latter's incompetence.[12] Meanwhile, Jawahar Singh beat the Sikh force to Jasrota and escaped with most of the coveted treasure to Jammu. The Sikh government was enraged at thus being outwitted. Reverting to its former tough stand, the darbar sent warnings to Gulab Singh, issued threats against his friends, and directed provincial governors to consider the Jammu chief an enemy of the kingdom. Gulab Singh's action thus prompted the darbar and the khalsa to a concerted effort, and a resolute decision was made to invade Jammu.[13]

Although Bhai Ram Singh succeeded in halting the attack temporarily by raising a false alarm that a British invasion of Panjab was imminent,[14] an army of about thirty-five thousand men under Raja Lal Singh and Sham Singh was finally sent toward Jammu during February.[15] However, its orders were not to exterminate the Dogra leader but to demand that he hand over three crores of rupees and surrender the possessions of Suchet Singh and Hira

Singh.[16] The Sikh troops encamped south of Jammu, but Gulab
Singh displayed no desire to give battle, realizing only too well that
any resistance might bring the rest of the khalsa from Lahore. Instead, he endeavored to dispel the danger to Jammu and to himself
by causing friction and disunity in the enemy's ranks with every
trick in his repertoire. Putting this strategy into operation, he sued
for peace and declared his readiness to negotiate a settlement with
anyone in the Sikh force. The soldiery quickly responded to Gulab
Singh's overture and, against the orders of its officers, decided to
send a delegation of the panches to Jammu. On the delegates'
arrival, the Raja, in a display of humility bordering on servility,
"placed his sword and shield on the ground at their feet and stood
with hands as a suppliant in their presence."[17] Having moved the
visitors with such an exhibition of submissiveness, the Dogra leader
proceeded to exploit the army's greatest weakness—its greed for
money—to bring it under his influence. He showered the panches
with gifts and promised to give every Sikh soldier a gold ring worth
a hundred rupees as a token of his personal friendship.[18] Furthermore, he coddled his guests with gourmet foods and epicurean wines.
The delegates were thus lulled into such a state of complacence and
conviviality that their determination to insist upon fulfillment of the
key Sikh demands evaporated. In the negotiations which were eventually held, no reference was made to the possessions of Suchet
Singh and Hira Singh. They did ask for the three crores of rupees,
but were satisfied with the Jammu Raja's explanation that he had
little to offer them because most of his treasure was still lying at
Jasrota. And the Sikh troops seemed ready to accept gratefully Gulab
Singh's offer to give them twenty-five lakhs of rupees if they would
return to Lahore.[19]

The panches were, as a matter of fact, so mesmerized by Gulab
Singh's pretense of amicability that they made a public statement
designed to please the Raja and at the same time to show their disdain of the Sikh government. They attributed to the duplicity and
impiety of the new rulers at Lahore the recent murders of Hira Singh
and Sohan Singh, crimes which the khalsa had in fact itself committed. Detecting this shift in the attitude of the panches, Gulab
Singh now took the offensive against the Sikh government and
blamed it for the anarchic state of affairs. In a move calculated to
arouse the army's apprehensions on a matter so dear to its heart, the
Raja glibly accused the new government at Lahore of pilfering the
Sikh treasury and ruining "the economic condition of the country
to such a limit, that it would no longer be able to supply bread to
the troops."[20] Gulab Singh's denunciations so stirred the panches

that they momentarily considered him the only genuine friend of the khalsa and offered him the vacant wazarat. The Raja was, however, too shrewd to accept such a proposal, not only because the army had no legal power to make it but also because past events had taught him that occupying the office of wazir was a highly risky business. He, therefore, respectfully declined the offer but, with vulpine cunning, recommended Kanwar Peshora Singh for the office.[21] The object of such a suggestion clearly was to bring further disorder to the already muddled situation in the Sikh kingdom.

Having thus neutralized the invading force, Gulab Singh now attempted to alienate its commanders from Lahore. During March he finally persuaded Lal Singh to send General Fateh Singh Mann and some other officers to Jammu for consultations. They, too, were warmly received, entertained for days, lavished with presents, and eventually won over by the Dogra leader. Bewitched by Gulab Singh's indomitable charm they also joined him in blaming Rani Jindan and her brother for the lawlessness in the Sikh state. Taking advantage of the Mann party's response, the Jammu Raja lashed out at the Lahore rulers and "contrasted the prosperity of the Sikh state when his family were employed, with the misgovernment of a debauched woman and a brutal brother."[22] Nonetheless, the Jammu Raja offered to make peace with Lahore by promising to give up several jagirs of the Dogra family in addition to the twenty-five lakhs he had pledged to the panches. The Raja actually handed over to Mann the promised sum of rupees, but as the delegates left town to return to their camp, they were ambushed by a party of disguised Dogras. In the melee that followed, Mann and some others were killed, and the assailants took the money given by Gulab Singh back to Jammu.[23] Why this assault took place and who carried it out is unclear. Although Gulab Singh would doubtlessly have wished to regain his money, it appears unlikely that the assault was authorized by him.[24] Such flagrant treachery would seem to completely negate the purpose of that policy he had so carefully formulated and followed since the entrenchment of the Sikh army near Jammu. The plot might very well have been master-minded by some over-zealous Dogra Mians.

Whether or not the Jammu chief was in any way implicated in this affair, he immediately denounced these murders and disowned responsibility for them.[25] But the army was so enraged by this dastardly attack that, for the moment, all factions at the Sikh camp banded together to seek revenge against Gulab Singh. As the Sikh army marched toward Jammu meeting little or no resistance, many terrified residents fled for safety into the neighboring hills. The area adjoining the river Tawi, on the banks of which Jammu is located, was occupied and the Sikhs needed to seize only a small fort to enter the city of Jammu itself. But instead of making a sustained effort to crush the power of Gulab Singh permanently, the army became side-tracked by other pursuits and carried out wholesale acts of plunder, abduction, and rapine in the environs of the city. Alluding to the army's conduct, Broadfoot reported such outrages were committed "that many women having lost their caste threw themselves into wells, and others to avoid dishonour were destroyed by their fathers, husbands or brothers."[26] Hardinge, Ellenborough's successor, also made reference to the sexual excesses indulged in by the army: "All sorts of atrocities were perpetrated—1000 women & boys carried by violence into the Camp."[27] Yet these execrable activities ironically enough saved the life of Gulab Singh as the soldiers expended their anger over Mann's death on the hapless population. In fact, their resentment ultimately tapered off to such an extent that, despite the urgings of their commanders to take over Jammu, the troops refused, declaring that "this country was given to Raja Gulab Singh by Maharaja Ranjit Singh, and we cannot take it back."[28] Taking advantage of this new situation the Raja again entered into negotiations with the army, seeking an agreement which would result in its withdrawal from the hills. An understanding was once more reached by which the Sikhs agreed to leave, but in return the Jammu chief was obliged to grant greater concessions than ever before. This latest pact stipulated that in addition to relinquishing the jagirs of Suchet Singh and Hira Singh and remitting the twenty-five lakhs of rupees, the Raja must also clear up his revenue debts and pay a fine of five lakhs of rupees per month for an unspecified length of time.[29]

Although this new settlement was denounced by Rani Jindan and Jowahir Singh, the army seemed satisfied and prepared to evacuate, but before departing Lal Singh and other officers went to bid farewell to the Dogra leader at Jammu. Inwardly delighted at the prospect of the Sikhs' withdrawal, Gulab Singh put up a façade of obeisance and penitence. The Jammu chief, "with his hands folded and sheet over his neck as a suppliant stood before the chiefs, and professed sorrow for his offences, leaving punishment or forgiveness in their hands."[30] Beguiled again by Gulab Singh's overwhelming humility, the visitors magnanimously comforted him and said he had committed no wrong. But when the officers returned to their camp they discovered that the army had undergone a change of heart and now declared that it would not go back unless ordered by Jowahir Singh. The khalsa's reaction "produced as much perplexity and alarm amongst the Surdars at Jummoo, as the treaty itself had done at Lahore."[31] As the tempo of anti-Dogra feelings again increased in the ranks of the impulsive troops, Gulab Singh decided to make a dramatic gesture which might persuade them to leave. Exhibiting considerable personal courage he arrived at the Sikh camp with only a small escort and thus, "by a bold stroke of policy, threw himself on the generosity of the troops."[32] While some of the Sikh soldiers, struck by the Raja's intrepidity, "saw in him the only possible reformer of the Lahore government"[33] and seemed eager to make him the wazir, others remained unimpressed and were ready to take his life. Heated arguments ensued, but the two sides ultimately reached an uneasy compromise by which it was agreed to remove the Dogra chief to Lahore before any final decision would be made about him.[34] Hence, as his fate hung in the balance, "one day condemned to die, the next day to be wuzzier, [Gulab Singh] marched with the troops to Lahore."[35] Although now facing the greatest trial of his life, the ambidextrous Raja managed to retain his composure and attempted to insure his personal safety by distributing more money among the returning Sikh troops and their officers.[36]

No sooner did the army bring Gulab Singh to Lahore in early April[37] than it became apparent that Rani Jindan and Jowahir Singh would prefer nothing more than to have the Dogra chief put to death. Several futile attempts were made on his life,[38] and the khalsa, afraid that the Jammu Raja might in sheer desperation try to escape or commit suicide, put a close guard upon his person. While the oscillating army debated the Raja's future, Jowahir Singh demanded that he be handed over to the darbar for punishment. However, the artful Jammu chief succeeded in twisting this command to his own benefit by eloquently arguing that he was the servant of the army, not of the darbar. This appeal to the khalsa's vanity had such an electrifying effect that the army now unanimously rejected the government's call for the Raja's surrender. Although the panches still did not permit him to return to Jammu, they "rebuked the Darbar and declared Gulab Singh to be the chief personage, after the Maharaja, in the state."[39] They also assailed Jowahir Singh's hostility toward the Dogra leader and "said that, as far as [he] was concerned he need not attend the Darbar."[40]

Gulab Singh was thus able to weather this latest storm, but he realized full well that he could fall victim to new circumstances. He therefore set into motion a number of maneuvers which might win for him his freedom. He first attempted to reconcile his differences with Rani Jindan by making overtures of friendship. When word of this move reached Ellenborough in England, he prophesied its doom and commented: "The lion or rather the lioness into whose mouth Golab Singh has put his head will bite it off unless he secures his own life for a time by taking hers, & her brother's, & making the young Duleep Singh a Roi faineant."[41] Although Ellenborough's forebodings proved inaccurate, the Rani did refuse to make peace with the Jammu Raja. During negotiations she accused him of Hira Singh's murder and, when he protested his innocence, the Rani snapped: "I have the correspondence and will produce it if you deny the fact."[42] Though Gulab Singh had not been a party to his nephew's death,[43] he quickly realized Jindan was in an uncompromising mood and, fearful of further arousing the Rani, terminated the parley.

Despite Jindan's snub the Jammu Raja did not despair and instead attempted to achieve his goal by dividing his enemies at the darbar. Aware of the bitter and incessant competition between Jowahir Singh and Lal Singh for the wazarat, he at first came out in favor of the Rani's brother[44] and gave him his blessings when he was finally permitted to assume the wazarat on May 14. But once Jowahir Singh took office Gulab Singh modified his strategy and alternated his support between the new wazir and his chief rival. It was reported during June that the three men "were well engaged in plans to assassinate each other, any two joining for a day against the third."[45] Though the Rani tried desperately to reconcile her brother and her lover, and once even attempted to divert their minds from the struggle for power "by sending each of them a handsome slave girl,"[46] the two men persisted in their squabble. In the meantime the wazir became quite addicted to alcohol and on occasion "he was too drunk to hold the Durbar."[47] Jindan herself now committed such excesses that she became "stupid instead of clever and lively; [and was] sometimes for days in a state bordering on fatuity."[48] Taking advantage of such moral dissoluteness and political mayhem, Gulab Singh once again sought permission to return to Jammu. Disgusted by the prevailing atmosphere of dissipation and the waves of intrigue and anarchy that had engulfed Lahore since Gulab Singh's arrival, the darbar concluded that the Raja's departure might be conducive to establishing some degree of normalcy and permitted him to return home. But before the Jammu chief left in August he once again went through the empty formality of signing a pact which granted sweeping concessions to the Sikh government. By this agreement the Dogra leader agreed to pay to Lahore sixty-eight lakhs of rupees and give up all territories belonging to the Jammu family except his own.[49] There is, however, no indication that he honored these terms any more than those previously negotiated.

Thus Gulab Singh, who had "a wonderful gift of evading assassination and violent death,"[50] returned home financially as well as physically unscathed.

Although the Sikhs had spared the Jammu Raja's life, he was now determined to become their most uncompromising enemy. Once in the security of the hills he again proposed an anti-Sikh alliance to the British.[51] He also incited Peshora Singh to raise a rebellion against Lahore. The unlucky Kanwar was, however, tricked into imprisonment by Chattar Singh Attariwala, who had aligned himself with the Lahore government upon his daughter's engagement to the young Maharaja in July. While in confinement the Kanwar was treacherously murdered, reportedly at the orders of Jowahir Singh. But when news of the Kanwar's death reached Lahore, the panches expressed deep indignation and ordered the wazir to appear before them to explain his conduct. On September 21 the petrified minister arrived at their camp accompanied by the Maharaja. He tried in vain to appease some of the panches by offering "a quantity of gold and jewels"[52] but "was shot down on his elephant, after the infant Maharaja had been torn from his side and conveyed to a place of safety."[53]

Jowahir Singh's execution plunged the capital into utter confusion. The Rani went into a state of shock, the little Maharaja hardly understood what had happened much less the significance of the event, and even the khalsa seemed uncertain about its future course of action. If it proposed to eliminate any other high dignitaries, there were not many more left. But the khalsa soon approached Gulab Singh, who had in the meantime formally conveyed his condolences to the Rani, and pressed him to assume the office of wazir. The Raja demurred, knowing only too well the perils of that position, and ingeniously tried to have himself taken out of consideration by responding that he was prepared to assume the wazarat if "he should have the full power of capital punishment, without any appeal from his decision."[54] This was a concession the panches were in no mood to grant, since it would have allowed Gulab Singh unlimited power over all parties in the state, including the khalsa.

But the army persisted in its hope that the Jammu chief would eventually accept the wazarat on its terms, and made a halfhearted attempt to purge Rani Jindan and Dalip Singh. While the Rani and her son were visiting Amritsar, the khalsa accused the two of having absconded and announced its intention of proclaiming an infant son of the late Sher Singh as the new Maharaja and Gulab Singh, albeit without his consent, as the wazir. Apprised of the conspiracy, the

Rani hurried back to Lahore and "arrived just in time to arrest the progress of these proceedings."[55] Finally, in view of the imminent war with the British, the khalsa during early November, though continuing to show interest in the elusive Jammu Raja, reluctantly approved Lal Singh's elevation to the wazarat and General Tej Singh's appointment as commander-in-chief.[56]

The events between December 1844, and September 1845, clearly demonstrate that Gulab Singh was not merely a calculating opportunist but also a master in the art of political and physical survival. During the Sikh army's siege of Jammu and his subsequent involuntary stay at Lahore he managed to stay alive by a skilful use of intrigue, bribery, and cajolery. His perilously close brush with death and continued vulnerability further convinced him of the need for total independence from Lahore. The Dogra chief waited for the right moment to strike and, as Anglo-Sikh relations deteriorated, he carefully deliberated how he could turn the situation to his advantage.

6 British Attitudes Toward Lahore and Jammu: 1839–1845

In case the British would be destroyed by the Afghans, huge treasures would fall into your hands. If the British would destroy the Afghans, it would be a matter of thanks to the Almighty.—Gulab Singh to the Sikh troops

The state of Punjab is . . . under my foot.
—Lord Ellenborough

*t*HE British East India Company had maintained the most amicable relations with the Sikh state until the death of Ranjit Singh. The Company respected and admired the Maharaja and throughout his long reign the British made no attempt to encroach upon his territories. The Sikh ruler, on his part, understood the importance and possible consequences of the rapid extension of the Company's power toward his southern frontiers and in order to maintain peace he granted significant concessions to the British in several treaties. As early as 1809 he relinquished his intention of annexing the Phulkian states south of the Sutlej.[1] In 1832 he literally abandoned his ambitions of conquering Sind, which would have provided his landlocked kingdom access to the Arabian Ocean, by acknowledging the maritime supremacy of the British in that region.[2] Finally, during 1838 the Maharaja consented to give moral and material assistance to the Company in its contemplated war with Afghanistan.[3] In 1839 he actually extended such aid when the British invaded and occupied that country and installed Shah Shuja, their puppet, in place of Dost Muhammad Khan as the Amir of Afghanistan.

However, such Anglo-Sikh understanding and solidarity endured only as long as the powerful Maharaja lived. In the years following Ranjit Singh's demise the Company noted the steady decline of the Sikh state and the role of various factions at the Lahore court which hastened that process. Nonetheless, the first British instinct was to hope that normalcy would soon return to Lahore. Such an attitude seems evident in this extract from a letter written early in 1840 by the Company's Board of Directors in London to Lord Auckland: "We repeat our great regret at the events which have taken place at Lahore . . . we should be happy to hear that success had crowned the effort to infuse a less violent spirit into the Durbar of Khurrick Sing."[4] But such good will toward the Sikhs gradually began to evaporate in the face of new developments. Reports that Lahore was attempting to establish diplomatic rapport with the Himalayan kingdom of Nepal caused the British authorities apprehension.[5] They also suspected that the new Sikh government was less than enthusiastic over the British presence in Afghanistan[6] and, when in late 1840 troop reinforcements were about to be dispatched to Kabul via the Sikh state, it was feared that Lahore might try to block their passage. The Board of Directors was so infuriated at the prospect of such an impediment that it spoke of marching the troops "through the Punjab with or without the consent of the Lahore Government," and even debated the possibility of a "contest with the ruler of the Punjab" to achieve the British objective.[7] In November, when news of the deaths of Kharak Singh and Naunihal Singh reached London, one of the most influential men in the Company's administration began to think in terms of annexing the Sikh state. H. B. Bayley, chairman of the Board of Directors, implied that the unexpected death of the young and aggressive Naunihal Singh would smooth the way for the expansion of British rule beyond the Sutlej and, in turn, usher in the final solution of the Afghan problem. On January 11, 1841, in a communication to John Hobhouse, the president of the Company's Board of Control, Bayley rationalized:

With Nao Nehal Sing we should, doubtless, have had a very pretty quarrel, as it stood. . . . These are sentiments which it would not be quite right to publish at Charing Cross, but which I may safely express in confidence to you.

I believe we should have no difficulty in withdrawing from Afghanistan if we occupied the line of the Indus. Our moral influence would, in that case, be more efficacious than the presence of a British force, holding complete occupation over Afghanistan. But, even if the holding of a force in Afghanistan should be necessary, we should find in the resources of the Punjaub, resources necessary for their maintenance; we could reinforce them without difficulty; and with Cashmere on our flank, the whole line of the Indus in our possession, we might defy all attacks whether from European or Asiatic enemies.[8]

Bayley's opinion was, of course, kept confidential. Even Auckland was not immediately told of this proposed change in policy toward the Sikhs, as is indicated by a letter written to him by Bayley and Lyall, a fellow director, on January 29. Although the two directors advised the Governor-General to insist that the Sikhs honor the 1838 treaty, they also cautioned that the Company "should carefully avoid all interference in the disputes which may arise among the different chiefs or parties [at Lahore]."[9] But during March of 1841 the Board of Directors gave Auckland an intimation of the tougher policy being envisaged against the Sikhs. Reacting to reports of the prolonged political chaos that was gripping Lahore in the wake of Kharak Singh's death, the Board told Auckland: "We ought by no means to discuss any matter of importance with a government unsettled as that of Lahore; and we would avoid interference in their internal disputes, as long as possible; but if called upon by circumstances to act, we should do so with promptitude and effect."[10] Even after being apprised that a degree of political stability had been restored at the Sikh capital under Sher Singh and Dhian Singh, the Board seemed reluctant to alter its stubborn viewpoint and concluded that "it would not be proper to compromise our character by appearing to tolerate the excesses at Lahore."[11]

Despite the expression of such intransigent opinions, the British refrained from taking any aggressive steps against the Sikh kingdom at that juncture. There was probably no unanimity of opinion on the policy to be pursued toward Lahore because many officials believed that the Company was then militarily unprepared to undertake the conquest of Panjab. There was perhaps also a growing feeling that internal dissension might eventually result in the disintegration of the Sikh state from within and facilitate the British advance to the north. The Company thus adopted a wait-and-watch policy while carefully observing the activities of the several feuding parties at the Sikh darbar, especially the one led by the Jammu Rajas. As rumors began to trickle into British India that Dhian Singh and Gulab Singh were entertaining ambitions of dominating the Sikh state, the Company officials expressed divergent views over the true intentions of the Dogra brothers. As late as December 1840, Herbert Maddock, the political secretary to the Governor-General, dismissed the possibility of a rupture between Jammu and Lahore, and theorized that the Dogra Rajas were not likely to break a long relationship with the Sikh kingdom, because "while they owe their fortune to its bounty [they] have also rendered to it the most important services."[12] However, by the spring of 1841, George Clerk had become convinced of the disloyalty of the Jammu Rajas, and appears to have been the first British official to foresee the possible advantages to be derived from an acknowledgment of their autonomy. In April he suggested to his government: "The recognition of the separate authority of the Jummoo Rajas would doubtless afford great facility to the British Government of establishing a due control over their aggrandizements."[13] By May, Clerk became further entrenched in his views and advocated the establishment of a direct link with Gulab Singh. Although the agent wrote that the Jammu Rajas were not then in favor of British interference in Panjab, he regarded Gulab Singh, as "a man of considerable sagacity" and believed that, if negotiations were opened with him, it would not be "difficult to lead him to comprehend that those advantages and that stability to the new Raj of his family might ensue from trusting to the guidance of the British Government which are unattainable through any other means."[14] Clerk's recommendation was, however, ignored by his superiors, who probably were unreceptive not only because the Company was reluctant to intervene so blatantly in the internal affairs of the Sikh kingdom, but also because the Jammu chief had been considered anti-British since the days of Ranjit Singh. In addition, he had recently angered the British by his operations in western Tibet.

The chariness and displeasure with which the British viewed Gulab Singh were once again revealed when during June they vehemently objected to Sher Singh's intention of replacing Paolo de Avitabile, the Italian-born general, with the Jammu chief as governor of the strategic province of Peshawar. Their reasons for doing so rested on the contention that Gulab Singh was personally hostile to their interests in Afghanistan. For example, Company officials suspected that in 1839 the Dogra leader had encouraged Khan Bahadur, the chief of the Malikdin Khel tribe,[15] to obstruct the march of the British troops into Afghanistan.[16] Moreover, the British believed that Gulab Singh enjoyed a close association with the Barakzai chiefs living at Peshawar who were blood relations of Dost Muhammad, the deposed Afghan ruler.[17] The Company, therefore, feared that Gulab Singh's appointment would place "the hills from the neighborhood of Kanggra to the Khyber Pass in the hands of men averse to the English and hostile to Shah Shooja."[18] These considerations led the British to exert relentless pressure on the Maharaja, who eventually capitulated. The governorship of Peshawar was not entrusted to Gulab Singh.[19]

But the bloody and ignominious rout of the British forces at the hands of the Afghan rebels near the end of 1841 helped to change the Company's attitude toward Gulab Singh. Although in the immediate aftermath of the disaster the British continued to mistrust the Raja, believing that he "will inwardly rejoice" at their misfortune,[20] ultimately certain unpleasant experiences with the Sikhs convinced them that Gulab Singh might be one of the few chiefs in the Panjab kingdom who could render them some valuable assistance at that critical time. For instance, in their eagerness to make a swift re-entry into Afghanistan the British first requested Avitabile, who was still the governor at Peshawar, to order the Sikh army's Nujeeb battalion, comprised only of Muslims, to cross the Khyber and give battle to the Afghans. The Nujeeb battalion, however, refused to fight their fellow Muslims in Afghanistan, mutinied, and defiantly withdrew all the way down to Attock. British appeals for help also met with a rebuff from General Mehtab Singh Majithia, then the commander of another Sikh force at Peshawar.[21] When Henry Lawrence and

Mackeson, two assistants of Clerk, sought an interview with Mehtab Singh, they were insolently informed that the general "would send word when it was convenient."[22] Later, Lawrence bitterly complained that the Sikh general treated the British as enemies while permitting the anti-British Afridi tribesmen "to enter his camp and sell grass and wood, and even the very clothing of our men lately killed in the Khyber."[23] The agents' criticism finally led Auckland to the conclusion that the Sikhs could not be expected to assume the burden of the fighting, and he decided to send a new British force under General Pollock to Afghanistan. But, fearful that Pollock's progress might be hampered by hostile elements in the northwest, the Governor-General requested Sher Singh to send Sikh troops to escort the British army into the Khyber. The Maharaja promptly obliged. And this time there were no protests when the Company officials heard that the Sikh force was to be led by Gulab Singh. Clerk especially had been so frustrated by the tactics of the intractable Sikh soldiery near Peshawar that he seemed most gratified by Lahore's decision, and exclaimed: "The only Punjaub troops from which I should expect useful co-operation at this time are those forming the force in the field with Raja Goolaub Singh."[24]

But if the British were now prepared to reconcile their differences with the Jammu chief, the latter seemed in no hurry to reciprocate. He had neither forgotten the Company's persistent criticism of Zorawar Singh's invasion of western Tibet nor forgiven it for its opposition to his proposed appointment as the governor of Peshawar. Thus, when Gulab Singh arrived near Attock in January at the head of twenty thousand men,[25] he was a less than enthusiastic supporter of the British cause. Since he camped on the right bank of the Indus directly opposite the spot where the Nujeeb battalion had stationed itself, the Company agents optimistically speculated that the Jammu Raja intended to teach the disobedient Nujeeb troops a lesson. But the British soon found that the Raja was not anxious to take any measures against the Muslim soldiers, as "he pretended himself to be afraid of them."[26] They discovered, too, that he had no intention of moving immediately to Peshawar. Gulab Singh's inaction resulted in extreme disillusionment among the Company officials, and Clerk, who had only recently set such high hopes upon him, now worried "that the Jummoo Rajah would rather contemplate the difficulties of the British Government in [the northwest], than be instrumental in removing them."[27] Henry Lawrence, who soon afterward arrived at Attock to receive Pollock's army approaching from the south, even feared that the presence of the Nujeeb troops might "serve Goolab Sing as an excuse to detain General Pollock at the [Indus]

Bridge."[28] The Raja, however, made no such attempt. In fact, when the Dogra leader lackadaisically turned up at the bridge, he was apparently impressed by the sight of Pollock and Lawrence taking their men and heavy artillery across, and said admiringly: "You Sahib-log [Englishmen] work hard."[29]

Discerning what he considered a slight shift in Gulab Singh's mood, Lawrence stayed behind at Attock to pressure the Raja into moving northward. The assistant agent was particularly afraid that the Jammu chief's anxiety over the continuing hostilities between the Dogras and the Tibetans in the Himalayas might cause him to simply withdraw from Attock and return home. Such concern was also voiced by Mackeson, who pungently exhorted Lawrence to prevent the Raja from leaving: "Recollect Rajah Goolab Singh is the fish of our net. Don't let him escape you. Tell him all friendship is at an end if he talks about Jammu and Chinese [Tibetan] affairs when he ought to be half way to Jalalabad."[30] Lawrence employed every importunity to stir the Dogra ruler into going to Peshawar. He told Gulab Singh that, if he cooperated, "it would be a matter of special gratification for the British and they would be amicable towards him forever."[31] He even offered to assist the Jammu Rajas in acquiring Peshawar and Jalalabad,[32] and such a proposal was actually forwarded to Clerk. Although the agent had some initial misgivings about the Jalalabad proposal and believed that "such a measure would be neither politic nor honest,"[33] yet he was later perhaps "not unwilling to place it permanently in [the Jammu Rajas'] hands by a stroke of finesse."[34] Again, while Clerk was not quite sure how the British could grant Peshawar to anyone since it was not under their control,[35] his government, in an effort to appease the Jammu chief and in a complete reversal of its obstinate stand of the previous year, now instructed the agent to request the Sikhs that Gulab Singh "be allowed to assume the government and direction of affairs at Peshawar."[36] In addition, Clerk sent a personal letter to the Jammu chief urging him to aid the British.[37]

Such efforts finally persuaded Gulab Singh to move from Attock, but he marched northward only grudgingly. He spent ten days covering a distance which normally took only four,[38] and finally arrived at Peshawar on February 14.[39] The British officers were baffled by the Raja's continued reluctance to collaborate with them. Governor Avitabile informed them "that nothing was ready in Goolab Sing's force; and it was out of the question to expect them to enter the Khyber."[40] Alexander Gardner, that inveterate prevaricator who was then posing as an American, warned the British that "it was the opinion of all that you will never again set foot in

Cabul."[41] Nevertheless, the British officers persisted in urging the Dogra leader to support them. But the Raja continued to hedge, first by claiming that he did not command the obedience of the Sikh army under his charge, then by declaring that he was still awaiting his government's instructions as to which of Lahore's troops were to enter the Khyber. Finally, the utterly frustrated Pollock and other British officials at Peshawar invited Gulab Singh to a conference on the evening of February 20. Soon after the meeting began, Mackeson bluntly asked the Raja "for what purpose the Sikh army had been sent to Peshawur and what order had been received from the Durbar?"[42] But the Jammu chief, while oozing graciousness and amiability from every pore, neatly circumvented the question and spent most of the evening talking about irrelevant subjects. Edwardes and Merivale, biographers of Henry Lawrence, provide this delectable description of the evasive tactics employed by the Raja:

[How] easily can those whose lot it has been to parley with that Ulysses of the hills, call up before them the sweet deference of attention, the guileless benevolence, the childlike simplicity, and the masterly prolixity of fiction, parenthesis and anecdote, with which Raja Goolab Sing stroked his silver beard while listening to the question, and then charmingly consumed the hours in avoiding a reply.[43]

Their patience exhausted by the Raja's protracted monologue, the British at last repeated Mackeson's query. This time Gulab Singh answered by announcing that it was time for him to retire, but before departing he embarked upon another discourse which, though more pertinent to the original question, confused the British even further. The final chapter of the evening's proceedings is once again delightfully narrated by Edwardes and Merivale:

But time was up. The Rajah's "opium hour" had arrived; and if detained he might even be so rude as to fall asleep. Hurriedly he produced a paper which he stated to be a Purwana [communication] from the Maharajah of Lahore, but which to the keen eyes of the British diplomatists seemed "drawn out by himself."
In very general terms it ordered him "to consult with General Pollock and Captains Mackeson and Lawrence as to the objects the British Government had in view; what they proposed to effect, and by what means;" and then "to act in support of the British troops agreeably to the terms of the treaty; and be guided in everything by the British officers' advice." And depositing this document in their hands, without asking any "views" or "proposals" or "advice," the master of the 20,000 allies yawned and took his leave.[44]

Pollock was so outraged by this encounter that he wrote to his government: "I confess that I have no expectation of any assistance from the Sikh troops."[45] But Clerk did not completely share such pessimism and, as soon as word of the Peshawar stalemate reached him, he decided to personally contact the Sikh government. Arriving at the darbar early in March, he complained to Sher Singh and Dhian Singh about the Jammu chief's temporizing conduct and pleaded that they urge him to extend his wholehearted cooperation to the British.[46] While the Maharaja was sympathetic, Dhian Singh at first remained unmoved by Clerk's entreaties. The wazir stoutly defended his brother's actions and, in a probable allusion to the suspicions the British had harbored against Gulab Singh for years, he declared: "Jo loha da jundra hovee, lukree nal na kolta [an iron lock cannot be opened with a wooden key]."[47] But in the end the minister yielded. Both he and the Maharaja wrote to Gulab Singh and prevailed upon him to aid Pollock.[48] Though by then the Jammu chief had received word of the Dogra debacle in Tibet and was anxious to return home, he stayed long enough to induce his soldiers to render assistance to Pollock and his men. Aware that the Sikh troops were in general inimical toward the British, he proceeded in his own peerless fashion to alter this state of affairs. He first lulled the soldiers into quiescence by distributing among them thousands of rupees worth of *halwa*,[49] a sweet delicacy particularly relished by the Sikhs. Then, while declaring himself to be in sympathy with the troops' attitude, the Raja nonetheless argued that under the pre-vailing circumstances their decision to help the British would, whatever the outcome of the Anglo-Afghan conflict, bring them dividends: "In case the British would be destroyed by the Afghans, huge treasures would fall into your hands. If the British would destroy the Afghans, it would be a matter of thanks to the Almighty."[50] Although such grandiose expectations were not destined to be fulfilled, they did prompt the Sikh army to assist Pollock across the Khyber, a step which ultimately led to the British reconquest of Afghanistan. The British manifested their gratitude for the timely succor provided by Gulab Singh. During April Clerk wrote to thank the Raja and pledged British friendship.[51] In May Ellenborough, the new Governor-General, sought the Sikh Maharaja's permission to decorate the Dogra in recognition of his services.[52] However, Sher Singh obviously resented the bestowal of so singular an honor on the Jammu chief by a foreign power and politely turned down Ellenborough's request by responding that Gulab Singh had already been rewarded with a medal "and in friendship, this is enough on the part of both the Governments."[53] Somewhat later, the Governor-General accepted his agents' earlier recommendations to grant Jalalabad to the Jammu chief because he felt that by doing so "we shall have placed an irreconcilable enemy to the Afghans between them and us."[54] But in return for Jalalabad Ellenborough demanded that the Raja withdraw from Ladakh.[55] The Jammu chief, however, rejected the offer.[56] He was certainly not prepared to surrender the vast Himalayan tracts he had spent years in acquiring for an isolated frontier town in extremely inhospitable surroundings.

Ellenborough's arrival in India once again revived the controversy over the policy to be followed toward the Sikh kingdom. Auckland's successor, who nurtured rapacious designs on the parts of India still free of British control, tenaciously contemplated the annexation of Panjab during his tenure of office. On the eve of his departure from England, Ellenborough had written a long letter in which he sought the endorsement of his plans from the Duke of Wellington, who had served in India as Arthur Wellesley at the turn of the century. After recounting the political ineptitude of Sher Singh, the growing power of the Jammu Rajas, and the increasing lawlessness in the Sikh army, he bluntly asked the Duke: "What I desired, therefore, was your opinion . . . as to the best mode of attacking the Punjab."[57] However, while Wellington advised Ellenborough to be prepared defensively[58] and seemed inclined toward the eventual acquisition of Kashmir, he opposed the annexation of the entire Sikh state:

. . . I would prefer to leave the Sikhs in possession of their Punjab. If we push to the West at all, it ought to be in the hills towards the sources of the rivers by which the Punjab is watered and defended, that is to say Cashmere.

I have always maintained this opinion; but I would prefer to leave the Sikhs as they are, and if possible to maintain peace.[59]

Ironically enough, Wellington's brother, Lord Richard Wellesley who, as Governor-General of India from 1798 to 1805, had acquired the reputation of being rather expansionist-minded, also spoke against further annexations and in July of 1842, wrote to Ellenborough: "No further extension of our territory is even desirable in India, even if war for conquest could be justified, or were legal."[60] The Board of Directors, too, were obviously aware of the belligerent policies advocated by the Governor-General, for in August it cautioned him and asked him to assure the Sikhs "that no foundation exists for the imputations against the British Government, of a desire to possess any portion of the Dominions of Lahore."[61] Despite the antipathy he encountered toward his projected policies, Ellenborough refused to alter his stand. In October he contended that the ensuing British withdrawal from Afghanistan would force the Sikhs to move the bulk of their army to the northwest, leaving Panjab relatively defenceless. That futurity, combined with the already bitterly polarized Lahore government, declared the contriving Governor-General, would soon pave the way for British intervention. Boasting that the "state of Punjab is therefore under my foot," Ellenborough in another communication to Wellington claimed:

[The Sikhs] will be obliged to keep their principal force [on the Afghan frontier], and Lahore and Umritsur will remain with insufficient garrison, within a few marches of the Sutlej, on which I shall, in twelve days, at any time, be able to assemble three European and eleven native battalions, one European regiment of cavalry, two regiments of native cavalry, and two of irregular cavalry, and twenty-four guns. . . . The conflict of parties in Punjab will render it more dependent every year, and, indeed, he who knows it best does not think the Government can last a year. I intend to be most courteous and liberal to both parties, and to wait till I am called in.[62]

But such an ultrazealous and grasping policy was again disapproved of by the Duke on various grounds:

I advisedly prefer the continuance of relations which have existed for 40 years between the Government of India, and that of Lahore. Divided as the Sikhs must be before we can justifiably enter their country, still the contest could not be short, and must be expensive. It would be one in which decisive success would only be obtained by the exercise of military talents of a high order, which the Government of India cannot always command, and it would terminate in an acquisition of territory which it would require the highest political ability in the head of the Government peacefully and satisfactorily to administer and preserve.[63]

During April of 1843 the Board of Directors advised Ellenborough to refrain from interfering in the internal policies of the Sikhs and declared: "Unless we terrify them into measures of hostility, we believe that we may calculate, if not on their cordial friendship, certainly on their abstinence from acts of aggression."[64] The Board also condemned the British press in India, which had so vehemently endorsed Ellenborough's bellicose stance that it had elicited an angry retort from Sher Singh. It complained: "So much has been written, and circulated, concerning the advantages which might be presumed to follow the extension of British dominion in the direction of the Sikh territory, that we cannot wonder at the jealousy with which every movement on our part has been watched by the Government at Lahore."[65]

Such criticisms, however, restrained the Governor-General only temporarily. The iniquitous annexation of Sind[66] in August whetted his appetite for more, and the simultaneous deaths of Sher Singh and his wazir during September revived his combative fervor. He wrote to Wellington that "the time cannot be very far distant when the Punjab will fall into our management."[67] Ellenborough also felt that these latest events had made Gulab Singh practically independent of Lahore[68] and wondered "what we shall do as respects the Hills."[69] Concluding that the Raja could be an important factor in the war he anticipated with the Sikhs, the Governor-General ordered Richmond, Clerk's successor, to collect information on the extent of Gulab Singh's territories, the number of his forts, and the quality of his troops.[70] Richmond's report on the Raja's strength,[71] combined with the growing intractability of the khalsa, convinced Ellenborough that the Sikh kingdom was moving toward a great internal convulsion, and early in 1844 he informed Queen Victoria and Wellington that he might be obliged to march across the Sutlej by the year's end.[72] Though conscious of the Board of Directors' disenchantment with his policies, he nonetheless warned it of the inevitability of war: "Let our policy be what it may the contest must come at last, and the intervening time which may be given to us should be employed in unostentatious but vigilant preparation."[73] The Board, however, again spurned Ellenborough's advice and counseled him "to avoid a policy of territorial extension towards Panjab despite lawlessness prevailing there."[74] But the stubborn Governor-General remained steadfast in his views. When word of the Jammu chief's altercation with Hira Singh reached him, he wrote to Wellington that it "has had the effect of entirely separating the Hills, under Gholab Singh, from the Plains," and surmised that it would now be easier for the British to take over Panjab. Indicating that he could be ready to wage war upon the Sikhs by December of 1844, Ellenborough almost jubilantly told the Duke: "Everything is going on there as we could desire, if we looked forward to the ultimate possession of the Punjab."[75]

However, the Governor-General remained undecided about the course of action to be pursued with respect to Jammu if hostilities with the Sikhs did erupt. He had maintained a close surveillance on Gulab Singh and learned soon after Dhian Singh's death that, though the Jammu chief might be interested in an alliance with the British, he would, if attacked, "never become a tributary without a struggle."[76] Early in April 1844, Ellenborough was informed by Richmond that in the event of an Anglo-Sikh war Gulab Singh would probably align himself with the British, but he would, in return, want to "be recognized as the independent sovereign of Peshawur and Cashmeer and also the Hill states between the Indus and the Sutlej."[77] As relations between the Jammu chief and Hira Singh became strained, the British agent reported that the former had made discreet inquiries about the possibility of a surreptitious arrangement by which the Company would recognize his future autonomy. Referring probably to the contact made by the British with Gulab Singh and Dhian Singh during the Anglo-Afghan War in 1842, Richmond wrote to his government that "the Governor-General was fully aware of the kind of hope which had from time to time been given to the Jammu family that their independence would not be displeasing to the British Government when a fitting time arrived for the recognition of their separate sovereignty."[78] But Richmond's communication irked Ellenborough. The agent was curtly informed that no promise of independence had been given to Gulab Singh and "if any such hope had been held out, it must have been without authority."[79] In addition, Richmond was ordered to refrain from responding in the future to any such overtures from the Jammu chief.[80]

However, before Ellenborough could formulate any plans regarding Gulab Singh or gain permission to invade the Sikh state, the Board of Directors recalled him from India in May of 1844. He was reportedly not unhappy to leave, for the Board had decided that, as far as Ellenborough was concerned, "the Punjab was to be forbidden fruit."[81] But if the Board had vigorously objected to Ellenborough's propositions regarding the Sikh state, the emergence of a strong anti-British sentiment in the Sikh army began to soften its firm stand against intervention in Panjab. Although the Board conveyed to Henry Hardinge, the Governor-General designate, its expressions of hope that friendly relations with Lahore would continue, he was nonetheless also told that "the supremacy of our power must be maintained when necessary by the force of arms."[82] However, on assuming the direction of affairs in India during July, Hardinge found the khalsa no immediate threat[83] and felt confident that, should such a situation arise, British defences could be promptly reinforced at the Sutlej. During September Hardinge informed Prime Minister Sir Robert Peel, a close friend: ". . . our force is respectable. In a few days we could concentrate [on the Sikh frontier] 20,000 men and 40 pieces of artillery, about 5,000 Europeans, and 15,000 natives."[84]

It was not very long before Hardinge noticed the special position of Gulab Singh in the Sikh state, and described him as the "most remarkable man in the country."[85] But like Ellenborough he, too, could not at first determine the exact policy to be followed toward him. Thus, when in the autumn of 1844 Jammu was threatened with an invasion by Hira Singh, the Dogra chief's secret offer of a pledge of loyalty to the Company in return for British recognition was ignored.[86] Nonetheless, the Governor-General seemed to feel that the Jammu Raja was capable of repulsing an invasion from Lahore and in October declared that "if the Hillmen make a successful resistance which it is expected they will do, Heera S. fate is sealed."[87] Hardinge must have quickly revised such an overestimation when the Sikh army, under Rani Jindan's orders, finally did attack Jammu in March of 1845. But even before that invasion actually commenced, Gulab Singh had made new approaches to the British. During January, Bhai Ram Singh sent a message to Broadfoot that the Jammu Raja would guarantee to pay the British fifty lakhs of rupees if they invaded Panjab at that moment.[88] Though rebuffed once again, the Raja did not give up and in February personally sent a communication to Broadfoot. In it he offered the British his assistance in the occupation of Panjab if they would in turn confirm him in his possessions and help him exact vengeance upon the Sikhs who, he charged, had mercilessly put several members of his family to death. He added that, since the Sikhs were now devoid of leadership capable of establishing a stable government, "the English must before long, of necessity, rule over the Punjab."[89] His proposals ignored for yet a third time, the Jammu chief made a direct overture to Hardinge through General Ventura, a French national in Lahore's employ, but it, too, was turned down. The Governor-General simply did not seem interested in the annexation of Panjab at that time and wrote to his son, Walter: "Golab Singh has through various channels sent us the same offers, which we have constantly rejected & desired all our agents to discountenance. . . . We desire no acquisition of territory."[90]

This stalemate in Anglo-Dogra relations was momentarily broken by the appearance at Jammu of an unemployed French mercenary named St. Amand. Aware of the Dogra leader's desire to befriend the Company, St. Amand "managed to bleed Gulab Singh pretty considerably"[91] by pretending to be a messenger sent by the British authorities "to propose [both] an alliance with the Raja & the conquest of the Punjaub."[92] The beguiled Jammu chief was so elated by this visitor that he immediately accepted the spurious offer and wrote to the British urging them to invade Panjab. The Frenchman's masquerade, however, was soon discovered, and so angered Hardinge that he dubbed St. Amand "a great scamp" and declared that he "will have his nose cut off or be hanged."[93]

Although Hardinge repeatedly rejected Gulab Singh's overtures early in 1845, he was gradually coming to the conclusion that he might eventually have to intervene in the Sikh state. Referring to the growing confusion at Lahore, he wrote that

if we can't bolster up this Sikh state, the govt. of which is carried on by a drunken prostitute—her councillors—her paramours, the only other alternative is [British] occupation. . . . The treasury has in it we hear not more than 2 months pay. . . . When these means are at an end most of the army will become plunderers and robbers and if we are to arrive at this result I confess I would prefer an abatement of the nuisance at *one blow* whilst it is an army, rather than be compelled at a later period to have to put it down in the shape of a Pindaree warfare.[94]

Later in February he hinted at a possible future alliance with Gulab Singh by noting that "fresh events may require fresh combinations."[95] However, aware of the criticism that might result from an unprovoked attack on Panjab, he wished to proceed cautiously, and added: "Come what may we shall have a case that will bear a House of Commons scrutiny."[96]

The attitude of the Board of Directors toward the Sikh state was also in the process of change. During March, it expressed the belief that if law and order did not return to Panjab, then a division of the kingdom between the Sikhs and the Dogras might be the only solution. The Board did not suggest that the British forcibly impose such a settlement upon Lahore and Jammu, but it wistfully hoped that the two antagonists would voluntarily turn for mediation to Hardinge, who should then advise

that both parties should forthwith establish peaceful relations with each other, and apply their best energies to the good government of their respective territories, and to the joint reduction of what with a view to that object alone, would be an overgrown military force. An arrangement of this description, honestly carried out, would not, as it appears to us, be either injurious to the two states themselves . . . separated from each other or prejudicial to the interests and the rights of the British Government.[97]

But that there was no room for such extreme optimism soon became evident when in April the Sikh army overwhelmed the Dogras at Jammu and removed Gulab Singh to Lahore. Hardinge was much perturbed by this event, and his sympathies clearly lay with the Jammu chief. Once again describing the Dogra leader as "able," he expressed concern for his safety.[98] Fearing that Gulab Singh would be executed, the Governor-General lamented that this "man's fate will not tend to establish a better order of things."[99] During the same month Hardinge also voiced his anxiety over the possibility that, because of the financial difficulties of the Lahore government, the impetuous Sikh "army may attempt to violate our Frontier."[100] However, he forecast no trouble for another six months, but declared that "after that time we must be guided by the Progress of events, which are perpetually changing."[101]

Despite Hardinge's partiality for Gulab Singh and his uneasiness over the state of affairs at Lahore, Company officials continued to spurn the Jammu Raja's bids for their friendship. For instance, Broadfoot scoffed at a message sent by Gulab Singh during May in which he maintained that he had tried in vain to persuade Rani Jindan to seek British assistance in curbing the growing menace of the khalsa. The agent labelled it a ruse "to support his claim hereafter to be the leader of the English party,"[102] and observed that this was yet another attempt by the Raja to "make his aid or neutrality worth buying by the English at a high price."[103] Again, after Gulab Singh managed to return to Jammu in August "with his head on his shoulders,"[104] he immediately sent a messenger to Broadfoot with the report that Lahore was making preparations for a showdown with the Company. The emissary added that "the English would be forced to make war and that it could not be delayed beyond the approaching cold season."[105] The Raja then repeated his offer to join the British if they would permit him to retain his hill territories. In return, he claimed that he could collect at least forty thousand troops, and possibly another fifty thousand, for an assault against the Sikhs. He further boasted that "every chief in Afghanistan, Tartary and Cashmere"[106] was under his influence and, if necessary, he could make them rebel against the Sikhs. Above all, the Jammu chief declared that, if the British desired, "he could so divide the Darbar, the country and the army that he could himself cause the destruction of the latter and leave the capital open to the British who would not have to fire a shot."[107] In order to allay any apprehensions that the British might still entertain about his loyalty, he even offered to send to them his only surviving son, Ranbir Singh, as a hostage. Broadfoot, with Hardinge's approval, firmly rejected these latest proposals from the Raja and replied, somewhat sanctimoniously, that the British "never made war till driven to it and still less took part in the intrigues or disaffection of the subjects of an ally."[108]

During September 1845 Hardinge told Peel of entreaties by Gulab Singh and other influential, though unidentified, Panjab chiefs to cross the Sutlej.[109] At the same time, he complained to the Company's Secret Committee in London of the "disgusting debauchery" rampant at Lahore under Jowahir Singh's wazarat.[110] While Hardinge stated that he was still opposed to the conquest of the Sikh state, he expressed fear that events might lead him to it. He conceded, however, that "the occupation will be a measure of great delicacy and difficulty."[111] Perhaps for this reason the Governor-General, despite his personal liking for Gulab Singh, briefly debated whether or not to expel him from the hills in a postwar settlement, and wrote: "The re-instatement of the dispossessed chiefs might be politic, because it would be fast and popular—and as these extend to Ladakh on the borders of China."[112] But he did not fully write the Raja off, for he added that the "disposal of property in [the] hills would depend on political considerations at the time."[113] The time for decisions, not only with respect to Jammu but also Lahore, approached rapidly after Jowahir Singh was assassinated at the end of September, and the Sikh kingdom rushed headlong toward catastrophe.

Ever since the death of Naunihal Singh there had been an increasing belief among Company officials that sooner or later the British would have to move against the Sikh kingdom. Gulab Singh eventually realized this and, in order to gain his own independence from Lahore, repeatedly offered to align himself with the British against the Sikhs. The Company's unwillingness to respond to Jammu's overtures can perhaps best be explained by the fact that, almost to the time war actually broke out, it had formulated no final policy toward Panjab. Despite this reluctance on the part of the British, it is noteworthy that Company officials carefully studied the contents of the Raja's communications and, what is even more significant, made no effort to reveal his incriminating actions to the Sikhs. Gulab Singh was well aware of this and probably considered it a diplomatic success, inasmuch as he had made it known to the British that he was not only anti-Lahore but could also be counted upon in the event of open Anglo-Sikh hostilities.

7 The Making of a Maharaja

The man whom I have to deal with, Golab Singh, is the greatest rascal in Asia—Henry Hardinge

As an enemy [Gulab Singh's] power of attack, with the divided forces of an irregular army, would have proved intolerably injurious; as a friend we may hope to find in him a steady adherent of that qualified British ascendancy to which he owes his rise—The *Times* (London)

Their fields, their crops, their streams
Even the peasants in the vale
They sold, they sold all, alas!
How cheap was the sale—Iqbal

𝓝O other aspect of Gulab Singh's long political career has perhaps aroused more controversy than his conduct in the First Anglo-Sikh War,[1] and it continues to evoke bitter argument. Whereas the debate at the end of the war concerned the Dogra chief's installation as the Maharaja of the independent state of Kashmir, in more recent years it has centered around Gulab Singh's part in the conflict which resulted in the partial dismemberment of the Sikh state. Two major assessments have been made which are diametrically opposed to one another. A school of Panjab historians judges the Jammu Raja's conduct to have been perfidious and brands him a traitor.[2] This conclusion is disputed by pro-Dogra historians who, while acknowledging his reluctance to fight against the British, imply nonetheless that he played an effective political role on behalf of the Sikhs which prevented the complete annexation of their state in 1846.[3] Such widely differing appraisals,[4] often made without sufficient historical data and characterized by political or regional prejudices, have done little to produce a balanced understanding of this highly controversial episode. This chapter, therefore, makes a special attempt to reconstruct and re-evaluate the Raja's role in the momentous events that took place in the history of the Sikhs between November 1845, and March 1846.

The appointment of Lal Singh to the wazarat in November 1845 failed to solve the numerous problems of the Sikh state. The khalsa had little confidence in him or in Rani Jindan, and it continued to intimidate both of them. The power of the Sikh army had steadily increased with the swift multiplication of its numerical strength,[5] and the Lahore government found it impossible to cope with its refractory attitude. Across the Sutlej the British were uneasily watching the growing state of anarchy in the Sikh kingdom. Hardinge, who had begun to fear an invasion by the khalsa as early as the spring of 1845, had reacted by systematically reinforcing the Sikh frontier[6] and, in anticipation of a conflict, personally arrived in Panjab during November. The Sikh government seized upon this British move as a possible means of resolving its own difficulties and actually decided to encourage the khalsa to cross the Sutlej. Whatever the outcome of such an enterprise, the darbar assumed that its own

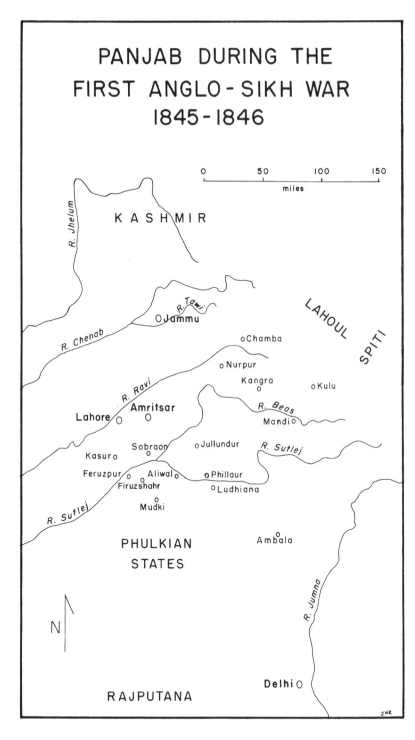

PANJAB DURING THE
FIRST ANGLO - SIKH WAR
1845 - 1846

0   50   100   150
miles

KASHMIR

R. Jhelum

R. Tawi

O Jammu

R. Chenab

LAHOUL

SPITI

o Chamba

o Nurpur

Kangra
o

o Kulu

R. Ravi

Amritsar

R. Beas

Lahore O   O

Mandi o

Sobraon
o

o Jullundur

R. Sutlej

Kasur o

Feruzpur o   Aliwal o

o Phillaur

Firuzshahr

o Ludhiana

o
Mudki

R. Sutlej

PHULKIAN
STATES

o
Ambala

R. Jumna

N

Delhi O

RAJPUTANA

JNR

position would be strengthened. If the Sikh army were defeated, the power of the most licentious element in the state would automatically be curbed. On the other hand, if the British were defeated, "the Sikhs joined by the Hindoos of Rajpootana & all the discontented were to over-run India & become a great military power."[7] Consequently, war was all but declared in the third week of November, though hostilities were not immediately launched. The soldiers were attracted by the opportunity of winning glory and lured by the prospect of booty, but they became apprehensive of the darbar's motives and threatened to murder various Sikh leaders. The unpredictable army deemed no one at Lahore worthy of its trust and contemplated "sending for Rajah Golab Sing to lead them."[8] On December 3, an angry exchange resulted when General Tej Singh defiantly confronted the Rani and the darbar. A British informer recorded the encounter:

[Tej Singh] to-day asked the Ranee and Sirdars, as they were sending him to make war on the English Government, to give him a written order; the Ranee said, "Why do you constantly ask for written orders? The army regular and irregular marched by the Maharajah's order, and now you are going by the same order." The Ranee asked what the army was plotting as to her? Tej Singh said, that this time the army would, undoubtedly, treat her ill; that she had sent them against the English to get them ruined, but that the army had found out this device, and now said that they would "comb" [torture] her, along with Rajah Lal Singh, and imprison the Sirdars, and deliver them to Rajah Golab Singh, who would settle their accounts.[9]

But in spite of their suspicions Tej Singh and the bulk of the Sikh army stationed near Lahore gradually began to move toward the Sutlej.[10] Even Lal Singh, though displaying little enthusiasm,[11] accompanied the troops. The panches, however, remained behind with a few regiments, demanding that the darbar offer the wazarat to Gulab Singh. This was refused, and the panches retaliated by communicating to the Raja their willingness to remove Rani Jindan from the regency if he would consent to administer the state during Dalip Singh's minority.[12] Perturbed by this unauthorized overture to Jammu, the Rani summoned an urgent meeting of the darbar. In the midst of its deliberations word arrived that Gulab Singh had accepted the khalsa's invitation. In a state of virtual panic the Rani wrote to the Raja and attempted to dissuade him from his plans: "You are an old faithful and well wisher of the Government. If you come without orders you will commit an offence against the Government. Do not act on the writings of the Khalsa. It is the same army which assailed you. Your brothers and relatives and dependents and sons and nephews sacrificed themselves. If you come to Lahore, you will gain nothing. Rely on this."[13] But the rumor-ridden Sikh capital had been misled about Gulab Singh's response. He had in reality declined to give a prompt answer to this latest invitation from the panches.[14]

On the other side of the Sutlej, British officials closely observed these developments in the Sikh state and speculated on Gulab Singh's part in the crisis. Frederick Currie, the political secretary to the Governor-General, suspected that the military movements had been instigated by the Jammu Raja to further his own interests: "I cannot but think that this late affair at Lahore is part of Goolab Singh's game, to induce the Ranee and Sirdars to urge the army to this demonstration, with a view to bringing a solemn remonstrance at least from us; this remonstrance and our impending danger to be used by the troops as a plea for putting those obnoxious to Goolab Singh to death, and thus smoothing his way to power."[15] Though Hardinge entertained similar misgivings,[16] his son Charles, who served as his private secretary, advanced a somewhat divergent opinion: "The Regent only consented to allow the troops to advance against the English to save her own life and lives of her lovers . . . [The Sikh soldiers] will retrieve their steps, murder the heads of the existing Govt. & Golab Singh."[17]

The Jammu Raja also surveyed the political scene but, despite reports that he intended to invade Lahore,[18] remained aloof in the hills. Nonetheless, he strengthened his army[19] and again offered to align himself with the British. A Dogra courier informed Brigadier Wheeler, commander of the troops at Ludhiana, that in the event of war Gulab Singh "wished to cast in his lot with the latter, as his existence depended on their success."[20] This was followed up by an overture to Broadfoot, in which the Jammu chief pledged his collaboration. The agent reported:

> The Rajah wishes to be taken by the hand . . . he wishes to cause disturbance in the whole Sikh Kingdom and he says he will carry out to the uttermost whatever orders may be given by the English Government. . . . If ordered he has force and will serve with life and property . . . that the jageerdars of the hills, those of Cashmeer, of Hazara . . . must be considered friends and servants of the English.[21]

Again the British declined to respond.

Gulab Singh, however, was not the only functionary in the Sikh state to approach the British. Determined to destroy the khalsa's strength, Lal Singh and even Tej Singh, upon their arrival at the Sutlej, "assured the local British authorities [at Feruzpur] of their secret and efficient goodwill."[22] There is some evidence that Rani Jindan and other members of the darbar were also involved in such activities.[23] Unaware of its government's chicanery, the army crossed the Sutlej on December 11. As resolved in advance, Lal Singh and Tej Singh helped pave the way for its defeat at the battles of Mudki on December 18 and of Firuzshahar on December 21 and 22.[24] But the British successes were not achieved before the Sikh troops, in spite of their leaders, had put up an extraordinarily stiff resistance, which prevented their total rout.[25] In London the influential *Times* summed up the situation with the comment: "The Sikh army has been repulsed, but not destroyed; and, although we have won a great battle, we have only begun the war."[26]

The failure to win swiftly and decisively shattered any dreams the British might have entertained of annexing the entire state of Panjab as a result of this conflict. This turn of affairs was not unwelcome to Gulab Singh who, as a subject of Lahore, howsoever unwilling, would have risked the loss of his territories in the event of a complete Sikh collapse. Taking advantage of the stalemate, Gulab Singh once more contacted the British. Lieutenant Edward Lake, a junior agent, became the recipient of this latest offer from Jammu, which was delivered by one Bansidhar Ghosh. The agent was favorably impressed and, acting on his own responsibility, returned an obscurely worded message designed to arouse and encourage the Raja's ambitions. Lake related the encounter to his immediate superior, Captain Mills:

[Bansidhar Ghosh] describes his master as willing to assist us on the following terms:
1. If we will confirm to him and his heirs forever the jaghiers which are at present held by himself and the different members of his family.
2. If we would leave him in possession of the territory at present under his rule, contenting ourselves with a tribute of [one-quarter] in every rupee of revenue which he derived from it.
As I am not in possession of the Right Honourable the Governor-General's views upon this subject I could return no explicit answer. I explained to the messenger the difficulty in which I was placed & told him to inform his master that I would lose no time in laying his views before the proper authorities.
In the meantime I gave him a letter . . . the purport of which is as follows.
"He who wishes to climb to the summit of a lofty mountain, must start at day break. Should he delay, night may close o'er him, 'ere he has gained the desire of his heart. The Treasure which is buried in the depths of the mountain will become the prize of that man who is the first to reach its summit."

In the absence of all instructions, I have made use of this ambiguous language, because I feel that while I may be promoting the interests of the British Government I have in no way compromised them. I have directed [Bansidhar Ghosh] to leave here a confidential servant, who will carry to Rajah Goolab Sing, any instructions with which the Right Hon'ble the Governor-General may think proper to honour him.[27]

Currie rebuked Lake for his action but nonetheless advised the agent "to refer the said emissary to me or to Major Lawrence,"[28] who had succeeded Broadfoot at Ludhiana.[29] Despite their refusal to commit themselves to Gulab Singh, the very willingness of high Company officials to receive his representative marked a significant shift in the British attitude toward Jammu. The policy of ignoring the Raja's initiatives was apparently being abandoned.

Unconscious of the Jammu chief's machinations, the Sikh troops not only continued to anticipate his assumption of the wazarat but expected him to come to the Sutlej, and declared that "the moment he arrives, they will fight again."[30] Though pretending to submit to the pressure of the panches,[31] the Raja, after careful deliberation, decided to visit the Sikh capital. He had come to the conclusion that only by assuming control of the Lahore government could he pursue policies which would persuade the British to be more receptive to him and his aspirations.

Aware of the various obstacles that lay ahead of him, Gulab Singh embarked upon a policy of calculated duplicity and deliberate vacillation. After a leisurely march the Raja, accompanied by an army said to number about twelve thousand men, approached Lahore on January 25.[32] This move raised high expectation among the Sikhs, but upon his arrival Gulab Singh politely declined to commit his army to the war. Yet he attempted to placate the Sikh forces by promising to supply them with "cash, ammunition, and food."[33]

With Gulab Singh at Lahore, the panches renewed their demand for a new wazir, but Rani Jindan adamantly refused. The Raja intensified the dispute by announcing that the wazarat was acceptable to him only if it included an absolute mandate to run the state. The panches now unconditionally agreed to support such a demand and promised that if he "agreed to exert himself in the cause of the Khalsa and would go out against the English, the whole Khalsa would accompany him. If on the contrary the Rajah disapproved of war, let him go and make peace—whatever the Rajah might order would be approved by the Khalsa."[34] Unmoved by such a rare display of docility, Gulab Singh instead undertook to exploit the army's obsession with him. He aimed to utterly baffle the khalsa by administering to it simultaneous dosages of despair and hope. He accused the Sikhs of cowardice at Mudki and Firuzshahar, charging that "when the time came, [they] fled, eight men out of ten."[35] And ridiculing the khalsa's war cry, "*Dehli takht per bethegi aap guru ki fauj* [Your guru's army will sit on the Mughal throne at Delhi]," he mockingly observed that it was "too small to accommodate the Sikh forces which numbered almost one hundred thousand."[36] On the other hand, he dangled before the army the prospect that he would take up arms against the British. The Raja reportedly "declared his determination to conquer the enemy or die in the attempt . . . [adding] that as soon as the whole of his men were collected, many being still in the rear, he would march to Ferozpore."[37] But if this encouraged the khalsa, the Rani put little faith in Gulab Singh's pledge and entertained grave apprehensions as to his true motives. She suspected that the Raja was, in fact, fomenting a conspiracy "to depose her and the infant Maharaja Dhuleep Singh, and throw them into prison."[38] To forestall such an eventuality she plotted to have the Raja murdered, but the attempt was foiled.[39]

Amid all this confusion Gulab Singh continued his intrigues designed to deepen the darbar-khalsa hostility. The news of yet another defeat at Aliwal on January 28 strengthened his position. With emotions running high among the Sikhs, the Raja made an appearance at the darbar on January 29, his first since arriving at Lahore. Feigning good will and loyalty, the Jammu chief announced that "he was the humble servant of the Government,"[40] yet, when asked to take part in the war, he took refuge behind wholesale prevarication. Nevertheless, on the following day he professed to the Rani his intention of fighting against the British, but added that he would not act in conjunction with the khalsa. The *Delhi Gazette* recorded this latest about-face:

Rajah Gholab Singh represented that he was fully prepared to undertake any duty which the Ranee might assign to him The Ranee said that he had better take what money was left in the treasury, and as much ammunition as might still be required, and proceed to join the camp. The Rajah replied that he had brought men, money, and ammunition with him, and was ready to place the whole at the disposition of the Sirkar, but he did not wish at the present moment to join the Sikh troops, being anxious to lead his troops on some service separate from theirs. He was, he said, determined to fight the British, but he did not in doing so wish to be mixed up with the Sikhs, who would run away instead of fighting.[41]

This promise, also, remained unfulfilled as the Raja whiled away his time censuring the khalsa rather than preparing for war. He condemned it for advancing against a power which was "sovereign down to the furtherest boundary of Sinde."[42] But when the panches protested that the Sikh troops had acted only under orders from the darbar, Gulab Singh, in yet another tergiversation, made the accusation that "the object of the officers of the state in sending them across was to destroy them."[43]

However, despite such double-dealing by the Raja, the panches refused to lose faith in him. On the morning of January 31 they issued a warning that, if Gulab Singh was not elevated to the wazarat by the day's end, the Rani, the Maharaja, and other high officials would be put to death. The terror-stricken Rani hastily convened a session of the darbar to which the Jammu Raja and the panches were also invited. In the stormy conference that followed, the panches launched into a rancorous tirade against the Rani, denouncing her for leading the kingdom down the path to destruction. Joining in the attack, Gulab Singh reproached the Sikh leaders for embezzling crores of rupees, an act which he said had led Lahore to the verge of financial disaster. In a particularly vituperative assault on Lal Singh, the Raja blamed the absent wazir for the outbreak of the war, "as his object was to destroy the Sikh army, and [demanded] that he ought now to be imprisoned and punished."[44] The Rani, unable to resist the mounting pressure, finally brought the altercation to an end by yielding to the panches' demand, and agreed to make Gulab Singh the wazir. At his inauguration that very evening, the Dogra chief proclaimed his intention of commencing guerilla warfare in the British territories beyond the Sutlej. Choosing pillage over actual combat, he

expressed his determination of dividing the cavalry into two bodies of about 5,000 men each, and sending them across the river at Loodianah, not to fight, but to plunder and cause destruction amongst the villages and towns, as far as they could penetrate, avoiding the regular British troops wherever they could. Should they meet with any, they were to pretend to fight, and then give way and take some other route, plundering as they went.[45]

Gulab Singh's pronouncement delighted the Sikh troops in the nearby camps, and they rejoiced by firing guns late into the night.[46]

But such exultation proved transitory as the Raja displayed no desire to implement the grand scheme he had unfolded. Instead, he stabbed the Sikhs in the back, for, "on being installed as Minister, [he] immediately put himself in communication with [the British], proferring every assistance in his power for the furtherance of any ends in regard to the State of Lahore which [they] might have in view."[47] In anticipation of a favorable response to this message, the Raja stiffened his attitude toward the Sikhs. Renewing his criticism of the war, he scorned the darbar's suggestions to participate in it.[48] He similarly ignored the wishes of the panches, but an attempt to get rid of them by bribing them to move to the Sutlej proved unsuccessful when they "refused the money, and said they would not go without the Rajah."[49] Undaunted by this failure, Gulab Singh again strove to undermine the khalsa's morale by vilifying its performance on the battlefield. Exercising the prerogative of his high office, he publicly condemned the troops "for their cowardice, and [told] them they were totally unfit for duty."[50] In spite of this latest humiliation, the army almost pitifully clung to the belief that the Raja alone could galvanize its spirit and lead it to victory. But when Gulab Singh was approached once more by the panches, he spoke of the inevitability of defeat and advised that Lahore sue for peace. Offering to mediate, the Raja demanded that the Sikhs reaffirm their pledge of unlimited authority to him,[51] to the extent that the Sikhs "would agree to stand by any treaty he made even if by that treaty the city of Lahore was offered as a peshkush [gift] to the English."[52] Contemptuously he remarked that those who disagreed with him could "fight to their hearts' content."[53] All parties at Lahore were so discouraged by the Dogra's intransigence that they repented their recent conduct and acquiesced in his demand,[54] but the panches on subsequent reflection withdrew their consent and decried Gulab Singh's unwillingness to join the Sikhs in the war.[55] The troops once again demanded his presence at the Sutlej[56] but the Raja declined, remarking acridly that "the Khalsa wanted him to be in the same plight as they were."[57]

Gulab Singh thus failed to win over the army to his point of view, but he did succeed in convincing the darbar of the advisability of seeking an accommodation with the British.[58] By February 6, the Jammu chief felt bold enough to announce "that he had sent an embassy to the English."[59] Unaware that the Raja had practically offered to sell out the Sikhs, the darbar supported his action and consented to further contact by declaring that "the fault [for the war] lay with the Khalsa, not the English."[60] But the army's intractability made any negotiations meaningless, and the prospect of another battle seemed imminent.

Though realizing that the khalsa was beyond the control of any one man,[61] the British were gratified by Gulab Singh's maneuvers to circumvent the Sikh determination to fight. This new turn of events made them increasingly optimistic that the war would end soon. In fact, Hardinge was so encouraged that he drew up a rough blueprint of postwar territorial arrangements less than three days after Gulab Singh succeeded to the wazarat. This plan, which included the creation of an independent kingdom under the Jammu Raja, was referred to by Hardinge in a letter to Peel:

A nephew came from Golab S. a day ago and a note this morning. I have desired Major Lawrence to let his native secretary answer it. . . . I antici-pate Golab S. will probably come here. The general operations will not be suspended. The chief difficulty will consist in controlling the Sikh army. Golab S. and the Rajpoot tribes should be made independent. Our frontier line may be improved by some annexations towards the hills exclusive of the Lahore territory confiscated on this side—and steps may be taken to come to a settlement before the hot weather sets in. . . . I write in great haste having just received Golab Singh's note an hour ago. If the [Sikh] nation and the army cling together and defend their footsteps our means and the advanced season render it impossible to carry the war to a successful termination this spring—if the Sirdars and the Ranee submit to our terms the termination is possible.

I must incur the risk or avoid it according to the progress of any nego-tiations with Golab Singh.[62]

The Governor-General directed Lawrence to acknowledge the Lahore minister's letters, and the agent informed the Raja that the British "appreciated his wisdom in not taking up arms . . . and that his in-terests would be taken into consideration."[63]

Strengthened by the British commitment and convinced of the army's resolute opposition to a peaceful settlement, Gulab Singh let the Sikhs drift toward another armed clash. In his determination to bring about the final defeat of the khalsa he took a series of steps designed to hinder its efforts and lower its morale. There was a sud-den irregularity in the dispatch of food supplies to the Sutlej.[64] Requests for additional war matériel were refused. One such appli-cation by Ranjore Singh Majithia, a prominent Sikh chief, was turned down with the jibe that he already had abandoned too much while fleeing from the scene of earlier defeats.[65] A complaint brought by Tej Singh against a group of his assistants was dismissed by the Jammu Raja, who encouraged insubordination by observing that "they were wise officers who thus refused to obey orders, and set a good example to the troops."[66] Finally, he removed all Sikh soldiers from Lahore and replaced them with his own. "His object evidently," an assistant agent pointed out in a letter to Currie, "is to bring about the extermination of the Sikh troops."[67] While thus crippling the khalsa, Gulab Singh ordered the captured British troops to be well treated. Elephants were frequently dispatched to conduct the pris-oners to Lahore, where the Raja honored them by granting audiences and bestowing gifts.[68] The cumulative effect of such measures was to create panic and desperation among the Sikh soldiers. Some of them expressed their readiness to accept any settlement with the British so long as it did not involve a reduction in their salaries. Others were so dismayed by Gulab Singh's conduct that they wanted Lal Singh reinstated as the wazir.[69]

But Lal Singh and Tej Singh were no more interested in winning the war than the Jammu chief himself. Once again at the battle of Sobraon on February 10 they led their forces astray and abandoned them,[70] thereby effecting a decisive Sikh defeat. The khalsa suffered thousands of casualties[71] and the survivors were forced to retreat, leaving behind the dead "as food for the jackal, the dog, and the vulture."[72] When news of the catastrophe reached Lahore, the panches reproached Gulab Singh for his failure to participate in the war. The Raja promptly placed the blame on the khalsa and charged, tongue in cheek, that it "had commenced to fight before his arrival."[73]

Having thus facilitated the British victory, Gulab Singh turned to the task of preparing the Sikhs for the penalties of defeat. Making the most of the general state of panic that gripped Lahore,[74] the Raja warned the darbar that the very existence of the Sikh kingdom was at stake.[75] The Rani, who was especially terrified that the British army would march into Lahore, remove her son from the throne, and molest the local women, now implored the Jammu chief to seek a compromise.[76] Gulab Singh, however, agreed to accept such an assignment only after the members of the darbar, the army officers, and even the panches had signed "a solemn declaration that they would abide by such terms as he might determine on with the British Government."[77] Once again Lahore fell prey to the Raja's schemes in the two-fold belief that he was genuinely concerned with their predicament and that he alone could save the kingdom from disastrous consequences. The Sikhs of course had no inkling that compliance with the British terms agreed to by Gulab Singh would inevitably advance his own aspirations at their expense.

Meanwhile the British forces moved rapidly into Panjab and halted at Kasur where, on February 14, Hardinge issued a proclamation expressing his readiness to negotiate a peace settlement with the Sikhs. His proposal was promptly accepted, and a delegation led by Gulab Singh arrived on the following day. The emissaries as a whole were coldly received. Condemning the Sikhs for committing aggression, Hardinge gravely warned of reprisals "which would mark to the whole world that insult could not be offered to the British Government."[78] But the reception of Gulab Singh was markedly different. Hardinge called him a "welcome ambassador,"[79] and praised his behavior during the war. This encounter was related in detail by the Governor-General in a communication to the Company's Secret Committee:

> I told the Rajah that I recognized the wisdom, prudence, and good feeling evinced by him in having kept himself separate from these unjustifiable hostilities of the Sikhs, and that I was prepared to mark my sense of that conduct in the proceedings which must now be carried through. I stated, in the most marked manner and words, my satisfaction that he who had not participated in the offence, and whose wisdom and good feeling towards the British Government were well known, had been the person chosen by the Durbar as their representative for negotiating the means by which atonement might be made, and the terms on which the Sikh Government might be rescued from impending destruction, by a return to amicable relations between the British Government and the Lahore State.[80]

While unfounded reports circulated in various parts of Panjab that Hardinge, Gulab Singh, and others had been slain by the Sikhs,[81] negotiations proceeded swiftly, and "the terms proposed were privately arranged between the Political Secretary and the Raja about 2 o'clock in the morning [of the 18th]."[82] Under the compelling persuasion of its leader, the Sikh delegation acceded to all the British demands, which included 1) the cession of territory between the Sutlej and the Beas, 2) the payment of one and one-half crores of rupees in indemnity, and 3) the drastic reduction of the Sikh army.[83]

Though it was not immediately revealed to the public, it was at this juncture that the British authorities devised a scheme by which they in due course would assist Gulab Singh to acquire Kashmir. Hardinge, who had previously informed Peel of his resolve to make Jammu independent of Lahore, now conveyed to the British prime minister his intention of selling Kashmir to the Raja.[84] Convinced that the financially bankrupt Sikh government would be unable to pay the stipulated indemnity, he obviously planned to maneuver Lahore into surrendering Kashmir and other hill territories as compensation and, in turn, to transfer them to Gulab Singh. The British desire to reward the Jammu chief was quite apparent, but Hardinge's reasons for following such a course were revealed *in toto* only in subsequent weeks.

At the end of the Kasur negotiations, Hardinge prepared to depart for Lahore to help draft a treaty based on the agreement made with the Sikh delegation. But before the Governor-General's departure, Gulab Singh summoned the Maharaja to meet him and directed that, if necessary, Dalip Singh accompany the British entourage to the Sikh capital. Hardinge seemed flattered by the gesture and recorded:

In the course of discussion, the minister [Gulab Singh] asked, if the young Maharaja should now return to the Ranee, at Lahore, or if it was my desire that he should remain at my camp, intimating that it was for me to dispose of the young chief as I pleased, and as I might consider best for His Highness's interests. I replied, that I thought it advisable that His Highness's camp should accompany mine, and that I should myself conduct him to his capital.[85]

The Raja took precautions to insure a safe passage by ordering those troops of the defeated Sikh army who had halted about eighteen miles from Lahore to remain in camp.[86] In addition, he replaced Sikh guards with Muslims at all the gates to the capital. On February 20, Hardinge marched into Lahore without incident and an official in his party boasted: "Thus we took the enemy's capital without firing a shot."[87] He should have given most of the credit for such a smooth entrance to Gulab Singh.

During the drafting of the Anglo-Sikh treaty, the Jammu chief's true role in the war began to be revealed. The Sikhs expressed bitter resentment over his tactics, and once more unsuccessful attempts were made on the Raja's life.[88] Rani Jindan dismissed him from the wazarat and reinstated Lal Singh.[89] In an angry letter to Henry Lawrence she warned "that if Kashmir were given to Gulab Singh she will appeal directly to Queen Victoria."[90] The vengeful Rani and her new wazir also endeavored to nullify the Raja's power by offering his territories to the British in reparation for the indemnity. Gulab Singh, assuming an air of injured innocence, used this as a pretext for a final break with the Sikhs. Ironically enough, Lahore's maneuver had led it straight into the Anglo-Dogra trap. The affair was reported in the *Times* as follows:

. . . the Ranee and Lall Singh, being determined to spite Gholab Singh if they could, agreed to propose the cession, including Jamoo. . . . This appears to have alarmed Gholab Singh exceedingly; and he openly declared that they might manage their affairs as they pleased, he would have no further concern with them . . . that he should take his departure, and make his own terms with the British. It is very probable, however, that the alarm and vexation were but a ruse of Gholab Singh's to get free of Lahore, and to throw himself entirely into the hands of the Governor-General. . . . Gholab Singh could pretend to be vexed at the idea of being transferred to the English. . . . He, therefore, preserved his appearance of having been affronted, and affairs took the course he desired, and which were probably desired by the Governor-General.[91]

According to plan, the British authorities accepted Gulab Singh's territories and, in addition, forced the Sikhs to cede the entire hill area between the Beas and the Indus, including Kashmir, in compensation for the indemnity. This was stipulated by article 4 of the Anglo-Sikh agreement known as the Treaty of Lahore. But the treaty also gave a broad indication that the British had acquired the Jammu Raja's territories merely on paper, since article 12 stated that he would be made an independent ruler of "such territories in the hills as may be made over to [him] by separate agreement between himself and the British Government."[92] The peace settlement was signed on March 9 amid ceremonies marking the resumption of Anglo-Sikh relations. Gulab Singh, though repudiated by the Sikhs and not a signatory to the treaty, was very much in evidence. An eyewitness observed: "The center of attraction was the Rae Saheb [Gulab Singh] in his plain suit of yellow, and his unadorned, but no doubt carefully loaded and capped, pistol stuck in his belt."[93]

The Lahore transaction was followed by negotiations between the British and the Jammu chief to settle the terms by which the latter was to become sovereign. During the course of these meetings Hardinge confided to Walter: "I believe I might have had £ 50,000 [worth of] secret presents from the Raja for the services and favours he has received."[94] Whether this was merely a jocular boast or such an offer was actually made by his protégé is conjectural. In any event the two sides reached an agreement by which the Jammu chief regained his territorial possessions, was ceded Kashmir, Hazara, and Chamba, and was recognized as a Maharaja.[95] In return he was to pay seventy-five lakhs of rupees to the British government.[96] When the Anglo-Dogra treaty (see Appendix B) was signed at Amritsar on March 16, Gulab Singh publicly acknowledged his deep debt to Hardinge. He reportedly "stood up, and with joined hands, expressed his gratitude to the British viceroy—adding, without, however, any ironical meaning, that he was indeed his 'Zur-khureed', or gold-boughten slave!"[97]

Both during and after the negotiations leading to the two treaties, Hardinge wrote letters in which he explained his reasons for the policies he pursued. Interestingly enough, they indicate that, despite the favorable settlement he awarded to Gulab Singh, his earlier admiration for the Raja had diminished somewhat. In remarkably candid comments to his family he manifested more disdain than admiration for the man. To his sister he described the Jammu Raja as "the ablest scoundrel in all Asia,"[98] and to his wife he wrote:

> The man whom I have to deal with, Golab Singh, is the greatest rascal in Asia. Unfortunately it is necessary to improve his condition, because he did not participate in the war against us & his Territories touching ours, we can protect them without inconvenience & give him a slice of the Sikh Territory which balances his strength in some degree against theirs & as he is a rascal and treat him better than he deserves.[99]

In a letter to the Secret Committee the Governor-General rationalized in detail his decision not to extend British rule over the hill territories. He argued that such a move would result in a clash with the neighboring powers, the new frontier would be hard to protect, and the mountainous and largely barren regions would be an economic liability.[100] Hardinge also advanced a religious reason for defending the creation of a northwestern kingdom under Gulab Singh. Exhibiting the anti-Muslim stance characteristic of British officials since the disastrous war against Afghanistan, he wrote to Peel: "I have done this on the principle that it is our policy to prefer Hindoo governments, or any race in preference to the Mahommedans on this great entrance into India."[101]

A heated debate, however, followed in the wake of these new arrangements. One of Hardinge's bitterest critics was General Charles Napier. Then the governor of Sind, he marched to Panjab with an army of twelve thousand men but arrived too late to give battle.[102] In several letters written to his brother during 1846 he denounced Hardinge's decisions. The General believed that he could have effected the complete annexation of Panjab if only the war had been continued. He believed that the "whole country along the Indus up to Dhera Ismael Khan, even higher, would have been in arms to aid us, both banks of the Sutlege in our possession, my army in full march on Lahore, and the Sikh army or its *debris* driven towards the hills on the eastward, where Golab Sing would oppose them."[103] Though the Jammu chief's aid in overwhelming the Sikhs was thus taken for granted, the General expressed indignation at Hardinge's decision to make Gulab Singh the Maharaja of Kashmir. The sanctimonious Napier wrote: "What a king to install! Rising from the lowest foulest sediment of debauchery to float on the highest surge of blood he lifted his besmeared front, and England adorned it with a crown!"[104] It seems, however, that most of Napier's invective during this period was primarily for fraternal consumption. Hardinge, though conscious of Napier's imperialistic views,[105] was not aware of the extent of his resentment. In fact, Charles Hardinge wrote that Napier "quite concurred with the Governor-General that annexation at that time was impossible."[106] Nonetheless, the younger Hardinge knew of the General's opposition to all native chieftains, including Gulab Singh, and eventually delivered a rejoinder to Napier and others who clamored for the total acquisition of the Sikh state:

Those, too, who cavil against Lord Hardinge's non-annexation policy, and who think, as Sir C. Napier did, that "no Indian prince should exist," must put to themselves this question: could the Governor-General, with the military means at his disposal, have achieved such a conquest after

Sobraon? There was at that time a deficit in the Indian treasury. The hot season was setting in, while four general actions had palpably weakened the strength of our European regiments.[107]

Another critic of Hardinge's policies was Ellenborough. Irritated by the creation of the new mountain state, he wrote to Hardinge that "there have been times when the treaties with Gholab Singh as the minister of the Lahore Govt. and the detaching from the Lahore dominions a very extensive Territory for the purpose of placing it under the independent authority of that minister, thus rewarding a Traitor, would have been measures a little too oriental in Principle."[108] Indignant at this criticism, Hardinge countered in a long letter by tracing the perennial differences between the Jammu chief and Lahore, and praising the personal risks that the Raja had taken to help secure British objectives. The Governor-General vigorously justified the grant of Kashmir to Gulab Singh and asked Ellenborough if the British were "to treat the only man who had not lifted his arm agt. us with indifference."[109]

The recognition extended to Gulab Singh was also defended by Henry Lawrence, who participated in both the war and the negotiations. He considered the Raja to be admirably suited for his new role and asserted: "If any native of India has the ability and the means of establishing a strong and beneficial government in the Northern Hills, Gulab Singh is the man."[110]

The reaction in London to the British victory and the treaties was one of jubilation. Hardinge was praised as a statesman and as a soldier. Peel informed him that there was "universal approval and admiration of your policy *from first to last.*"[111] The Board of Directors conveyed its "most cordial admiration, thanks and gratitude."[112] Commendatory speeches were delivered in Parliament, and the Queen honored Hardinge by making him a viscount. The press added its approbation, and the *Times* termed the treaty with the Jammu chief the "most striking feature in these arrangements."[113] In the belief that the British would benefit by the agreement with Gulab Singh, the newspaper emphasized: "As an enemy his power of attack, with the divided forces of an irregular army, would have proved intolerably injurious; as a friend we may hope to find in him a steady adherent of that qualified British ascendancy to which he owes his rise."[114]

The polemic over the Treaty of Amritsar reasserted itself after the complete annexation of Panjab in 1849 and continued throughout most of the second half of the nineteenth century. Its advocates, however, prevailed, and Kashmir remained under the control of Gulab Singh and his successors until the British withdrawal from India.

The more recent debate which has arisen over Gulab Singh's role in the war[115] should be examined in the light of other alternatives available to him. If he had bowed to the pressure of the khalsa, he could have taken immediate control of the Lahore government and attempted to guide the Sikhs to victory. But the Raja decided that the consequences of such a course would be suicidal to him. In the event of success, the suddenly reinvigorated Sikhs, who generally abhorred the Jammu chief's special status in their kingdom, might then turn upon him. On the other hand, if the Sikhs lost, Gulab Singh stood the risk of incurring British retribution. It is also doubtful whether the Jammu chief had the ability to lead the Sikh army throughout the length and breadth of India and drive the British into the sea. Though credited with a chain of conquests in the hills, his overall experience as a soldier was too narrow to permit an undertaking of this magnitude. Furthermore, despite the outstanding fighting ability of the khalsa, it is unlikely, if not impossible, that this chronically insubordinate and insatiably avaricious body could have carried out the task of uniting a country which had suffered from deep political divisions since the beginning of the eighteenth century.

Another course open to the Raja lay in secluding himself at Jammu and letting the two antagonists settle their differences on the battlefield. But there were also hazards in treading this path. His territories could be negotiated away in case of a sudden Anglo-Sikh settlement, or his indifference could invite the vengeance of the unpredictable khalsa which, if it survived the war, might decide to destroy him once and for all.

There was a third alternative. The Raja could have become instrumental in stirring up revolts in various parts of the kingdom and thus added to Lahore's problems. In return, however, he wanted an Anglo-Dogra alliance, but the lack of response from the British discouraged him from making such a bold move.

Finally, Gulab Singh, on assuming the wazarat, could have reinforced the khalsa and assisted it in denying to the British a decisive victory at Sobraon. If the fighting had been prolonged indefinitely, the British, who were beginning to experience financial and physical fatigue, might have been inclined to negotiate a peace settlement more honorable to the Sikhs.

Undoubtedly the Machiavellian Jammu Raja gave serious consideration to such alternatives before pursuing the calculated course that he did. He concluded that his interests would best be served by producing a decisive Sikh defeat in collusion with the British. When such an opportunity presented itself in the later stages of the war, the Raja turned it to his advantage.

Gulab Singh's conduct during the war and ensuing negotiations is decidedly not above reproach. He can be indicted for making overtures from Jammu to a foreign power at war with the Sikhs. There is also no doubt that the Raja's transactions during his brief though fateful tenure of the wazarat were full of deception and treachery. To attain his own ends he confounded, frustrated, and duped Lahore, and secretly reached an understanding with the British detrimental to the very government he headed. He again betrayed the Sikhs at the Kasur parleys. He negotiated the surrender of the territory between the Sutlej and the Beas and was chiefly responsible for the extinction of Sikh rule in the vast mountain region between the Beas and the Indus. If the Sikh state escaped complete obliteration it was not due to the exertions of Gulab Singh but, as the evidence indicates, because the British had neither the will nor the means to accomplish that end in 1846.

However, in spite of all the incriminating testimony, the Jammu chief cannot be held entirely responsible for the Sikh defeats. He was not involved in the first three battles and can only partially be blamed for the carnage at Sobraon. The larger responsibility for the overall debacle must rest with Lal Singh and Tej Singh, who deliberately deserted the battlefield and betrayed their own troops by surreptitiously contacting British officials. If Gulab Singh is to be called a traitor, a similar charge must be leveled at these two leaders. Such an accusation can also be made against Rani Jindan, who in all probability knew and approved of Lal Singh's inculpatory link with the enemy and might have made overtures of her own. The dangerously naïve darbar is equally guilty for conspiring to send the khalsa to its destruction while overlooking the fact that such a result would inevitably endanger the very survival of the Sikh state. Gulab Singh was merely one among many villians, though he alone had the clairvoyance to set a viable goal and the peculiar genius to attain it.

8 The Birth of the Dogra State

If I am to have only Kohistan, then I shall have nothing
but stones & trees.—Gulab Singh to Henry Lawrence

I am grieved that such complaints . . . should have been
uttered; for it seems to me, & to all India, & will doubtless
appear to all in England that your Highness had cause
only for thankfulness, in that you had received much
in return for very little.—Henry Lawrence to Gulab Singh

Oh! Goolab Sing,
We made you king,
All our of moderation!
But says Cashmere,
You shan't come here,
And all is botheration!—Charles Napier

*t*HE Treaty of Amritsar did not automatically extend Gulab Singh's jurisdiction to all the land it had apportioned for the creation of the Dogra kingdom. Many of these territories lay directly under Lahore's control and an expeditious Sikh withdrawal was necessary before the state could really emerge. Nor did the treaty specify the steps to be adopted if its implementation was obstructed by the Sikhs or the local chiefs. The British obviously did not feel duty-bound to extend armed assistance in the event such a problem arose. They were, however, prepared to lend diplomatic support and were anxious that Gulab Singh should promptly proceed to occupy his new territories. But to their chagrin the new Maharaja at first exhibited little interest in the task and, when at last he did move into Kohistan, which included such princely states as Jasrota, Jubal, Basohli, Ramnagar, Poonch, and Rajauri, he bitterly complained of Sikh attempts to block his progress. He protested that all the important forts in Kohistan had been handed over by the Sikhs to anti-Dogra rebels.[1] Disturbed by this complaint, the British authorities asked Lahore to arrange the immediate transfer of the forts to Gulab Singh.[2] But when shortly afterward the Dogras occupied Jasrota almost effortlessly, Henry Lawrence, now the British Resident at Lahore, questioned the validity of Gulab Singh's accusations and suspected that the situation in Kohistan might have been exaggerated to further alienate the British from the Sikhs. As the Dogra chief continued to postpone his entry into the other Kohistani states despite reports of disturbances in Poonch and Jubal,[3] Henry Lawrence tried flattery in an effort to pressure Gulab Singh into action. In a letter the Resident wrote to him "that the Maharaja being now a great sovereign should cheerfully forget small matters and employ all his energies in acquiring possession of his extensive territory, & in them, by forbearance, consideration & mercy [establish] his reputation & [perpetuate] his name."[4] Gulab Singh was finally persuaded to act, but before embarking upon his mission he warned ominously "that in a short time no man will be able to breathe in his presence."[5] That he had not delivered an empty threat soon became evident when the Dogras terrorized the residents of Rajauri by burning their houses. Such oppressive measures were employed against other parts of Kohistan that its deposed Rajas petitioned Henry Lawrence to intervene. In exasperation the Resident warned the Maharaja not to ignore "the rights & claims of its chiefs and inhabitants"[6] and urged him to pacify Kohistan. The reign of terror subsided and, under a British guarantee, Gulab Singh agreed to give to the Rajas an annual remuneration of 62,200 rupees. The former rulers were allowed to remain in his kingdom and at first they elected to do so, but eventually most retired to British India.[7]

While the Kohistan controversy was raging, Gulab Singh also strove to lay his hands on some additional Sikh territory not allocated to him by the Amritsar treaty. In several communications to Lawrence he asserted his right to a strip of land known as the Daman Koh (skirt of the hills), arguing that segments of it were actually a part of Kohistan. Aware of the British interest in Himalayan commerce, he contrived to gain their consent by making the tantalizing offer to build a road from Kashmir to Jullundur "with a view of drawing the trade of the Hills direct into the British Territory."[8] But he hastened to point out that, since such a road must pass through the Daman Koh, it was essential that this territory be under his control. To further strengthen his case, the Maharaja even attempted to invoke pity by complaining: "If I am to have only Kohistan, then I shall have nothing but stones & trees."[9] Lawrence, however, was unimpressed and, accusing Gulab Singh of misinterpreting the treaty, rejected his claim. He took particular exception to the implied criticism of the potential of Kohistan and lashed out at Gulab Singh with uncharacteristic fury:

> I am grieved that such complaints . . . should have been uttered; for it seemed to me, & to all India, & will doubtless appear to all in England that your Highness had cause only for thankfulness, in that you had received much in return for very little. And I in belief of your wisdom & forethought was a party to the above arrangement. It is therefore strange that I should have trouble & care from your acts, or you should think that in your affairs I would deviate a hair's breadth from the terms of the Treaty.[10]

In a similar vein the Resident refused to sympathize with the Maharaja's lamentation that he would need an army to occupy all of his territories, retorting: "You surely did not think that without an Army & without expense, the settlement of so large a tract of country could be effected."[11]

Just as he had delayed moving into Kohistan, the Jammu chief seemed in no hurry to establish control over Kashmir. When the Amritsar treaty was signed, the Sikh province was still being governed by his reputed protégé, Sheikh Mohi-ud-Din. Gulab Singh had confidently announced that he and the governor "were on an understanding with each other, and that his possession of Cashmere would be accomplished without difficulty."[12] The Maharaja remained unruffled at Mohi-ud-Din's death in early April and upon the succession of his son, Sheikh Imam-ud-Din, declared that the new governor "was, equally with his father, in his (Golab Singh's) interest."[13] Thus anticipating no opposition, the Dogra ruler, during the third week of April, sent Lakhpat Rai at the head of a few regiments to take control of Kashmir. On his arrival in Srinagar, Lakhpat Rai established his headquarters at the historic Hari Parbat fort and quickly contacted Imam-ud-Din to arrange for the transfer of Kashmir. Simultaneously, the Dogra agent conveyed to Imam the Maharaja's offer to maintain him as governor" with a salary of one lakh of rupees."[14] But the Sheikh, to the surprise and shock of Lakhpat Rai, refused to turn over Kashmir to the Dogras.

Several theories were advanced as to the reasons and motives behind the controversial[15] governor's defiant attitude. It was argued that Imam was acting at the behest of the Lahore government, which was reluctant to surrender Kashmir. It was also rumored that the two Sheikhs had succeeded in smuggling out only part of a vast fortune they had amassed during their rule, and Imam was upset because recent events had prevented them from making off with the rest.[16] There was speculation, too, that Imam had deliberately turned away from the Dogras because he believed that the British "would be very glad to have Cashmeer and would throw Golaub Singh over to gain their object."[17] Later, it was even conjectured that the governor was marking time "to play entirely for his own hand and strike for the sovereignty of Kashmir."[18]

Whatever the real motive of Imam, his refusal to cooperate constrained Gulab Singh to dispatch additional troops under Wazir Ratnu to reinforce Lakhpat Rai's contingent in Kashmir. The Dogras now ordered Imam to leave the valley, but the Sheikh, professing preoccupation with financial matters, "delayed from week to week his departure from Cashmere."[19] The mounting hostility on both sides ultimately led to an armed clash in which several Dogras, including Lakhpat Rai, were killed. The surviving Dogras took shelter in Hari Parbat, but Imam swiftly surrounded the fort and besieged it for forty days.[20] When the news of the bloody setback reached Jammu, the Maharaja decided to proceed to Kashmir personally, and on August 12 he arrived in his future capital at the head of yet another Dogra force. Two British officials, Captain Broome and Lieutenant John Nicholson, who since early April had been assigned to train the Jammu army, also accompanied him.[21] But even Gulab

Singh was ignored by Imam who, upon hearing of his approach, retired into the countryside. While an uneasy peace prevailed, the Maharaja attempted to make a show of strength by parading his troops through the streets of Srinagar. During one such march a sniper attempted to assassinate Gulab Singh but "missed him by inches."[22] Though claiming credit for rescuing the Maharaja, Broome and Nicholson were so unnerved by the incident that they beat a hasty retreat out of Kashmir, leaving Gulab Singh behind.[23] Taking advantage of the confusion that ensued, the Sheikh's force attacked the Dogra troops[24] and killed about one hundred of them.[25] As a result Gulab Singh, too, pusillanimously fled to Jammu, though some of his men, including Ratnu, remained entrenched at Hari Parbat.[26]

Bouyant over his triumph, the Sheikh persuaded the neighboring princes of Rajauri and Rampur to join the standard of rebellion. He also urged Ladakh to throw off the Dogra yoke and encouraged the Khyber and Hazara tribes to march on the Indus.[27] Though the Ladakhis and the tribesmen of the northwest made no discernible move, numerous hill chiefs in Kashmir's immediate neighborhood rose and made common cause with Imam. Herbert Edwardes, then serving as one of Henry Lawrence's assistants, observed: "The people, who looked forward with horror to the rule of Golab Singh, declared like one man in [Imam's] favour, and the refugee scions of old depressed and ruined royal families in the surrounding hills flocked round him with their scanty band of faithful ruffians, and determined to win back, under his banner, some of their ancient lands."[28]

Henry Hardinge, who had been keeping an eye on Kashmir, expressed grave concern over the new developments.[29] Although blaming Gulab Singh for his initial delay in occupying Kashmir,[30] Hardinge now advised him "to exert himself, and . . . to advance at once with his disposable force to Cashmere."[31] The Governor-General alerted Brigadier Wheeler at Jullundur to move his force, if necessary, toward Jammu to guard Gulab Singh's "rear, and, should he wish it, to hold his territory for him during his absence."[32] Hardinge also rebuked Lahore for the actions of its governor and coerced the reluctant Sikh government into sending a force to assist the Dogras in Kashmir.[33] But he emphatically rejected the suggestion that British forces should fight on behalf of Gulab Singh and declared early in October: "I am by no means satisfied that there is an obligation on our part to put down the rebellion by British bayonets."[34] Later that month he was still adamant on this point. "I do not intend," he asserted, "to let a Br. soldier into Cashmeer—the Native Lahore &

Jummoo soldiery must effect this object."[35] It turned out, however, that Gulab Singh himself was anxious not to have British troops set foot on his soil, fearing, perhaps, that they might remain indefinitely. He sent to Simla his agent, Jawala Sahai, who unequivocally informed the British government that his master "not only did not expect or desire that a British force should be actually employed against Cashmere, but, on the contrary, preferred that his own troops, aided by the Sikh forces, should be employed for the purpose."[36]

Though no British troops, therefore, were sent against the Sheikh, Hardinge nonetheless ordered Henry Lawrence to personally lead some of the Sikh regiments into Kashmir and appointed John Lawrence to act as Resident at Lahore during his brother's absence.[37] The Governor-General also asked Lieutenant William Hodson, an assistant agent in Panjab, to accompany Henry Lawrence. Other Sikh columns were led by General Tej Singh and the influential Attariwala chief, Chattar Singh, and his son, Sher Singh. In addition, Herbert Edwardes was dispatched to Jammu to raise the morale of Gulab Singh's troops and to accompany them on the expedition. The Dogra soldiers rendezvoused with the Sikhs, and the combined force, numbering almost thirty thousand men,[38] marched into Kashmir during October. As news of their advance spread, Mirza Fakirullah, the Rajauri chief, broke with Imam and announced his allegiance to the new Maharaja. The other hill chiefs soon followed suit. As his ranks dwindled and pressure from the advancing army increased, the Sheikh decided to surrender without a showdown. He handed over Srinagar to the beleaguered Wazir Ratnu[39] and on November 1 presented himself before Lawrence. Thus the expedition accomplished its mission without any bloodshed and cleared the way for Gulab Singh's peaceful entry into the capital on November 9. According to Henry Lawrence, the Maharaja's arrival was "by no means displeasing to the inhabitants of the province, who were loud in their complaints of the tyranny and oppression of Sheikh Imamooddeen."[40]

While Gulab Singh busied himself with consolidating his position in Kashmir, the Sheikh claimed that he had challenged the Dogras only at Raja Lal Singh's urging. The alleged involvement of the Lahore wazir forced Hardinge to appoint a five-man court to investigate the matter. At the inquiry, which opened in December, Imam charged that he had received from Lal Singh both oral and written messages exhorting him not to surrender Kashmir. To substantiate his contention the Sheikh submitted several letters which had purportedly been signed by the wazir. One of the letters read:

My friend, you are not ignorant of the ingratitude and want of faith which Rajah Golab Sing has exhibited towards the Lahore Sirkar. It is indeed sufficiently glaring. I now write, therefore, to request, my friend, that you will not set before your eyes the example of your late father's intercourse with the aforesaid Rajah, but consider both your duty and your interest to lie this way, and inflict such injury and chastisement upon the said Rajah, that he shall have reason to remember it. It is to be hoped that if the Rajah makes but one false step, he will never be able to re-establish himself again. For your security and confidence, my friend, I have sent you a separate written guarantee, that you may have no misgivings as to the consequences. Let me hear often of your welfare.

P.S. Tear up this paper when you have read it.[41]

"The Raja," according to John Lawrence who sat on the court, "[was] in a devil of a funk,"[42] but he vehemently denied that he had sent those communications.[43] Dewan Dina Nath defended Lal Singh and countered that the Sikh government, desiring the orderly transfer of Kashmir, had instructed the Sheikh several times during April and May to extend full cooperation to the Dogra officials. He argued that the whole Kashmir affair was the result "of the machinations of Maharajah Golab Sing, whose creature the Sheik was, and had always been, and that this infamous plot was contrived by the Maharajah for the destruction of the Durbar."[44] The protestations of Lal Singh and Dina Nath were, however, of no avail. The court held the wazir solely responsible for the recent episode and exonerated Imam who, by willfully defying the Treaty of Amritsar, should have shared at least part of the blame.[45] But whatever the merits of this verdict, it did obligate the Sikh government to dismiss Lal Singh and expel him from Lahore.[46]

After the occupation of Kashmir was completed, the Dogras turned to pacifying the Kakka Bamba chiefs of the adjoining territories, who were said to be some of "the most formidable opponents of Maharaja Gulab Singh."[47] They included, among others, the Rajas of Buniar, Chattar, Kot, and Madopuria, and the Sultans of Muzaffarabad, Uri, Kathai, and Dopatta. Gulab Singh reconciled these adversaries by acknowledging their claims to the jagirs granted to them by the Sikhs and they, in turn, recognized his sovereignty.[48]

But other problems of territorial adjustment emanating from the Lahore and Amritsar treaties remained to be solved. One of these involved a dispute over Chamba whose Raja, during 1846, protested to the British the proposed transfer of his state to Kashmir. Under Henry Lawrence's arbitration Gulab Singh received the territories of Lakhanpur and Chandgraon, and his claim to disputed Bhadarwah, which he already occupied, was recognized. However, the state of Chamba on both sides of the Ravi remained independent of Kashmir.[49]

Another altercation resulted when, during August of 1847, Gulab Singh's nephews laid claim to some of the territories of the new state. Jawahar and Moti Singh, the two surviving sons of Raja Dhian Singh, filed a suit with Frederick Currie, then acting as Resident at Lahore during Henry Lawrence's absence in England, demanding Poonch and Jubal, which had been given in jagir to their father by Ranjit Singh. They also demanded the jagirs of their brother, Raja Hira Singh, in Jasrota and half the fortune of their uncle, Raja Suchet Singh. After considerable deliberation, Currie, in May of 1848, rejected their claims to the properties of their late brother and uncle. He did recognize their right to Poonch and Jubal, but these territories were to be considered a part of the Kashmir kingdom. Moreover, the two brothers were forbidden to dispose of any part of their jagirs without Gulab Singh's consent.[50] In 1852, Jawahar Singh and Moti Singh quarreled, and the Maharaja befriended Moti Singh by awarding him several new jagirs.[51] Deep hostility between Gulab Singh and his other nephew continued unabated, and during 1854 the Maharaja accused Jawahar Singh of instigating a rebellion.[52] In April 1855 the Dogra ruler sent a force into Poonch and besieged a number of his nephew's forts, but the British authorities forced the Maharaja to withdraw his troops.[53] This intrafamily squabble ended only after Gulab Singh's death. During 1859, Jawahar Singh renounced his rights in Poonch and moved to Ambala on a British pension.[54] Poonch was then declared the jagir solely of Moti Singh, and his descendants continued to enjoy a privileged position in the Dogra kingdom.[55]

Trouble was brewing as well in Hazara, which also passed under Dogra occupation in 1846. Gulab Singh seemed to anticipate no opposition to his rule there, and even Henry Lawrence predicted that the Dogra takeover would "be hailed as a welcome deliverance from the government of the Sikhs."[56] Such optimism, however, was not justified. Several Muslim chiefs, whose jagirs had been seized by the Dogras, organized a widespread insurrection during January 1847. When Gulab Singh decided to advance personally upon Hazara, the Resident interposed, asking that instead he dispatch Jawala Sahai, now the Prime Minister of Kashmir, to restore order.[57] Nettled by the treatment accorded the Hazara chiefs, Henry Lawrence insisted that the Maharaja honor all Sikh-conferred jagirs[58] and warned that the British "had not accepted to support him for the oppression of his subjects."[59] Ignoring these admonitions, Gulab Singh complained for weeks in his darbar that he had been driven to the brink of bankruptcy by being forced to barter away rich lands for such barren territories as Hazara and Kohistan. Indignant at such criticism, Henry Lawrence issued a stern warning: "Any irresponsible talk, even one tenth of what has been reported, is undesirable."[60] Continual British pressure and the fierce resistance of the Hazara rebels, who reportedly kept "full 10,000 men [of Gulab Singh] at bay,"[61] led the Maharaja to conclude that the new territory was a dubitable asset. He therefore sought British assistance in exchanging Hazara for some Sikh territory adjoining Jammu. Although the ensuing negotiations were marred by anti-Dogra hostility at Lahore,[62] Gulab Singh's proposition was ultimately accepted, and an agreement was signed in May 1847. Hazara reverted to the Sikhs, "and the Jhelum became the Western boundary of the State of Kashmir, roughly speaking, between the towns of Jhelum and Muzaffarabad."[63] Captain James Abbott, another assistant agent, was appointed to fix the boundary. The task was completed by December.[64]

During 1846 and 1847 the British authorities also attempted to define and demarcate the other boundaries of Gulab Singh's territories. One of its commissions completed its assignment by May of 1847, fixing the border between Ladakh and the British-occupied territories of Lahoul and Spiti to the south.[65] Two other commissions, however, failed to set the boundary between Ladakh and Tibet. The first could not reach the frontiers because of Imam-ud-Din's rebellion. The second was ignored by the Tibetans and the Chinese. However, Vans Agnew, a member of one of the commissions, optimistically observed that "the line was . . . already sufficiently defined by nature, and recognized by custom, with the exception of its two extremities."[66] But those on the other side apparently did not accept the boundary as such, and the long-simmering dispute finally culminated in the Chinese invasion of Ladakh in 1962. Kashmir's eastern limits thus have remained undemarcated to this day.

The new state's frontier to the north and northwest also remained undefined. Such a task was made impossible not only by the almost impenetrable mountainous terrain of this area, but also by the fiercely independent spirit of its inhabitants. At the turn of the nineteenth century the region had been composed of several petty states, including Gilgit, Hunza, Nagar, Punial, Yasin, Ghizr, and Ashkuman, which were all ruled by Muslim chiefs. By 1842, however, the Sikhs had imposed their authority on this region and Nathu Shah, an official appointed by Lahore, ruled as governor. When Gulab Singh became the Maharaja, Nathu Shah transferred his loyalty to him, and the area officially passed under Dogra hegemony. But the people of that region, who had only reluctantly accepted Sikh domination, remained unreconciled to their new rulers. As early as 1847 an anti-Dogra uprising occurred during which Nathu Shah was murdered.[67] The rebels were subdued, but additional insurrections in the 1850s marked the end of Gulab Singh's control,[68] and Dogra rule was revived only nominally under his successors.[69]

While some English officials considered it imperative to render some sort of assistance during the rather laborious birth of the Dogra kingdom, others did so only on orders from their superiors. And there were those who were ready to strangle the new state at its very inception. Critics found in Imam-ud-Din's revolt a pretext to resurrect the controversy over the transfer of Kashmir. The London newspapers "attributed to Gholab Sing every sort of treachery and ingratitude."[70] The new Maharaja was "doubted, denounced, and vilified in anonymous journals."[71] Bitter condemnations, though mostly in private, were also voiced by several British officials in India. Once again Charles Napier appeared as the foremost calumniator. Fire-breathing and bumbling as usual, he castigated Hardinge and his protégé, Gulab Singh, and blamed the outbreak of the Kashmir insurrection on the shortsighted and indecisive policies of the Governor-General.[72] During the height of the Kashmir crisis, he condemned both the decision not to commit British troops to crush the rebellion and the very wisdom of installing Gulab Singh as the Maharaja:

If the first we admit folly in supporting a man we have not force to put in possession of what he has paid us for. We shall then be in a false position, cramming down the throats of the Cashmerian people a hated and hateful villain, of whom Hardinge said to me, "He is the most thorough ruffian that ever was created; he is a villain from a kingdom down to a halfpenny." Yet he makes him a king! and this is called "moderation!"[73]

The irrepressible Napier was so thrilled by the embarrassment caused by Imam that he gleefully penned a poem giving vent to his emotions:

> Oh! Goolab Sing,
> We made you king,
> All our of moderation!
> But says Cashmere,
> You shan't come here,
> And all is botheration!
>
> Oh! Lord Hardinge,
> You made me king,
> For a con-sid-eration!
> Now give me back
> Some hundred lac
> Paid for your moderation.

Quoth Hardinge No!
I can't do so,
For I have got no money
But the chamber door
Of the sweet La whore,
I'll watch for you my honey!

Lall Sing and Punk,
May both get drunk
While you may take Cashmere.
Repay your cash!
'T would be too rash,
I cannot be cashier.[74]

Finally, he advocated the ouster of Gulab Singh as a solution to the
British predicament. Envisioning himself as Kashmir's liberator, he
predicted rich returns from such a venture:

... it is almost certain that I could take steamers into the heart of Cashmere, and form magazines at Mazafurabad. We could then, early in the
spring, run into Baramula when the job would be done. And when Cashmere was ours, a dozen good officers spread through the valleys, doing
justice vigorously and protecting the ryots and manufacturers, would in
three months make the grand valley of Cashmere devoted to us; and in
a year or two, a happy people would pay 50 lacs a year in money and
kind.[75]

The Maharaja was also denounced by several officials involved in
the operations against Imam. Among them, Herbert Edwardes was
one of the most vociferous. A man marked by his pathological disdain for all Indians,[76] he called Gulab Singh "the worst native I have
ever come in contact with, a bad King, a miser, and a liar."[77] Edwardes termed the decision to sell Kashmir a "strange mixture of
political wisdom and imperial generosity,"[78] and during the insurrection he envisioned himself as the man who could turn Kashmir
into near Utopia: "Oh, what field is that valley at this moment for
that noble animal, *a just ruler!* In five years I would undertake to
raise its revenue to a million, and its people from *Irish poverty* to
what Providence designed them to enjoy—scriptural milk and
honey."[79] Hodson described Gulab Singh as "the cleverest hypocrite
in the world,"[80] and revealed his sympathy for Imam by confessing
"that if *he* was in the same position he would not give in while he
still had a man to pull the trigger."[81] Nicholson, too, who had so
ungallantly sped the scene of the Srinagar insurrection in August,
seems to have had little admiration for the Maharaja. He left Kashmir, as it was later claimed, because he had "no wish to be sacrificed
for loyalty to a flayer."[82]

It was also during this period that *A History of the Reigning Family of Lahore* appeared at Calcutta. The book attempted an extensive exposé of the Jammu family's intrigues and manipulations during the rule of the Sikhs, but many of its charges must be considered grossly exaggerated.[83] Its virulently anti-Dogra editor, G. Carmichael Smyth, declared in the introduction: "I have now been twenty-six years in India, and during the whole of my sojourn in the East, I have never heard of so infamous a miscreant as the Rajah of Jummoo."[84] He also felt that, as far as the Kashmiris were concerned, the supplanting of Sikh rule by that of the Dogras was merely a transfer "from Scylla into Charybdis."[85]

But fortunately for the Dogra leader, most of his critics and enemies carried little influence with the two men—Henry Hardinge and Henry Lawrence—who at this time actually formulated British policies affecting northwestern India. During the remainder of his term in office, Hardinge entertained no thought of ejecting Gulab Singh. And Lawrence, despite occasional wranglings with the Maharaja, emerged as his strongest proponent. Though conceding that he was a "bad man," he talked of his "courage, energy, and personal purity."[86] Apparently unaware of the depth of his own assistants' resentment toward Gulab Singh, he wrote: "The general tenor of the reports of the score of English travellers who have visited him during the years 1846 and 1847 is, that though grasping and mercenary, he is mild, conciliatory, and even merciful."[87]

Thus the new state of Kashmir, which had been sanctioned on paper during March of 1846, did not fully take shape until the end of the year. The intervening months revealed, among other things, the military weakness of the Dogras and the repugnance with which several British officials continued to view Gulab Singh. But for the firm commitment of Henry Hardinge and Henry Lawrence to the new Maharaja, the Dogra kingdom could indeed have been dealt a death blow in its very infancy. It was Lawrence's faith in Gulab Singh especially which was to serve the Dogra ruler well in the coming years, and it marked the beginning of a close, though at times vexatious, friendship between the two men.

9 The Death of the Sikh State

Goolab Sing . . . is cleverest man ever India produced.
—Charles Napier

Maharaja Golab Sing ought not to be trusted, and will
not be trusted by me for one minute.—Dalhousie to the
Duke of Wellington

Had Golab Sing shown as much valor and resolution as
you have, the Sikhs would now be in possession of the
Sovereignty of Lahore.—Dost Muhammad to Mul Raj

. . . it may well be said of this your humble friend that
you have performed the miracle of Christ in raising me
from the dead.—Gulab Singh to Dalhousie

tHE establishment of Gulab Singh's suzerainty over his new state did not erase his controversial image. Some Company officials expressed grave doubts over his ability to rule (see Chapter 11) and, ironically enough, the specter of a new anti-British movement among the Sikhs led others to cast a shadow of doubt on the extent of the Dogra ruler's loyalty to his benefactors. Despite the bitter parting between Lahore and Jammu, a trace of suspicion remained that a Sikh-Dogra coalition might emerge to the detriment of British interests. Pointing to the continued presence of Gulab Singh's partisans at the Sikh capital, some of the Company's directors warned that his character did not "in any way tend to diminish the danger to be apprehended on his account."[1] When in 1847 a certain Preyma was charged with conspiring to murder Sikh leaders and assault British troops stationed at Lahore, it was feared that he might have been associated not only with Rani Jindan but also with Gulab Singh and his followers. A careful British investigation, however, failed to discover any clandestine Dogra link with either Preyma or Jindan,[2] which led John Lawrence to remark: "It is almost impossible to believe that Maharajah Golab Sing was concerned in any intention to make a disturbance."[3] But the alleged conspiracy resulted in life imprisonment for Preyma and exile for Jindan to Sheikhupura. In sheer desperation, the Rani even sought Gulab Singh's support but, to the relief of the British, her plea was firmly rejected.[4]

Nevertheless, the eruption of an anti-British revolt in Panjab during April 1848 revived the mistrust of the Dogra ruler. The uprising, led by Dewan Mul Raj, the Sikh governor of Multan, set the stage for the Second Anglo-Sikh War. As the situation deteriorated, it was discovered that at the end of 1847 the embittered Rani Jindan had formulated schemes to oust the British from Panjab. Currie, who was still acting as Resident, charged that a full-fledged plot had existed against the British. The Rani reputedly had sought not only the assistance of all prominent Panjab chiefs but also that of Amir Dost Muhammad of Afghanistan whom she attempted to win over by offering to him Peshawar, a province he had lost to Ranjit Singh in 1834. Gulab Singh was also approached again. Though the acting Resident did not specify the nature of the pledge made to Kashmir, he wrote that the Dogra chief unquestionably had been "in secret communication with the Maharanee, in December or January last."[5] Currie's claim of a general conspiracy was, however, dismissed by Lord Dalhousie, the new Governor-General, yet he tended to suspect the Dogra leader's involvement. "The Maharaja Gholab Sing is deep in this," he wrote, "tho' he will carefully stop short of committing himself, I have no doubt."[6]

Some of Gulab Singh's alleged messages to the Rani were subsequently procured by Currie. In one of the communications the Dogra ruler supposedly wrote: "Don't be afraid; they [the British] will not remain many days longer. I have arranged my plans. The Dooranee [Afghan] people have joined me, and I have sent a force from Cashmere to Jummoo. From the latter place they will be sent on."[7] This evidence is, however, not sufficient to incriminate Gulab Singh. Not only the sweeping promises of help contained in the letter, but also its uncharacteristically straightforward tone tend to create the impression that it was probably forged. The validity of such a premise is enhanced by a second letter in which the Maharaja declared that the "order of the English is not to be opposed by me."[8] This flatly contradicts the role Gulab Singh had seemingly assigned to himself in the first letter. The forgery might have been the work of conspirators who wanted either to convince the Sikh leaders that Gulab Singh was on their side or to discredit the Dogra leader in the eyes of the British.

The Dogra chief undoubtedly worried about the possible ramifications of Mul Raj's rebellion. His primary concern was obviously the security of his kingdom. Anticipating a new round of Anglo-Sikh fighting, he took precautionary measures by enlarging his army and reinforcing his frontier posts.[9] He also apparently decided that his interests would best be served by adopting a cautious pro-British posture while at the same time avoiding direct involvement in the Multan affair. But his plans were somewhat shaken when certain Sikh soldiers, whom he had employed at the end of the First Anglo-Sikh War, announced in May their intention of marching to Multan and joining the rebels. Currie took a serious view of this development and issued a trenchant warning to the Kashmir government: "Out of consideration for the Maharaja's subjects any one of them proceeding to Multan [is] liable to be revenged with the sword along with Dewan Mul Raj."[10] The British authorities were further irritated when during the same month Gulab Singh, probably as part of his consolidation moves, instructed four thousand of his troops to proceed to Muzaffarabad, a town directly opposite the Sikh province of Peshawar. At Currie's insistence, the Maharaja rescinded these orders,[11] and during June chastised several Sikh soldiers who were desirous of going to Multan.[12] Moreover, when news of the initial British successes began to reach Kashmir, Gulab Singh felt confident enough to indulge in a scurrilous condemnation of Mul Raj in his court. Calling the Multan governor a "bastard," he predicted "that ultimately Mul Raj would be seized by his own troops and receive the punishment due to him from the British officers."[13] On learning of the British triumph of July 1, which took them to the very walls of Multan, the Maharaja ordered official celebrations to be held in his capital. One hundred guns were fired from Sher Garhi, his fortified palace, and another forty from the Hari Parbat fort to mark the occasion.[14]

While the British success at Multan was followed by a deadlock, another political storm broke in Hazara. Since the early months of 1848 its governor, Chattar Singh Attariwala, had been suspected of nurturing unfriendly designs against the British by James Abbott, who was then serving as the assistant agent in that Sikh province.[15] The governor had been much incensed at British attempts to block the wedding of his daughter to Maharaja Dalip Singh, and feared that they planned to remove the young ruler from his throne.[16] An abortive anti-Attariwala insurrection among the Hazara tribesmen, which seems to have been encouraged by Abbott, further enraged him. The end result was mutual distrust and hostility which early in August led to an irreparable breach between Chattar Singh and the British. While the Sikh government at Lahore remained silent over the dispute, the Attariwala leader, in his desire for an all-out effort against the British, turned to his old comrade,[17] Gulab Singh, for armed assistance. Appeals were also made to the Amir of Afghanistan and his brother, Sultan Muhammad Barakzai, who resided at Peshawar. Aware of Dost Muhammad's obsession with Peshawar, Chattar Singh, like Jindan, attempted to win him over by promising that, in the event of a Sikh victory, the province would be returned to him.[18]

As signs of disaffection began to appear among the ranks of the Sikh soldiers in the northwest, Abbott concluded that it was the result of a plot to which Gulab Singh was a party. In August he claimed that he had intercepted letters from Chattar Singh to the Maharaja of Kashmir which pleaded for aid and urged him to write to the Sikh troops at Peshawar to join the rebellion.[19] In the following month Abbott charged that Gulab Singh had not only "promptly complied with" the Attariwala leader's request by dispatching a few regiments, but had also granted him financial assistance "to keep together his army."[20] However, George Lawrence, another brother of Henry who was at that time the assistant agent at Peshawar, stated that the Dogra leader had refused to respond to the Attariwala overture.[21] But he also reported that he had intercepted a letter dated August 30 from Chattar Singh to Sultan Muhammad boasting of Dogra support and claiming, "Troops and guns have been already sent from Jummoo."[22] As Chattar Singh's partisans "paraded the name of Maharaja Goolab Sing in all their inflammatory proclamations,"[23] a host of rumors involving the Dogra chief spread like wildfire. It was said in Kashmir that the Maharaja was not only in correspondence with Chattar Singh but, as a special gesture, had had pashmina dresses made for him.[24] There was even speculation that he had exchanged gifts with Dost Muhammad.[25] It was also claimed that "one whole Regiment of Infantry, with the exception of the officers, and 250 men of another Regiment, hitherto in the service of the Maharaja,"[26] had joined the rebels. Gossip had it that some of these troops might proceed to Multan[27] and others, under the Attariwala chief's son, Attar Singh, might march to Rawalpindi.[28] There was talk that Gulab Singh had "collected 70,000 or 80,000 men,"[29] and it was believed he was recruiting more.[30] Word also spread that some of the Maharaja's troops had appeared "in a village on the Ravee opposite Bussowlee."[31] Lastly, reports were circulated that some of the Sikh rebels from Multan had received shelter in the Dogra kingdom.[32]

Such imputations against Gulab Singh brought a swift response from British officials. Describing the Dogra chief as "a hart of many tynes,"[33] Dalhousie declared that "there is more than suspicion that Maharajah Goolab Sing is implicated."[34] Though Currie's initial reaction was to discount this latest round of accusations against the Maharaja "as a thing one can hardly believe possible,"[35] the Attariwala leader's intercepted message to Sultan Muhammad made him revert to his former suspicions. "This letter," he told Commander-in-Chief Sir Hugh Gough, "seems to leave scarcely a doubt of complicity of Rajah Goolab Sing."[36] Gough, however, was not fully convinced that the Kashmir ruler would risk open involvement at this juncture, but feared that if he "is in earnest we shall have to look sharp everywhere."[37] The crotchety Charles Napier, who had returned to England earlier in the year, worked himself up into another frenzy. Asserting that he was receiving reports from Amritsar merchants ("and I know [them] to be positively true")[38] he claimed that Gulab Singh had been reappointed the wazir of Panjab.[39] Fearing serious repercussions as a result of this imaginary Dogra-Sikh axis, Napier warned: "I expect it will be a dreadful war."[40] Calling Gulab Singh the "cleverest man ever India produced,"[41] the General lamented that Currie was not the man to cope with him. Others revived the possibility of removing the Dogra sovereign from his throne. General Sir John Littler suggested that, if charges against the Maharaja were true, his state should be annexed.[42] Major Robert Napier, the future Lord of Magdala, condemned him summarily with the words: "I believe Goolab Sing must be guilty."[43]

Another official to join the chorus of critics was Herbert Edwardes, then involved in operations against Mul Raj. His first instinct was to reject Abbott's charges, responding that "a man should be very sure of his facts before he asks one to believe (in preference to any other theory) that our greatest [enemy is the] one man to whom we have given a kingdom."[44] He had also been impressed by the declaration of Sher Singh Attariwala, another son of Chattar Singh who had been sent by the Lahore government to assist the British at Multan, that "his father might raise the whole country if he liked, but he and Golab Sing would be the first to pitch into him."[45] But the continuous doubts of other British officials and the views of some Panjab leaders who met with him during the Multan campaign altered his views. For instance, he was warned by the bitterly anti-Dogra Shamsher Singh Sandhawalia that if Chattar Singh rebelled "he [would] be supported through thick and thin by Maharajah Golab Sing."[46] However, his mind was perhaps most influenced by Sheikh Imam-ud-Din, one of Gulab Singh's chief tormentors during 1846,[47] who also was at Multan. During the course of several meetings with Edwardes, Imam succeeded in convincing him of the Dogra leader's equivocation by arguing "that Maharajah Golab Sing is not at all unlikely to instigate Chuttur Sing to ruin himself, for some secret project of his own; but will never give him an open assistance, or leave the smallest trace of having even interfered against the British."[48] Sher Singh's unexpected defection to his father in the middle of September deepened Edwardes's suspicions all the more. He bombarded Currie with letters, clamoring for action against Kashmir. Branding Gulab Singh an enemy,[49] he advised that the Kohistani chiefs and the Kakka Bambas be encouraged "to rise up against a sovereign they detest."[50] In a later communication, inspired by yet another conference with Imam, Edwardes declared that Kashmir's Pir Panjal chiefs were prepared to oppose Gulab Singh and "that the Sheikh himself desires nothing more than to have the conduct of a campaign against his ancient enemy."[51]

Edwardes's suggested course of action was, however, rejected by Currie, who had again changed his mind about Gulab Singh. He questioned the credibility of the Attariwala announcements of Dogra support, characterizing their claims as "rather what they desire, than what they believe, to be the fact."[52] Nevertheless, Currie was so disturbed by the criticism of Edwardes and others that he now decided to write to the Maharaja and set "before him in plain terms, all that is said about him."[53]

From Srinagar Gulab Singh himself was closely scrutinizing the Panjab scene in the wake of the Hazara outbreak.[54] The Attariwala agents had indeed brought the Maharaja messages from their master, but he had refused to respond, at least in writing. Although he was tempted to continue "a policy of masterly inactivity,"[55] mounting British pressure forced him to reconsider his position. He held prolonged deliberations with his officials as to the course of action he ought to adopt. Despite the incessant Attariwala pleas,[56] the Maharaja eventually concluded that there was little prospect of a Sikh victory and decided to enter the conflict on the side of the British. Fully aware of the commotion caused in British circles by the Attariwala claims and the desertion of some of his own troops, Gulab Singh, in response to Currie's letter, pledged his full support:

My whole force is ready to act in any way that may be desired by the British Govt., and any service you may require at my hands, I am ready and most anxious to perform. Do not, I beg of you, let the idea enter your mind that I am in any way friendly to the course of Chutter Sing. I esteem the enemies of the British Govt. mine own, and am ever ready to oppose them as such.[57]

Protesting his loyalty to the British while blaming "malicious tongues" for defaming him, the Maharaja termed his former friend a "rebel" and a "traitor," and offered to punish him in battle. "How then can it be believed," he asked, "that I should engage in any matter which would be displeasing to you who are my protector?"[58]

At the end of September the Dogra leader also dispatched Dewan Nihal Chand as his emissary to Currie in a further attempt to mollify British grievances. During the ensuing discussions Nihal Chand scrupulously defended his master. Dismissing as spurious the Attariwala professions of Gulab Singh's collaboration, he declared that they had been "set forth partly in the hope of injuring him with the British Govt., and out of enmity because he refused the aid they have required of him, and partly to give importance and weight and influence to their cause."[59] While conceding that two of Kashmir's regiments had joined the Attariwalas, Nihal Chand protested that they had been part of the three thousand disbanded khalsa troops the Maharaja had been obliged to employ in 1846. This had been done, he added, at the urging of Henry Lawrence who, with Hardinge's approbation, had argued that Gulab Singh needed the additional troops to control his new territories. The Dogra chief reportedly had tried unsuccessfully to warn Lawrence that these troops "would be a perpetual source of embarrassment to him while they remained, and would certainly join the first rebellion or disturbance that should occur."[60] The Dogra envoy further informed Currie that Gulab Singh had already discharged fifteen hundred of these Sikh soldiers during the territorial adjustments involving Hazara in 1847 but, on hearing of the revolt, had retained the rest because he feared that "the dismissed men would, in all probability, go to Mooltan to join Moolraj."[61] He also claimed that the Maharaja had tried in vain to entice the Sikh deserters into returning, with offers of higher salaries and other benefits, and asserted that the remaining Sikh soldiers had been disarmed and put under surveillance. When confronted with the reports of new army enlistments, Nihal Chand acknowledged their veracity, explaining that Gulab Singh wished to replace the Sikhs with three new regiments. However, he added that, because of British apprehensions, such plans had been abandoned indefinitely.[62]

Currie seemed at least partially satisfied with the explanations offered by Nihal Chand. On checking the records he found that Lawrence had indeed pressured Gulab Singh into employing the former Lahore soldiery. He was also convinced that the Maharaja had not deliberately encouraged the desertion of these troops and dismissed Abbott's contention that the Sikhs "mutinied by orders from Cashmere."[63] However, he did blame Gulab Singh for failing to prevent their departure.[64] Nonetheless, he expressed "great gratification" at the Maharaja's reiteration of loyalty. Accepting his offer to back the British, Currie asked the Dogra chief to assist Abbott in putting down the Hazara rebellion, stressing that if "[you are] ready and anxious to put down the nefarious proceedings of the 'Atarees' . . . the reports of your calumniators would be proved false and their mouths closed for ever."[65] Currie considered his outright acceptance of Gulab Singh's overture a masterful tactic which would help drive the crafty Dogra into a corner. He believed that it would provide the British with "the advantage of learning whether . . . to look upon him, in the coming operations, as friend or foe."[66] To further tie the hands of Gulab Singh, he made the Anglo-Dogra correspondence public and, with a certain sense of relief, remarked that the Maharaja's "protest and his declarations of obligations and gratitude are before the world, and if he proves false, he is altogether without excuse."[67]

But if Currie still entertained a few reservations about Gulab Singh, Dalhousie and Napier put no confidence in him at all. Dalhousie, for instance, remained dissatisfied with the Maharaja's explanations. Though agreeing that the available evidence was insufficient to incriminate him, the Governor-General informed Currie: "I do not trust Maharaja Gholab Sing or believe one word he says."[68] He also told the Secret Committee that the British authorities had "a right to demand from him something more than neutrality."[69] From England, Charles Napier continued to hurl charges of Dogra-Sikh collusion, claiming that Gulab Singh was sending twenty-five thousand of his troops to assist Chattar Singh. He ominously warned that "there is a great game playing at Lahore and Kashmere; and it is very extraordinary none of the politicals knew it, or could guess at it."[70] He even went so far as to suggest that the Dogra chief and the Multan governor were acting in concert. Alluding to the relative calm prevailing at Multan since July, Napier conjectured that Mul Raj was "following the plan of Goolab Sing, not to give the English the pleasure of a general action."[71]

The Kashmir ruler, however, responded not only by accepting Currie's demands but also by attempting to provide further proof of his friendship. During October the Maharaja submitted to the acting Resident the original copies of the communications from Chattar Singh and delivered up some Sikh insurgents who had been apprehended in his state.[72] When another Attariwala agent, Hira Nand, arrived in Kashmir, he was promptly arrested and also dispatched to Currie.[73] Above all, Gulab Singh sent five regiments, four guns, and thirty thousand Kashmiri rupees for Abbott's use in Hazara. The assistant agent accepted the monetary assistance but firmly refused to receive the Maharaja's troops, fearing that they might be lured away by the rebels with offers of better salaries.[74] Furthermore, Abbott maintained that the five Dogra regiments were no match for the fourteen or fifteen under Chattar Singh, and argued that a confrontation between the two "would oblige the Maharaja in self-defence to join the Sikhs."[75] But if the British authorities were dissatisfied with the commitment of merely five regiments, they made no formal demands at this time for a greater number of Dogra troops. Thus, though Gulab Singh seemed well-inclined to take part in the conflict, the British, because of inherent fears and suspicions, failed to fully utilize his services.

While this Anglo-Dogra impasse prevailed, Gough marched to Ramnagar[76] on the east bank of the Chenab to do battle with Sher Singh's force, which was encamped on the opposite shore. Again Gulab Singh endeavored to display openly his support of the British by sending a force of three thousand men to assist Gough. But once more the attempt was rebuffed, this time on the grounds that the

Maharaja Ranjit Singh, Raja Dhian Singh, and Raja Hira Singh. Plate 7 in
W. G. Osborne's *The Court and Camp of Runjeet Sing* (London, 1840).

Gulab Singh, with his son, inspecting his bodyguard. By an unknown Indian artist. From the *Illustrated London News*, April 4, 1846.

Raja Suchet Singh. By an unknown artist. From the *Illustrated London News*, March 7, 1846.

Gulab Singh as the Raja of Jammu. By an unknown Indian painter. Courtesy of the Kashmir Government Museum, Srinagar.

Gulab Singh and General Zorawar Singh. By an unknown Indian painter.
Courtesy of the Kashmir Government Museum, Srinagar.

Sir Henry M. Lawrence. Frontispiece in F. P. Gibbon's *The Lawrences of the Punjab* (London, 1908).

Sir Henry Hardinge. Frontispiece in Charles Hardinge's *Viscount Hardinge* (Oxford, 1891).

General Sir Charles J.
Napier. Frontispiece in
W. F. Butler's *Sir Charles
Napier* (London, 1890).

A view of Jammu in 1846. By Charles Hardinge, in his *Recollections of
India* (London, 1847).

A fort of Gulab Singh in the Jammu hills. By Charles Hardinge, in his *Recollections of India*.

Maharaja Gulab Singh in 1846. By Charles Hardinge, from his *Recollections of India*.

James Ramsay, 1st Marquis of Dalhousie. By Sir John Watson Gordon.
Courtesy of National Galleries of Scotland, Edinburgh.

Sultan Dost Muhammad. By
G. T. Vigne. Frontispiece in
his *Personal Narrative of a
visit to Ghuzni, Kabul, and
Afghanistan*, 2nd ed.
(London, 1843).

Sheikh Imam-ud-Din in 1846. By Charles Hardinge, from his
Recollections of India.

Memorial on the site of Gulab Singh's cremation, Srinagar. Photographed by the author.

Dogra troops "could not be depended on, perhaps, to act against the Sikhs."[77] However, any fears that the Kashmir ruler might side with Sher Singh were dismissed by Gough with the remark: "I am certain he is too cunning a fox to do so."[78] Nevertheless, he took precautions "by sending a detachment across the Beas, to prevent any communication between Lahore and Gholab Singh."[79]

In the actual Anglo-Sikh skirmishes that ensued near the Chenab during November and December, the British, in spite of some success, encountered stiff opposition, and Sher Singh remained far from vanquished. Their frustrations were further aggravated by the news of the Sikh siege of British-occupied Attock, by the arrival of Dost Muhammad with three thousand men on the Indus, and by the fact that Mul Raj was still holding out at Multan. Matters were made even worse by Abbott's claim that envoys of Dost Muhammad and Chattar Singh had recently entered Kashmir "disguised as merchants," and that even Mul Raj's agents were present there. Pointing to the unexpected but apparent Sikh-Afghan alignment, Abbott reasoned that the "junction of Maharaja Goolab Singh seems also improbable, for the same reasons of self-interest—but we must not be astonished if it takes place."[80] Abbott also reported the desertion of yet another Sikh regiment of the Dogra Maharaja to Chattar Singh, and observed bitterly: "Surely a little energy would have sufficed to disarm them."[81]

Harassed by a flood of problems, Dalhousie exploded with anger when he heard of the latest complaints against Gulab Singh. Early in December he wrote to the Duke of Wellington that the Maharaja "ought not to be trusted, and will not be trusted by me for one minute."[82] A fortnight later, in another communication to the Duke, he seemed even less compromising. "I will not," he thundered, "trust him for half a minute."[83] Therefore, he promptly concurred with Gough's decision not to use Gulab Singh's troops, but seemed perturbed by the possibility of a Dogra ambush from the rear.[84] Even after Gough succeeded in crossing the Chenab in the middle of December, Dalhousie expressed the fear that the Kashmir ruler "might cut down on us from his hills at any hour, as an enemy."[85] Furthermore, he believed that the British effort was being hampered because "Maharajah Gholab Singh must be provided against."[86] The Governor-General remained steadfast in his distrust of the Kashmir ruler and even rejected Nicholson's request to employ Dogra troops in an attempt to rescue British prisoners from Sikh custody. He ordered that "no use should be made of Gholab Sing's troops for any purpose on which anything depends."[87] When Hodson complained that Dogra territories were being used as a haven by Sikh rebels and notorious Panjab robbers with the full knowledge of local officials,[88] Dalhousie was provoked into retaliating. In spite of Jawala Sahai's assurances that he would investigate the matter and punish the culprits,[89] the Governor-General commanded that the British authorities not hesitate to enter Kashmir in order to curb the troublemakers.[90] But when such an incursion was made, even Hodson admitted that the Dogra troops extended active cooperation to him.[91]

Dalhousie's suspicions and vituperations were surpassed only by those of Napier.[92] Still suspecting a Sikh-Dogra plot, he continued to consider the conquest of Kashmir an essential step toward a permanent solution of the Panjab problem. Once more Napier devised a grand strategy and nourished the hope that General William Whish, the commander in charge of the Multan operations, would be chosen to implement it. He recommended:

When Mooltan falls Whish should mount the river with the Bombay troops to Rhotas, forty miles north of Ramnuggur; thus he would sweep the doabs, concentrate the operations, and cut the communications between Jumnoo and the Hazaree country. I would then leave the Bombay force at Rhotas and with the Bengal corps march upon Jumnoo, which would probably end the war: if not the Bombay corps should march upon Attock, and the Bengal corps enter Cashmere either by the Bimber, if the hot weather had arrived, or by Muzufferabad if the snow still covered the passes. By this plan Goolab would not dare to quit Jumnoo, either as friend or foe; he would be isolated, and our people concentrated and in command of the rivers.[93]

Contending that the Kashmiris themselves would welcome the removal of their ruler, the inimitable Napier declared: "Goolab is hated in Cashmere: it was there *'He take most pleasure to skin de men alive'* as a half Scotch, half Sikh man told me; adding *'And dey likes it, and tinks it very proper.'* Still they don't like being fleeced as well as flayed!"[94] Because of the lack of additional troops to bolster Gough's army, he forecast grave consequences unless his suggested course of action was pursued. Attributing preposterous designs to the Dogra chief, Napier warned that if Gough's "convoys be cut off who is to relieve him? The march upon Delhi would then be as free to Goolab Sing as it was to Nadir Shah, and Goolab is just the chap to make it as terrible."[95]

This new skepticism of high-ranking British officials toward the Kashmir ruler began to be mirrored in the views of their subordinates. Often given to rumor-mongering, they had a natural tendency to exaggerate. One complained that the Maharaja "inspite of the favours heaped upon him is a doubtful friend."[96] Another implied that several chiefs, including the Dogra leader, were actively aiding the rebels.[97] A third laid the blame squarely on Gulab Singh for "simply helping the Rebels with Money, Men, and Provisions!!"[98]

But as the British and the Sikhs prepared for the first major battle of the war, which began on January 13 at Chillianwala, it became evident that, far from being sympathetic to the Attariwala-Barakzai alliance, Gulab Singh was, in fact, gravely apprehensive over the imminent Afghan entry into the Panjab conflict. The Maharaja feared that Dost Muhammad's true motives were not merely to regain Peshawar but also to reoccupy Kashmir. Petrified at the prospect of Afghan aggression, he appealed for British assistance in the event of an invasion of his kingdom. This anti-Afghan entreaty seemed to mitigate somewhat Dalhousie's suspicions, and he grudgingly consented to a reconciliation. Though blaming the Dogra ruler for his failure to provide "real proof of his trustworthiness and amity" and declaring that his government "sets no value on half and half friends," the Governor-General, in a letter dated January 2, told Currie:

If the Maharaja shall really do effective service against the Sikh army now in arms against the British Govt., or against Dost Mahomed, in the event of that person attempting to aid the Sikh army, he may rest assured that Dost Mahomed will not be permitted to injure him.[99]

However, he warned that, if

the Maharaja does not render such service, it is impossible that the British Govt., can place any reliance on his friendship, and they will proceed to take such measures against . . . [him] as their own interests and security may seem to require.[100]

Dalhousie's blunt remarks were conveyed to Gulab Singh,[101] but again no firm request for armed assistance was made insofar as the British failed to indicate either the extent of aid expected, or where, when, and to whom it was to be delivered.

Gulab Singh was quite smitten by the aspersions cast on his fidelity but carefully refrained from issuing an immediate rejoinder. Despite the Governor-General's vaguely worded demand, he nonetheless attempted to comply with it by alerting his army, ordering his forts stocked with provisions, and directing Kashmiri blacksmiths to manufacture additional guns.[102] He had already stationed a force of four thousand men[103] under Steinbach at Mirpur to take the field against Sher Singh, but Gough "protested against their approaching the scene of operations, for the fear that they might fraternize with the insurgents."[104] Thus no Dogra troops were permitted to participate in the battle at Chillianwala[105] where the Sikhs scored an initial success and forced the British to retreat. But the ultimate result was a stalemate.

As the two combatants regrouped for the final battle at Gujarat, significant developments were taking place in other areas of Panjab. Mul Raj at last surrendered at Multan on January 22, and Whish's forces were finally free to reinforce Gough at the Chenab. Meanwhile, Dost Muhammad had crossed the Indus and captured the fort at Attock. This permitted Chattar Singh and his forces to join Sher Singh. The Afghan ruler also sent his son, Akram Khan, with a force of fifteen hundred men to assist the Sikhs, but decided personally to stay at Attock "with a view to collect together all the Affghans in these parts and afford aid if necessary."[106] However, at the same time the Amir claimed that he was being detained because of Gulab Singh who, despite promises to the contrary,[107] had refrained from supplying him with military and financial support. Unaware of Mul Raj's troubles, Dost communicated this complaint to the Multan governor and prophesied: "If [Gulab Singh does] not now lend his assistance in supplying us with money, and [neglects] to join our cause, he will eventually repent it: for it is written."[108] Bristling with indignation at the Kashmir ruler's behavior, he told Mul Raj: "Had Golab Sing shown as much valor and resolution as you have, the Sikhs would now be in possession of the Sovereignty of Lahore."[109] Nevertheless, the Amir once again dispatched envoys to Kashmir to solicit the Maharaja's aid. Yet he simultaneously sought the cooperation of several hill chiefs to help restore Afghan rule to Kashmir, promising territorial rewards for their backing.[110]

Confounded by the latest turn of events, Gulab Singh constantly closeted himself with his advisers, some of whom were infinitely impressed by the Sikh show of arms at Chillianwala. Almost convinced of an imminent British defeat, they recommended that, as the Attariwalas were "expected to conquer Lahore in the near future, it would be prudent to send money and troops to Chattar Singh."[111] According to one report, the Maharaja wavered momentarily,[112] but if so, he must have decided to reject their counsel. Perceiving that an Attariwala-Barakzai victory over the British would inevitably enhance the danger of an Afghan invasion into Kashmir, he forwarded the original communications from Dost Muhammad to Currie and reaffirmed his devotion to the British. The Maharaja proclaimed that he would not alter his stand "even if the mountains should rock," and lashed out at his detractors, declaring "that the face of those who have defamed me may be blackened."[113]

The outcome of the battle at Chillianwala produced the predictable reaction from Dalhousie. Never known for maintaining unruffled calm under pressure, he burst into a fiery rage. Nor did Gulab Singh escape its heat. Implying that the Maharaja of Kashmir ought to share at least part of the blame for the fiasco, Dalhousie charged him with lack of support and threatened to penalize him if he continued to pursue such a course. Through his subordinates he conveyed the grim warning to Gulab Singh that, in the case of noncompliance with his wishes, the British

will be compelled to regard His Highness not as a friend, but as, in truth, an enemy; and will proceed in due time, to seize such portions of His Highness's territory as may give reparation for his breach of treaty, and compensate for the expense which will be caused thereby, or to inflict upon His Highness such other punishment as the Governor-General may think suited to the faithlessness of his conduct.

The Governor-General trusts that the Maharajah, by prompt and vigorous action, will avert this misfortune.[114]

In this same communique he demanded that the Maharaja destroy any Sikh troops who might escape into the hill territories as a result of the impending contest. For the first time, therefore, the Governor-General clearly defined one of the roles he expected Gulab Singh to play. But again he drifted into vague generalities by calling "upon him, further, to put forth every exertion for the destruction of the army of the Sikhs, now in arms against the British Government."[115] Whether this meant that the Maharaja was to fight independently against the Sikhs on the plains, or alongside the British, or both, Dalhousie made no effort to specify.

This time Gulab Singh responded quickly to Dalhousie's threats and demands in a long letter described by Henry Lawrence, who had returned as Resident on February 1, as "a bold and indignant reply to what he considers an unjust accusation."[116] In this letter the Maharaja attempted to defend his conduct from the beginning of the Anglo-Sikh hostilities. While he made no mention of his failure to volunteer troops for the Multan campaign, he claimed that he had attempted to quell the Hazara disturbance at the outset by ordering his troops to Muzaffarabad as early as May of 1848. But he declared that his efforts had been nullified by the opposition of Abbott. He complained, with justification, that his offers of armed assistance in October had been similarly rejected. Asserting that he had planned to march personally to Hazara, Gulab Singh added, somewhat ambiguously: "[As] I imagined that evil disguised people might misconstrue and misrepresent my intentions, I remained where I was."[117] He argued that, if permission had been granted at that time, "I could have easily defeated" the rebels, but the conflict had now acquired such proportions that "I can of myself do nothing without joining the British Troops."[118] However, he reaffirmed his commitment to the Treaty of Amritsar and indicated his intention of assisting the British even at the risk of imperiling his own kingdom.[119] The Maharaja provided the Resident with the exact location of his forces and, as if chiding the British officials, especially Dalhousie, for their ambiguous demands, asked for "speedy, plain and explicit orders."[120] He also endeavored to refute the insinuations contained in the Governor-General's letter of January 2 to Currie and made one of the more ironical statements of his career. "I am not," he declared, "accustomed to wear two faces."[121]

Gulab Singh's letter did alleviate some of Dalhousie's grievances, and the Governor-General's response revealed a marked moderation in tone. "His Lordship," the Maharaja was told, "does not question your fidelity, or goodwill, but requires to see its fruit."[122] Mindful of Gulab Singh's complaint against the lack of perspicuous instructions, Dalhousie defined the role he expected him to play in the final Anglo-Sikh showdown:

. . . when the Sikhs are defeated by the British army, his Lordship expects that the Jummoo troops will, with heart and soul, pursue, attack, and, to their utmost ability, destroy them, in the hill country, not only on the border, but withersoever they may fly, whether towards Noorpoor, or beyond the Jhelum, in the direction of Pind Dadun Khan, or elsewhere.[123]

Lawrence elaborated on the instructions by informing the Maharaja that

you may envince your good faith; by closing the ferries and forts to the supplies and troops of the enemy; by attacking their attached parties that pass through your lands; by delivering up their emissaries; and by furnishing grain and fodder to the British army; in short, by actively showing to the world that you are our friend, and their enemy.[124]

This exchange led to a distinct improvement in Anglo-Dogra relations. Even Abbott, whose allegations had in the first place opened the floodgates of criticism against Gulab Singh, was now overflowing with gratitude. "The Maharaja," he wrote, "continues his liberality. May his shadow never be less."[125] He also now seemed pleased with the Dogra leader's attitude toward the Afghans, and described him as "a bad thorn in the Uumier's [Dost's] side."[126] Some Dogra troops finally received permission to participate in the fateful battle of Gujarat on February 21, which was fought amid a fallacious rumor that Gulab Singh had been assassinated in Kashmir.[127] Although a Dogra commander named Dewan Ram Singh was killed in the engagement,[128] the general contribution of his troops to the British victory seems to have been insignificant. However, another Dogra force under Dewan Hari Chand and Steinbach performed quite effectively in its pursuit of the fleeing adversary.[129] The Sikhs eventually surrendered in the middle of March, and the Afghans retreated to their homeland. The British annexation of Panjab at the end of the month sounded the death knell of the Sikh state.

Gulab Singh seemed ecstatic over the result and, in a congratulatory message filled with metaphorical rhetoric and unabashed flattery, he told Dalhousie:

If the whole surface of the earth were to become paper, the trees pens, and the rivers turn into ink, they would all be insufficient to express my unbounded pleasure.

It is well known that I owe to the British Government the preservation of my life, my country and everything that I have; and it may well be said of this your humble friend that you have performed the miracle of Christ in raising me from the dead.[130]

In any assessment of Gulab Singh's conduct during the Second Anglo-Sikh War, several British officials must be held responsible for spasmodically jumping to ill-founded conclusions which caused innumerable misapprehensions and strained Anglo-Dogra relations. Dalhousie, Abbott, Napier, and Edwardes can especially be blamed for pursuing a policy of extreme distrust and inordinate overreaction toward the Maharaja of Kashmir. There is no concrete proof to substantiate the incessant accusations of Dogra collusion with the enemies of the British. However, there is sufficient evidence that some of the British officials were in such a state of hysteria that they seemed incapable of rationally deciding whether or not to accept assistance from the Maharaja.

Gulab Singh, on his part, deliberately chose to pursue a policy of friendly neutrality toward the British at the start of the conflict. He was indeed a self-seeking man and considered non-entanglement to be politically and financially the most expedient course open to him. But once the British authorities demanded his active cooperation, he seemed ready and willing to give it. It would be absurd to presume that he desired a British defeat. Though predictably troubled by occasional calls from some Englishmen for Kashmir's annexation, he nonetheless could not foresee any immediate danger from the British government. On the other hand, he must have realized almost immediately that a Sikh victory would inevitably revive at Lahore the painful memories of his role in the last war and encourage a Sikh attempt to regain the Himalayan territories so reluctantly surrendered in 1846. Even if the Dogra chief had joined Chattar Singh and Dost Muhammad on the condition that Kashmir's sovereignty would be respected, and if such a joint venture had resulted in a British defeat, it is debatable whether the Sikhs and the Afghans would have honored their pledge. Despite the indubitably obsequious tone of his felicitations to Dalhousie, Gulab Singh's exultation over the results of the war was probably quite genuine. The British victory saved the Dogra state not only from the threat of a Sikh invasion but also from the sudden peril posed by the Afghans.

10 Anglo-Kashmir Relations 1849-1857

Gholab Singh has hitherto been eager to lick the dust below my feet.—Dalhousie

. . . Goolab will be able to play a stiff game: rock, sun, snow! all on his side. Diable!—Charles Napier

. . . [Gulab Singh] caught my dress in his hands, and cried aloud, "Thus I grasp the skirts of the British Government, and I will never let go my hold."—Dalhousie

nO sooner had the excitement over the annexation of Panjab subsided somewhat than rumors of an impending British invasion of Kashmir began to circulate in England. Such speculation gained credence because of several news stories from India which appeared in the *Times* of London. It was reported in August that Dalhousie planned to mount an attack against Kashmir during the autumn because of Gulab Singh's refusal to surrender his reputedly formidable artillery to the British.[1] Word arrived during September that in anticipation of war "nearly whole of the steamers belonging to the Indus flotilla had been ordered up, so that there would be one or more in each of the great tributaries of the Indus."[2] According to other rumors, the Dogra ruler was also reinforcing his army and "large bodies of Sikhs [were] flocking towards Cashmere, prepared, no doubt, once more to try the fortune of war if Gholab should be rash enough to lead them against our troops."[3] Disturbed by the prospect of a new war, the *Times* in an editorial expressed concern that, if the Maharaja chose to fight the British, "his standard once displayed in rebellion would serve instantly as a rallying point to the discontented spirits and disbanded soldiery of the Punjab, and his forces would be swelled by recruits of all ranks and castes."[4] Dalhousie, however, dismissed as gossip the reports that he had asked Gulab Singh to relinquish his guns or that another round of fighting was imminent. "Never believe anything you see in the newspapers about India, unless my letters confirm it," he told a friend.[5] The misgivings which had been aroused in the Governor-General's mind during the course of the recent hostilities were fast dissipating, and he seemed satisfied with the postwar attitude of the Maharaja. "Gholab Singh," he observed, "has hitherto been eager to lick the dust below my feet."[6]

Dalhousie's new posture toward Kashmir, however, was soon challenged by one of the most zealous advocates of Gulab Singh's removal. In the tremulous aftermath of Chillianwala, the Company's directors had appointed Charles Napier to replace Gough as Commander-in-Chief and to take charge of the Second Anglo-Sikh War operations. Even before his departure from England, Napier singled out the Kashmir sovereign as one of his chief targets by telling his brother that "my first blow will probably be at Goolab Sing."[7] He denounced those London officials who seemed inclined to exonerate the Dogra ruler because of the lack of incriminating evidence, and worried that Dalhousie might be unsympathetic toward his proposed course of action. Declaring that "Goolab is not to be trifled with," the General threatened that he would resign if his advice were disregarded.[8] The war was already over upon his arrival in India during May of 1849, but Napier continued to express his fear of aggression from Kashmir and claimed that "a great army with some hundreds of guns was ready, under Gulab Singh, to threaten British India."[9] He even warned Dalhousie of the prospect of a third Anglo-Sikh war in which Gulab Singh could be expected to play an active role against the British.[10] The Governor-General, however, refused to be stampeded into precipitous action and rejected Napier's pleas to allow him to carry out military operations against Kashmir. This disagreement was the beginning of a bitter controversy between the two mercurial-tempered men. Dalhousie soon complained of Napier's incessant garrulity: "He is talking everywhere very wildly, and mischievously—prognosticating an immediate attack from Gholab Sing, and asserting the certainty of a row—all of which is the very likeliest mode of producing the evil he prophesies."[11]

Despite a cordial meeting with Gulab Singh at Jammu during December of 1849,[12] Napier's distrust continued undiminished. When an abortive anti-British Sikh mutiny broke out at Gobindgarh during the same month, he saw it as the prelude to a war with Kashmir and Afghanistan.[13] Dalhousie, however, challenged his supposition. Only after Wellington in England also questioned Napier's judgment[14] did the Commander-in-Chief yield, but he declared nonetheless: "Had all happened, that might have happened, the Queen's troops, comparatively few in number, would have been isolated at each station. Sikhs and Affghans would inevitably have been in arms. What the Maharaja would have done no man can tell, but he would have had *power* to do us all possible mischief."[15] But he still remained obsessed with the notion of ousting Gulab Singh. During August of 1850, an unfounded rumor that Henry Lawrence, then touring Kashmir, had been imprisoned by the Maharaja stirred Napier to demand an immediate invasion of the Dogra state. Once more he devised an elaborate strategy to achieve his object in the face of what he considered to be heavy odds:

... after hard fighting, those tremendous heights are forced; you get into Cashmere, and are at once in the midst of swamps and fevers, and must bring up your provisions by the terrible passes you have forced—in itself a job of no ordinary nature, even when not opposed; but Goolab will surely close them behind you if he can. Yet only half the danger is told. While working up the sides of the mountains the Sikhs will rise in rear, and a single defeat places hosts between your army and your supplies. Even Delhi will be in danger, for all the protected states detest us. If events should come too fast for me to escape the direction of the war, I think I shall form my force at Puneh [Poonch], and so threaten the Baramula pass and that of Pir Punjal; order [Brigadier General Colin] Campbell to march from Peshawur, and crossing the Indus march on Baramula: this will force Goolab to divide his forces and I can then act according to my information.[16]

The General declared that he "could give that monster Goolab Sing such a thrashing that he deserves."[17] Although Napier at first claimed that he could finish the job by December, he eventually admitted that success might elude him until spring. Citing the approaching cold weather as the reason for his reappraisal, he ejaculated: ". . . Goolab will be able to play a stiff game: rock, sun, snow! all on his side. Diable!"[18]

In spite of Dalhousie's indifference toward such schemes, the constant clamoring of his Commander-in-Chief persuaded him to make an on-the-spot check in the northwest at the end of the year, and he asked Gulab Singh to meet him in Panjab.[19] The Maharaja expressed grave concern over the consequences of such an interview. Conscious of Dalhousie's irascibility and his unfriendliness during the Second Anglo-Sikh War, the superstitious Maharaja sought the advice of an astrologer, Haji Inayatullah, before accepting Dalhousie's invitation. Inayatullah was "directed to determine by calculating the position of the stars as to what would be the nature of the audience with *sahiban alishan* [Dalhousie], what fruit it would bear, and what sort of treatment would be extended to [the Maharaja]."[20] Assured by the astrologer that the Governor-General would be favorably inclined toward him, Gulab Singh made preparations for the trip and ordered gifts worth thirty thousand rupees which were to be presented to Dalhousie.[21] The two men met at Wazirabad on December 26 in the Governor-General's camp after a deputation of British officials led by Henry Elliot, the political secretary, escorted the Maharaja from his camp on handsomely decorated elephants over a route lined with thousands of the Company's troops.[22] Though Dalhousie was not particularly overjoyed at the prospect of meeting Gulab Singh,[23] he soon succumbed to his visitor's irresistible charm and unabashed sycophancy. Determined to allay the suspicions of the Governor-General once and for all, Gulab Singh startled Dalhousie when he unblushingly grabbed his "dress in his hands, and cried aloud, 'Thus I grasp the skirts of the British Government, and I will never let go my hold.' ''[24] The gesture impressed the Governor-General immensely, and put him in a congenial frame of mind for the rest of the conference. Taking advantage of Dalhousie's changed mood, the Maharaja fed his host's vanity by describing him "as a young man" and remarking that the "other Governor-Generals he had seen were grey-bearded."[25]

While pleasantries were thus being exchanged, groundless rumors of Gulab Singh's arrest spread through Wazirabad,[26] and there was a sigh of relief in the Dogra camp when he returned safely. On the following day Dalhousie "passed with a train of 22 caparisoned elephants down a street of about 7000 troops"[27] to visit the Maharaja. Additional pledges of friendship and loyalty were given by Gulab Singh. He also expressed his fond hope of joining Dalhousie in a future invasion of Afghanistan.[28] To further strengthen this new rapport with the Governor-General, the Maharaja even begged him to pay a visit to the beautiful vale of Kashmir. Dalhousie recorded Gulab Singh's rhetorical pleas: "It is yours; why should you leave it? Cashmere is your house, the boats are on the lake—they are yours; the horses are on the land—they are yours; the climate is good—it is yours; everything is yours—why leave it?"[29] Although favorably disposed toward such a trip, the pressure of official business prevented Dalhousie from accepting the invitation.[30] Nevertheless, the parleys with Gulab Singh created a lasting impression on his mind, and he did not question the Dogra's trustworthiness during the rest of his term as Governor-General.[31]

But the Wazirabad conference only temporarily dampened the pugnacious spirit of Charles Napier. During the autumn of 1851, when speculation became rife that the Kashmir sovereign was on his death bed, Napier once again contemplated an attack on Kashmir. Dalhousie, however, refused to alter his policy toward the Dogra state and retorted that, if Napier persisted in his belligerence, "I shall take care to tie him up hand and foot."[32] The personal discord and animosity between the two men finally resulted in the Commander-in-Chief's resignation, and he returned home without fulfilling his dream of conquering Kashmir. But Napier continued to harbor resentment against Dalhousie, who did not really comprehend the full extent of Charles Napier's fanaticism until his brother published his private letters in 1857. Seething with indignation, Dalhousie responded: "These two Napiers were vineyards on a volcano. They would have been gay and genial but for the perpetual flames bursting out and scorching and blasting all that was good in them."[33]

While in India, Charles Napier had suspected that Dalhousie's northwestern policies were in reality being formulated by the Lawrence brothers. This was a fallacious supposition, since the Governor-General was by nature too egocentric to surrender such an executive privilege to his subordinates.[34] In fact, Henry Lawrence, like Napier, was involved in disputes of his own with Dalhousie. The Governor-General had resented Henry's sympathetic attitude toward Gulab Singh during the last war and his opposition to the annexation of Panjab. Determined to curb the extensive powers he wielded as Resident, Dalhousie in 1849 appointed a three-member board to administer the new British province of Panjab. Though Henry was to be its president, the two other members, for all practical purposes, were made independent of him. One of the appointees to the board was John Lawrence, an ambitious and opportunistic man, who henceforth consistently backed Dalhousie against his brother.[35] But in spite of these difficulties, Henry maintained close relations with Panjab's neighbor to the north. While denying charges that he held Gulab Singh in high personal esteem,[36] he nevertheless made it a point to squelch unwarranted criticism against him and can thus be credited, at least in part, with diminishing Dalhousie's antipathy toward the Dogra ruler. After a visit to Kashmir late in 1849, he rejected Napier's exaggerated claims of the state's military might[37] and his contention that Gulab Singh was poised for attack. He denounced the Dographobes and, in a letter to the Governor-General, analyzed the situation in Kashmir: "Like most natives [Gulab Singh] is a watcher of events, but a very clever and a far-seeing one . . . . If we allow him to be our humble friend and ally he will be so; but there are so many Europeans panting for the possession of this valley, that it will not be an easy task to keep the peace."[38] However, Henry continued to encounter bitter opposition from both Dalhousie and John Lawrence over what they considered his partisan attitude toward Gulab Singh. The Governor-General raised objections when he embarked on another tour of Kashmir in 1850.[39] Later, Dalhousie blamed him for the territorial settlement of 1847 involving Hazara and complained: "To this bad bargain we have succeeded and we must now make the best of it."[40] Finally, when Henry attempted to pressure his brother into altering a censorious report which he had prepared against the Maharaja, John "doubled his strictures and forwarded them to the Government."[41]

Such antagonism led to the resignation of Henry Lawrence in December 1852. Dalhousie thereupon swiftly abolished the board of administration and rewarded John for his indubitable subservience by appointing him Chief Commissioner of Panjab. But before Henry departed to assume the Residency of Rajputana, Gulab Singh, even at the risk of arousing Dalhousie's wrath, requested a meeting with his friend. The two men bade each other a sentimental farewell on January 22, 1853, near Sialkot. Recalling their conversation, Lawrence wrote: "I told him I was going away, that we shall probably not meet again in this world."[42] The Maharaja described Henry's pending departure as "a heavy blow to him" and inquired if he "would accept a remembrance of him."[43] But Dalhousie's resentment against Henry Lawrence continued to linger even after he returned to England. This is illustrated by his reaction to a laudatory article in the *Times* after Henry's violent death during the Mutiny at Lucknow. Betraying both jealousy and pettiness, he seemingly included even John Lawrence in his outburst: "[I] who am supposed to have been merely a bystander looking on while other men were building up a pedestal for my reputation to stand on . . . I have sometimes, in reading over these folios, stood astonished at how much I bore and forbore, and how temperately I worked out my own objects, through Lawrences on one side, and Sir Charles Napier on the other."[44]

Other British voices, in addition to those of Dalhousie, Napier, and Lawrence, were heard on the Kashmir issue during this period. George Clerk stoutly championed Gulab Singh and considered his control of Kashmir favorable to British security in India.[45] J. D. Cunningham also came to the Maharaja's defense. Although he bitterly assailed the British conduct during the First Anglo-Sikh War in his book which appeared in 1849, he wrote that it was wrong to presume that Gulab Singh

is a man malevolently evil. He will, indeed, deceive an enemy and take his life without hesitation, and in the accumulation of money he will exercise many oppressions; but he must be judged with reference to the morality of his age and race, and to the necessities of his own position. If these allowances be made, Golab Singh will be found an able and moderate man, who does little in an idle or wanton spirit, and who is not without some traits both of good humor and generosity of temper.[46]

But other contemporary writers took a divergent view. One called the creation of the Dogra state "an unfortunate choice of policy," and predicted that Kashmir would meet the fate of Panjab.[47] Another entertained a similar hope, and asserted that, with the occupation of Kashmir, "we shall have, to the North and North-west, one of the most magnificent boundaries which an empire could desire."[48] It seems that even a plan to colonize Kashmir with three million Englishmen or Anglo-Indians was suggested, but was eventually discarded because it was considered politically unfeasible.[49]

Gulab Singh was not unaware of the demands being made for the annexation of Kashmir,[50] and adopted several measures in his internal administration calculated to prevent such an eventuality (see Chapter 11). He also took additional steps to keep the British government in good humor. Expensive gifts were periodically dispatched to Queen Victoria.[51] The Maharaja took a keen interest in the progress of the Crimean War, and once in unseemly haste he ordered a premature celebration of British victory.[52] He kept a close vigil, too, on the Anglo-Iranian conflict over Herat which flared up in 1856. As soon as the news of the Iranian retreat reached Kashmir, he sent his felicitations to the British.[53]

With the eruption of the Sepoy Mutiny in 1857, shadows of doubt were once again cast on Gulab Singh's good faith. The Deputy Commissioner at Sialkot angrily questioned the motives behind the presence of a Dogra force on the Jammu border. However, he was pacified by the explanation that the troops had been stationed there long before the outbreak occurred.[54] There was also uneasiness over the continued presence of an anti-British faction at Gulab Singh's darbar and the influence it might exert on him during the course of the Mutiny.[55] But despite some trepidation, the Maharaja[56] apparently resolved from the outset to adopt a pro-British stand. It is said that, when word of the uprising reached Gulab Singh, he prophesied: "Well, it will give the English some trouble, cost them a good deal of money, but in a few months they will be alright again."[57] He made a somewhat similar prediction to Lieutenant Harriett Urmston, the Assistant Commissioner of Peshawar, who was then on vacation in Kashmir. During a boat-ride conference with him, the Maharaja glanced at a passing cloud and reflected that "the Mutiny will be just like that fleeting cloud."[58] Although Urmston reported a certain degree of anti-British sentiment among the natives,[59] he was much impressed by Gulab Singh's sympathetic attitude.

The Kashmir ruler was prompt in responding to British appeals for assistance. He lent ten lakhs of rupees to the Panjab government to pay its troops, whose salary was in arrears because of the delay in receiving funds from Calcutta.[60] Gulab Singh thus might have helped the British stave off the possibility of any insubordination in the ranks of their Sikh soldiery. At the urging of the British, he also forbade the mutineers to seek asylum in any part of Kashmir. Some two hundred rebels of the Fourteenth Native Infantry located at Jhelum, who managed to escape into Jammu, were apprehended and handed over to the British.[61] Another group of mutineers, who belonged to the 55th Native Regiment, made a desperate attempt to escape to Kashmir, unwilling to believe that Gulab Singh, "who had a foot in each boat in the war of 1848–49, would not in this more awful crisis leap into the argosy of rebellion."[62] However, they never reached their destination.[63] A similar move by some Sialkot mutineers likewise ended in failure.[64]

The Maharaja also agreed to send a Kashmiri force to assist the British during the siege of Delhi. When the British authorities expressed the fear that his troops might defect to the mutineers, they were assured that only troops of proven loyalty would be employed.[65] Continued British doubts and irresolution,[66] however, kept the Dogra force immobile for several months. It was only after Gulab Singh's death in August that this force, consisting of two thousand infantrymen, two hundred cavalrymen, and six guns,[67] was allowed to depart from Jammu under Lieutenant Richard Lawrence, the youngest of the Lawrence brothers. John Lawrence, who inspected the troops at Jullundur, was not wholly impressed by them. Although he described the soldiers as "a fine body of men, young, active, and well-made," he felt they were not "first-class fighting men,"[68] and lacked "the bone and muscle of the Sings."[69]

Nevertheless, the Kashmir contingent proceeded to Delhi where, because of the aspersions cast on its reliability and effectiveness, it saw only limited action. It "took part in the attack on the Kishengunge suburb on the 14th September; it guarded the British camp while the Europeans were storming the city; it was largely employed in the re-occupation of the Delhi territory."[70] However, the psychological significance of Gulab Singh's decision to commit his troops far outweighed their actual contribution in combat. His action was a clear warning that Kashmir was opposed to the mutiny and, therefore, perhaps diminished the probability of a serious conflagration in the erstwhile Sikh state. Even Edwardes considered Gulab Singh's pro-British stance "an interposition of Providence" and declared: "Had he chosen to revolt, had he chosen to call upon the Sikhs, his late comrades in the Punjab, to rise against us, no doubt they would have risen at his command, and we should have been unable to hold that province."[71]

The marked improvement in Anglo-Kashmir relations which took place between 1849 and 1857 must be attributed in large part to the change in Dalhousie's attitude toward Gulab Singh. Had the Governor-General so desired, he could have found a pretext for attacking Kashmir, since he did have the military strength necessary to occupy the Dogra state. But Dalhousie chose otherwise, and contemptuously rebuffed Napier and the others who recommended such an invasion. His policy underwent no discernible shift even after the controversial departure of Henry Lawrence from the northwest. Gulab Singh was, of course, acutely aware of the increased peril to his kingdom from the British in the wake of Panjab's annexation. The Maharaja, therefore, not only welcomed Dalhousie's overture, but also deliberately and consistently pursued a course designed to preserve and strengthen the new understanding with the Company. This is best exemplified by his performance at Wazirabad, his endurance of British criticism, and his assistance during the Mutiny. Thus there was a significant decline in the level of that suspicion and distrust which had characterized Anglo-Dogra relations until 1849.

11 Internal Administration
1846-1857

Every living man is to [Gulab Singh] a blade of golden
corn, which he will never leave till he has gathered,
and threshed, and winnowed, and garnered.
—Herbert Edwardes

The king is avaricious . . . and he won't look beyond his
money-bags. There is a capitation tax on every
individual practising any labour, trade, profession,
or employment, collected *daily*.—William Hodson

My good friends the English Government having
discovered their mistake, in supposing that the shawl
wool is a product of my country, seem disposed to shear
me.—Gulab Singh

*t*HE Afghan conquest of Kashmir during the eighteenth century had reduced its people's existence to a deplorable plight. Ranjit Singh expelled the Afghans in 1819, but did little to alleviate the miseries of the Kashmiris. In fact, it seems their lot worsened under the Sikhs. While touring Kashmir in 1824, Moorcroft noted that more than one-sixteenth of the cultivatable land was lying barren because many farmers, unable to endure the exorbitant rate of taxation imposed by the government, had quit their occupation.[1] The shawl manufacturers, engaged in one of the province's most important industries, paid a twenty-six percent tax on their total output plus a levy for importing wool.[2] It seems no one was spared. Moorcroft observed that "butchers, bakers, boatmen, vendors of fuel, public notaries, scavengers, prostitutes, all paid a sort of corporation tax and even the Kotwal, or chief officer of justice, paid a large gratuity of thirty thousand a year for his appointment, being left to reimburse himself as he might."[3] Vigne encountered a similar situation in 1835 and was particularly disturbed by the desolate conditions in Kashmir.[4] This state of affairs was aggravated by the Sikhs' retention of the system of begar (forced labor), which had been practiced by the Afghans. Since most of the laborers were commandeered from the ranks of the farmers, this, too, encouraged many of them to give up agriculture.

The situation in Kashmir further deteriorated after 1839 and was perhaps at its worst under the last two Sikh governors, Mohi-ud-Din[5] and Imam-ud-Din. Younghusband describes the conditions on the eve of the Dogra rule:

The Government took from two-thirds to three-fourths of the gross produce of the land. . . . One half was taken as the regular Government share, and additional amounts were taken as perquisites of various kinds, leaving one-third or even only a quarter with the cultivators. . . . The whole system of assessment and collection was exceedingly complicated and workable only in the interests of the corrupt officials; and Government [also] held a monopoly in the sale of grain.[6]

Upon the establishment of Dogra hegemony, several Company officials wondered if Gulab Singh had any intention of solving the enormous economic problems of Kashmir. They found the prospect for correcting the situation, which required a broad and altruistic effort, rather discouraging in view of the parsimonious reputation enjoyed by the new Maharaja. Such sentiments were epitomized in Herbert Edwardes's gloomy rhetoric: "And now he *is a King*, and has a wide field wherein to reap. Every living man is to him a blade of golden corn, which he will never leave till he has gathered, and threshed, and winnowed, and garnered."[7] Henry Hardinge, however, was more optimistic. In view of the relatively prosperous state of the farmers around Jammu, he believed that Gulab Singh would similarly improve the economic conditions in Kashmir by reorganizing its taxation system.[8] The British desire for reform was personally conveyed to the Maharaja by Henry Lawrence at the end of 1846.[9] But since Gulab Singh stood to gain by continuing the coercive and corrupt practices of his predecessors in Kashmir, he displayed little interest in discarding them. This attitude evoked a chorus of British complaints in the first half of 1847, symbolized by Charles Hardinge's stricture: "He has all his life been a huckster on a large scale, is undoubtedly avaricious, and he no doubt finds great difficulty in ridding himself from habits of self-enrichment which have been year by year growing upon him."[10]

By the middle of 1847, the Company felt compelled to adopt a policy of direct interference by pressuring the Maharaja to initiate reform. Early in June it asked the Kashmir government to reduce prices on foodstuffs and to make available in the market an abundant supply of rice.[11] Simultaneously, Henry Lawrence dispatched to Srinagar a mission under one of his assistants, Lieutenant Reynell Taylor, who was given the formidable task of recommending necessary reforms after consultation with the people as well as the government.[12] While extending a warm welcome and ostensible cooperation to the mission, Gulab Singh skillfully blocked it from completing its work. Attempts were made to convince the visitors that the Kashmiris were generally content with the Maharaja's rule, and that the cause of their grievances came from other quarters. For example, in July over four thousand shawl weavers staged a demonstration against their local Kashmiri employers and went on strike,[13] but it was suspected that their protests were inspired by Gulab Singh himself to impress the mission with his own innocence.[14] During his three-month stay, Taylor's attempts to secure the populace's viewpoint were thwarted not only by the manipulations of the Maharaja's officials but also by the timidity of the people themselves. Khuihami, a Kashmiri historian, recorded the futile exertions of Taylor:

In 1847 Mr. Taylor Sahib came to Kashmir to inquire into the conditions in Kashmir and to suggest reforms in the Maharaja's administration. For some time he studied the local laws and revenue regulations. He called a general darbar in the Maisuma grounds [at Srinagar], and in a very loud voice he inquired "O you, the people of Kashmir, are you happy with the Maharaja's rule or not." Some of the people who had been tutored by Pandit Raj Dhar Kak [a high government official] shouted back, "Yes, we are." When Taylor Sahib heard this he felt disgusted with the character of the people of Kashmir and went back to [British] India.[15]

Taylor himself had mixed feelings about his assignment. On the one hand while in Kashmir, he expressed serious misgivings about the justness of his mission: "The manifest danger of an inexperienced man dabbling in the affairs of a kingdom, and with one word consenting to arrangements affecting the prosperity and happiness of thousands, or unfairly tying the hands of a ruler in his own country for years to come, has encountered me at every step."[16] Yet on the eve of his departure in September, Taylor confessed: "I have a heartbreaking feeling that there is much left to be done."[17]

Thus the British intervention produced no concrete results. For a while, Gulab Singh's expressions of pious intentions to Taylor led the British authorities to the erroneous conclusion that he had committed himself to a course "calculated to improve the country generally, and ameliorate the condition of his subjects."[18] Specifically, it was felt that the Maharaja had been induced to abolish the begar system and abandon the state's monopoly on the sale of rice.[19] But Gulab Singh, who had become gravely alarmed at the prospect of persistent meddling by the Company in his administrative affairs, continued to procrastinate and failed to carry out any salutary reforms.

Although Taylor's mission failed, Henry Lawrence remained interested in reform and, at least partly for this purpose, visited Kashmir during 1849 and 1850. His first trip was termed a vacation, but the Maharaja, with some justification, worried that it might have also been undertaken for other reasons. Mirza Saif-ud-Din, the Company's secret informer at Srinagar (see Appendix D), reported that the Maharaja "could not at all believe or trust that sahib kalan bahadur's [Lawrence's] visit was without [political] purpose and that it was exclusively a holiday trip."[20] Filled with apprehension, he repeatedly urged his officials to use caution during Lawrence's sojourn. Gulab Singh ordered that he must be kept informed of the Resident's "minute by minute activities" and that the Kashmiri malcontents should be denied access to the important visitor. Fearful of arousing the Resident's suspicions, he ordered the government's arms and ammunition in Srinagar to be kept out of the visitor's sight.[21] Though Lawrence personally despised the Kashmiris and once described them as "filthy, idle, [and] litigious,"[22] he was nonetheless interested in bettering their lot. He assailed Gulab Singh for disregarding the assurances made to Taylor, and exhorted him to work toward the economic improvement of his subjects. While the Maharaja reiterated his intention of bowing to the wishes of the British, he offered no satisfactory explanation for his failure to carry out his earlier pledges. After Lawrence's departure, Gulab Singh put the blame for his administration's shortcomings on his officials, but once more refrained from introducing any changes in the system.[23] Lawrence's efforts were politely snubbed by the same evasive tactics during his second visit.[24] But as long as Henry remained in the northwest, he continued to dwell upon the advisability of reform, and even during their parting interview in 1853 he told Gulab Singh "that if I heard that his subjects were happy, and his chiefs and army contented, [then] I too should be satisfied."[25]

However, Henry Lawrence's exhortations were all in vain and, to the relief of the Dogra ruler, British pressure had actually begun to slacken even before Henry's departure. As a matter of fact, while the Company, after 1850, maintained a close vigil on Kashmir developments through the extensive confidential dispatches of Saif-ud-Din, relatively few attempts were made to interfere in Gulab Singh's domestic affairs during the remainder of his reign.

Although it is unclear as to what precisely prompted this significant change in the Company's position, it probably was due to a combination of reasons. First, there was perhaps a growing conviction that the British, short of employing actual force, could not persuade Gulab Singh to make the necessary changes. Second, the British had no legal right to dictate economic reforms to the Dogra ruler. The Amritsar treaty had granted no such prerogative to the Company, and Gulab Singh, once he had assumed control of Kashmir, carefully avoided joining the tricky and often suicidal Subsidiary Alliance. Third, the Second Anglo-Sikh War in 1848 and 1849 diverted British attention away from Kashmir to Panjab. And lastly, the postwar shift in Dalhousie's relationship with Gulab Singh must have discouraged other British officials from intervening in his internal affairs.

The new British attitude gave the Maharaja carte blanche in the administration of his new acquisition. He had neither the inclination nor perhaps the ability to launch a broad program of reconstruction. In addition, he seemed to consider his purchase of Kashmir a financial investment and was determined to wring rich economic dividends from it. Thus the harsh taxation system of the pre-Dogra period was not only maintained, but in some ways broadened. Hodson, a frequent visitor to Kashmir, recorded in 1850: "The king is avaricious . . . and he won't look beyond his money-bags. There is a capitation tax on every individual practising any labour, trade, profession, or employment, collected *daily*."[26] Similarly, Mirjanpuri, another Kashmiri historian, lamented: "In the extortion of money he used a hundred arts and opened new doors of tyranny."[27]

Gulab Singh did indeed inaugurate a rapacious economic program to earn such notoriety. He confiscated a very large number of tax-free jagirs, including those belonging to Hindu and Muslim priests, which enabled the authorities to collect an additional two hundred thousand *khirwars* (a donkey's load)[28] of grain per year.[29] The farmers producing *shali* (unwinnowed rice), the major agricultural crop of Kashmir, were forced to remit at least fifty percent of their harvest to the government.[30] The Maharaja not only retained a full monopoly on the sale of *shali* but doubled its price from one to two rupees per *khirwar*,[31] a policy which resulted in widespread hoarding and black-marketing.[32] The annual tax on *sangharas* (water chestnuts) was raised from fourteen thousand to as much as a hundred thousand rupees.[33] These assessments, combined with the land taxes and the devaluation of the rupee,[34] increased the government's total annual revenue from about thirty-five lakhs to over forty-six lakhs of rupees.[35] Such taxation produced a great hue and cry, particularly among the farmers. To deter them from abandoning their occupation, the government equalled the fee "on the transfer of land to the amount for which it was sold."[36] The Maharaja's tax measures aggravated the peasants' condition to such a degree that for them "there seemed no way to live their lives and sustain themselves except by the grace of God."[37]

Nor did Gulab Singh spare those engaged in the pashmina trade. The annual tax on the industry was raised from four to twelve lakhs of rupees.[38] The merchants paid anywhere from 180 to 5,500 rupees to the government, depending upon the number of weavers employed in their factories.[39] These ruinous levies, coupled with constant meddling by officials, brought the pashmina industry to a virtual halt in 1849.[40] Unable to endure such onerous conditions, so many shawl workers began to leave Kashmir that in 1851 the government forbade them to emigrate.[41]

The Kashmiri populace also continued to be oppressed by the servile practice of begar which remained in vogue. The Maharaja himself employed forced labor on more than one occasion.[42] Gulab

Singh likewise retained the *nikah* (wedding) tax which had been exacted by Kashmir's former rulers, and even drastically raised it. "The flames of tyranny," to quote the eloquent phraseology of Mirjanpuri, "rose to such heights that the wedding tax was increased from ten to one hundred rupees."[43] Saif-ud-Din records that some people, probably the very affluent, had to pay exorbitant *nikah* assessments amounting to thousands of rupees.[44] However, in the latter part of his reign Gulab Singh, under British pressure, abolished this unpopular tax.[45]

The Maharaja introduced several other stringent measures designed to augment his treasury. These included a government monopoly on the sale of tobacco and a tax on gambling houses.[46] He also forced the gravediggers to relinquish a part of their wages,[47] imposed duties on the sale of animals, and even taxed the sale of dried cowdung[48] used as fuel, although these last two tolls were eventually revoked. In addition, the proprietors of large shops were required to pay up to fifteen hundred rupees per annum in taxes,[49] and each Afghan trader had to pay an exit fee of one hundred rupees.[50] There is also a reference to the collection of a certain levy from Hindu temples.[51]

The vulturous quality of Gulab Singh's taxation system aroused bitter resentment among the normally docile Kashmiris. Protests and strikes were held, and twice there was widespread uproar. During the fall of 1848, Srinagar's shopkeepers retaliated by temporarily closing their stores and demanding a reduction on the prices of goods sold to them by the government. Other merchants and the industrial workers joined the agitation.[52] Again, in January of 1850, the smoldering hostility toward the Maharaja's economic policies erupted in the form of serious riots throughout the valley. The local officials, however, firmly crushed the disturbances, and the agitators were severely punished. One of the victims was forced to walk across the partially frozen Wular Lake and drowned when the thin ice gave way beneath his weight. Complaints against such ruthlessness were ignored by Gulab Singh,[53] and the outbreaks failed to have any effect on his policies. Although the Maharaja was not again confronted with any crises of the magnitude of those during 1848 and 1850, there is evidence that his subjects were never fully reconciled to their economic lot.[54]

Gulab Singh regularly held his darbar in Srinagar. At the summit of his officialdom was Jawala Sahai, who for years had been his trusted lieutenant and who now, in addition to being his Prime Minister, also emerged as his top diplomat. The Maharaja employed several other high officials who either performed specific duties or were dispatched on special missions. Unlike the Sikh maharajas, he was reluctant to grant Muslims a significant role in his administration and, upon assuming power, he discharged most of the Muslim officials who were serving in the all-important revenue department.[55] Few Muslims served in the upper echelons of the bureaucracy and, after Mazhar Ali, who had served Gulab Singh for several years, resigned in 1851,[56] none were appointed to high positions.[57] Among the Maharaja's Hindu officials an acrimonious struggle for power developed between the Kashmiris and the so-called Panjabis. The Kashmiris contemptuously considered all those who hailed from Jammu as Panjabis, although by doing so they were also unwittingly scorning Gulab Singh himself, without whose blessing they could hardly expect to triumph over their rivals. Raj Dhar Kak, the leader of the Kashmiri faction who had sole control over the Maharaja's vital revenue department, especially aroused the deep antagonism of the non-Kashmiris. At one point Kak was actually beaten by some unknown miscreants, and the Kashmiri official's underlings warned him "that the Panjabis in the service of the Maharaja are after your life."[58] The hostility toward Kak reached a climax when Jawala Sahai, who hailed from Jammu, accused him of maladministration in revenue affairs.[59] By means of his extraordinary influence, the Prime Minister persuaded the Maharaja to weaken Kak by forcing him to share his power with Devi Ditta Mal, a native of Jammu. That Gulab Singh himself now seemed eager to curb Kashmiri preponderence in the important department of revenue is evident from the instructions he issued to Devi Ditta on the assumption of his new duties: "Now you should collect revenue from every quarter and root out Kashmiri influence from every quarter." The Maharaja tendered similar advice to the lesser revenue officials.[60] The appointment of Devi Ditta aroused bitter indignation among the Kashmiris, and seven to eight hundred protesting farmers presented themselves before the Maharaja to express their unhappiness. But Gulab Singh dismissed their complaints by accusing them, rather hypocritically, of harboring anti-Jammu prejudices.[61] Nevertheless, a certain degree of unrest persisted among the farmers, which Devi Ditta and other Jammu officials blamed on the machinations of Kak and his Kashmiri cohorts.[62] This charge might indeed have had some basis, since Kak remained irreconciled to the Jammu faction in the Kashmir administration, and his obstinacy so angered the Maharaja that in 1853 he imposed a fine of eighty thousand rupees on him.[63]

The Dogra kingdom was divided into several provinces, including Jammu, Kashmir, and Ladakh, each of which was administered by a governor in the name of the Maharaja. Every province was in turn divided into several parganas (districts). The top officials in each pargana were the *zilahdar* (district officer), the *thanadar* (police officer), and the *qanungo* (revenue officer).[64] These officials were responsible for maintaining peace and collecting revenues in the area under their jurisdiction. Gulab Singh frequently toured the parganas, and during the latter part of his reign displayed special interest in the production of cotton, silk, saffron, chestnuts, tobacco, and opium.[65] However, few concrete measures were taken to promote or expand these industries. A plan to establish a sugar factory with the assistance of Martin Honigberger, the Transylvanian physician, also did not materialize.[66]

But if Gulab Singh failed to introduce a well-defined administrative system, his subjects did benefit from his penchant for law and order. The Maharaja imposed exemplary fines on dishonest shopkeepers and eventually decreed that all weights and measures used in the stores must be checked by the government and bear its seal.[67] Humiliating punishment was inflicted on thieves, who were often paraded in the streets with mud plastered on their faces.[68] The Maharaja was also concerned with administering speedy justice. Whenever the Maharaja rode out in public, any subject could gain his attention by holding up a rupee as a *nazarana* and by proclaiming, " 'Maharaj, arz hai!', that is, 'Maharaja, a petition!' " The Dogra ruler, it is said, "would pounce down like a hawk on the money, and having appropriated it would patiently hear out the petitioner."[69] Saif-ud-Din records another ingenious innovation: "[Gulab Singh] has installed a cage which hangs on cotton cords running from his palace to the [outside]. A complainant drops his petition into the cage which is personally pulled in and read by the Maharaja. If necessary a decision is immediately rendered, otherwise [the petition] is forwarded to the appropriate official for action."[70] But occasionally his obsession with justice bordered on the ludicrous. Once, when he suspected that his gardeners were making personal profit by selling roses from the royal gardens, he not only threatened to penalize them but ordered his policemen to "arrest anyone found holding a rose in his hand."[71]

Perhaps the Maharaja's most progressive accomplishment was in the field of social reform. At the urging of the British, he paid serious attention to the customs of sati and female infanticide, which were still prevalent in his kingdom. Outlawing these abominable practices, he imposed penal retribution on any offenders.[72] He also discouraged the killing of illegitimate infants and opened orphanages to protect them and other unfortunate children.[73]

Gulab Singh did little to improve his army. Up to 1845 the Company had formed a very exaggerated notion of the quality of the Jammu forces. Some British officials had indulged in such fantasies about the Dogra combative capabilities that they considered the Sikhs "to be inferior in martial qualities to the population of the Jummoo hills."[74] But such a laudatory estimate underwent a drastic revision at the end of the First Anglo-Sikh War when Gulab Singh solicited his benefactors' aid in training the Dogra troops.[75] Hardinge granted his request and assigned the job, as previously noted, to Captain Broome and Lieutenant Nicholson. But soon after their arrival at Jammu during April of 1846, they discovered that the Maharaja had no intention of "anglicizing" his troops. Nicholson complained: "I did not believe the Maharaja was really desirous of having our system of discipline introduced into his army; so it has turned out he merely asked for European officers because he was aware of the moral effect their presence would have at his Durbar in showing the terms of intimacy he was on with the British Government."[76] By the year's end Hardinge was so disgusted with the Dogra ruler's attitude that he not only recalled Broome and Nicholson but declared: "I do not intend to have any B. offr. for the purpose of superintending the discipline and drill of his army."[77] However, in spite of this incident, the British did make another attempt to impress upon Gulab Singh the need for army reform,[78] but to no avail. The salaries of his troops were pitifully low and often in arrears,[79] which occasionally encouraged desertion or unruly activities.[80] Such conditions obviously did not imbue his soldiers with a true sense of dedication or service. Nevertheless, Gulab Singh demanded high moral conduct from his troops. They were forbidden to gamble[81] or to visit brothels. One soldier, accused of carousing with a prostitute, was strung upside down in a cage and exhibited in public.[82] Another who was convicted of stealing was punished by having his hair burned and then being thrown into prison.[83] But such measures alone could not improve the quality of the Maharaja's forces. While visiting Kashmir in 1849, Henry Lawrence discovered on close scrutiny that the Maharaja's "army had at most 12,000 regular troops of poorish quality."[84] Edwardes was even less impressed. Describing the Dogra army as "ill-equipped, ill-clothed, and ill-paid," he concluded, "I think there cannot be anything more unfounded than the alarm so prevalent, both in India and England, about Goolab Sing's military resources."[85]

It is, therefore, easy to comprehend why the Maharaja lost Gilgit to the local rebels in 1851. During the same year Gulab Singh's troops also had difficulty in putting down an insurrection in Chilas, a territory adjoining Gilgit. Hundreds of Dogras were killed in a futile attempt to occupy the Chilas fort. When news of the disaster reached Srinagar, the Maharaja made frantic efforts to send reinforcements to the battleground. Resorting to begar, he rounded up thirty-four thousand men from Kashmir and Jammu and sent them to Chilas. In the fever of excitement he even conscripted children but subsequently spared most of them from the ordeal. Foodstuffs were often collected without payment, and on one occasion three to four hundred men, who had gathered at the Jama Masjid for the traditional Friday prayers, were marched to the Hari Parbat fort where they were forced to carry ammunition destined for Chilas to the boats in the lake below.[86] Though such actions deeply aroused the people, their complaints fell on deaf ears. Referring to Gulab Singh's complete preoccupation with the revolt, Saif-ud-Din recorded: "Nowadays Maharaja Sahib is, day and night, worrying and talking about Chilas. There is nothing else on his tongue except this subject."[87]

The Dogra-led forces finally reached Chilas and besieged its fort, but the Chilasis fought valiantly, their men defending the fort at night and their women keeping guard by day. The rebels inflicted heavy casualties on the Maharaja's forces and as many as fifteen hundred of his soldiers lost their lives during the hostilities.[88] However, despite the stubborn resistance of the Chilasis, Gulab Singh's efforts eventually bore fruit, and his troops entered the Chilas fort on the night of September 11.[89] The successful occupation of this fort, which reputedly had not fallen to a foe in fourteen hundred years,[90] so elated Gulab Singh that to mark the occasion he ordered eighty guns to be fired from Hari Parbat. Many Chilasi rebels were put to death,[91] but their chiefs, including Rahmatullah Khan and Dhuri Khan, were taken to Srinagar in chains and presented to the Maharaja. Fortunately for the leaders, they were released after taking an oath of allegiance to the Kashmir government and delivering up their sons as hostages.[92] The mildness of their punishment was a remarkable contrast to what they could have anticipated at the hands of Gulab Singh in similar circumstances during the 1830s.

Another problem which considerably agitated the Maharaja arose from the activities of the large number of junior Company officials and their families who began to use Kashmir as a resort. Many of these visitors were frightfully arrogant, acting as if Gulab Singh was personally indebted to each one of them for the grant of Kashmir and often proceeding to treat the valley as their own private fief. The Maharaja attempted to keep them in good humor by offering gifts and providing entertainments, but such attention was generally taken for granted. These officials frequently paid little or nothing for the goods procured from the natives,[93] and one English visitor even made off with money collected from the Kashmiris under false pretenses.[94] The Maharaja himself lamented that many visitors were taking "with them very large quantities of saffron, and other products of the country."[95] The Srinagar authorities also were offended by the open fraternization of some young English officials with the local prostitutes.[96] It was not long before the Company became aware of these problems, and Henry Lawrence personally spoke disgustedly of the misconduct of some of his countrymen.[97] In 1848 the British government ordered that all of its officials must first receive permission before setting foot in Kashmir.[98] This, however, did not eliminate the difficulties, as even the authorized tourists began to indulge in improper practices. After repeated protests by Gulab Singh, the British in 1852 negotiated an agreement with the Maharaja whereby a Company official was to serve in the valley every summer and regulate the conduct of European visitors.[99] From 1856 a special British representative was stationed in Kashmir for six months during a year and given wide powers to deal with the offenders.[100]

Gulab Singh was also successful in opposing British efforts to acquire a share of the pashmina trade and once, alluding to the fact that the product came from Tibet, remarked in sardonic jest: "My good friends the English Government having discovered their mistake, in supposing that the shawl wool is a product of my country, seem disposed to shear *me*."[101] Some British officials, like Napier and Edwardes, expressed an interest in terminating Gulab Singh's monopoly over the "China trade,"[102] which was conducted from Leh[103] and included not only the shawl wool from Tibet but also goods from Sinkiang. During 1846 and 1847 Henry Hardinge attempted to encourage the Tibetan wool traders to do business in British-held territories, but his endeavors were ineffectual.[104]

Although Gulab Singh resisted outside interference in his internal affairs, he always rolled out the red carpet for highly placed British officials, fully realizing the importance of remaining in their good graces. The senior officials, on their part, seemed as anxious to join the "Kashmir rush" as their subordinates, and the list of such guests reads like a *Who's Who* of India's British bureaucracy during that period. In the spring of 1846, even before Gulab Singh himself had entered Kashmir, a party of important English officials, including the Governor-General's two sons, Charles and Arthur Hardinge, and Bombay's future governor, Mountstuart Elphinstone, embarked on a trip to the vale. Arriving in Jammu during the second week of April, they were warmly received and showered with gifts by the

Maharaja.[105] The travelers then continued on to Kashmir[106] and spent several weeks there.[107] Other visitors included John Lawrence, Charles Napier, Colin Campbell, and Robert Montgomery. Even though many of the Maharaja's guests were privately so critical of him, they seldom hesitated to partake of his liberality.[108] He made arrangements for their trips into the interior, entertained them with fireworks and music, and pampered them with culinary delicacies from the royal kitchens.[109] But while entertaining his guests, Gulab Singh, in his eagerness to amuse them, at times naïvely revived memories of his sordid past. For instance, Charles Hardinge wrote that the Maharaja "produced a sort of panorama painted by a native artist, portraying the events of his life. In one there was a group of men pouring what was evidently molten lead down a prisoner's throat. We asked what they were doing, upon which he laughed heartily, and pointing to the caldron said, 'They are making tea!' "[110] Nicholson also recorded another sample of his host's morbid humor:

"Alas!" said Gulab Singh, "one of my best cooks tried to poison me."
"And what did you do?" asked Nicholson.
"I had him brought before me," explained the Maharajah gently, "and I ordered my people to separate the skin of the head from the neck behind the throat, then to flay the head, and then to put up the skin over the skull."
"Did he die?"
"Oh dear no! he lived for weeks."[111]

Incidents of such extreme barbarity, however, receded during his years as Maharaja. This perhaps resulted both from the mellowing influence of his advancing years and from his fear of adverse British reaction. After 1846 the very brutal punishments seem to have been mostly reserved for those accused of cow-killing. He often ordered the cow-killers' noses and ears cut off, and once burned down the houses of several farmers convicted of the same wrong-doing. Another offender's hair was sprinkled with oil and set aflame.[112] Although the Maharaja on occasion threatened to make cow-killing a capital crime, the maximum penalty he ever seems to have imposed was life imprisonment.[113]

A devout Hindu, Gulab Singh often went on pilgrimages. He celebrated Hindu festivals with considerable zeal and devotion, and ordered the closing of butcher shops during Dussehra and Dewali.[114] It was probably on the eve of these festivals that once, in a rare burst of generosity, he ordered a quantity of coins, equivalent in sum to his own weight, distributed among the impoverished.[115] But despite his own religious enthusiasm, the Maharaja continued to allow universal freedom of worship and, besides the dismissal of Muslims from high administrative positions, there are few instances of discrimination against adherents of other faiths. For example, the Saif-ud-Din papers reveal that, although Gulab Singh once permitted the erection of a temple over the site of a mosque, on another occasion he expressed disapproval at a similar occurrence, and personally intervened to save yet another mosque from demolition.[116] Again, while he denounced Hindu-Muslim marriages and conversions of Hindus to Islam,[117] he did not ban either of the practices. Thus Gulab Singh's religious policies must on the whole be considered moderate. A shrewd ruler, he was well aware of the advantages accruing from religious harmony in a kingdom inhabited by men of many creeds. He apparently considered this imperative in the province of Kashmir, which was predominantly Muslim.

It is perhaps because of his rigid adherence to religious conventions that not enough is known about the Maharaja's private life and the immediate members of his family. Unlike the licentious conduct of many at the Lahore court, including some flamboyant members of his own family, Gulab Singh seems to have been somewhat more restrained in his moral behavior. At the time of his death he had three wives,[118] but, as previously noted, only the youngest of his three legitimate sons, Ranbir Singh, still survived. Once known by the inelegant nickname of Pheenoo (pug-nosed), he served as governor of the Jammu province and acquired a controversial reputation as an administrator. Fanatically religious, he urged Hindus and Sikhs to boycott the *halal* (Muslim-butchered meat) shops and patronize instead the *jhatka* (Sikh-butchered meat) markets, and expressed indignation upon discovering that his advice was not fully heeded.[119] He was even more bitterly opposed to cow-slaughter than his father, and once ordered the body of a culprit, who had been starved to death in prison, thrown into a river. On another occasion, he had a female offender's head shaved and her tongue cut out before parading her in several villages as a warning to others.[120] Apart from such monomaniacal prejudices, Ranbir Singh may be considered to have been to a certain degree both progressive and judicious. He took measures to prevent the bloody Sunni-Shia clashes which took place among the Muslims on the occasion of the Muharram mournings.[121] Once he punished some men for their deliberate and mischievous failure to put out a fire in their neighbors' homes by ordering them to help in the rebuilding of the gutted property.[122] He was a learned man who displayed keen interest in Hindi,

Urdu, Persian, and Arabic, and even recommended that English replace Persian as the state's official language, but the proposal was rejected by his father.[123]

In addition to Ranbir Singh, one of the Maharaja's sons born out of wedlock, Jamiat Singh, was still living, but there is no reference to the whereabouts of the other illegitimate son, Chiman Singh. During the fifties a serious estrangement developed between Jamiat Singh and his father because of the former's affair with a Brahman widow. Gulab Singh was so enraged by such conduct that he had his bastard son viciously beaten, expelled from the palace, and threatened with disinheritance.[124] Jamiat Singh might conceivably be the half-brother so sadistically tortured to death by Ranbir Singh in 1857. Hesketh Pearson describes the gruesome execution in these words: "When the Indian Mutiny broke out Rhumbeer's brother rebelled, was caught, sentenced to death, suspended by his hair from a beam and lowered one inch into a cauldron of boiling oil; the next day two inches, the next three, and so on until he was extinct."[125]

Equally scant is the knowledge about the Maharaja's favorite pastimes. There is evidence that he enjoyed watching hog-dog bouts,[126] and also took delight in performances by musicians and dancers who accompanied him and his aides on chakwari (royal boat) rides.[127]

Some scattered information is also available on the Maharaja's appearance and manners during his reign. Although the advancing years had brought grey hair and made him somewhat corpulent, he was still quite handsome. Despite a lingering illness, he remained mentally alert and retained a good sense of humor. Even the British officials who were suspicious and ready to condemn Gulab Singh found him soft-spoken and sweet-tempered. Hodson characterized him as "a fine, tall, portly man, with a splendid expressive face, and most gentlemanly pleasing manner, and fine-toned voice."[128] Taylor termed him a "good-looking fellow, handsomely dressed."[129] Charles Hardinge called the Maharaja "a fine handsome old man"[130] and further described him as follows: "His features are regular, and the expression of his countenance more than usually mild, with an affectation of openness. Indeed, it has been remarked that a 'man might almost take him for his grandmother.' "[131] A talented artist, Charles sketched a portrait of Gulab Singh during his visit to Jammu in 1846. It appeared during the following year in a large volume along with several other fascinating pictures he had drawn in India.[132] In view of his faithful executions of numerous historical and scenic spots in Kashmir and Panjab, Charles' sketch of the Dogra leader may be considered among the few true-to-life portraits of the man in existence.[133]

Despite Gulab Singh's gradual abandonment of some of the most repugnant traits so evident in his early career and the relative political stability of his kingdom, most British officials remained disenchanted with his overall image as Maharaja. Dalhousie, notwithstanding his change of heart toward Gulab Singh since the Wazirabad conference, typified such disillusionment on the eve of his retirement: ". . . in 1846, we unwittingly handed over [Kashmir] to a chief who has proved himself a veritable tyrant, and who already appears to be the founder of a race of tyrants."[134]

Deeply apprehensive of these persistent British misgivings and only too conscious of the arbitrary methods employed by Dalhousie to annex several other princely states, Gulab Singh worried that an orderly succession might not follow his demise. Failing health increased his concern. Determined to insure the continuance of the Dogra dynasty, he abdicated early in 1856 in favor of Ranbir Singh, the heir apparent. The new Maharaja was installed amidst pomp and show on February 8, 1856, and Gulab Singh thereupon assumed the governorship of the Kashmir province. For all practical purposes, however, Gulab Singh continued to be the real sovereign of the kingdom until his death. But this maneuver did not relieve him of all his anxieties. As late as 1857, when he became aware of the disparaging reports about the Dogra administration being published in the London press, he nervously resorted to astrologers in an attempt to ascertain British intentions regarding his state. In an act unworthy of his status, he even attempted to collect testimonials from British visitors in Kashmir to refute the newspaper charges.[135] Nonetheless, controversy over the Dogra rule did not dissipate but continued for decades after his death.[136]

Gulab Singh first revealed signs of diabetes in 1851[137] and, despite various treatments[138] over the years, his condition failed to improve.[139] As the disease advanced, the Dogra ruler became progressively more superstitious and even turned to men who were considered well versed in witchcraft to restore his health.[140] During the summer of 1857 he suffered from an attack of typhoid, which further weakened him. He eventually lost consciousness on July 28 and succumbed on Sunday, August 7, at 2 P.M.[141] As word of his death spread, Srinagar went into a state of mourning. Arrangements for his funeral began immediately but were complicated by the insistence of Gulab Singh's three Ranis to commit sati with their husband. When this request was refused, one of the Ranis jumped from an upper-story window of the royal apartments in a vain attempt to kill herself.[142] Referring to the stubborn determination of the widows, Mrs. Urmston, who was with her husband in Kashmir at the time, wrote: "If denied a public suttee, they would still perish with their husband, using daggers or poison to accomplish the last sacrifice of religion and affection. Already they sat decked in their richest jewels, as brides for the celestial marriage."[143] It was only after considerable persuasion that the Ranis were prevented from carrying out their threat.[144]

The day after his death Gulab Singh was given a royal funeral, which was attended by a multitude of mourners. Saif-ud-Din penned a vivid eyewitness account of the funeral ceremonies:

At last Maharaja Sahib's remains were laid upon the bier and with all stately honors carried towards Ram Bagh. [Men] mounted on an elephant showered coins, gold and silver, worth about 5,000 rupees over the bier of Maharaja Sahib. From the parade grounds to Ram Bagh black-turbaned troops stood at attention and saluted. The bier was preceded by the bands and standard [bearers] of all the regiments. The bands played the funeral march theme. Ornately decorated horses and elephants also accompanied the procession. From Sher Garhi to Ram Bagh, a distance of about two miles, there was a mass of people, including the Panjabis and Kashmiris [of Srinagar], and the Hindu and Muslim villagers who had poured in from the mountains. It is estimated that between fifty and sixty thousand persons had assembled on both sides of the road, and there were hundreds of boats in the river.[145] . . . At about three in the afternoon the procession reached Ram Bagh and the Maharaja Sahib's remains were laid upon a huge royal pyre made of fuel, almonds, and raisins. Around the body were placed a few maunds of sandalwood. Then Mian Pratap Singh [Ranbir Singh's son] put a flame to the pyre and it was reduced to ashes. Afterwards thousands of people, including the members of the royal family, civilian and army officials, soldiers, servants and subjects of the Maharaja Sahib excepting Brahmans, Muslims, and Sikhs, shaved their heads and beards. Also on that day all the Hindus in their sorrow cut off their hair . . .[146]

The government decreed an unusually strict mourning for a prolonged period. Mrs. Urmston recorded:

Every shop here has been closed since the death of the Rajah. No meat is allowed to be slaughtered, nor marriage celebrated. . . . No meat or fish is to be eaten for a whole year. All nets have been seized, the Brahmins teaching that the soul of the late Prince might change into a fish. Not a light is allowed after sunset, for the people are ordered to sit in darkness.[147]

When Gulab Singh died, Ranbir Singh was in Jammu and could not reach Srinagar in time for the funeral. He returned[148] in a state of shock "tearing his hair, rending his clothes, putting dust on his head, and giving way to all Eastern expressions of grief."[149] Considering the extent of his personal sorrow and the historic significance of the passing of the man who had dominated the Dogra scene for over forty years, it was perhaps only after some time that Ranbir Singh realized that he had become the Maharaja in fact as well as in name.

12 Conclusion

*t*HE foregoing study should establish beyond doubt that Gulab Singh was one of the most controversial figures in the history of India during the nineteenth century. His successful career indeed invokes admiration. Born into a princely but petty hill family in Jammu, he rose to be the founder of the Dogra dynasty of the state of Kashmir. Through his commander, Zorawar Singh, he conquered Ladakh and, for the first time in India's long history, made it a part of the subcontinent. One of the shrewdest diplomats that India has produced in recent times, he practised this art in so masterly a fashion that his contemporaries were led to characterize him as the "Ulysses of the hills" and "the Talleyrand of the East." It is surely this skill, combined with his sharp wit and remarkable levelheadedness, which helped him survive both physically and politically in the very bloody and turbulent times in which he lived.

But the life of Gulab Singh also invites contempt. He was an unprincipled liar and a self-seeking opportunist who would stoop to any means to achieve his ends. He was a ruthless tyrant who could brook no opposition to his rule. He remorselessly inflicted the most sadistic punishments upon his opponents although, mercifully, the application of torture as an instrument of his policy gradually decreased in the later part of his life. He was faithful to no one except himself, and his treacherous betrayal of the Lahore government at the end of the First Anglo-Sikh War and immediately thereafter provides perhaps the most glaring proof of this trait. Moreover, although he brought a degree of tranquillity to Kashmir during the eleven years of his reign as Maharaja, in the imposition and collection of taxes he acted as a veritable economic vampire.

Above all, the Dogra ruler was a pragmatist who was probably the first to perceive that, in the anarchy which followed at Lahore after Dhian Singh's assassination, the extension of the Company's power across the Sutlej was inevitable, and he concluded that his future could only be insured by collaborating with the British. The Dogra ruler was a scheming, calculating, and crafty strategist. He did not believe in taking unnecessary risks, and he had no scruples about switching loyalties if the exigencies of the situation required it. He had the uncanny foresight to avoid hasty military involvement in a clash of arms between adversaries stronger than himself, and the unerring instinct to choose the right moment to align himself with the winning side and exploit it to his advantage. In a memorable passage, Herbert Edwardes sums up rather well the true character and role of Gulab Singh: "His was the cunning of *the vulture.* He sat apart in the clear atmosphere of passionless distance, and with sleepless eye beheld the lion and the tiger contending for the deer. And when the combatants were dead, he spread his wings, sailed calmly down, and feasted where they fought."[1]

Appendixes
List of Abbreviations
Notes
Glossary
Bibliography
Index

Appendix *a*

A Folk Song of the Poonch Warriors

This folk song,[1] which was composed primarily in the Panjabi tongue with a sprinkling of Urdu and Poonchi words, has been handed down orally through the years. A highly partisan but none-theless poignant ballad, it traces Shams-ud-Din's determined attempt to throw off the Dogra yoke, his allies' repudiation of him after Gulab Singh's invasion of Poonch, and finally his heinous murder at the home of the Terola chief. Although the song is commonly entitled *Shams te Malli Sabzalli di War* [The Ballad of Shams, Malli, and Sabzalli], it mentions Malli and Sabzalli only once. How-ever, it does contain several references to Shams-ud-Din's nephew, Raj Wali, who collaborated with him and shared his fate.

Praised be the Lord and his black-robed Prophet.
Praised be the Saint of Baghdad who rescued the wrecked ships from the sea.
Great was Raja Rustam, lord of all Poonch,
After him was born Wali Khan Shams-ud-Din, the warrior,
Who from his youth dreamt of independence.

He mounted a black stallion and rode to Jammu
Where Gulab Singh inquired, "You are a soldier? From what state?"
"O, Raja," said Shams, "Poonch is my land and I am a warrior of the Maldyal tribe."
And Gulab Singh bestowed on him a robe of honor, a horse, and a pair of gold bangles.

Then Shams Khan daringly demanded,
"Hand over the administration of Poonch to me."
The Raja agreed, but warned him, "Do not steal my revenues."
And Shams promised to remit the taxes faithfully.

Shams returned home, opened free kitchens for the poor, and arranged feasts.
But soon the village elders and accountants met to determine the amount of revenue owed to Gulab Singh.

"Thirty-six thousand rupees," they told Shams, "are due."
Stung by such oppressive taxation, Shams and his nephew Raj Wali
  decided to rebel.
"Let us recruit a force of valiant solders," they said.

What a wonderful pair God had created in Shams and Raj Wali.
The forts of Tatwala and Bhalangai Wala Shams took by storm,
A dozen other fortresses fell, and Tara Dogra was captured.
He begged for mercy in the name of God and offered submission.
Shams Khan then sent emissaries to the tribes of Kakka and Bamba,
Which assured Shams of their full support.

When news of the revolt reached Gulab Singh, he became exceedingly
  angry,
And commanded Dewan Dhannoo with five hundred soldiers to march on
  Poonch.
Shams advanced to meet him.
Looking scornfully at the Dogra commander he exclaimed,
"I know you are Dewan Dhannoo. But I am Shams Khan, the warrior.
"I shall give you such a battle that people will sing tales about it,
"I shall rip you apart with my sword and scatter your limbs around."

Dewan Dhannoo beat a hasty retreat down the hill from Chappra
And galloped back to Jammu. There he raised a hue and cry and told
  Gulab Singh,
"O Raja, if you remain at Jammu, you shall have to wash your hands of
  Poonch,
"Shams has now risen in open rebellion."

When Gulab Singh heard this he trembled with rage
And at once ordered his forces to return from Kishtwar.
He recruited additional soldiers and collected laborers to work as porters;
The iron of the blacksmiths was confiscated for casting shells;
The yarn of the weavers was taken for making tents.

Gulab Singh himself assumed command and hastened to Poonch.
Hearing this, the Kashmiri camp followers deserted Shams.
The Raja first marched to Pindi Jhelum and then entered Pothhar.
His third camp he established at the village of Bagh.
There he flayed alive Malli and Sabzalli and stuffed their skins with
  straw,
Even innocent young children he flayed alive.

Then the Raja searched for Shams and questioned Muzaffar Khan of Uri,
Who feigned complete ignorance to save his own skin.
But Fate led Shams and Raj Wali to the village of Dhagwala
Where Nur Khan Terola, the Chief, invited them to dinner
In order to ensnare and disarm them.
At midnight Raj Wali woke and cried, "O, Uncle! I have had a terrible
  dream.

"I have seen myself being served a dish full of blood.
"Surely it is a sign that our death is near."

The ill-omened dream foretold the truth; they were betrayed.
Shams felt deep chagrin at the way he had been tricked,
And in the dead of night tried to escape over the wall,
But Nur Khan saw him and dragged him down.
Then Agar Khan of Rajauri unsheathed his sword to kill Shams.
The cornered rebel looked to the left and looked to the right, but no
    friend did he find.
Alas! Who could be his ally at this, his final hour?
Shams turned to Nur Khan and cried, "O, brother! You seem determined
    to commit this treachery.
"But remember that valiant soldiers are not afraid to sacrifice their lives
    for the sake of the Holy Quran."
His enemies remained unmoved.
They beheaded Shams and Raj Wali and carried their heads to Bagh.
There Gulab Singh saw the severed heads and was filled with joy.

Praise be to your mother, O, Shams Khan,
A son like you no other mother will ever bear.

Appendix **B**

The Treaty of Amritsar, March 16, 1846

Treaty between the British Government on the one part, and Muharaja Golab Singh of Jummoo on the other, concluded, on the part of the British Government, by Frederick Currie, Esq., and Brevet Major Henry Montgomery Lawrence, acting under the orders of the Right Honorable Sir Henry Hardinge, G.C.B., one of Her Britannic Majesty's most Honorable Privy Council, Governor General, appointed by the Honorable Company to direct and control all their affairs in the East Indies, and by Muharaja Golab Singh in person.

Article 1. The British Government transfers and makes over, for ever, in independent possession, to Muharaja Golab Singh, and the heirs male of his body, all the hilly or mountainous country, with its dependencies, situated to the eastward of the river Indus, and westward of the river Ravee, including Chumba and excluding Lahool, being part of the territory ceded to the British Government by the Lahore State, according to the provisions of article 4 of the treaty of Lahore, dated March 9th, 1846.

Article 2. The eastern boundary of the tract transferred by the foregoing article to Muharaja Golab Singh shall be laid down by commissioners appointed by the British Government and Muharaja Golab Singh respectively, for that purpose, and shall be defined in a separate engagement, after survey.

Article 3. In consideration of the transfer made to him and his heirs by the provisions of the foregoing articles, Muharaja Golab Singh will pay to the British Government the sum of seventy-five lacs of rupees (Nanukshahee), fifty lacs to be paid on ratification of this treaty, and twenty-five lacs on or before the 1st of October of the current year, A.D. 1846.

Article 4. The limits of the territories of Muharaja Golab Singh shall not be at any time changed without the concurrence of the British Government.

Article 5. Muharaja Golab Singh will refer to the arbitration of the British Government any disputes or questions that may arise between himself and the Government of Lahore, or any other neighboring State, and will abide by the decision of the British Government.

Article 6. Muharaja Golab Singh engages for himself and heirs, to join, with the whole of his military force, the British troops, when employed within the hills, or in the territories adjoining his possessions.

Article 7. Muharaja Golab Singh engages never to take, or retain, in his service any British subject, nor the subject of any European or American State, without the consent of the British Government.

Article 8. Muharaja Golab Singh engages to respect, in regard to the territory transferred to him, the provisions of articles 5, 6, and 7, of the separate engagement between the British Government and the Lahore Durbar, dated March 11th, 1846.

Article 9. The British Government will give its aid to Muharaja Golab Singh, in protecting his territories from external enemies.

Article 10. Muharaja Golab Singh acknowledges the supremacy of the British Government, and will, in token of such supremacy, present annually to the British Government one horse, twelve perfect shawl goats of approved breed (six male, and six female), and three pairs of Cashmere shawls.

This treaty, consisting of ten articles, has been this day settled by Frederick Currie, Esq., and Brevet Major Henry Montgomery Lawrence, acting under the directions of the Right Honorable Sir Henry Hardinge, G.C.B., Governor General, on the part of the British Government, and by Muharaja Golab Singh in person; and the said treaty has been this day ratified by the seal of the Right Honorable Sir Henry Hardinge, G.C.B., Governor General.

Done at Umrutsir, this 16th day of March, in the year of our Lord 1846, corresponding with the 17th day of Rubbee-ool-awul, 1262, Hijree.

Appendix **C**

Did Gulab Singh
Pay for Kashmir?

According to the third article of the Treaty of Amritsar, Gulab Singh was required to pay the stipulated sum of seventy-five lakhs of rupees in two installments, "fifty lacs . . . on ratification of this treaty, and twenty-five lacs on or before the 1st of October of the current year, A.D. 1846." Some sources, like the anonymous author of *Kashmir-ke-Halaat*, have implied that the sale of Kashmir was a hoax, and that the British never really collected the required sum from the Dogra ruler.[1] Such gossip continues to be heard occasionally on the Indian sub-continent till this day. However, there is substantial evidence that, though late, Gulab Singh did pay the amount in full. In a letter dated May 12, 1846, Hardinge informed Ellenborough, that the Maharaja "has paid his first instalment of 50 lacs."[2] The Governor-General communicated similar information to the Secret Committee in September.[3] Even more important, however, is the following table of payments prepared on October 10, 1848, by the Company's financial department at Calcutta, which clearly indicates that by the end of July 1848 Gulab Sing had paid most of his debt:

In 1845/46		497,204– 4– 9
In 1846/47		5,619,581–10– 0
In 1847/48		858,541–12– 8
In 1848/49		
May	97,997–13– 0	
June	48,156– 7– 6	
July	0– 0– 0	146,154– 4– 6
		7,121,481–15–11
Balance due to the British Government		
on the 31st July 1848		378,518– 0– 1[4]

The rest of the amount, totalling less than four lakhs of rupees, was paid by the end of March 1850, and a copy of "The Final Receipt for the Purchase of Kashmir," signed by the members of the Board of Administration of Panjab, is on exhibition at the Panjab Record Office Museum in Lahore.[5]

Appendix O

The Secret Dispatches
of Saif-ud-Din

The confidential dispatches of Mirza Saif-ud-Din, written from Srinagar between 1846 and 1859 to the British authorities at Lahore,[1] provide one of the most important sources for the early history of the Dogra rule in Kashmir. For some inexplicable reason Saif-ud-Din went through the laborious task of making two copies of his Persian letters. The British, after studying their copies, in all probability destroyed them. But Saif-ud-Din or someone else carefully concealed the duplicates in the hollow of a wall inside his home where they remained until their discovery in 1960 by Mirza Kemal-ud-Din, a descendant. This enormous manuscript, comprising twelve volumes, has since been deposited with the Government of Kashmir's Research and Publication Department at Srinagar. It consists of over seventeen hundred 15 x 9½ inch folios. Each page averages about twenty-five lines of Persian shikasta.[2] The manuscript is to a large extent in excellent condition. Though white ants destroyed portions of the first fifty-three folios of the tenth volume, the other volumes have escaped with only scattered and minor holes.

It was Saif-ud-Din's father, Mirza Abad Beg, who first became a British informer[3] in the 1830s through the efforts of the noted traveler, Godfrey Thomas Vigne.[4] After Abad Beg's death Henry Lawrence recruited his son to perform the same task, and from 1846 Saif-ud-Din was engaged as a *khufia navis*[5] (secret writer).

Gulab Singh became aware of Saif-ud-Din's activities soon after he became the Maharaja. Immensely displeased, the Dogra sovereign forbade Saif-ud-Din's attendance at his darbar, and confiscated his jagirs,[6] but refrained from inflicting further punishment for fear of infuriating the informer's employers. In 1848 Gulab Singh accused him of reporting news "right and wrong, true and false."[7] Five years later the Kashmir ruler was delighted to learn that the British authorities were contemplating the termination of Saif-ud-Din's services because of postal delays in receiving his reports.[8] But his relief was only temporary. Saif-ud-Din's dispatches continued and so did Gulab Singh's discomfiture. As late as 1857 the Maharaja remained unreconciled to the presence of the Company's spy in his capital and asked his Prime Minister, Jawala Sahai, "to get this seditious and imprudent man dismissed from British service by any possible means."[9]

Saif-ud-Din had the unenviable position not only of being stigmatized for being in the pay of the British but also of living under constant fear of reprisal at the hands of the Maharaja. He often complained of official harassment. At one time he begged the British to secure him employment outside Kashmir and wrote: "The displeasure of the ruler has made it impossible for me to live here."[10]

Saif-ud-Din's dispatches capture in minute detail the everyday occurrences during the entire reign of Gulab Singh and the first few years of Ranbir Singh's rule. The information in his communications is arranged in chronological order. Each dispatch either bears a specific date or refers to the months it covers. To some degree this work may be compared to the now famous "Umdat-ut-Tawarikh" written by Sohan Lal Suri, who provided extensive eyewitness accounts of the Sikh rule in Panjab. But unlike Suri, Saif-ud-Din was not an official scribe and, as noted, was prohibited from appearing at Gulab Singh's court. He collected most of his information from others who were allowed admittance, but claimed he never sent it to the British before verifying it.[11] He also gathered news of events taking place in Srinagar and intelligence reaching the capital from other parts of the Dogra kingdom. His reports, for the most part, must be considered impartial[12] because Saif-ud-Din, whatever his own sentiments toward Gulab Singh, was aware that the British authorities had employed him mainly to acquaint them with the true state of affairs in Kashmir. Consequently, baseless and fabricated accounts could have jeopardized the informer's credibility with the British upon whom he depended both for his economic livelihood and physical security. His writings, therefore, betray little personal malevolence toward the Maharaja, and his dispatches, as the last four chapters of this book indicate, contain both disparaging and commendatory accounts of Gulab Singh's reign.[13]

List of Abbreviations

"AIP'"
"Abstract of Intelligence from the Punjaub," in *Panjab On The Eve of First Sikh War*, ed. H. R. Gupta (Hoshiarpur, 1956).

ASW
Ganda Singh, ed., *Private Correspondence Relating To the Anglo-Sikh Wars* (Madras, 1955).

"BDSL"
"Board's Drafts of Secret Letters," MSS in the India Office Library, London.

BGLD
Papers relating to the Articles of Agreement concluded between the British Government and the Lahore Durbar (London, 1847).

"CSD"
"Chattar Singh Collection of Documents," Persian MSS in the Panjab State Archives, Patiala.

Dalhousie's Minute
A Minute by the Marquis of Dalhousie, etc. (London, 1856).

DG
Delhi Gazette.

Edwardes Memorials
Emma Edwardes, *Memorials of the Life and Letters of Major-General Sir Herbert B. Edwardes* (London, 1886).

"EP"
"Ellenborough Papers," MS in the Public Record Office, London.

"ESLI"
"Enclosures to Secret Letters from India," MSS in the India Office Library, London.

FPNWF
Further Papers relating to the Late Hostilities on the North-Western Frontier of India (London, 1846).

"Gulab Nama"
Kirpa Ram, "Gulab Nama," MS in the Panjab State Archives, Patiala.

IOL
India Office Library, London.

"LI"
"Lahore Intelligence," in "Political Correspondence," transcribed records in the Panjab State Archives, Patiala.

LN
Lahore News, reprinted from the *Delhi Gazette* by the *Times* (London).

"PA"   "Panjab Akhbar," in *The Panjab In 1839–40*, ed.
                            Ganda Singh (Amritsar, 1952).

"PBI"   "Panjab Intelligence," in Secret Department,
                            "Enclosures to Secret Letters from India," MSS
                            in the India Office Library, London.

"PC"   "Political Correspondence," transcribed records
                            in the Panjab States Archives, Patiala.

PHNI   *Papers relating to the Late Hostilities on the
                            North-Western Frontier of India* (London, 1846).

"PI"   "Panjab Intelligence," in *The Panjab In 1839–
                            40*, ed. Ganda Singh (Amritsar, 1952).

PMP   *Papers relating to the Mutiny in the Punjab, in
                            1857* (London, 1859).

"PPHH"   "Private Papers of Henry Hardinge," MSS in the
                            possession of Lady Helen Hardinge, Penshurst,
                            Kent.

PRAL   *Papers relating to the Articles of Agreement for
                            the Administration of the State of Lahore* (Lon-
                            don, 1847).

PRP   *Papers relating to the Punjab, 1847–49* (London,
                            1849).

PSA   Panjab State Archives, Patiala.

RD   Record Department

RPD   Research and Publication Department, Srinagar.

SC   Secret Committee

SD   Secret Department

"SDS"   Mirza Saif-ud-Din, "Secret Dispatches," MSS in
                            the Research and Publication Department, Srin-
                            agar.

"Umdat-ut-Tawarikh"   Sohan Lal Suri, "Umdat-ut-Tawarikh," tran-
                            scribed Persian chronicle in Panjab State Ar-
                            chives, Patiala.

Notes

Preface

1. H. M. L. Lawrence, *Adventures of An Officer in The Punjaub*, 2 vols. (London, 1846; reprint ed., Delhi, 1970), 2:364n.

2. Kirpa Ram succeeded his father, Dewan Jawala Sahai, as the Prime Minister of Kashmir under Ranbir Singh. He wrote another book entitled *Gulzar-e-Kashmir* (Lahore, 1870), which also contains complimentary references to Gulab Singh but deals largely with the geography and economy of the Dogra kingdom.

3. A second impression of this book was produced in 1953 under the title *The Founding of the Kashmir State*.

4. See Prem Nath Bazaz, *The History of Struggle for Freedom in Kashmir* (New Delhi, 1954), p. 129.

5. They include Khushwant Singh, *A History of the Sikhs*, 2 vols. (Princeton, 1963, 1966), and *The Fall of the Kingdom of the Punjab* (Calcutta, 1962); Ganda Singh, ed., *Private Correspondence relating to the Anglo-Sikh Wars* (Madras, 1955); Sita Ram Kohli, *Sunset of the Sikh Empire* (New Delhi, 1967).

6. Foremost among these are Godfrey T. Vigne, *A Personal Narrative of a visit to Ghuzni, Kabul, and Afghanistan*, 2nd ed. (London, 1843), and *Travels In Kashmir, Ladak, Iskardo, etc.*, 2 vols. (London, 1842); Herbert B. Edwardes, *A Year on the Punjab Frontier, in 1848–49*, 2 vols. (London, 1851); Emma Edwardes, *Memorials of the Life and Letters of Major-General Sir Herbert B. Edwardes*, 2 vols. (London, 1886); William Napier, *The Life and Opinions of General Sir Charles James Napier* (London, 1857), vols. 3 and 4.

7. Smyth's work appeared in 1847; Gardner's memoirs in 1898.

8. Both are characterized by their inordinate attention to violence, intrigue, and scandal in the Sikh state, and indeed make interesting reading. But C. Grey, *European Adventurers of Northern India, 1785 to 1849*, ed. H. L. O. Garrett (Lahore, 1929), labels the memoirs edited by Pearse as a "Roguemontic narrative" (p. 11), and conclusively proves that Gardner, who served under both the Sikhs and Gulab Singh, twisted facts and conjured up fantastic tales to exaggerate his own part in the politics of the northwest (pp. 78, 241, 265–91). As a result, Smyth's *History* also cannot be depended upon, since he himself acknowledges (p. xv) that he compiled his book "chiefly from the notes of" Gardner.

1 The Years Under Ranjit Singh

1. Gulab may be translated "rose" or "rose-water"; Singh means "lion" or "warrior."

2. "Gulab Nama," p. 111.

3. Gulab Singh's name and his long association with Lahore might lead some to the erroneous conclusion that he was a Sikh. But in addition to the Sikhs who use Singh as their middle or last name, many Hindus from the warrior castes also add that appellation as a cognomen. Therefore, although every Sikh is a Singh, every Singh is not necessarily a Sikh.

4. It has been generally accepted that the Dogras belonged to the distinguished Rajput class. But Vigne, *Narrative*, p. 254, challenged the validity of such a claim by arguing that the components of the word *Dogra*, " 'do', two; and 'rug', a vein,"

connoted an individual "of mixed blood and low caste." However, P. N. K. Bamzai, *A History of Kashmir* (Delhi, 1962), p. 588, writes that the term *Dogra* originated from the Sanskrit word *dogirath* (two lakes) and alludes to the Mansar and Siroinsar lakes near Jammu.

5. According to "A Journey to Cashmeer," p. 19, European MS in IOL, the Dogras "are the Rughoolbunsee Rajpoots descending from the old solar race, and have been in possession of this country [Jammu] since immemorial times." Lepel H. Griffin, *Ranjit Singh* (Oxford, 1911), p. 189, writes that Jammu was "ruled for several thousand years by a Hindu dynasty of Rajput blood." "Gulab Nama," p. 97, traces the Dogras' origin to the *Ramayana*. Bamzai, p. 588, believes that the Dogra principalities were carved out of the Jammu territories by warriors from Delhi and Avadh about the time of Alexander's incursion into India. K. M. Panikkar, *Gulab Singh* (London, 1930), p. 9, states that the Dogras are the descendants of Rajputs from Panjab who escaped into the Jammu hills in the wake of Muhammad bin Ghori's invasions during the twelfth century.

6. Shahamat Ali, *The Sikhs and Afghans* (London, 1847), p. 79.

7. *A note on the Jammu and Kashmir State* (Jammu, 1928), p. 2.

8. Bamzai, p. 588.

9. S. Ali, pp. 82–83.

10. An appellation of respect given to highborn Dogras.

11. "Tarikh Nama," p. 32, Persian MS in PSA.

12. Debi Parshad, *Gulshan-e-Panjab* (Bareilly, 1850), p. 21.

13. S. Ali, p. 87.

14. "Gulab Nama," pp. 108–9.

15. *History of the Panjab* (London, 1846), 2:202.

16. Vigne, *Narrative*, p. 254.

17. *A History of the Sikhs* first appeared during 1849 in London.

18. J. D. Cunningham, p. 189.

19. See his appendix xxv.

20. See p. 469n. For an extensive account of Gulab Singh's forebears, read Ganesh Das Badhrah, "Raj-Darshani," fols. 201a–259b, Persian MS in the British Museum, London.

21. Edwin Arnold, *The Marquis of Dalhousie's Administration of British India* (London, 1862), 1:33n.

22. Victor Jacquemont, *Letters From India* (London, 1834), 2:9. However, Alexander Burnes, *Travels into Bokhara*, 2nd ed. (London, 1839), 1:287, attests that the Dogra was not completely illiterate by stating that he "can read."

23. "Gulab Nama," p. 127.

24. Ibid., pp. 128–29.

25. Kanihya Lal, *Tarikh-e-Panjab* (Lahore, 1877), p. 465.

26. *Edwardes Memorials*, 1:67–68. Other sources, however, provide different reasons for Gulab Singh's recruitment. According to the "Tarikh Nama," p. 39, the Sikh ruler hired Gulab Singh to fulfill a pledge made to his own father, Mahan Singh, who "at the time of his death left a will with him to show consideration to Mian Mota or his descendants." On the other hand, John H. Gordon, *The Sikhs* (London, 1904), p. 101, asserts that Ranjit Singh purposely enlisted diverse people like the Dogras and the Muslims into his army because the "opposing elements were useful to him on occasions."

27. See *Edwardes' Memorials*, 1:68; Muhammad Latif, *History of the Panjab* (Calcutta, 1891; reprint ed., New Delhi, 1964), pp. 439–40; Panikkar, p. 19; James P. Ferguson, *Kashmir* (London, 1961), p. 52.

28. Vigne, *Narrative*, p. 250.

29. "Gulab Nama," p. 132, claims that Gulab Singh started as the commander of a regiment at a monthly salary of 275 rupees. This statement seems exaggerated when compared to several other writers, who indicate that the Jammu brothers started out far more modestly. Latif, *History*, p. 440; J. D. Cunningham, pp. 189–90; Vigne, *Narrative*, pp. 250–51; Henry Steinbach, *The Punjaub: being a brief account of the country of the Sikhs* (London, 1845), p. 20; S. Ali, p. 92; *Edwardes Memorials*, 1:66, all agree that Gulab Singh enlisted as a "ghorcharah", or horseman. Although Steinbach and S. Ali write that Gulab Singh was recruited at one and two rupees per day respectively, according to *Edwardes' Memorials*, he started at merely twenty rupees per month.

30. Masson once accused Alexander Burnes and other Englishmen in Afghanistan of being "too lax in their relations with the Kabuli women." This earned him the abiding hostility of Henry Lawrence, who "lost no opportunity of deriding, ridiculing, or even abusing him in the pages of the Calcutta Review." See Grey, pp. 198–99. While Grey himself is highly complimentary to Masson, even he suggests (p. 203) that on at least one occasion he might have been given to a "certain amount . . . [of] brag and exaggeration."
31. Charles Masson, Narrative of Various Journeys in Balochistan, Afghanistan, and the Panjab (London, 1842), 1:441.
32. G. Carmichael Smyth, ed., A History of the Reigning Family of Lahore (Calcutta, 1847), p. 99.
33. Lawrence wrote the Adventures of An Officer in The Punjaub as a novel on Sikh politics in which fact was intentionally intermingled with fantasy. His wife, Honoria, collaborated with him, and her lively imagination added an aura of romance to the story. Until recently, several historians, including C. Grey, mistook the Adventures to be a reliable work and utilized it as a book of reference. For more details on the circumstances leading to the appearance of this piquant novel, see John L. Morison, Lawrence of Lucknow (London, 1934), pp. 93, 98–102.
34. Lawrence, 1:33.
35. "Gulab Nama," p. 138.
36. Ibid., p. 155.
37. K. Lal, pp. 470–71.
38. Ibid., p. 476.
39. "Gulab Nama," pp. 154–56.
40. Amar Nath, Zafarnama-e-Ranjit Singh, ed. Sita Ram Kohli (Lahore, 1928), p. 141.
41. "A Journey to Cashmeer," p. 22.
42. Ganeshi Lal, "Siyahat-e-Kashmir," fols. 13–14, Persian MS in PSA; K. Lal, p. 480.
43. K. Lal. pp. 483–84.
44. "Gulab Nama," pp. 166–67.
45. K. Lal, p. 484.
46. Ibid.
47. Ibid.
48. Latif, History, p. 414.
49. This route probably passed through the city of Jammu. According to one source, eighteenth-century Jammu "was a town of considerable commercial resort, as it was then an entrepot between Cashmere and Hindostan." See The History of the Sikhs (Calcutta, 1846), p. 19.
50. For more on the pashmina commerce, see my Chapter 2.
51. Copy of an agreement between Maharaja Ranjit Singh and the Jammu family, November 15, 1820, "CSD."
52. "Umdat-ut-Tawarikh," vol. 2, pt. 1, pp. 282–83.
53. S. Ali, p. 94.
54. See Henry T. Prinsep, Origin of the Sikh Power in the Punjab (Calcutta, 1834), p. 125; S. Ali, pp. 101–2.
55. "Umdat-ut-Tawarikh," vol. 2, pt. 3, p. 288.
56. K. Lal, p. 479. But Vigne, Travels, 1:181, provides a different version of the episode. According to him, the Dogra leader feigned friendship for his former master and advised him to reinforce his defences because a Sikh attack was imminent. Upon receiving the warning, writes Vigne, Raja Tegh Singh "and his people prepared for resistance, and sent an answer to say that they had done so." However, Vigne continues, Gulab Singh then changed his tune, claiming falsely that Tegh Singh's own counsellors had secretly invited the Sikhs to march upon Kishtwar, and informed the Raja "that he must be joking to talk of resistance when the chief men of his country, who pretended to be his friends, were opposed to him."
57. "Gulab Nama," p. 183.
58. History of the Panjab, 2:204; Hugh K. Trevaskis, The Land of the Five Rivers (London, 1928), p. 204; Vigne, Travels, 1:182–83. Vigne also states that the Dogra "bribed Tegh Singh's servant to poison his master for a reward of 10,000 rupees; and his death was effected by mixing the poison in a cup of sherbet."
59. "Gulab Nama," p. 219.
60. C. U. Aitchison, Collection of Treaties, Engagements and Sanads relating to India and Neighboring Countries (Calcutta, 1909), 11:245.
61. See copy of an agreement between Maharaja Ranjit Singh and the Jammu brothers, June 3, 1822, "CSD."

62. See copy of an agreement between Chet Singh and the Jammu brothers, June 13, 1822, "CSD." Following this transaction, Chet Singh and his family left Jammu and migrated south of the Sutlej. However, S. Ali, p. 90, writes that after Chet Singh died, his son, Devi Singh, was employed by the Lahore darbar but once made certain remarks which so aroused the ire of the Jammu brothers that he recrossed the Sutlej to save his life.

63. Latif, *History*, p. 440.

64. S. Ali, pp. 95–96.

65. Lepel H. Griffin, *Punjab Chiefs* (Lahore, 1890), p. 323. According to J. D. Cunningham, p. 246, Hira Singh "had really, if not formally, been adopted by the old Maharaja."

66. "A Journey to Cashmeer," p. 19. According to other sources, Jamiat Singh, nicknamed Mian Huttoo, was the offspring of the Jammu Raja's intimacy with a *kaniz* (maid servant). See Saif-ud-Din's report to John Lawrence, news of Aug. and Sept. 1857, "SDS," vol. 10, fol. 81/1, and Ghulam Hassan Khuihami, "Tarikh-e-Hassan," vol. 2, fol. 344, both Persian manuscripts in RPD.

67. Emily Eden, *Up the Country* (London, 1866), 2:162, is quite positive on this point. She records: "It is the practice of that [Jammu] family never to allow a female infant of their race to live; they marry wives from other very high Rajpoot families, but they will not give their daughters to inferior princes nor let them live unmarried, so they are all put away as soon as they are born."

68. S. Ali, p. 94, writes that "his attendance at court was merely confined to the festivals of the [Baisakhi] and the [Dussehra], when he received the usual *Khilats* [robes of honor] and returned to Jammoo." But there is evidence that the Jammu chief also appeared at Lahore on certain other occasions. See my Chapter 1.

69. Hari Ram Gupta, ed., *Panjab on the Eve of First Sikh War* (Hoshiarpur, 1956), p. 37n.

70. "Umdat-ut-Tawarikh," vol. 3, pt. 2, p. 207.

71. Ibid., p. 210.

72. One lakh equals one hundred thousand.

73. "Umdat-ut-Tawarikh," vol. 2, pt. 3, p. 331. According to Edwardes, *Punjab Frontier*, 2:28, the wazir in 1837 actually induced the Maharaja to permit Gulab Singh to take Multan from Sawan Mal, but at the last minute the ruler withdrew his permission.

74. S. Ali, pp. 103–6, writes that Gulab Singh controlled twenty-six jagirs; Dhian Singh, twenty-nine; Suchet Singh, twenty; and Hira Singh, ten.

75. See copy of an agreement made by the members of the Jammu family, December 16, 1837, "CSD." The pact designated the following order of seniority within the household: 1) Raja Gulab Singh, 2) Raja Dhian Singh, 3) Raja Suchet Singh, 4) Mian Udham Singh, 5) Raja Hira Singh, 6) Mian Sohan Singh, 7) Mian Jawahar Singh, 8) Mian Ranbir Singh, 9) Mian Moti Singh, 10) Mian Huttoo Singh. There is no reference to Mian Chiman Singh.

76. For example, Leopold von Orlich, *Travels in India including Sinde and the Punjab*, trans. H. Evans Lloyd (London, 1845), 1:173, suggests that Dhian Singh so jealously guarded his standing with his master that he even "attempted to kill his own son, Heera Singh (Diamond Lion), the handsomest boy in the country, because the Maharaja appeared to take a liking to him." Remarks ascribed to Dhian Singh by Lawrence (2:73), also hint at family tensions: " 'Oh, if I could rouse my own boy [Hira Singh?] to ambition! If he lets the prize slip, his uncle will not. And then these plaguey women—I shall make a fresh breach with Suchet Singh, by releasing the girl he had his eye on. But never mind, it will suit Gulab Singh to be on my side, and if it did not, he would find ground of complaint, whatever I might do!' "

77. "Umdat-ut-Tawarikh," vol. 3, pt. 2, pp. 338–39.

78. Ibid., pt. 1, p. 8; pt. 2, pp. 161, 330, 404.

79. Ibid., pt. 1, p. 89.

80. Hari Ram Gupta, "The Yusafzais and the Sikhs" in *Sir Jadunath Sarkar Commemorative Volume*, ed. H. R. Gupta (Hoshiarpur, 1958), p. 148.

81. Lawrence, 2:363n, put the number of Poonchi victims in the thou-

sands when he wrote that Gulab Singh "inflicted such terrible vengeance on the people of Sudan (a large district south-east of Mozafarabad), cutting up, maiming, flaying to the amount, it is said, of twelve thousand persons, that the men of Dundi and Satti, two adjoining territories, sent in their submission, but begged *not to see his face.*" Lawrence's estimate of the dead is echoed by Trevaskis, p. 204, who says that the Raja "was commonly believed to have needlessly put to death over 12,000 persons."

82. Vigne, *Travels*, 1:241.

83. Khuihami, vol. 2, fol. 339.

84. Ibid. In a personal communication to this scholar, Principal Hassan Shah writes that the chains used to bind the two men before their death were hung on an old tree at Mung near Bagh in Poonch until 1935. Vigne, who passed through this area during 1838, records in his *Travels:* "The heads of two of the prisoners I saw grinning from iron cages over the path at Ada Tak, by way of affording a wholesome lesson to travellers" (1:241). Whether these were the skulls of Malli and Sabzalli, Shams-ud-Din and his nephew (see note 85 below), or some other victims is not clear.

85. See Appendix A. The heads of Shams and his nephew, who was murdered with him, were put into two separate cages and hung in the Bhimber Pass. See A. Cunningham in the *Asiatic Society Journal* as quoted by Lawrence, 1:130n.

86. "Umdat-ut-Tawarikh," vol. 2, pt. 4, pp. 432–33.

87. *Edwardes Memorials*, 1:72–73.

88. Ibid., p. 73.

89. W. Napier, *Life of Charles Napier*, 3:474.

90. Eden, 1:192.

91. William Barr, *Journal of a March from Delhi to Peshawar* (London, 1844), p. 274, who met Gulab Singh in 1839, also termed him "very politic and unassuming."

92. As quoted by Arnold, 1:33–34n.

93. Jacquemont, 2:2.

94. Ibid.

95. Ibid., pp. 2–3. Jacquemont wrote that "as I found him a good fellow, understanding from the first my Hindoostanee, which I have strangely Persianized and Punjabized . . . I remained conversing with him till night."

96. On his departure Gulab Singh dutifully informed Lahore that "Jacquemont Sahib had been supplied with entertainment and other necessities, according to the orders of the Maharaja." See "Umdat-ut-Tawarikh," vol. 3, pt. 1, p. 22.

97. Jacquemont, 2:180, was particularly touched by the last present and wrote: "I shall feel real pleasure in continuing my tour in India on Gulab Sing's horse; because he did not give it to me merely from etiquette, but evidently as a token of remembrance. Is not this familiar friendship with a demi-savage of the Himalayas, very curious?"

98. Ibid., p. 178.

99. Ibid., p. 1.

100. Ibid., p. 166.

101. William L. M'Gregor, *The History of the Sikhs* (London, 1846), 2:30, also wrote that the Raja was "shorter in stature than either Dhyan Singh or Soochet Singh." However, Barr, p. 274, described him as "a tall, powerful-looking man."

102. V. Jacquemont, *Letters From India*, trans. C. A. Phillips (London, 1936), p. xxviii.

103. See "Umdat-ut-Tawarikh," vol. 3, pt. 2, pp. 292, 295; pt. 4, pp. 390, 498; pt. 5, p. 93.

104. Ibid., pt. 2, p. 256.

105. Vigne, *Travels*, 2:372.

106. Ibid., 1:179–80.

107. Ibid., p. 180. Vigne inadvertently refers to Gulab Singh's eldest son as Urjun Singh.

108. Jacquemont, 2:166–67. M'Gregor, 1:246, was likewise well inclined toward Udham Singh and wrote that he "is a promising youth." Alexander Cunningham, *Ladak* (London, 1854), p. 343n, also described the Jammu chief's eldest son as "a fine soldier-like young man."

109. Vigne, *Travels*, 1:183.

110. Ibid.

111. Ibid., p. 184. Vigne writes that when a non-Muslim grumbled "that the Mullah's cry disturbed his devotions," the Raja wryly responded "that he would order him to desist, if the applicant will take the trouble to collect the flock for him."

112. Ibid.

113. Ibid.

114. Ibid., pp. 187–318 passim. Vigne was a good artist and sketched various men he encountered and places he visited during his journeys through the northwest. Several of these drawings are contained in his *Travels* and *Narrative*.

115. Charles Hugel, *Travels in Kashmir and the Panjab* (London, 1845), p. 288.

116. Ibid., p. 69.

117. Burnes, 1:287.

118. "Umdat-ut-Tawarikh," vol. 3, pt. 1, p. 37.

119. Ibid., pp. 37, 58.

120. Wade to Macnaghten, political secretary to the Governor-General, Jan. 1, 1838, "PC," vol. 143, no. 57.

121. Ibid., Nov. 17, vol. 145, no. 26.

122. Henry Edward Fane, *Five Years In India* (London, 1842), 1:127.

123. Barr, pp. 117–18, estimated that the wazir's private army numbered between 25,000 and 30,000 men.

124. M'Gregor, 1:242.

125. Ibid.

126. Lawrence, 1:35.

127. William G. Osborne, *The Court And Camp of Runjeet Sing* (London, 1840), p. 75.

128. Eden, 1:14.

129. Hugel, p. 288.

130. Vigne, *Travels*, 1:218; 2:375.

131. Vigne, *Narrative*, pp. 251–52.

132. Ibid., p. 253. A similar charge against Gulab Singh was made by Barr, p. 274.

133. Vigne, *Narrative*, pp. 253–54.

134. J. D. Cunningham, p. 214.

135. Lawrence, 1:34.

136. Edwardes, *Punjab Frontier*, 2:28.

137. Masson, 1:441.

138. Hugel, p. 288.

139. "Umdat-ut-Tawarikh," vol. 3, pt. 4, pp. 471–72; pt. 5, pp. 8, 43–49.

140. Vigne, *Travels*, 2:371.

141. "Umdat-ut-Tawarikh," vol. 3, pt. 4, pp. 470–74.

142. Kahan Singh, *Tarikh-e-Rajgan Jammu-va-Kashmir* (Lahore, 1932), p. 119.

143. Vigne, *Travels*, 2:373.

144. Ibid., p. 374.

145. Ibid.

146. "Umdat-ut-Tawarikh," vol. 3, pt. 5, p. 49.

147. Ibid., pp. 63–64, 69.

148. Emily Eden, *Up the Country*, ed. E. Thompson (London, 1937), p. 199.

149. Ibid., p. 226.

150. Osborne, p. 76.

151. Wade to Maddock, political secretary to the Governor-General, June 27, 1839, "PC," vol. 147, pt. 2, no. 117.

152. "Umdat-ut-Tawarikh," vol. 3, pt. 5, p. 156. According to another source, Kharak Singh and other Sikh chiefs "threw their turbans at his feet to dissuade him, alleging that without him the affairs of the State would be deranged." See "PA," June 28, 1839, p. 61.

153. "Umdat-ut-Tawarikh," vol. 3, pt. 5, p. 156; "PA," June 28, 1839, p. 61.

154. "Umdat-ut-Tawarikh," vol. 3, pt. 5, p. 156.

155. "PA," June 28, 1839, p. 63. European writers also confirm the wazir's attempt to immolate himself. Von Orlich, 1:171, writes that he "appeared to be about to throw himself into the flames, but the descendants of the Maharaja . . . held him back." Osborne, p. 225, records that the minister "threw himself twice on the pile, and said he could not survive his master, but was dragged away by main force." However, Vigne sneeringly suggests that Dhian Singh's "pretended attempt to throw himself upon [the Maharaja's] funeral pyre, was nothing but a masterly piece of humbug." See his *Narrative*, p. 250.

2 Triumph in Ladakh and Baltistan; Disaster in Tibet

1. For further details on Ladakh's geography, see A. Cunningham; E. Thornton, *A Gazetteer of the Coun-tries Adjacent to India on the North-West*, 2 vols. (London, 1844).

2. For Ladakh's early history, see A.

H. Francke, A. *History of Western Tibet* (London, 1907); Ferguson; Zahiruddin Ahmad, "Tibet and Ladakh: A History" in G. F. Hudson, ed., *Far Eastern Affairs: Number Three* (Carbondale, Ill., 1963), pp. 23–28; Margaret W. Fisher, Leo E. Rose, and Robert A. Huttenback, *Himalayan Battleground* (New York, 1963).

3. De-lek also embraced Islam and took the name of Akabat Khan, but his successors returned to the fold of Buddhism. However, the *gyalpos* used Akabat Khan as a title until the nineteenth century. See Ferguson, pp. 92–93; Fisher, p. 38.

4. William Moorcroft and George Trebeck, *Travels in the Himalayan Provinces of Hindustan and the Panjab* (London, 1841), 1:419–20.

5. Thornton, 2:12.

6. Moorcroft, 1:419.

7. Ibid., pp. 420–21.

8. Article 1 of this treaty stipulated that "the British Government will have no concern with the territories and subjects of [Ranjit Singh] to the northward of the River Sutlej." See J. D. Cunningham, p. 384. The Company might have concluded that the Sikh ruler could claim the Ladakhis as his "subjects" because of their tributary status to Kashmir.

9. Moorcroft, 1:421.

10. For more on the Leh trade, see Chapter 11, note 103.

11. The pashmina used by the Kashmiris to manfacture their famous shawls was imported from "the high table land of Tibet, where alone the shawl goat producing it will thrive." For more on the source and production of pashmina, see *The History of the Sikhs*, pp. 42–43.

12. A. Lamb, "Tibet in Anglo-Chinese Relations: 1767–1842" in the *Journal of the Royal Asiatic Society of Great Britain and Ireland*, 1958, pt. 2, pp. 38–40.

13. Francke, pp. 137–38.

14. Ibid., p. 138.

15. Thornton, 2:12.

16. Francke, p. 139.

17. Gholaum Hyder in the *As. Jour.* (Sept.-Dec. 1835) as quoted by Thornton, 2:12.

18. He was born in 1786 near Kalhoor, now in the Bilaspur district of Himachal Pradesh, and joined Gulab

Singh's service during 1817. See Narsingdas Nargis, *Zorawar Singh* (Jammu, 1964), pp. 1, 7.

19. Francke, p. 139.

20. A. Cunningham, pp. 333–35; Francke, pp. 139–42.

21. Francke, p. 142, refers to him simply as Tsepal. A. Cunningham, p. 338n, writes that his real name was Tonduk Namgyal.

22. Hugel, p. 101.

23. Ibid., pp. 101–2. Henderson was actually an eccentric nonconformist in the Company's service whose "restless mind could not be satisfied with the quiet routine of his professional duties." He had obtained a few months' vacation to travel by foot from Ludhiana to Calcutta, but decided instead to explore the western Himalayas. He arrived incognito in Ladakh wearing "Mohammedan garb, and [using the] fictitious name of Ishmael Khan." Henderson had apparently not anticipated becoming a center of controversy.

24. Ibid., p. 102.

25. Ibid. It is not clear what action, if any, the Company took against Henderson on his return.

26. A. Cunningham, p. 335. However, Francke, p. 144, puts the total number of this force between 15,000 and 20,000 men. Either way this must be considered a dramatic increase in the size of the Ladakhi army, which was said to have been less than 4,000 (see my Chapter 2). It would also seem to indicate that the *gyalpo* enrolled a large percentage of his subjects into his army. The 1961 census put Ladakh's total population at only 88,651. It was presumably less in the 1830s.

27. A. Cunningham, pp. 335–36. Francke, p. 143, refers to him as Bangkapa.

28. A. Cunningham, pp. 335–36.

29. Ibid., p. 336.

30. Ibid., pp. 336–37.

31. Francke, pp. 146–47.

32. A. Cunningham, p. 339, writes that 37,000 rupees of the indemnity were paid immediately, with the remainder due in the following months. However, according to Francke, p. 147, the Ladakhi sources "give only 9000 as the annual tribute, and do not mention the war indemnity at all."

33. A. Cunningham, p. 339. But his

brother, J. D. Cunningham, p. 214, states that Ladakh was to pay a tribute of 30,000 rupees.

34. A. Cunningham, pp. 339–40.

35. Francke, p. 148. However, J. D. Cunningham, p. 214, states that before leaving, the Dogra commander "placed a garrison in the fort [at Leh, and] he retained some districts along the northern slopes of the Himalayas."

36. J. D. Cunningham, p. 241n.

37. Vigne, Travels, 2:337.

38. J. D. Cunningham, p. 214.

39. "Umdat-ut-Tawarikh," vol. 3, pt. 3, p. 306. At first glance it might seem that Zorawar Singh was merely expressing his desire to occupy Tibet and not China, since the Sikhs and the Dogras often referred to the Tibetans as Chinese. But a message from Gulab Singh to the Maharaja in 1838 indicates that the General was perhaps echoing his master's views and might really have meant what he said. In this communication, characterized both by an inordinate overconfidence and a certain vagueness about the enormity of China, Gulab Singh declared that if Ranjit Singh was "anxious to exact tribute or conquer the hill areas by the grace of the glory of the Sirkar he could bring the entire area upto the Chinese wall and the country of Kashgarh under his sway." See Wade to Maddock, June 27, 1839, "PC," vol. 147, no. 155.

40. Francke, p. 148.

41. A. Cunningham, p. 342.

42. Francke, p. 150. A. Cunningham, p. 342, refers to him as Moru-pa Tadsi; Vigne, Travels, 2:354, calls him Marut Tunzin.

43. A. Cunningham, p. 342.

44. Ibid., p. 343. However, Francke, p. 151, writes that this revolt was probably not instigated by Ngorub and concludes that he was deliberately blamed for this latest disturbance because Gulab Singh had disapproved of his elevation to Ladakh's throne, and the Dogras used the uprising as a pretext to remove him.

45. A. Cunningham, pp. 343–44.

46. Ibid., pp. 344–45.

47. Francke, p. 155.

48. A. Cunningham, pp. 345–46.

49. Vigne, Travels, 2:235, writes that the gyalpo "said that he was sending his respectful salaam to the King

[William IV] of England, that he was his slave, and wished for his protection."

50. Clerk to Torrens, deputy political secretary to the Governor-General, Aug. 25, 1840, "PC," vol. 149, no. 56.

51. Torrens to Clerk, Aug. 31, 1840, "PC," vol. 127, no. 31. Zorawar Singh had, through a lieutenant, unsuccessfully attempted earlier to seize the Jussorah fort. See the "Cashmere Intelligence" of June 16 to July 1, 1840, in Panjab In 1839–40, ed. Ganda Singh (Amritsar, 1952), p. 232.

52. J. D. Cunningham, p. 255.

53. A. Cunningham, p. 347, adds: "About 400 men only managed to find their way back to the Dogra camp with the tale of their defeat."

54. Ibid., p. 348.

55. Ibid. According to Francke, p. 157, the invaders crossed the river by means of "a bridge of ice and wood" constructed for them by men from Da, a village on the Ladakh-Baltistan border.

56. A. Cunningham, pp. 348–49.

57. This fort was located on the imposing rock of Iskardu, which Vigne, Travels, 2:246, found somewhat comparable to Gibraltar.

58. A. Cunningham, p. 349.

59. Ibid.

60. Francke, pp. 158–59.

61. See Clerk to Torrens, Aug. 24, 1840, "PC," vol. 149, no. 60; Clerk to Maddock, Nov. 23, 1840, "PC," vol. 152, no. 75. Mohi-ud-Din was suspected of being an ally of Gulab Singh. See my Chapter 3.

62. Clerk to Maddock, Jan. 2, 1841, "PC," vol. 151, no. 53.

63. Maddock to Clerk, Jan. 25, 1841, "PC," vol. 128, no. 17.

64. Mackeson's opinion is cited in a letter by Maddock to Clerk, Feb. 2, 1841, "PC," vol. 128, no. 45. However, there seems to be some justification for Clerk's charges. As early as 1839, the "PA," of June 26, p. 65, reported that Zorawar Singh "is going to take possession of Yarkund, where there are very few troops." In addition, J. D. Cunningham, p. 256, states that after the conquest of Baltistan, the Dogra commander "claimed fealty from Ghilgit; he was understood to be desirous of quarrelling with the Chinese

governor of Yarkund." Similarly, A. Cunningham, p. 351, writes that Zorawar Singh "threatened the neighboring states, and even talked of invading Yarkand."

65. A. Cunningham, p. 351; Francke, p. 161.

66. A. Cunningham, p. 351. Francke, p. 162, estimated this army to number between six and seven thousand men.

67. J. D. Cunningham, pp. 256–57.

68. A. Cunningham, pp. 351–52; Francke, pp. 162–63.

69. J. D. Cunningham, p. 257.

70. Clerk to Maddock, May 13 and 25, 1841, "PC," vol. 151, nos. 57 and 63, respectively.

71. Clerk to Maddock, June 22, 1841, "PC," vol. 152, no. 7.

72. Undated letter of Zorawar Singh to the Sikh government received at Lahore on Aug. 18, 1841, enclosed in a communication from Clerk to Maddock, Sept. 10, 1841, "PC," vol. 151, no. 41.

73. Clerk to Maddock, Aug. 20, 1841, SD, "ESLI," vol. 79, enc. 77, letter 133.

74. Clerk to Maddock, Aug. 10, 1841, SD, "ESLI," vol. 79, enc. 77, letter 119.

75. Clerk, quoting Lushington, to Maddock, Sept. 4, 1841, "PC," vol. 152, no. 41.

76. Clerk to Maddock, Oct. 10, 1841, "PC," vol. 155, no. 114.

77. J. D. Cunningham, p. 257n, states that the Dogras and the Nepalese government were actually in correspondence.

78. Clerk to Maddock, Sept. 4, 1841, "PC," vol. 152, no. 41. J. D. Cunningham, p. 257, writes that "it was deemed inadvisable to allow the Lahore and Nepal dominions to march with one another behind the Himalayas."

79. Clerk to Maharaja Sher Singh, Oct. 19, 1841, "PC," vol. 155, no. 132.

80. J. D. Cunningham, p. vi. According to J. C. Marshman, The History of India (London, 1867), 3:276, a "day was fixed for restoring the town of Garo to the Grand Lama, and a British officer was deputed to witness the surrender."

81. Copy of undated letter from the Lahore government to Gulab Singh, "PC," vol. 155, no. 128.

82. Undated letter of Sher Singh to Clerk received on Oct. 31, 1841, "PC," vol. 155, no. 133.

83. In a communication that probably never reached his commander, Gulab Singh ordered him to return to Ladakh and extend cooperation to J. D. Cunningham. See "PI," Nov. 30, 1841, p. 267.

84. A. Cunningham, p. 352; J. D. Cunningham, p. 258n.

85. J. D. Cunningham, p. 258.

86. A. Cunningham, p. 352. However, Herbert B. Edwardes and Herman Merivale, Life of Sir Henry Lawrence (London, 1872), 1:323, state that Zorawar Singh committed suicide "rather than fall alive into the hands of the Chinese." Two other accounts of Zorawar Singh's death have been reported. According to Francke, p. 163, after the Dogra had been wounded, "a Tibetan horseman thrust his lance through Zorawar Singh's breast." On the other hand, Gwasha Lal Kaul, Kashmir Through the Ages (Srinagar, 1960), p. 77, writes that the Tibetans shot Zorawar Singh "with a golden bullet as they believed that the General was endowed with supernatural powers and no lead bullet could penetrate his body." He also adds that "the testicles and one hand of Wazir Zorawar Singh are kept in a Buddhist monastery near Taklakot."

87. A. Cunningham, p. 353. Alluding to the disaster, J. D. Cunningham, p. 258, writes that "a few principal men" were seized by the Tibetans, "but the mass was left to perish, huddled in heaps behind rocks, or at the bottoms of the ravines."

88. A. Cunningham, p. 353.

89. Ibid., p. 354.

90. Francke, p. 165, refers to him as Jigsmed.

91. Ibid. There was also a rebellion in Baltistan itself, but it was crushed by Lakhpat Rai. See A. Cunningham, p. 354n.

92. Ellenborough to the Duke of Wellington, June 7, 1842, in Lord Colchester, ed., History of the Indian Administration of Lord Ellenborough (London, 1874), p. 254.

93. J. D. Cunningham to Clerk, May 20, 1842, "PC," vol. 153, no. 50.

94. Clerk to Maddock, Feb. 15, 1842, "PC," vol. 153, no. 31.

95. Clerk to Maddock, May 11, 1842, "PC," vol. 153, no. 103.
96. Francke, p. 165.
97. A. Cunningham, p. 355.
98. See Edwardes and Merivale, 1: 323.
99. Saif-ud-Din, "Khilasat-ut-Tawarikh," p. 53, Persian MS in the private papers of Mirza Kemal-ud-Din at Srinagar. Birbal Kachroo, "Tarikh-e-Kashmir," fol. 297/2, Persian MS in RPD, also confirms that the preparations for the Ladakhi expedition were made in Kashmir. However, Bamzai, p. 570, seems to imply that Mohi-ud-Din supplied no troops to Gulab Singh but did obtain for the Dogras "fifteen days' rations and ten thousand villagers for carriage of their baggage to the inhospitable regions of Ladakh."
100. Bamzai, p. 570.
101. This road covers a distance of some 200 miles from Srinagar to Himis in Ladakh. The pass is 11,580 feet at its highest elevation. See Enakshi Bhavnani, "A Journey to 'Little Tibet' " in National Geographic Magazine 99 (1951), 607.
102. Francke, p. 166. Fisher, Rose, and Huttenback, p. 55, however, suggest that the new Tibetan force was composed of nearly 5,000 men.
103. Francke, pp. 166–67.
104. J. D. Cunningham to Clerk, Oct. 28, 1842, "PC," vol. 113, no. 48.
105. At least two drafts of the Lhasa-Jammu treaty exist. For the Dogra version, see "Gulab Nama," p. 264. The Tibetan version is contained in a letter from Erskine to Clerk, April 1, 1843, "PC," vol. 50, no. 74. However, the substance of these two drafts is essentially the same.
106. Ferguson, p. 62.
107. Francke, p. 167.
108. Nargis, p. 4.

3 The Rise and Fall of Dhian Singh

1. Lawrence, 1:35.
2. Fane, 1:127.
3. Eden, ed. Thompson, p. 199.
4. Lawrence, 1:35.
5. Osborne, p. 74.
6. M'Gregor, 1:242.
7. Fane, 1:127–28, and Eden, ed. Thompson, p. 199, also found Dhian Singh to be exquisitely dressed. Vigne, Narrative, pp. 279–80, was struck by the Western influence on the Raja's attire, and Osborne, p. 74, wrote that he "dressed in a magnificent helmet and cuirass of polished steel, embossed with gold, a present from King Louis Philippe of France."
8. Charles Gough and Arthur D. Innes, The Sikhs and the Sikh Wars (London, 1897), p. 50.
9. Hugh Pearse, ed., Memoirs of Alexander Gardner (Edinburgh, 1898), p. 212.
10. Griffin, Punjab Chiefs, p. 323.
11. The concept of the khalsa originated with the last of the Sikh gurus, Gobind Singh. It continued to gain strength during the eighteenth century and acquired its more modern shape and organization under Ranjit Singh.
12. Osborne, pp. 192–93.
13. J. D. Cunningham, p. 236.
14. Eden, ed. Thompson, p. 208.
15. John M. Honigberger, Thirty-Five Years in the East (London, 1852; reprint ed., Calcutta, 1905), p. 104.
16. M'Gregor, 2:4.
17. "PA," July 13, 1839, p. 82.
18. According to M'Gregor, 2:5, and Latif, History, p. 497, the new Maharaja actually removed Dhian Singh from the wazarat and replaced him with Chet Singh, but this is not confirmed by others.
19. Latif, History, p. 497.
20. "PA," Oct. 2, 1839, p. 137.
21. Wade to Maddock, Dec. 31, 1839, "PC," vol. 147, no. 196.
22. J. D. Cunningham, p. 238.
23. "PA," Sept. 24, 1839, pp. 126–27.
24. "PA," Sept. 21, 1839, p. 259.
25. "PA," Sept. 24, 1839, p. 127.
26. Parshad, p. 42.
27. Latif, History, p. 497.

28. Ibid.

29. Ibid.

30. According to Ganesh Das Badhrah, "Chirag-e-Panjab," fol. 75/1, Persian MS in IOL, the Jammu chief had escorted Naunihal Singh back to the capital and attached himself to the prince "as a *bulbul* [songbird] does to the flower bush."

31. J. D. Cunningham, p. 238.

32. "Gulab Nama," p. 277.

33. Latif, *History*, p. 498.

34. "Gulab Nama," p. 278.

35. J. D. Cunningham, p. 238n.

36. Latif, *History*, p. 498. However, "Gulab Nama," p. 279, maintains that Chet Singh was killed by the Jammu chief.

37. "PA," Oct. 9, 1839, pp. 138–39. M'Gregor, 2:5, mistakenly believes that Beli Ram also lost his life at this time. He did not die until 1843. See my Chapter 3.

38. M'Gregor, 2:5.

39. "PA," Oct. 9, 1839, p. 139.

40. S. Ali, pp. 544–45.

41. S. Ali, who accompanied Wade, records (pp. 543–44) that Kharak Singh "was now strictly watched and kept in a state of arrest" by Naunihal Singh. He adds that the "Maharaja was said to have been bewildered by the savage and cruel treatment of his son."

42. Wade to Maddock, Dec. 11, 1839, "PC," vol. 147, pt. 3, no. 176. In reference to the confiscations, the agent observed in his letter of Dec. 18, no. 185, that the Jammu Raja "maintains a perfect silence. God knows what would be the result."

43. Wade to Maddock, Jan. 15, 1840, "PC," vol. 148, pt. 1, no. 17.

44. Wade to Maddock, Jan. 13, 1840, "PC," vol. 148, pt. 1, no. 14.

45. Wade to Maddock, Jan. 24, 1840, "PC," vol. 148, pt. 1, no. 19.

46. "PI," July 4–5, 1840, pp. 218–19.

47. Ibid., July 5, 1840, p. 221.

48. Ibid., July 20, 1840, p. 249.

49. See J. D. Cunningham, pp. 242–43; K. Singh, *History*, 2:10–11.

50. "PI," June 5, 1840, p. 192.

51. J. D. Cunningham, p. 242.

52. K. Singh, *History*, 2:11.

53. "PI," July 3, 1840, p. 216.

54. Ibid., July 25, 1840, p. 255.

55. Ibid., p. 256.

56. Bikrama Jit Hasrat, *Anglo-Sikh Relations: 1799–1849* (Hoshiarpur, 1968), p. 195.

57. J. D. Cunningham, p. 244.

58. According to Latif, *History*, p. 497, Kharak Singh "was a man of weak intellect. . . . Physiognomically he was the counterpart of his royal sire, but he possessed none of his diplomatic qualifications." Hasrat, p. 183, describes him as "an unimaginative and irresolute weakling." K. Singh, *History*, 2:5, who is particularly critical of Kharak Singh, writes: "He was an indolent, easy-going debauchee with neither the restless energy that had animated his illustrous father nor the down-to-earth simplicity that had endeared his predecessor to the masses."

59. M'Gregor, 1:252.

60. Ibid., 2:5–6.

61. K. Singh, *History*, 2:12n.

62. J. D. Cunningham, p. 244; K. Singh, *History*, 2:12. However, M'Gregor, 2:6, states that Naunihal Singh was killed outright.

63. Honigberger, p. 106.

64. J. D. Cunningham, p. 244.

65. Steinbach, p. 24.

66. *Edwardes Memorials*, 1:69.

67. K. Singh, *History*, 2:12–13n, who cannot be considered pro-Dogra, dwells at some length on this controversy and argues convincingly against the likelihood of Dogra culpability in the incident.

68. This figure is given by Grey, app. I, p. viii. But according to K. Singh, *History*, 1:295n, Ranjit Singh married twenty-two times and fathered seven sons.

69. See Grey, app. I, p. viii.

70. Among contemporaries who allude to his illegitimacy are J. D. Cunningham, p. 245; Fane, 1:120; and M'Gregor, 2:4.

71. Fane, 1:120.

72. Eden, ed. Thompson, p. 210.

73. J. D. Cunningham, p. 245.

74. See Eden, ed. Thompson, pp. 210, 221, 238.

75. J. D. Cunningham, p. 237n.

76. Grey, app. I, p. ix. According to Thomas Keightley, *A History of India* (London, 1847), p. 192, the "Ranee was a woman of the most dissolute habits, and devoid of all prudence and regard to decency."

77. Hasrat, pp. 197–98; K. Singh, *History*, 2:15.

78. J. D. Cunningham, p. 246. According to Grey, app. I, p. viii, the widow did deliver a posthumous son, but it was stillborn.

79. Auckland to Hobhouse, Dec. 5, 1840, in Hasrat, p. 198.

80. Grey, app. I, pp. ix–x.

81. "Umdat-ut-Tawarikh," vol. 4, pt. 2, p. 6.

82. Grey, app. II, p. xi.

83. Clerk to Maddock, Dec. 25, 1840, "PC," vol. 150, no. 52.

84. Auckland to Hobhouse, Dec. 7, 1840, in Hasrat, p. 199.

85. J. D. Cunningham, p. 246.

86. K. Singh, *History*, 2:14–15.

87. M'Gregor, 2:7.

88. Ibid.

89. "Umdat-ut-Tawarikh," vol. 4, pt. 2, pp. 10–11.

90. Clerk to Maddock, Jan. 2, 1841, "PC," vol. 151, no. 2.

91. M'Gregor, 2:7–8.

92. Grey, app. II, pp. x–xi.

93. M'Gregor, 2:8. Although the Anglo-Sikh Treaty of 1809 had fixed the Sutlej as the main boundary line between the two powers, Ranjit Singh was nonetheless allowed to hold some territories east of the Sutlej.

94. J. D. Cunningham, p. 248.

95. M'Gregor, 2:9–10.

96. Clerk to Maddock, Jan. 21, 1841, "PC," vol. 151, no. 16. However, Latif, *History*, p. 504, writes that "the whole army of 70,000 infantry, with 50,000 followers, rushed infuriated in the direction of the fort, filling the air with the war-cry, 'Wah, Guru ji ki Fateh,' 'Wah, Guru ji ki Khalsa-ji' [To God belongs the victory, to God belongs the khalsa]."

97. "Umdat-ut-Tawarikh," vol. 4, pt. 2, pp. 10–11. Grey, app. II, p. xi, writes that Gulab Singh picked only those troops "he thought trustworthy, disarmed the remainder, comprising some 1,200 Sikhs of the regular army, who were imprisoned in the vaults, under the citadel, and overawed by guns placed at the only two doorways leading therefrom."

98. It is probable that this money was not his own but had been taken from the Sikh treasury located in the fort. See Grey, app. II, p. xi.

99. "Umdat-ut-Tawarikh," vol. 4, pt. 2, p. 11.

100. While describing the Jammu chief's role in this dispute, Mohammad Naqi Peshawari, in his *Sher Singh Nama*, trans. Vidya Sagar Suri, in *Panjab University Historical Society Journal* 8 (1944), 105, flatteringly compares him, in flowery Persian, to several legendary figures in the East: ". . . that wise commander and forefront of the battle, that tempered sword of daring and courage, that being endowed with the bravery of Rustum, the frame of Tahmten, the cunning of Bizhan, the vengefulness of Behram, the audacity of Jove, namely, Raja Gulab Singh Bahadur."

101. Clerk to Maddock, Jan. 19, 1841, "PC," vol. 151, no. 14.

102. J. D. Cunningham, p. 248.

103. Clerk to Maddock, Jan. 19, 1841, "PC," vol. 151, no. 14.

104. Clerk to Maddock, Jan. 21, 1841, "PC," vol. 151, no. 16.

105. Grey, app. II, p. xiii.

106. M'Gregor, 2:10.

107. K. Lal, pp. 389–90.

108. J. D. Cunningham, p. 248.

109. Peshawari, p. 105.

110. "Tarikh Nama," pp. 132–33.

111. J. D. Cunningham, pp. 248–49.

112. According to the "Gulab Nama," pp. 300–301, the jagir produced nine lakhs of rupees in annual revenue.

113. Latif, *History*, p. 506.

114. J. D. Cunningham, p. 249.

115. M'Gregor, 2:11.

116. Latif, *History*, pp. 506–7. Parshad, p. 46, writes that the treasure was removed in carriages which were covered at the top with ammunition to hoodwink the Sikhs.

117. "Tarikh Nama," p. 141. According to Smyth, p. 60, the valuables purloined by Gulab Singh included the famed Koh-e-Nur (the mountain of light), which, nevertheless, he returned to Sher Singh before leaving Lahore. It may be debated whether the Koh-e-Nur, if it had found its way to Jammu, would ever have become part of England's royal crown jewels.

118. Clerk to Maddock, Feb. 8, 1841, "PC," vol. 151, no. 26.

119. Clerk to Maddock, March 3, 1841, "PC," vol. 151, no. 34.

120. Mackeson to Clerk, April 23, 1841, "PC," vol. 40, pt. 2, no. 103.

121. See Sita Ram Kohli, "The Organization of the Khalsa Army," in *Maharaja Ranjit Singh Centenary Volume*, ed. Teja Singh and Ganda Singh (Amritsar, 1939), pp. 67–85.

122. Ibid., pp. 70, 74, 80.

123. Lawrence, 2:309–10.

124. J. D. Cunningham, pp. 249–50.

125. "Umdat-ut-Tawarikh," vol. 4, pt. 3, p. 35.

126. J. D. Cunningham, pp. 253–54.

127. Ellenborough to Queen Victoria, Oct. 20, 1843, in Colchester, p. 97.

128. J. D. Cunningham, p. 254.

129. Clerk to Maddock, May 17, 1841, "PC," vol. 151, no. 58.

130. Clerk to Maddock, May 25, 1841, "PC," vol. 151, no. 63.

131. Clerk to Maddock, June 10, 1841, "PC," vol. 151, no. 69; Aug. 10, "PC," vol. 152, no. 23.

132. Clerk to Maddock, Oct. 3, 1841, "PC," vol. 152, no. 40.

133. The Sheikh was perhaps all the more indebted to Gulab Singh because he had begun his "life as a shoemaker; he was a man of no family, character, or influence." See the Governor-General's letter to SC, Sept. 19, 1846, *PRAL*, p. 194. J. D. Cunningham, p. 259, even felt that Mohi-ud-Din's appointment made the Jammu chief "the virtual master of the [Kashmir] valley."

134. Latif, *History*, p. 508.

135. J. D. Cunningham, p. 269n. Referring to the manner of Jawala Singh's death, Latif, *History*, p. 508, writes: "He was thrown into a dark and deep dungeon. . . . While in prison, he was flogged daily, after which he received his prison allowance of food, which consisted of half a measure of flour and an equal quantity of salt, mixed together. Hot irons were applied to the soles of his feet, as an additional punishment. Under these tortures he lingered for forty days, and expired in the fort of Shekhupura, whither he had been removed ten days previously to his death."

136. The bitter feud between the two had continued. In May 1841 the Rani protested that Sher Singh had restricted her freedom of movement. When the Maharaja retorted that the "Sundhanwalla Chiefs had gone to complain to the British Government merely at her instigation . . . [the] Ranee shed tears but answered not." See "PI," Nov. 29, 1841, p. 266.

137. J. D. Cunningham, p. 269. There are hints that Dhian Singh himself could have been involved in the plot to murder Chand Kaur. Latif, *History*, p. 509, believes that Sher Singh bribed the Rani's maids to kill her. He adds that Dhian Singh "proceeded to punish the assassins, and had their noses, ears, and hands cut off publicly. . . . Their tongues, however, were not mutilated, and they related the circumstances under which they had been tempted to perpetrate the horrible crime at the instance of both the Maharaja and his minister." On the other hand, K. Singh, *History*, 2:19n, writes: "The culprits were apprehended but before they could divulge the motives of their crime, their tongues were cut off and they were executed by the order of Dhian Singh Dogra."

138. *History of the Panjab*, 2:273. However, J. D. Cunningham, p. 246, writes that the wazir had announced the existence of Dalip Singh as early as 1840.

139. According to M'Gregor, 2:30, Dalip Singh, "with his mother, had been under the protection of Goolab Singh at Jummoo."

140. J. D. Cunningham, p. 269.

141. Ibid., pp. 269–70.

142. M'Gregor, 2:12; K. Singh, *History*, 2:26.

143. J. D. Cunningham, p. 267. According to a writer in the *Calcutta Review* presumed to be Henry Lawrence, Sher Singh would have sought unconditional British protection if he had not feared an attempt on his life (instigated by Dhian Singh?). See J. D. Cunningham, p. 267n.

144. Ellenborough to Queen Victoria, May 11, 1843, in Colchester, p. 79.

145. Richmond to Currie, Feb. 24, 1844, "PC," vol. 159, no. 25.

146. J. D. Cunningham, p. 270.

147. Richmond to Currie, Feb. 24, 1844, SD, "ESLI," vol. 96, letter 15.

148. Dhian Singh is said to have rebuked the Sandhawalias "for killing the young prince, but they merely ob-

served, 'that what was done could not be helped.' " See M'Gregor, 2:16.
149. Ibid., pp. 16–17.
150. Ibid., p. 18.
151. Suchet Singh was ill at the time and hence unable to take an active part in the events that followed

his brother's death. See M'Gregor, 2:19.
152. Ibid., p. 18.
153. J. H. Gordon, p. 126.
154. M'Gregor, 2:19–20; J. D. Cunningham, p. 271.
155. J. D. Cunningham, pp. 271–72.

4 The Wazarat of Hira Singh

1. Eden, ed. Thompson, p. 199.
2. M'Gregor, 1:243.
3. Osborne, pp. 77–78.
4. J. D. Cunningham, p. 279.
5. Ellenborough to Queen Victoria, Oct. 20, 1843, in Colchester, pp. 96–97.
6. Ibid.
7. Ibid., pp. 97–98.
8. J. D. Cunningham, p. 272.
9. Ellenborough to the Queen, Nov. 20, 1843, in Colchester, p. 102.
10. M'Gregor, 2:36.
11. Gough and Innes, p. 57.
12. Osborne, pp. 62–63, who met Suchet Singh during 1838, called him "one of the handsomest of the Sihk [sic] chiefs." M'Gregor, 2:26, termed him "the *beau ideal* of a Sikh soldier."
13. J. D. Cunningham, p. 272.
14. Richmond to John Thomason, foreign secretary to the Governor-General, Nov. 2, 1843, "PC," vol. 158, no. 142.
15. Ellenborough to Queen Victoria, Oct. 20, 1843, in Colchester, p. 97.
16. Ibid., Nov. 20, p. 102.
17. Richmond to Currie, Nov. 28, 1843, "PC," vol. 158, no. 169. The Sikh troops were, however, not very frightened by the presence of the Dogra troops at Lahore, as indicated by this encounter between them: "The Sikhs laugh at the mountain soldiers of the Raja, & say to them—How can you fellows . . . [who earn only] a seer [about 2½ pounds of weight] of atta [wheat flour] a day carry such heavy matchlooks? Why do you not demand more pay? The hill men answer that if they do so, Raja Golab Singh will put their families to death." See Richmond to Currie, Dec. 22, 1843, SD, "ESLI," vol. 95, enc. 8.
18. Richmond to Currie, Dec. 12, 1843, "PC," vol. 158, no. 174.

19. "Tarikh Nama," p. 295.
20. Richmond to Currie, Dec. 12, 1843, "PC," vol. 158, no. 174.
21. Richmond to Currie, Nov. 28, 1843, "PC," vol. 158, no. 169.
22. Ibid. This incident occurred on Nov. 24. The khalsa was especially provoked by Jowahir Singh's threat to flee to British India and take the Maharaja with him unless the soldiers acted against the Jammu chief.
23. "AIP," Jan. 10, 1844, p. 30. This development probably led Ellenborough to report to the Queen on Feb. 16, 1844, in Colchester, p. 114, that in "the hills, Raja Gholab Singh is extending his power with his usual unscrupulous disregard of the rights of others and of the supremacy of the State he pretends to serve."
24. "AIP," Jan. 7, 1844, pp. 24–25.
25. Latif, *History*, p. 522.
26. Richmond to Currie, Dec. 30, 1843, SD, "ESLI," vol. 95, enc. 8.
27. "AIP," Dec. 31, 1843, pp. 12–13.
28. Richmond to Currie, Jan. 21, 1844, SD, "ESLI," vol. 95, enc. 12, letter 59.
29. Honigberger, pp. 112–13; Griffin, *Punjab Chiefs*, p. 276; M'Gregor, 2:25.
30. "Tarikh Nama," p. 317.
31. According to Richmond, the "young men are the reputed, but really the adopted sons of the old Maharaja." See his letter to Currie, March 23, 1844, SD, "ESLI," vol. 96, enc. 22, letter 20.
32. J. D. Cunningham, p. 274.
33. Richmond to Currie, Jan. 9, 17, and 19, 1844, SD, "ESLI," vol. 95, enc. 12.
34. Richmond to Currie, Jan. 9, 1844, SD, "ESLI," vol. 95, enc. 12.
35. Richmond to Currie, March 23,

1844, SD, "ESLI," vol. 96, enc. 22, letter 20.

36. Richmond to Currie, Dec. 30, 1843, SD, "ESLI," vol. 95, enc. 8.

37. Richmond to Currie, Jan. 10, 1844, SD, "ESLI," vol. 95, enc. 12.

38. Richmond to Currie, Jan. 22, 1844, SD, "ESLI," vol. 95, enc. 12.

39. Richmond to Currie, Jan. 15, 1844, SD, "ESLI," vol. 95, enc. 12.

40. Richmond to Currie, Jan. 21, 1844, SD, "ESLI," vol. 95, enc. 12.

41. Richmond to Currie, Jan. 22, 1844, SD, "ESLI," vol. 95, enc. 12.

42. Richmond to Currie, March 27, 1844, "PC," vol. 159, no. 42.

43. "AIP," Jan. 8, 1844, p. 26.

44. Richmond to Currie, March 27, 1844, "PC," vol. 159, no. 42.

45. Ibid.

46. Richmond to Currie, Jan. 24, 1844, SD, "ESLI," vol. 95, enc. 12, letter 59.

47. Richmond to Currie, March 27, 1844, "PC," vol. 159, no. 42.

48. Richmond to Currie, Nov. 16, 1843, "PC," vol. 158, no. 142; Currie to Richmond, Jan. 31, 1844, SD, "ESLI," vol. 95, enc. 12, letter 60. Richmond believed that the hill populace, too, was opposed to the Jammu Raja and observed: "The people of the Hills between the Jehlum and Sutlej have one and all turned their eyes towards their ancient chiefs—who on their part are ready to take advantage of circumstances and rise upon Raja Golab Singh should he break with the Sikhs." See his letter to Currie, Feb. 13, 1844, "PC," vol. 159, no. 17.

49. Richmond to Currie, March 23, 1844, SD, "ESLI," vol. 96, enc. 22, letter 20.

50. Ibid.

51. "Umdat-ut-Tawarikh," vol. 4, pt. 2, p. 6.

52. "AIP," Feb. 12, 1844, p. 86.

53. Ibid.

54. K. Lal, pp. 502–3.

55. "AIP," Feb. 13, 1844, p. 87.

56. Ibid., March 1, p. 104.

57. Ibid.

58. "Tarikh Nama," p. 335.

59. J. D. Cunningham, p. 274.

60. Latif, History, p. 527.

61. M'Gregor, 2:29. According to "AIP," March 31, 1844, p. 137, fifty-five women cremated themselves with Suchet Singh.

62. "AIP," May 2, 1844, p. 172.

63. Ibid., March 31, p. 137.

64. Ibid., April 23, p. 162.

65. Ibid., May 20, pp. 192–93.

66. "Umdat-ut-Tawarikh," vol. 4, pt. 3, p. 60.

67. "AIP," April 3 and 4, p. 141.

68. One crore equals ten million.

69. "AIP," April 11, p. 150. Ellenborough estimated Suchet Singh's personal property at 150,000 pounds. See his letter to the Queen, June 10, 1844, in Colchester, p. 128.

70. "AIP," April 27, p. 167.

71. According to J. D. Cunningham, p. 277, Suchet Singh had loaned this money to the British during the Anglo-Afghan War.

72. "AIP," May 25, p. 199.

73. Ibid., May 28, p. 201. This was in sharp contrast to the later years of Ranjit Singh's reign when he used to collect anywhere from 148 to 302 lakhs of rupees in revenue annually. See H. S. Dhillon, "Taxation System" in Maharaja Ranjit Singh Centenary Volume, ed. Teja Singh and Ganda Singh, (Amritsar, 1939), pp. 139–40.

74. "Tarikh Nama," p. 397.

75. Ibid. Unlike Hira Singh, these two had never acquired prominence at Lahore, and lived under the supervision of Gulab Singh in the Jammu hills.

76. "AIP," June 8, p. 211.

77. Ibid., June 16, pp. 219–20; June 28, p. 232; June 29, p. 233.

78. Ibid., June 10, p. 212.

79. Ibid., July 4, p. 239.

80. Ibid., July 17, p. 250.

81. Ibid., July 19, p. 252.

82. Ibid., p. 253.

83. Ibid., July 21, p. 255.

84. Ibid., pp. 254–55.

85. Ibid., July 26, p. 257.

86. Ibid., Aug. 5, p. 264.

87. Ibid., July 26, p. 258.

88. Ibid., July 22, pp. 255–56; July 23, p. 256; Aug. 3, p. 263.

89. Ibid., July 23, p. 256.

90. Ibid., July 29, p. 259.

91. Ibid., Aug. 8, p. 268.

92. Ibid., Aug. 19, p. 279.

93. Ibid., Aug. 11, p. 271.

94. Ibid., Aug. 15, p. 274.

95. Ibid., Aug. 1, p. 261.

96. Ibid., Aug. 8, p. 268.

97. Ibid., Aug. 5, p. 264. He was also under pressure from the Dogra

Mians at Jammu to take revenge against Julla.

98. Ibid., Aug. 12, p. 272.

99. Ibid., Aug. 5, p. 264.

100. Ibid., Aug. 6, p. 266.

101. Ibid., Aug. 5, p. 264; Aug. 6, p. 266; Aug. 7, p. 266; Aug. 20, p. 279.

102. Ibid., Aug. 5, p. 264. Julla was so annoyed by Hira Singh's refusal to act promptly that he sulked and boycotted the darbar for two days. See "AIP," Aug. 6, p. 266.

103. Ibid., Aug. 7, pp. 266–67.

104. Ibid., Aug. 23, p. 280.

105. These facts were personally provided by the Kanwar to Broadfoot. See the latter's communication to Currie, Dec. 16, 1844, "PC," vol. 164, no. 15. But according to an intelligence report that reached Lahore, Peshora Singh spurned Gulab Singh's bid for an anti-Lahore alliance. See "AIP," Aug. 25, p. 282.

106. "AIP," Aug. 12, p. 272; Aug. 20, p. 279; Sept. 3, p. 290.

107. The Jammu Raja tried to dissuade him, "saying he should not go to the enemies of the late Raja Soochet Singh," but Jawahar Singh answered that he "would remain [at Lahore] two or three days only." See "AIP," Aug. 24, p. 281.

108. Ibid., Aug. 26, p. 282.

109. Ibid., pp. 282–83.

110. Ibid., p. 283.

111. Ibid., Sept. 1, pp. 287–88.

112. In his futile petitions for permission to leave the Sikh capital, Jawahar Singh claimed that "he could not aid in any business of the court and felt generally ill when at Lahore." See "AIP," Sept. 6, p. 294.

113. Ibid., Sept. 8, p. 296.

114. Ibid., Sept. 12, p. 300.

115. Ibid., Sept. 5, p. 293. Julla himself feared that the Jammu Raja "might persuade some Meeans of the Hills to assassinate [Hira Singh] and himself." See "AIP," Sept. 8, p. 297.

116. Ibid., Sept. 5, p. 293.

117. Ibid.

118. Ibid., Sept. 7, p. 295.

119. Ibid., Sept. 6, p. 294.

120. Ibid., pp. 294–95.

121. The land surrounded by two converging rivers.

122. "AIP," Sept. 12, p. 300.

123. Ibid., Sept. 6, pp. 294–95.

124. Ibid., Sept. 12, p. 299.

125. Ibid., Sept. 24, p. 311.

126. Ibid., Sept. 9, p. 297.

127. Ibid.

128. Ibid., Sept. 16, p. 303; Sept. 17, p. 304; Sept. 18, p. 306.

129. Ibid., Sept. 24, p. 311.

130. Ibid., Sept. 18, p. 305. The Raja's claim led Julla to retort that Gulab Singh "himself designed to oppose the Khalsa and really wished that the English should possess the Punjaub." See Richmond to Currie, Sept. 30, 1844, SD, "ESLI," vol. 98, enc. 66–91.

131. "AIP," Sept. 28, p. 316. In addition, the Jammu Raja threatened Julla "that on the first shot fired against Jummoo, he shall have joints of his brother served up to him." See Henry Hardinge to Ellenborough, Oct. 22, 1844, "EP," ref. 30/12/21, no. 7. It was also reported that Gulab Singh had sent twenty men to Lahore to murder Julla. See "AIP," Oct. 5, pp. 326–27.

132. The Rani felt that Hira Singh and Julla had usurped Dalip Singh's powers and complained "that her son was merely called Maharaja but never sat in the Durbar." See "AIP," July 15, p. 249.

133. Ibid., Sept. 23, p. 311.

134. Ibid., Oct. 1, p. 320.

135. Ibid., Oct. 2, p. 320.

136. Ibid., Sept. 29, p. 317.

137. J. D. Cunningham, p. 280. Although Broadfoot does not charge Gulab Singh with actually starting the rebellion, he writes that once it broke out the Raja "used every means to attach the people of Cashmeer, and its neighbourhood to himself, and to detach them from Lahore." See his letter to Currie, Oct. 9, 1844, "PC," vol. 164, no. 12.

138. "AIP," Oct. 3, p. 323.

139. Ibid., Sept. 26, p. 313.

140. "Tarikh Nama," p. 406.

141. "AIP," Sept. 27, p. 314; Oct. 4, p. 324.

142. Ibid., Oct. 3, p. 323; Oct. 6, p. 328; Oct. 19, p. 336.

143. "Tarikh Nama," p. 409; "AIP," Oct. 19, p. 336.

144. "AIP," Oct. 15, p. 334.

145. Ibid., Oct. 24, pp. 341–42.

146. Ibid., Oct. 18, p. 335; Oct. 24, pp. 341–42.

147. Broadfoot to Currie, Nov. 9,

1844, "PC," vol. 164, no. 3. The matter of the Feruzpur treasure was further complicated by Rani Suchet Singh, who requested the British authorities not to surrender it to Lahore. See "Umdat-ut-Tawarikh," vol. 4, pt. 3, p. 60.

148. Broadfoot to Currie, Jan. 22, 1845, "PC," vol. 164, no. 40.

149. Broadfoot to Currie, Nov. 13, 1844, "PC," vol. 164, no. 3.

150. "AIP," Oct. 22, p. 337.

151. During August and September rumors were rife that Jindan was pregnant by Lal Singh. See "AIP," Aug. 7, p. 267; Sept. 17, pp. 304–5; Sept. 20, p. 308; and Honigberger, p. 121. On Sept. 21, when the Rani fell critically ill, the darbar warned her paramour that "if it appeared she were now with child and lost her life the Misser should be put to death." See "AIP," Sept. 21, p. 308.

152. The Jammu Raja also castically inquired of Hira Singh: "Now that Lal Singh has been raised to the status of a Raja, what title should be used for you?" See "Tarikh Nama," pp. 420–21.

153. Broadfoot to Currie, Nov. 24, 1844, "PC," vol. 164, no. 8.

154. M'Gregor, 2:35–36.

155. J. D. Cunningham, p. 281.

156. Hardinge to Robert Peel, Jan. 7, 1845, "PPHH," vol. 5.

5 Lahore under Rani Jindan

1. J. D. Cunningham, p. 282.

2. Broadfoot to Currie, Jan. 5, 1845, "PC," vol. 164, no. 30.

3. "Umdat-ut-Tawarikh," vol. 4, pt. 2, p. 70.

4. Broadfoot to Currie, Jan. 4, 1845, "PC," vol. 164, no. 29.

5. Broadfoot to Currie, Jan. 7, 1845, "PC," vol. 164, no. 31.

6. Broadfoot to Currie, Jan. 2, 1845, "PC," vol. 164, no. 26.

7. Broadfoot to Currie, Jan. 4, 1845, "PC," vol. 164, no. 29.

8. Broadfoot to Currie, Jan. 22, 1845, "PC," vol. 164, no. 40.

9. Broadfoot to Currie, Jan. 16, 1845, "PC," vol. 164, no. 36.

10. Broadfoot to Currie, Jan. 22, 1845, "PC," vol. 164, no. 40. Broadfoot also wrote that the Sikh government, too, was anxious to acquire the entire resources of the Jammu chief, and it "therefore desired by any means to obtain part of them as facilitating the acquisition of the rest."

11. Broadfoot to Currie, Jan. 25, 1845, "PC," vol. 164, no. 41.

12. Ibid.

13. Broadfoot to Currie, Feb. 5, 1845, "PC," vol. 164, no. 27.

14. Henry Hardinge to Walter Hardinge, Feb. 8, 1845, "PPHH," vol. 7.

15. Hardinge to Ellenborough, March 8, 1845, "EP," ref. 30/12/21, no. 7; Badhrah, "Raj-Darshani," fols. 137/1–138/1.

16. Latif, History, p. 532.

17. Broadfoot to Currie, Feb. 23, 1845, "PC," vol. 165, no. 47.

18. Ibid. Charles Hardinge, Viscount Hardinge (Oxford, 1891), p. 72, wrote that Gulab Singh "gave £250,000 to be distributed among the men," but this figure seems overstated.

19. Broadfoot to Currie, Feb. 23, 1845, "PC," vol. 165. no. 47.

20. Ibid.

21. Ibid. Peshora Singh was continuing to be a source of irritation to the Sikh government. He was holding court daily at Sialkot and receiving deputations from the khalsa. Gulab Singh provided him with more ammunition for mischief by sending him five lakhs of rupees.

22. Broadfoot to Currie, March 18, 1845, in William Broadfoot, The Career of Major George Broadfoot (London, 1888), p. 300.

23. Ibid. See also J. D. Cunningham, p. 283.

24. J. D. Cunningham, p. 283, seems in general to exonerate the Jammu Raja of involvement in this ambuscade, but suggests that he might have been interested in eliminating a member of the Mann party named Batchna "who had been variously employed by

[the Raja] and who knew the extent of his resources."

25. It is not known, however, whether the Dogra leader ever apprehended and punished the culprits.

26. Broadfoot to Currie, March 18, 1845, "PC," vol. 165, no. 12.

27. Hardinge to Ellenborough, June 7, 1846, "EP," ref. 30/12/21, no. 7.

28. K. Lal, pp. 506–7.

29. Broadfoot to Currie, March 18, 1845, "PC," vol. 165, no. 12.

30. Ibid.

31. Ibid.

32. Hardinge to his wife Emily, April 21, 1845, "PPHH," vol. 6.

33. Broadfoot to Ellenborough, April 21, 1845, in W. Broadfoot, p. 310.

34. According to K. Lal, p. 507, the Sikh government sent repeated orders to the troops not to bring the Jammu chief to Lahore but instead to seize his lands and property. However, they declined to comply.

35. Hardinge to Emily, April 21, 1845, "PPHH," vol. 6.

36. "Umdat-ut-Tawarikh," vol. 4, pt. 3, pp. 71–72.

37. So excited were the people of Lahore on the Jammu Raja's arrival that, as his escorts conducted him on an elephant to his quarters, they hid his face with a handkerchief to save him from the peering eyes of the curious spectators. See Broadfoot to Ellenborough, April 21, 1845, in W. Broadfoot, p. 311.

38. M'Gregor, 2:37.

39. Broadfoot to Ellenborough, April 21, 1845, in W. Broadfoot, p. 315.

40. Ibid.

41. Ellenborough to Hardinge, June 5, 1845, "EP," ref. 30/12/21, no. 7.

42. Hardinge to Ellenborough, June 3, 1845, "EP," ref. 30/12/21, no. 7.

43. It is true that during September 1844, at the height of his quarrel with Lahore, the Raja had tried to turn Rani Jindan against Hira Singh (see Chapter 4), but there is no proof that he was in any way implicated in the eventual death of his nephew. As surely as it was impossible for Gulab Singh to be involved in his first son's death in 1840, he could not now have been a party to a plot in which his second son was killed. If incriminating correspondence did exist, as implied by the Rani, historians have yet to find any trace of it.

44. Hardinge to Ellenborough, June 3, 1845, "EP," ref. 30/12/21, no. 7.

45. Richmond to Currie, June 20, 1845, PHNI, p. 168.

46. Richmond to Currie, June 13, 1845, PHNI, p. 167. Richmond, however justifiably he may have deplored such behavior, seemed all too eager to censure the morals of all Sikhs when he added: "Such is Sikh morality in this matter, and taste also, for Lal Singh is one of the Ranee's own lovers."

47. Richmond to Currie, June 14, 1845, PHNI, p. 168. According to Keightley, p. 194, Jowahir Singh "often got so drunk among horse-jockeys, common servants, and dancing-girls, that he was for days unable to hold a durbar."

48. Richmond to Currie, Aug. 6, 1845, PHNI, pp. 168–69. Dwelling on the same subject, Keightley, p. 194, wrote that "the Ranee herself drank to such excess that her faculties began to be impaired, and she was sinking into stupor: her lust also knew no bounds; Lal Sing, but not he alone, was her known paramour."

49. J. D. Cunningham, p. 284.

50. Morison, p. 92.

51. Broadfoot to Currie, Aug. 25, 1845, "PC," vol. 167, no. 15.

52. J. D. Cunningham, pp. 285–87.

53. C. Hardinge, Viscount Hardinge, p. 73. Arnold, 1:41, charged that the wazir was murdered at Gulab Singh's instigation. This conclusion is, however, not corroborated by other sources.

54. Hardinge to Ellenborough, Oct. 23, 1845, "EP," ref. 30/12/21, no. 7. At the same time, Gulab Singh is reported to have indicated his lack of interest in the wazarat by scornfully observing that "he wished to live for more than six months."

55. Hardinge to SC, Nov. 18, 1845, PHNI, p. 175.

56. Keightley, p. 194, provides this amusing though undoubtedly exaggerated version of how the wazir was chosen: "The troops, like the praetorian guards at Rome, actually put the viziriat up to auction; Lal Sing offered fifteen rupees a man, but they

would not have *him* on any account; another offered eighteen rupees. Gholab Sing was the person they wished to have, provided he would raise their pay, and give them a liberal donation. . . . The Ranee then proposed to decide the question by a lot. . . .These names were Gholab, Tej, and Lal Sing; the young Maharajah drew the lot, and by chance or management, it proved to be that of the last named."

6 British Attitudes Toward Lahore and Jammu: 1839–1845

1. J. D. Cunningham, pp. 384–85.

2. Ibid., pp. 389–92.

3. Ibid., pp. 395–400.

4. R. D. Jenkins and W. B. Bayley to Auckland, Jan. 29, 1840, RD, "BDSL," vol. 12.

5. T. N. Waterfield to Auckland, Aug. 7, 1840, RD, "BDSL," vol. 13.

6. T. N. Waterfield to Auckland, July 31, 1840, RD, "BDSL," vol. 13.

7. Bayley, G. Lyall, and W. Astell to Auckland, Nov. 30, 1840, RD, "BDSL," vol. 12.

8. Bayley to Hobhouse, Jan. 11, 1841, RD, "Home Miscellaneous Correspondence," 836:184–85, MSS in IOL.

9. Bayley and Lyall to Auckland, Jan. 29, 1841, RD, "BDSL," vol. 14.

10. Bayley, Lyall, and Astell to Auckland, March 31, 1841, RD, "BDSL," vol. 14.

11. Lyall and L. I. Lushington to Auckland, June 5, 1841, RD, "BDSL," vol. 14.

12. Maddock to Clerk, Dec. 28, 1840, "PC," vol. 150, no. 121.

13. Clerk to Maddock, April 8, 1841, "PC," vol. 151, no. 41.

14. Clerk to Maddock, May 7, 1841, "PC," vol. 151, no. 53.

15. Cuthbert C. Davies, *The Problem of the Northwest Frontier* (Cambridge, 1932), pp. 136–37 n.

16. See Mackeson to Wade, July 11, 1839, "PC," vol. 11, no. 23.

17. Maddock took particular note of the suspected Dogra-Barakzai bond and directed Clerk to inform the Sikh government that "the connection of the Jummoo family with the Barukzys . . . is too close to admit of any of its members being a proper representative of the Sikh Government, charged with interests of all the states in that quarter." See his letter of Aug. 2, 1841, "PC," vol. 128, no. 127.

18. J. D. Cunningham, p. 260.

19. Clerk to Maddock, Sept. 9, 1841, "PC," vol. 151, no. 43.

20. John W. Kaye, *History of the War in Afghanistan* (London, 1851), 2:319.

21. Ibid., pp. 319–20.

22. Edwardes and Merivale, 1:32.

23. Ibid.

24. Clerk to Maddock, Dec. 8, 1841, "PC," vol. 152, no. 84.

25. Edwardes and Merivale, 1:325. However, on p. 318 they put the strength of the Raja's force at only 10,000.

26. Ibid., p. 318.

27. Kaye, *History*, 2:321n.

28. Edwardes and Merivale, 1:318.

29. Ibid., p. 319.

30. Mackeson to Lawrence, Feb. 3, 1842, "PC," vol. 40, pt. A, no. 63. Jalalabad, a town north of the Khyber Pass, was then under British occupation.

31. "Gulab Nama," p. 317.

32. Edwardes and Merivale, 1:327–28. Mackeson later proposed that Gulab Singh might be given Shikarpur in Sind instead of Jalalabad. See Kaye, *History*, 2:322–23.

33. Kaye, *History*, 2:322.

34. Ibid., p. 322n.

35. Edwardes and Merivale, 1:328.

36. Maddock to Clerk, Feb. 10, 1842, "PC," vol. 130, no. 39.

37. Clerk to Gulab Singh, Feb. 1, 1842, Persian "Marasalajats," ref. 4381, fol. 36/2, MSS in PSA.

38. Edwardes and Merivale, 1:319.

39. Kaye, *History*, 2:321.

40. Edwardes and Merivale, 1:320.

41. Ibid.

42. Ibid., p. 324.

43. Ibid.

44. Ibid., pp. 325–26.

45. Kaye, *History*, 2:321; Charles R. Low, *The Life and Correspondence of Field-Marshall Sir George Pollock* (London, 1873), p. 247.

46. Kaye, *History* 2:323–26.
47. Clerk to Maddock, March 6, 1842, "PC," vol. 153, no. 41.
48. Kaye, *History*, 2:326–27.
49. *Halwa* is usually made with flour, sugar, ghee (purified butter), and nuts. The Sikhs also consider it a holy food since it is served in the *gurdwaras* (Sikh temples) to the congregation after most services.
50. "Gulab Nama," pp. 316–19.
51. Clerk to Gulab Singh, April 20, 1842, Persian "Marasalajats," ref. 4381, fol. 38/2. Despite the appreciation expressed by other British officials, Pollock did not forgive the Dogra leader's procrastination. In April he grumbled: "I have . . . been much disappointed by the delay of the Rajah Golab Sing, in not sooner having moved up his troops. . . . Although I have never expected any very active operations from them." See Low, p. 253.
52. Clerk to Maddock, July 28, 1842, "PC," vol. 154, no. 27.
53. Undated letter of Maharaja Sher Singh to Ellenborough received by Clerk on July 18, 1842, "PC," vol. 155, no. 181.
54. Ellenborough to Wellington, June 7, 1842, in Colchester, p. 254.
55. J. D. Cunningham, p. 264.
56. Ibid., pp. 264–65.
57. Ellenborough to Wellington, Oct. 26, 1841, in Colchester, p. 160.
58. Wellington to Ellenborough, Dec. 29, in Colchester, p. 200.
59. Wellington to Lord Fitzgerald, April 6, 1842, in Colchester, p. 247.
60. Wellesley to Ellenborough, July 4, in Colchester, p. 175.
61. Lushington and Cotton to Ellenborough, Aug. 31, 1842, RD, "BDSL," vol. 16.
62. Ellenborough to Wellington, Oct. 18, 1842, in Colchester, p. 299.
63. Wellington to SC, Jan. 20, 1843, in *India Under Lord Ellenborough*, pp. 49–50.
64. Lushington, Cotton, and Astell to Ellenborough, April 3, 1843, RD, "BDSL," vol. 17.
65. Ibid.
66. General Charles Napier, who conquered Sind, reported his achievement to Ellenborough by quipping in Latin: "Peccavi [I have sinned]." See R. C. Majumdar, H. C. Raychaudhuri,

and K. Datta, *An Advanced History of India*, 2nd ed. (London, 1963), p. 763.
67. Ellenborough to Wellington, Oct. 20, 1843, in Colchester, p. 399.
68. Ellenborough to Wellington, Dec. 18, in Colchester, p. 411, and Ellenborough to Queen Victoria, Dec. 19, in Colchester, p. 107.
69. Ellenborough to Wellington, Oct. 20, in Colchester, p. 399.
70. Currie to Richmond, Jan. 31, 1844, SD, "ESLI," vol. 95, enc. 12, letter 59.
71. Richmond to Currie, Feb. 13, 1844, SD, "ESLI," vol. 96, enc. 14, letter 8.
72. Ellenborough to Wellington, Feb. 15, 1844, and Ellenborough to the Queen, Feb. 16, 1844, in Colchester, pp. 423–24 and p. 114, respectively.
73. Ellenborough to SC, Feb. 11, 1844, in *India Under Lord Ellenborough*, p. 114.
74. Shepherd and Willock to Ellenborough, April 30, 1844, RD, "BDSL," vol. 18.
75. Ellenborough to Wellington, May 9, 1844, in Colchester, p. 437.
76. Richmond to Thomason, Oct. 26, 1843, SD, "ESLI," vol. 128, enc. 158.
77. Richmond to Currie, April 3, 1844, SD, "ESLI," vol. 96, enc. 22, letter 23.
78. Richmond also postulated that "Raja Golab Singh is an able man as was his brother Dhian Singh and they could draw their inferences and conclusions from the tone of our conversations from our wishes and from our desire to have their men employed on specific duties as well as [those] of the state." See his letter to Currie, June 3, 1844, "PC," vol. 159, no. 92.
79. Currie to Richmond, June 15, "PC," vol. 134, no. 40.
80. Ibid.
81. Hardinge to Peel, Aug. 1, 1844, "PPHH," vol. 5.
82. C. Hardinge, *Viscount Hardinge*, p. 50.
83. Hardinge to Peel, Aug. 1, 1844, "PPHH," vol. 5.
84. Hardinge to Peel, Sept. 21, 1844, "PPHH," vol. 5.
85. C. Hardinge, *Viscount Hardinge*, p. 71.
86. Richmond to Currie, Sept. 10

and Oct. 5, 1844, "PC," vol. 160, nos.
48 and 60, respectively.
87. See Hardinge to Ellenborough,
Oct. 22, 1844, "EP," ref. 30/12/21, no.
7. Hardinge also wrote that, "altho' an
able man & good soldier, [Gulab
Singh] is a tiger even amongst the cut
throat Sikhs."
88. Broadfoot to Currie, Jan. 25,
1845, "PC," vol. 164, no. 4. Hardinge
referred to this offer in a communication to Peel: "Golab Singh is evidently
in great alarm. He has made proposals
through his friends at Lahore to Major
[Broadfoot] to march a British force
into the Punjaub." See his letter dated
Feb. 7, 1845, "PPHH," vol. 5.
89. Broadfoot to Currie, Feb. 4,
1845, "PC," vol. 164, no. 45.
90. Hardinge to Walter, Feb. 8,
1845, "PPHH," vol. 7.
91. Grey, p. 349.
92. Hardinge to Ellenborough, Feb.
28, 1845, "EP," ref. 30/12/21, no. 7.
93. Hardinge to Ellenborough, Feb.
20, 1845, "EP," ref. 30/12/21, no. 7.
The impostor did, however, escape
physical punishment. He remained at
Jammu until the end of the First Anglo-Sikh War and was then deported
from India. See Grey, p. 349.
94. Hardinge to his step-son, Gra-
ham, "PPHH," vol. 7. The letter bears
no date but was probably written in
February, 1845, since it is filed with
other letters of that month.
95. Hardinge to Emily, Feb. 20,
1845, "PPHH," vol. 6.

96. Ibid.
97. Shepherd and Willock to Hardinge, March 24, 1845, RD, "BDSL,"
vol. 18.
98. Hardinge to Peel, April 8, 1845,
"PPHH," vol. 5.
99. Hardinge to Emily, April 21,
1845, "PPHH," vol. 6.
100. Hardinge to Peel, April 21,
1845, "PPHH," vol. 5.
101. Hardinge to Emily, April 21,
1845, "PPHH," vol. 6.
102. Broadfoot to Currie, May 5,
1845, "PC," vol. 165, no. 31.
103. Ibid.
104. Hardinge to Ellenborough,
Sept. 8, 1845, "EP," ref. 30/12/21, no.
7.
105. Broadfoot to Currie, Aug. 25,
1845, "PC," vol. 167, no. 15. Broadfoot
also reported that Shiv Datt, the messenger, recounted how he personally
had beheld signs of the coming conflict while at Lahore: "Yakeen Januua
—Zuroor Jung hoonda—asi khood
vekhya—Rely on it, there will assur-
edly be war—I have myself seen it."
106. Ibid.
107. Ibid.
108. Ibid.
109. Hardinge to Peel, Sept. 8, 1845,
"PPHH," vol. 5.
110. Hardinge to SC, Sept. 6, 1845,
PHNI, p. 167.
111. Hardinge to Peel, Sept. 8, 1845,
"PPHH," vol. 5.
112. Ibid.
113. Ibid.

7 The Making of a Maharaja

1. This author published a large
part of this chapter as an article entitled "Raja Gulab Singh's Role in the
First Anglo-Sikh War" in *Modern
Asian Studies* 5 (1971), pp. 35–59. It is
reprinted here by permission of Cambridge University Press.
2. Such a position is supported by,
among others, Jagmohan Mahajan,
*Circumstances Leading to the Annexa-
tion of the Punjab* (Allahabad, 1946);
Ganda Singh, ed., *Private Correspondence relating to the Anglo-Sikh
Wars*; K. Singh, *Fall of Punjab.*
3. The strongest proponent of such

a belief is Panikkar. Others who express similar views include Bamzai;
G. L. Kaul; Salig Ram Koul, *The Biography of Maharaja Gulab Singh*
(Srinagar, 1923); Mohammad Aslam
Khan, *The Dogra Occupation of
Kashmir* (Srinagar, 1946); Hashmat
Ali Khan, *Tarikh-e-Jammu* (Lucknow,
1939).
4. Varying opinions on Gulab Singh
have also been put forward by the
writers who have dwelt upon the India-Pakistan dispute over Kashmir.
However, their treatment of the man,
covered in brief introductory surveys,

tends to be superficial. These writers can be divided into two groups. The first is quite partisan and includes Bazaz; Aziz Beg, *Captive Kashmir* (Lahore, 1957); M. M. Rahman Khan, *The United Nations and Kashmir* (New York, 1956); Sisir Gupta, *Kashmir, A Study in India-Pakistan Relations* (New Delhi, 1966); Balraj Madhok, *Kashmir: Centre of New Alignments* (New Delhi, 1963). Among the second group, portraying a more dispassionate viewpoint, are Lord Birdwood, *India and Pakistan* (New York, 1954); Michael Brecher, *The Struggle for Kashmir* (New York, 1953); Alastair Lamb, *Crisis in Kashmir* (London, 1966).

5. Kohli, basing his estimates on the darbar's records, states that the numerical strength of the khalsa rose from 46,037 in 1838 to 65,835 in 1843 and again to 89,821 in 1845. These statistics include the infantry, artillery, and the cavalry, but not the levies supplied by the fief-holders. See pp. 60–98, with special reference to pp. 70–87.

6. C. Hardinge, *Viscount Hardinge,* p. 77, discloses that the British strength at the Ambala cantonment was increased "from 13,600 men and 48 guns in January, 1844, to 32,500 men and 68 guns in December, 1845."

7. Hardinge to Peel, Feb. 19, 1846, "PPHH," vol. 5. Hardinge also reported that, according to Gulab Singh's postwar explanation of Lahore's objectives, the khalsa was to "sweep away" the frontier stations of Feruzpur and Ludhiana. If triumphant, the darbar expected the Company's Hindu sepoys and the Phulkian states to join hands with the khalsa and believed "that they would in a month be in possession of Delhi." The Sikhs also looked to "Nepal to be ready in case of a first success against [the British]."

8. Broadfoot to Currie, Nov. 20, 1845, in *The War In India* (London, 1846), p. 21.

9. Kishan Chand to Broadfoot, Dec. 3, 1845, as quoted in the *Times* (London), March 2, 1846, p. 2.

10. Though no official figures are available, M'Gregor, 2:64, estimated the invading force to consist of "nearly 50,000 infantry, 25,000 cavalry

and 200 guns." It seems that a part of the army remained stationed in such provinces as Kashmir, Peshawar, and Multan.

11. When Bhai Ram Singh attempted to dissuade the wazir, the latter answered: "Bhaee Sahib, what can I do? if I remain, the soldiery seize me by the throat." Peel quoted Lal Singh's response from a letter written by an informer at Lahore dated Nov. 24, 1845, in a speech before the House of Commons on March 2, 1846. See *Hansard's Parliamentary Debates* (London, 1846), 84:393.

12. "LI," Dec. 6, 1845, "PC," vol. 169.

13. Ibid. However, according to K. Lal, p. 507, the Rani in fact urged the Dogra chief to assume the wazarat soon after the war commenced.

14. "LI," Dec. 6, 1845, "PC," vol. 169.

15. Currie to Broadfoot, Nov. 25, 1845, in W. Broadfoot, p. 370.

16. Hardinge to SC, Dec. 2, 1845, in *The War In India,* pp. 9–10.

17. C. Hardinge to his mother Emily, Dec. 4, 1845, "PPHH," vol. 6.

18. "LI," Dec. 1, 1845, "PC," vol. 169.

19. Hardinge to SC, Dec. 4, 1845, in *The War In India,* p. 28.

20. See Currie to Broadfoot, Nov. 25, 1845, in W. Broadfoot, pp. 372–73. The messenger claimed that he had actually carried a written communication from the Raja but that as "he was about to be searched at the Phillaur Ferry, he dropped the letter into the river [Sutlej] and swam across to save his life."

21. "LI," Dec. 10, 1845, "PC," vol. 169.

22. J. D. Cunningham, p. 304.

23. A hint of such implication is found in a letter from Lal Singh to Peter Nicholson, assistant agent at Feruzpur, wherein the wazir informed the British officer "to consider him and the bibi sahiba (Jindan) as their friends and cut up the burchas (ruffians, i. e. the khalsa) for them." See K. Singh, *History,* 2:48. An indirect reference to messages from the Rani and other leaders was also made by Hardinge in a letter dated Jan. 13, 1846, to Hugh Gough, the Company's commander-in-chief: "such is the

treachery, low cunning & perverse policy of the Durbar & even of Raja Golab Sing, that no dependence can be placed on the professions which every party is ready to make for its own interested objects & in the present state of the Sikh Army neither the Ranee nor any chief can offer any guarantee for the performance of their promise." See SD, "ESLI," vol. 103, enc. 2, letter 14.

24. The extensive testimony regarding the incriminating role of Lal Singh and, to a lesser degree, Tej Singh is provided by, among others, J. D. Cunningham, pp. 304–9; M'Gregor, 2:80–82; Latif, History, pp. 541–43; Hesketh Pearson, The Hero of Delhi (London, 1939), pp. 79–80.

In retrospect, the Jammu chief, too, questioned the wisdom of the Sikh strategy at Firuzshahar: "Teja Singh committed a great blunder; he should never have gone near you [the British], but should have marched at once upon Delhi!" Quoted in W. W. W. Humbley, Journal of a Cavalry Officer (London, 1854), p. 104.

25. British writers, among them some eyewitnesses, who commended the khalsa's performance include J. D. Cunningham, pp. 301–10; J. W. Fortescue, A History of the British Army (London, 1927), 12:390; H. Knollys, ed., Life of General Sir Hope Grant (London, 1894), 1:58–59; M'Gregor, 2:46–53, 111–28; Trevaskis, pp. 205–6.

26. The Times, March 2, 1846, p. 4. Pearson, p. 80, quotes Hardinge's stinging observation: "Another such victory and we are undone!"

27. Lake to Mills, Jan. 15, 1846, SD, "ESLI," vol. 103, enc. 2, letter 3.

28. Currie to Mills, Jan. 17, 1846, "ESLI," vol. 103, enc. 2, letter 24.

29. Broadfoot was killed at Firuzshahr.

30. LN, Jan. 7, 1846, DG, Times, March 2, 1846, p. 5.

31. According to Honigberger, p. 125, Gulab Singh permitted himself to be drawn "from Jummoo, his den" by the panches, who had dubbed him the "bear."

32. The Times, March 25, 1846, p. 5. However, the Illustrated London News, April 4, 1846, p. 220, reported that the Raja came with 20,000 men.

33. LN, Jan. 26, 1846, DG, Times, March 25, 1846, p. 5, reported that the Raja "has brought immense quantities with him; the number of bullocks with his camp is enormous—some say 300,000. He has left orders with his lieutenants in Jamoo and other places to send more as soon as they could be collected."

34. "LI," Jan. 29, 1846, "PC," vol. 170.

35. Illustrated London News, April 4, 1846, p. 220.

36. "Gulab Nama," p. 425.

37. Illustrated London News, April 4, 1846, p. 220. According to the "Tarikh Nama," p. 589, Gulab Singh told the panches that he would move upon receipt of the Rani's written orders.

38. History of the Campaign on the Sutlej and the War in the Punjaub (London, 1846), p. 36.

39. Ibid., p. 37; LN, Jan. 29, 1846, DG, Times, April 1, 1846, p. 6.

40. "LI," Jan. 29, 1846, "PC," vol. 170.

41. LN, Jan. 30, 1846, DG, Times, April 1, 1846, p. 6.

42. "LI," Jan. 30, 1846, "PC," vol. 170.

43. Ibid., Jan. 31.

44. Ibid.

45. LN, Jan. 31, 1846, DG, Times, April 1, 1846, p. 6.

46. Ibid.

47. Hardinge to SC, FPNWF, p. 67.

48. "PBI," Feb. 1, 1846, SD, "ESLI," vol. 103, enc. 6.

49. LN, Feb. 1, 1846, DG, Times, April 1, 1846, p. 6.

50. LN, Feb. 2, 1846, DG, Times, April 1, 1846.

51. Ganesh Das Badhrah, "Char Bagh-e-Panjab," fol. 376/2, Persian MS in IOL.

52. "LI," Feb. 2, 1846, "PC," vol. 170.

53. Ibid.

54. Badhrah, "Char Bagh-e-Panjab," fols. 376/2–377/1.

55. "PBI," Feb. 4, 6, and 8, 1846, SD, "ESLI," vol. 103, enc. 6.

56. "PBI," Feb. 7, 1846, SD, "ESLI," vol. 103, enc. 6.

57. "PBI," Feb. 8, 1846, SD, "ESLI," vol. 103, enc. 6.

58. "PBI," Feb. 1, 4, and 5, 1846, "ESLI," vol. 103, enc. 6.

59. "PBI," Feb. 6, 1846, SD, "ESLI," vol. 103, enc. 6.

60. "PBI," Feb. 8, 1846, SD, "ESLI," vol. 103, enc. 6.

61. Hardinge to SC, Feb. 19, 1846, FPNWF, p. 67.

62. Hardinge to Peel, Feb. 3, 1846, "PPHH," vol. 5. In a letter to SC, Feb. 3, 1846, FPNWF, p. 54, Hardinge spoke of a similar postwar solution.

63. J. J. M. Innes, *Sir Henry Lawrence* (Oxford, 1898), p. 208.

64. According to William Edwardes, *Reminiscences of a Bengal Civilian* (London, 1866), p. 104, a soldiers' deputation complained to the Rani of a shortage of food at the front. When told that Gulab Singh had sent sufficient supplies, the soldiers retorted: "No he has not, we know the old fox; he has not sent breakfast for a bird."

65. "PBI," Feb. 5, 1846, SD, "ESLI," vol. 103, enc. no. 6.

66. LN, Feb. 8, 1846, DG, Times, April 1, 1846, p. 6.

67. Mackeson to Currie, Feb. 10, 1846, SD, "ESLI," vol. 103, enc. 6, letter 23.

68. Honigberger, p. 126; LN, Feb. 7, 1846, DG, Times, April 1, 1846, p. 6; "PBI," Feb. 9, 1846, SD, "ESLI," vol. 103, enc. 6.

69. LN, Feb. 8, 1846, DG, Times, April 1, 1846, p. 6.

70. Badhrah, "Raj-Darshani," fol. 306/1. Several British writers also have alluded to the cowardly conduct of the Sikh generals at Sobraon. J. D. Cunningham, p. 327, wrote: "The traitor, Tej Singh, indeed, instead of leading fresh men to sustain the failing strength of troops on his right, fled on the first assault, and, either accidentally, or by design, sank a boat in the middle of the bridge of communication." Calling him "a base traitor," Humbley, p. 179, charged that Tej Singh "deserted his post; he fled at the first brush." He also noted that Lal Singh "lay with his cavalry higher up the river in a careless, unmilitary position, conscious of being closely watched by the English." Trevaskis, p. 205, condemned Sikh and British generals alike and commented that the war "may be described as one between lions led by asses."

71. J. D. Cunningham, p. 328n, puts the number of dead and wounded between 5,000 and 8,000, but Humbley, p. 180, believes it was between 12,000 and 15,000.

72. M'Gregor, 2:177.

73. "PBI," Feb. 12, 1846, SD, "ESLI," vol. 103, enc. 6. It also reported Gulab Singh's boast "that had he gone, he would have died like the other Sirdars, & not have run away like the Khalsa."

74. Badhrah, "Raj-Darshani," fol. 306/2.

75. "PBI," Feb. 12 and 13, 1846, SD, "ESLI," vol. 103, enc. 6.

76. According to Badhrah, "Raj-Darshani," fols. 306/2–307/1, Gulab Singh resorted to poetry in an effort to calm Jindan's nerves. He recited eight verses, which, in essence, told the Rani that she had little to fear if she would follow the Dogra chief's advice.

77. Hardinge to SC, Feb. 19, 1846, FPNWF, p. 68.

78. Ibid.

79. Hardinge to Emily, Feb. 17, 1846, "PPHH," vol. 6.

80. Hardinge to SC, Feb. 19, 1846, FPNWF, pp. 68–69.

81. See Mackeson to Currie, Feb. 19, 1846, SD, "ESLI," vol. 103, enc. 7, letter 29. Curiously enough, Mackeson discounted the rumors of all the murders except that of the Jammu Raja. However, according to LN, Feb. 18, 1846, DG, Times, April 20, 1846, p. 6, "a rumor got abroad [at Lahore] that Rajah Gholab Singh and others, who had gone to the British camp had been seized and made prisoners by the British, which greatly alarmed the people."

82. Hardinge to Peel, Feb. 19, 1846, "PPHH," vol. 5.

83. Hardinge to SC, Feb. 19, 1846, in *The War in India*, p. 102.

84. Hardinge told Peel, Feb. 19, 1846, "PPHH," vol. 5, that in anticipation of independence Gulab Singh "wished us to [let him] adopt the subsidiary system & a Resident. This was refused."

85. Hardinge to SC, Feb. 19, 1846, in *The War In India*, p. 104.

86. The *Illustrated London News*, April 4, 1846, p. 222, reported that this force numbered "from 14,000 to 20,000 horse and foot, with about 35 guns."

87. H. L. Pester, *Papers*, p. 14, European MS in IOL.

88. R. N. Cust, *Papers*, p. 76, European MS in IOL. Cust, an assistant to Lawrence, claimed to have witnessed an attempt by unknown snipers to kill Gulab Singh on Feb. 24. C. Hardinge, *Viscount Hardinge*, pp. 138–39, also refers to a conspiracy by Lal Singh to murder the Raja.

89. *LN*, Feb. 21, 22, and 23, 1846, *DG*, *Times*, April 20, 1846, p. 6.

90. "Gulab Nama," p. 443.

91. "The Treaties of Lahore" in the *Times*, May 25, 1846, p. 8.

92. J. D. Cunningham, pp. 406–11.

93. John C. Marshman, *Memoirs of Major-General Sir Henry Havelock* (London, 1860), pp. 161–62.

94. Hardinge to Walter, March 11, 1846, "PPHH," vol. 7.

95. The new state under Gulab Singh was not to include such eastern hill areas as Kulu, Kangra, Nurpur, and Mandi. The British considered the region strategically important and annexed it. Justifying the territorial division, Hardinge told SC, March 4, 1846, *FPNWF*, p. 89: "It is highly expedient that the trans-Beas portion of Kooloo and Mundi, with the more fertile district and strong position of Noorpoore, and the celebrated Fort Kangra —the Key of the Himalayas, in native estimation—with its district and dependencies, should be in our possession." Further territorial adjustments which did not affect Kashmir were made later.

96. J. D. Cunningham, pp. 413–15. For more on the sale of Kashmir, see my Appendix C.

97. Ibid., p. 332n. In spite of such a display of servility, the Dogra leader protested against the slaughter of cows by the British party at Amritsar, and suggested that they eat goat meat instead. He even ordered free mutton to be supplied to the British during their sojourn there. Gulab Singh's efforts finally met with partial success when Hardinge prohibited the butchering of female cows. See Babu Ram, *Mukhtsar-Sair-Gulshan-e-Hind* (Kanpur, 1878), pp. 192–94.

98. Hardinge to Sarah, Feb. 19, 1846, "PPHH," box no. 1 of unfiled letters.

99. Hardinge to Emily, March 2,

1846, "PPHH," vol. 6.

100. Hardinge to SC, March 4, 1846, *FPNWF*, p. 89.

101. Hardinge to Peel, March 19, 1846, "PPHH," vol. 5.

102. C. Hardinge, *Viscount Hardinge*, p. 131.

103. W. Napier, *Life of Charles Napier*, 3:391.

104. Ibid., p. 400.

105. Napier's militant attitude was no secret to the inhabitants of northwestern India. A news item entitled "India and China—The Overland Mail" in the *Times*, March 6, 1846, p. 5, revealed that they had tagged him "Sheitan ka bhaee, 'the Devil's brother.'"

106. C. Hardinge, *Viscount Hardinge*, p. 131.

107. Ibid., pp. 132–33. Charles also wrote about the "impolity and the difficulties of annexation" soon after the cessation of hostilities: "Peshawar 300 miles in advance of the Sutlege with 4 deep rivers intersecting it—and the military occupation of Cashmeer touching Chinese Tartary with our troops extending down to Mooltan would by no means improve our frontier line." See his letter to Walter, March 4, 1846, "PPHH," vol. 7.

108. Ellenborough to Hardinge, April 22, 1846, "EP," ref. 30/12/21, no. 7.

109. Hardinge to Ellenborough, June 7, 1846, "EP," ref. 30/12/21, no. 7.

110. Morison, p. 158.

111. C. Hardinge, *Viscount Hardinge*, p. 143.

112. H. Willock, J. Hogg, and W. Astell to Hardinge, April 4, 1846, RD, "BDSL," vol. 19.

113. *Times*, May 5, 1846, p. 4.

114. Ibid., May 21, p. 4.

115. Although the poet Iqbal never actually wrote on the conduct of the Jammu chief in the First Anglo-Sikh War, yet he was perhaps responsible for reviving the old controversy over the issue by alluding to the sale of Kashmir in the now famous verse quoted below:

Their fields, their crops, their streams
Even the peasants in the vale
They sold, they sold all, alas!
How cheap was the sale.

8 The Birth of the Dogra State

1. Gulab Singh to Currie, undated letter included in correspondence of April and May, 1846, SD, "ESLI," vol. 104, enc. 10, letters 7–12.

2. Herbert Edwardes to Henry Lawrence, March 27, 1846, SD, "ESLI," vol. 104, enc. 10, letter 99.

3. Henry Lawrence to Currie, March 29, 1846, SD, "ESLI," vol. 104, enc. 10, letter 26.

4. Henry Lawrence to Currie, March 31, 1846, SD, "ESLI," vol. 104, enc. 10, letter 27.

5. Henry Lawrence to Currie, April 11, 1846, SD, "ESLI," vol. 104, enc. 11, letter 35.

6. Henry Lawrence to Currie, April 17, 1846, SD, "ESLI," vol. 104, enc. 12, letter 45.

7. Aitchison, 11:252; Hardinge to SC, Dec. 4, 1846, PRAL, p. 194.

8. Henry Lawrence to Currie, April 11, 1846, SD, "ESLI," vol. 104, enc. 11, letter 35.

9. Ibid.

10. Henry Lawrence to Gulab Singh, April 11, 1846, SD, "ESLI," vol. 104, enc. 11, letter 17.

11. Ibid. Henry Lawrence's outbursts were the culmination of his mounting resentment over Gulab Singh's tactics. On March 29 he had complained to Currie (enc. 10, letter 26) that instead of gratitude the Maharaja "still adheres to so much of his old petty & grasping line of policy." Again, on April 9, he told Currie (enc. 11, letter 33) that Gulab Singh "still affects poverty. He seems to expect everything & to be very little disposed to give in return, more than fair words."

12. Hardinge to SC, Sept. 19, 1846, PRAL, p. 186.

13. Ibid., pp. 186–87. Gulab Singh considered Imam-ud-Din to be under his thumb because he had in the past been instrumental in obtaining for him the administration of Jullundur Doab. Moreover, during the Dogra leader's bitter dispute with Hira Singh in 1844, Imam had adopted a pro-Jammu stance.

14. C. Hardinge, Viscount Hardinge, p. 148. But Henry Hardinge wrote to SC, Oct. 4, 1846, PRAL, p.

191, that Gulab Singh only "requested the Sheik to remain till he sent full reinforcements to assume military occupation."

15. Contemporaries made very divergent estimates of Imam-ud-Din. One anonymous source called him "the best-dressed and best-mannered man in the Punjab." See Frederick P. Gibbon, The Lawrences of the Punjab (London, 1908), p. 129. Herbert Edwardes wrote that he had "all the qualities which win popular applause, and less than the usual share of those vices which, in the East, make governors detested." See Edwardes Memorials, 1:63. On the other hand, an acquaintance described him as a man of "ambition, pride, cruelty, and intrigue, strangely mixed with indolence, effeminacy, voluptuousness, and timidity." See R. Bosworth Smith, Life of Lord Lawrence, 2nd ed. (London, 1883), 1:225. Charles Hardinge called him "a thickheaded and foolish fellow." See his letter to Walter, Sept. 2, 1846, "PPHH," vol. 7. Comparing the Sheikh to the Jammu chief, John Lawrence once said: "If Golab Sing flayed a chief alive, Imamuddin boiled a Pundit to death: they are certainly a pair of amiables." See R. B. Smith, 1:225.

16. Hardinge told SC, Sept. 19, 1846 (PRAL, pp. 187–88), that Mohiud-Din was delinquent in revenue payments to Lahore, and on the eve of the Anglo-Sikh War had sent "across the Sutledj" embezzled goods worth a crore of rupees.

17. Charles to Walter, Sept. 2, 1846, "PPHH," vol. 7.

18. Gibbon, p. 129.

19. Hardinge to SC, Sept. 19, 1846, PRAL, p. 186.

20. Har Gopal Kaul, Guldasta-e-Kashmir (Lahore, 1883), p. 194.

21. Lionel J. Trotter, The Life of John Nicholson (London, 1897), p. 60.

22. Pearson, p. 85.

23. Ibid.

24. It is interesting to note that, on the very day that Imam's troops struck, it was "industriously circulated at the Bazar of Cashmere, that the British troops had been attacked

and defeated at Lahore and the young Maharajah killed." See Hardinge's letter to SC, Sept. 19, 1846, *PRAL*, p. 188. Apprehensive of the consequences of this lingering crisis, the Governor-General decided to "continue to hold Lahore by a strong British garrison" (p. 191).

25. Hardinge to Walter, Sept. 18, 1846, "PPHH," vol. 7.

26. Trotter, *Nicholson*, p. 60.

27. Hardinge to SC, Oct. 4, 1846, *PRAL*, p. 190.

28. *Edwardes Memorials*, 1:63–64.

29. However, he suspected that the rebellion was not "the rising of the people agt. Golab S. but of the Hill States paid by Shiek." See his letter to Walter, Oct. 22, 1846, "PPHH," vol. 7.

30. Hardinge to Walter, Sept. 18, 1846, "PPHH," vol. 7.

31. Hardinge to SC, Sept. 19, 1846, *PRAL*, p. 188.

32. Ibid. Hardinge also ordered another four regiments and twelve guns moved from Lahore to Sialkot to assist Wheeler (p. 190).

33. When John Lawrence sought the Sikh leaders' aid, they "made excuses, and procrastinated as best as they could. But [he] was firm, and compelled them to do what was naturally so distasteful to them." See R. B. Smith, 1:224.

34. Hardinge to SC, Oct. 4, 1846, *PRAL*, p. 190.

35. Hardinge to Walter, Oct. 22, 1846, "PPHH," vol. 7.

36. Hardinge to SC, Oct. 4, 1846, *PRAL*, p. 189.

37. John Lawrence wanted the command for himself. He is quoted as having said: "I should like nothing better . . . I would soon settle our friend the Sheikh." See R. B. Smith, 1:224. Henry Hardinge, too, entertained a similar desire, and confided to Walter, Sept. 18, 1846, "PPHH," vol. 7: "If I were a Brigadier instead of a GG [Governor-General] I should like to have the management of the Cashmere campaign."

38. Hardinge to Peel, Dec. 21, 1846, "PPHH," vol. 5; Morison, p. 167.

39. Hardinge to SC, Nov. 3, 1846, *PRAL*, p. 192.

40. Hardinge to SC, Nov. 21, 1846, *PRAL*, p. 193.

41. See Minutes of the Court of Inquiry, Dec. 3, 1846, *BGLD*, p. 208.

42. Morison, p. 169.

43. Minutes of the Court of Inquiry, Dec, 3, 1846, *BGLD*, p. 214.

44. Ibid., p. 216.

45. Ibid., p. 219.

46. Innes, p. 69.

47. Aitchison, 11:252.

48. Ibid.

49. Ibid., p. 250.

50. Frederick Currie's Award on the Jawahar Singh-Gulab Singh Dispute, May 5, 1848, Persian "Marasalajats, ref. 628.

51. These jagirs included Koth, Siala, Sudankot, and Chaliar. See *sanads* (titles or deeds) issued by Gulab Singh, March 21, 1852, and Sept. 25, 1852, Persian "Marasalajats," ref. 669.

52. See H. G. Kaul, p. 195.

53. See Jawahar Singh to John Lawrence, April 6, 1855, Persian "Marasalajats," ref. 674; John Lawrence to Gulab Singh, May 6, 1855, Urdu "Marasalajats," ref. 616.

54. See copy of a *sanad*, Feb. 18, 1859, Urdu "Marasalajats," ref. 621.

55. See Aitchison, 11:251.

56. Lawrence to Currie, March 29, 1846, SD, "ESLI," vol. 104, enc. 10, letter 26.

57. Lawrence to Gulab Singh, Jan. 5, 1847, Persian "Marasalajats," ref. 4382, pp. 2–4.

58. Lawrence to Jawala Sahai, Feb. 17, 1847, Persian "Marasalajats," ref. 4382, pp. 25–27.

59. Lawrence to Jawala Sahai, Feb. 2, 1847, Persian "Marasalajats," ref. 4382, p. 22.

60. Lawrence to Gulab Singh, April 4, 1847, Persian "Marasalajats," ref. 4382, pp. 72–73.

61. Currie to Edwardes, Jan. 4, 1848, *PRP*, pp. 135–36.

62. At one stage Dina Nath, the Sikh negotiator, taunted the Dogra representatives that Gulab Singh was too stingy to make the financial investment necessary to retain Hazara. See "Umdat-ut-Tawarikh" vol. 5, pt. 1, p. 52.

63. Aitchison, 11:248. For a full copy of the Anglo-Dogra agreement, see Aitchison, 11:266–67.

64. See Currie to the political sec-

retary of the Governor-General, Dec. 27, 1847, *PRP*, pp. 127–28.

65. For details of the delimitation, see Aitchison, 11:248n.

66. Ibid., p. 249.

67. Ferguson, pp. 62–63; Thomas Thomson, *Western Himalaya and Tibet* (London, 1852), p. 249.

68. Referring to Gulab Singh's difficulties, Henry Lawrence observed in 1850 that Gilgit "is as expensive to him as Peshawar is to us." See Morison, p. 239. The most serious revolt came in 1852 when almost a thousand Dogras lost their lives. See Ferguson, pp. 63–64. Despite innumerous efforts during 1855 and 1856, the Maharaja failed to regain control of the region. See Saif-ud-Din to John Lawrence, June 27 and Aug. 15, 1855, "SDS," vol. 8, fols. 71/2, 102/2; March 22, May 2, June 1, July 4, 7, Aug. 20, 25, 30, Sept. 5, 8, 11, and Oct. 7, 1856, vol. 9, fols. 37, 53/2, 67/2, 91, 92/2, 149/2, 154/2, 160/2, 168/2, 170/2, 176, 208.

69. Gilgit was recaptured in 1860 by Maharaja Ranbir Singh, but the real power there eventually passed to a British political agent who was permanently stationed in Gilgit from 1889. See Aitchison, 11:256–59; Lamb, *Crisis in Kashmir*, p. 26.

70. Peel to Hardinge, July 7, 1846, "PPHH," vol. 4.

71. Edwardes and Merivale, 2:62.

72. See Charles to William, Oct. 16, 1846, in W. Napier, *Life of Charles Napier*, 3:455.

73. Charles to William, Nov. 2, 1846, in W. Napier, *Life of Charles Napier*, 3:458.

74. Charles to William, Nov. 6, 1846, in W. Napier, *Life of Charles Napier*, 3:459.

75. Charles to William, Nov. 8, 1846, in W. Napier, *Life of Charles Napier*, 3:469–70.

76. The following excerpts from his letters in *Edwardes Memorials*, vol. 1, lead to this conclusion: "When we think we have estimated them rightly, some new prejudice, or some old superstition, an almost impossible suspicion, or a downright mad contrivance, flits before their eyes, and leads these grown-up children in full chase after a *feu follet*" (p. 65); "Their utter depravity is one thing which always involves natives in a mesh of their own spinning. They cannot imagine such a thing as honesty for honesty's sake" (p. 65); "I have laid it down . . . as a rule on which I mean invariably to act . . . *never to assume that a native* will do anything, but hope that he will *do the best, and prepare for his doing the worst*" (p. 66); "There is something noble in putting the hand of civilization on the mane of a nation like the Punjab" (p. 76).

77. As quoted by R. B. Smith, 1:225.

78. *Edwardes Memorials*, 1:62.

79. Ibid., p. 75.

80. Lionel J. Trotter, *Life of Hodson of Hodson's Horse* (London, 1901), pp. 47–48.

81. Barry J. Cork, *Rider On A Grey Horse* (London, 1958), p. 27.

82. Pearson, p. 85.

83. See my discussion of this book in the Preface, especially note 8.

84. Smyth, p. xx. Smyth was a major in the Third Bengal Light Cavalry.

85. Ibid., p. xxn.

86. Edwardes and Merivale, 2:62.

87. Ibid.

9 The Death of the Sikh State

1. Hogg, Tucker, and Wigram to Hardinge, Oct. 19, 1846, RD, "BDSL," vol. 18.

2. Abstract of Depositions in Preyma's Case enclosed with Henry Lawrence's letter to Hardinge, Aug. 2, 1847, *PRP*, pp. 78–83.

3. Ibid., p. 83.

4. Ibid., pp. 102, 112.

5. Currie to Henry Elliot, political secretary to Dalhousie, July 31, 1848, *PRP*, p. 300. Hodson also suspected Gulab Singh of complicity. On Sept. 3, 1848, he wrote that several chiefs, including the Kashmir ruler, "have been for months and months securely plotting, without our having more than the merest hints of local distur-

bances, against the supremacy of the British Government." See Trotter, *Hodson*, p. 78.

6. Dalhousie to Currie, Sept. 16, 1848, *ASW*, p. 95.

7. This communication appears in an undated letter to Rani Jindan from her priest, Shiv Dayal, who quoted it from a letter by Sardar Kahn Singh at Multan. The Sardar, who had been sent to Multan to succeed Mul Raj, defected to the rebels and reportedly contacted Gulab Singh at the Rani's behest. The British confiscated a lengthy correspondence, including the letter under review, from a servant of Shiv Dayal. See Currie to Elliot, Dec. 18, 1848, *PRP*, p. 537.

8. Ibid., p. 539. This particular message from Gulab Singh was contained in another undated letter to Jindan from an anonymous writer.

9. Currie to Elliot, July 31, 1848, *PRP*, p. 300.

10. Currie to Jawala Sahai, May 25, 1848, Persian "Marasalajats," ref. 43803, fol. 63/1.

11. Currie to Gulab Singh, June 1, 1848, Persian "Marasalajats," ref. 43803, fol. 70/1.

12. Currie to Jawala Sahai, June 27, 1848, Persian "Marasalajats," ref. 43803, fol. 95/1.

13. Saif-ud-Din to Currie, July 12, 1848, "SDS," vol. 1, fol. 70/2.

14. Saif-ud-Din to Currie, July 17, 1848, "SDS," vol. 1, fol. 73/2. According to Grey, p. 326, Gulab Singh made yet another gesture of friendship by dispatching a Dogra force under Henry Steinbach, now in the service of the Kashmir government, to assist the British at Multan. But Grey adds that the wily chief, still not sure of the conflict's final outcome, was wary of committing himself completely, and "Steinbach's troops were by his orders so long on the road that not only this, but the Second Punjab war was over before they joined the British." This information is, however, partially contradicted by evidence which indicates that the Dogras under Steinbach did see action late in the war (see my Chapter 9).

15. Gough and Innes, p. 159; George Bruce, *Six Battles For India* (London, 1969), p. 201. For more on the dispute between Abbott and the

Attariwala leader, and subsequent developments, see Mehtab Singh, "Tawarikh-e-Mulk-e-Hazara," fols. 112/1–119/1, Persian MS in IOL.

16. Bruce, p. 233.

17. The two men were friends of long standing. During 1844 Chattar Singh had openly sided with the Jammu chief against Hira Singh and, as a token of fellowship, had exchanged turbans. See "AIP," Aug. 15, 1844, p. 274; Edwardes to Currie, Aug. 29, 1849, *ASW*, p. 261. Currie described the Attariwala chief as a "confidential friend of Maharajah Golab Sing." See his letter to Elliot, Aug. 15, 1848, *PRP*, p. 324.

18. If the statement of a certain Bahadur Surat Singh Majithia, which was recounted to the British by Lal Singh Kaleewala, a Sikh informer, is to be believed, Chattar Singh and some other Sikh leaders had also approached the Kashmir ruler during 1847 with an invitation to participate in an anti-British conspiracy. Majithia claimed that Gulab Singh decided to help, but only after the Attariwala leader had taken an oath of loyalty to him on the Holy Granth. The Maharaja then reportedly met an Attariwala messenger in a secret hideout where the latter was shown "a great quantity of arms and ammunition" which Gulab Singh had collected, presumably to oppose the British. Displaying unusual sympathy for the Sikh government, the Dogra ruler was said to have accused the British of not allowing Lahore to retain even a semblance of sovereignty and advised Chattar Singh that he "should commence operations by creating a disturbance in Hazara." The Maharaja, added Majithia, also suggested that Chattar Singh seek the assistance of Dost Muhammad and Sultan Muhammad in his venture. See Currie to Elliot, Dec. 18, 1848, *PRP*, p. 543.

19. Abbott to Currie, Aug. 13, 1848, *PRP*, p. 342.

20. Diary of Abbott, Sept. 17–19, SD, "ESLI," vol. 117, enc. 78.

21. George Lawrence to Currie, Aug. 17, 1848, *PRP*, pp. 328–29.

22. Currie to Elliot, Sept. 12, 1848, *PRP*, p. 388.

23. Currie to Elliot, Oct. 6, 1848, SD, "ESLI," vol. 117, enc. 2, letter 249.

24. Saif-ud-Din to Currie, Dec. 2, 1848, "SDS," vol. 1, fols. 105/2–106/1.
25. Saif-ud-Din to Currie, Feb. 16, 1849, "SDS," vol. 2, fols. 13–14. Charles Napier, in a letter dated Oct. 6, 1848, to his brother William, also believed that Gulab Singh was corresponding with Dost Muhammad. See Napier, *Life of Charles Napier*, 4:126–27.
26. Currie to Elliot, Oct. 6, 1848, SD, "ESLI," vol. 117, enc. 2, letter 249; John Nicholson to Currie, Sept. 13, 1848, *ASW*, p. 427.
27. Edward Lake, commander of the Bahawalpur troops, to Currie, Aug. 30, 1848, *ASW*, p. 402.
28. Raja Dina Nath to his brother, Dewan Kedar Nath, Sept. 9, 1848, SD, "ESLI," vol. 117, enc. 78.
29. Charles to William, Oct. 6, 1848, in Napier, *Life of Charles Napier*, 4:124.
30. Currie to Elliot, Oct. 6, 1848, SD, "ESLI," vol. 117, enc. 2, letter 249.
31. George Lawrence to Currie, Sept. 20, 1848, *PRP*, p. 406; George Lawrence to John Inglis, Sept. 20, 1848, SD, "ESLI," vol. 117, enc. 78.
32. C. B. Saunders to John Lawrence, Sept. 11, 1848, *PRP*, pp. 385–86.
33. R. B. Smith, 1:333.
34. Dalhousie's memorandum, Sept. 30, 1848, SD, "ESLI," vol. 117, enc. 78. Dalhousie, in a letter dated Oct. 8, 1848, told Currie: "How far [Gulab Singh] has committed himself remains yet to be seen. If he has done, he shall smart for it." See *ASW*, p. 102.
35. Currie to Elliot, Sept. 12, 1848, *PRP*, p. 387.
36. Currie to Gough, Sept. 12, 1848, SD, "ESLI," vol. 117, enc. 78.
37. Gough to Currie, Sept. 15, 1848, *ASW*, pp. 183–85.
38. Charles to William, Oct. 6, 1848, in Napier, *Life of Charles Napier*, 4:127.
39. Ibid., p. 124.
40. Ibid., p. 125.
41. Ibid., p. 127.
42. Littler's Minute, Sept. 30, 1848, SD, "ESLI," vol. 117, enc. 78.
43. Robert Napier to Currie, Oct. 3, 1848, *ASW*, p. 361.
44. Edwardes to Currie, Aug. 10, 1848, *PRP*, p. 314.
45. Edwardes to Currie, Sept. 3, 1848, *ASW*, p. 264.

46. Edwardes to Currie, Aug. 29, 1848, *ASW*, p. 261.
47. Edwardes recorded that Imam's "hatred of Maharaja Golab Sing, and the Attaree party, who, side with him, exceeds, if possible, that which he bears to the Sikh race generally, which he is fond of characterizing as 'filthy!!'" See his letter to Currie, Sept. 16, 1848, *PRP*, p. 397.
48. Edwardes to Currie, Sept. 10, 1848, *PRP*, p. 381.
49. In another letter to Currie on Sept. 26, 1848, *ASW*, pp. 279–80, Edwardes expostulated: "Myself I quite believe that G. S. is actively engaged against us, and the sooner he is unveiled, the better."
50. Edwardes to Currie, Sept. 22, 1848, *ASW*, p. 278.
51. Edwardes to Currie, Oct. 3, 1848, *ASW*, p. 283.
52. Currie to Edwardes, Sept. 23, 1848, SD, "ESLI," vol. 117, enc. 78, letter 467.
53. Currie to Elliot, Oct. 6, 1848, SD, "ESLI," vol. 117, enc. 2, letter 249.
54. The capital city itself was then buzzing with rumors of a British defeat at Lahore. See Saif-ud-Din to Currie, Sept. 10, 1848, "SDS," vol. 1, fol. 92/1.
55. Gough and Innes, p. 194.
56. Saif-ud-Din to Currie, Dec. 2, 1848, "SDS," vol. 1, fols. 105/2–106/1.
57. Gulab Singh's undated letter to Currie included in Currie's communication to Elliot, Oct. 6, 1848, SD, "ESLI," vol. 117, enc. 2, letter 249.
58. Ibid.
59. Currie to Elliot, Oct. 6, 1848, SD, "ESLI," vol. 117, enc. 2, letter 249.
60. Ibid.
61. Ibid.
62. Ibid.
63. Ibid.
64. Ibid.
65. Currie's undated letter to Gulab Singh, in Currie to Elliot, Oct. 6, 1848, SD, "ESLI," vol. 117, enc. 2, letter 249.
66. Ibid.
67. Ibid.
68. Dalhousie to Currie, Oct. 25, 1848, *ASW*, p. 113.
69. Dalhousie to SC, Nov. 1, 1848, *PRP*, p. 413.
70. Charles to William, Oct. 28, 1848, in Napier, *Life of Charles*

Napier, 4:130. Charles also declared that preparations for war were "going on very extensively at Kashmere, Jumnoo, and all over the Punjaub hills" (pp. 128–29).

71. Ibid., p. 130.

72. Currie to Dalhousie, Oct. 12, 1848, *ASW*, p. 107; Currie to Gough, Oct. 13, 1848, SD, "ESLI," vol. 117, enc. 2.

73. According to Currie, Hira Nand had actually been sent by the Attariwala leader to Gulab Singh "to beg his intercession to procure terms for him with the British Government." See his letter to Elliot, Nov. 6, 1848, *PRP*, p. 444.

74. Currie to Elliot, Nov. 3, 1848, *PRP*, p. 440; Abbott to Currie, Oct. 29, 1848, *ASW*, p. 417.

75. Abbott to Currie, Nov. 2, 1848, *ASW*, p. 420.

76. Robert S. Rait, *The Life and Campaigns of First Viscount Field-Marshal Gough* (London, 1903), 2:181, states that Gough deliberately chose Ramnagar "because it afforded possibilities of communicating with Golab Singh, should that wily chief be inveighed into rebellion."

77. These troops were stationed at Minawar, northwest of the Chenab. The Acting Resident suggested to the commander-in-chief that, once he had crossed the river, he should order the Dogras to return to "their own territory, and not to pass their own border to the plains, without positive instructions." See Currie to Gough, Nov. 30, 1848, *PRP*, p. 479.

78. Rait, *Gough*, 2:172.

79. Ibid. Robert S. Rait, *The Life of Field-Marshal Sir Frederick Paul Haines* (London, 1911), p. 52, states that "it was necessary to send a detachment across the Beas to secure the loyalty of Golab Singh."

80. Excerpts from the Diary of Abbott, Dec. 18, 1848, contained in Currie's letter to Elliot, Dec. 28, 1848, SD, "ESLI," vol. 11, enc. 3. According to Dalhousie, a representative of the Amir was "to ascertain the feeling of Golab Sing towards him, and to request his aid in money." See his letter to SC, Jan. 22, 1849, *PRP*, p. 529.

81. Excerpts from the Diary of Abbott, Dec. 18, 1848, contained in Currie's letter to Elliot, Dec. 28, 1848, SD, "ESLI," vol. 11, enc. 3.

82. Dalhousie to Wellington, Dec. 7, 1848, in Williams Lee-Warner, *The Life of the Marquess of Dalhousie* (London, 1904), 1:194.

83. Dalhousie to Wellington, December 22, 1848, in Lee-Warner, 1:198.

84. Dalhousie to Currie, Dec. 12, 1848, *ASW*, p. 132.

85. Dalhousie to Sir George Couper of the 92nd Highlanders, Dec. 22, 1848, in J. G. A. Baird, ed., *Private Letters of the Marquess of Dalhousie* (London, 1910), p. 39. The *Times*, March 6, 1849, p. 5, seems to echo Dalhousie's views. In an editorial, it observed: "Gholab Singh's force, fresh and uninjured, still hangs like a thundercloud on the hills above us."

86. Dalhousie to Couper, Dec. 22, 1848, in Baird, p. 39.

87. Dalhousie to Currie, Dec. 25, 1848, *ASW*, p. 142.

88. Hodson to Currie, Jan. 1, 1849, *PRP*, pp. 572–73.

89. Currie to Elliot, Jan. 3, 1849, SD, "ESLI," vol. 118, enc. 3.

90. Dalhousie to Currie, Jan. 8, 1849, *ASW*, p. 150.

91. Hodson to Currie, Jan. 4, 1849, SD, "ESLI," vol. 118, enc. 3.

92. The *Times* was well aware of Napier's temperament and, during the height of the debate in London over the war, editorially commented: "Unhappily . . . Sir Charles possesses a tongue and a pen as sharp and as reckless as his sword. His indignation once aroused, justly or unjustly, knows neither friend nor foe" (March 5, 1849, p. 4).

93. Charles to William, Dec. 10, 1848, in Napier, *Life of Charles Napier*, 4:136–37.

94. Ibid., p. 137.

95. Charles to William, Dec. 18, 1848, in Napier, *Life of Charles Napier*, 4:140.

96. R. N. Cust made this comment on Dec. 25, 1848. See his *Papers*, p. 99.

97. Edward J. Thackwell, *Narrative of the Second Sikh War, in 1848–49* (London, 1851), p. 116. He was an aide-de-camp to his father, General Thackwell, who participated in the war.

98. George G. Pearse, who commanded the British Horse Artillery

during the war, reached this conclusion on Nov. 19, 1848. See his "Journal," p. 112, European MS in IOL.

99. *ASW*, p. 147.

100. Ibid.

101. Resident's abstract of Persian correspondence ending Jan. 6, 1849, SD, "ESLI," vol. 118, enc. 3. Currie also told the Maharaja that the Governor-General considered his support "lukewarm" and his monetary assistance to Abbott insufficient evidence of loyalty.

102. Saif-ud-Din to Currie, Feb. 16, 1849, "SDS," vol. 2, fols. 13–14, 46.

103. Henry Lawrence to Elliot, Feb. 12, 1849, SD, "ESLI," vol. 118, enc. 4, letter 8.

104. Thackwell, p. 119.

105. However, K. Singh, *History*, 2:79n, writes that Gulab Singh's troops did take part in this battle.

106. See Dost Muhammad's letter to Mul Raj of Jan. 18, 1849, which was intercepted by the British and enclosed with Lawrence's communication to Elliot, Feb. 12, 1849, SD, "ESLI," vol. 118, enc. 3.

107. Ibid. According to Dost Muhammad's letter, these pledges were made by the Maharaja in messages to the Barakzais at Peshawar in which he also exhorted them to "join the Sikhs and encounter the British."

108. Ibid.

109. Ibid.

110. Currie to Elliot, Jan. 30, 1849, *PRP*, p. 606.

111. Saif-ud-Din, in his dispatch to Henry Lawrence, May 31, 1849, "SDS," vol. 2, fol. 47, wrote that when one courtier named Maulvi Mazhar Ali advised against such a move by referring to the Company's enormous resources, "he was taunted and ridiculed because they thought its power and prestige had been greatly exaggerated."

112. Ibid. Subsequently, Edwardes even went to the extent of claiming: "We may suspect, nay, we may know, that he truckled with the Sikhs before the battle of Goojurat" (*Year on the Punjab Frontier*, 1:200).

113. See Gulab Singh's undated letter to the Acting Resident enclosed in Currie's communication to Elliot, Jan. 30, 1849, *PRP*, pp. 606–7. The

Times, March 23, 1849, p. 4, commented that the Afghan interest in Kashmir had "promptly confirmed [Gulab Singh] in his fidelity to his patrons" and that "by a singular result of the same policy [the British] cause will be strengthened in a much greater ratio."

114. Elliot to Currie, Jan. 27, 1849, *PRP*, p. 606.

115. Ibid.

116. Lawrence to Elliot, Feb. 12, 1849, SD, "ESLI," vol. 118, enc. 3.

117. Gulab Singh to Currie, Feb. 8, 1849, SD, "ESLI," vol. 118, enc. 3. The Maharaja was at that time unaware of Lawrence's return.

118. Ibid.

119. Ibid. Acknowledging his gratitude once again for the "bestowal" of the Himalayan province in 1846, he told Currie: "Cashmere, my friend, is not my hereditary country."

120. Ibid.

121. Ibid.

122. Excerpts from Elliot's letter contained in Lawrence's communication to Gulab Singh, Feb. 16, 1849, *PRP*, p. 630.

123. Ibid.

124. Ibid.

125. Abbott to Reynell G. Taylor, Feb. 5, 1849, European MS in IOL.

126. Ibid.

127. According to the *Times*, April 18, 1849 p. 6, the news "of Gholab Singh's death was current at Lahore, Jullundur, [and] at all the principal towns and villages on the frontier." The newspaper further reported that, because of the Dogra chief's failure to aid Sher Singh, "one Jowahir Singh, a Sikh, had stabbed the wily chieftain to the heart." Another news item on the same page stated "that Gholab Singh had been poisoned by his Khunsamah [cook], at the instigation of his nephew."

128. "Gulab Nama," p. 515.

129. Dalhousie to SC, March 7, 1849, *PRP*, p. 632; the *Times*, April 18, 1849, p. 6; Badhrah, Char Bagh-e-Panjab," fol. 420/1.

130. Gulab Singh to Dalhousie, April 9, 1849, English translation of a Persian communication in the *Dalhousie Papers*, ref. GD 45/6/260, Scottish Record Office, Edinburgh.

10 Anglo-Kashmir Relations: 1849–1857

1. The *Times*, Aug. 20, 1849, p. 4. Another news item on the same page read: "The chances of another war . . . stand at high quotations on the political exchange. Gholab Singh . . . has, it is said, shown his teeth." The issue of Aug. 21, p. 4, reported that the Jammu fort alone was equipped with "150 pieces of heavy cannon."

2. Ibid., Sept. 26, 1849, p. 6.

3. Ibid., Aug. 20, 1849, p. 4.

4. Ibid., Aug. 21, 1849, p. 4. That the *Times* was then quite preoccupied with the Maharaja of Kashmir is indicated in another editorial which, while ridiculing what it considered overexertions in the cause of peace by a European conference then being held at Paris, mockingly commented: "Should any little difference again arise between England and Gholab Singh, the Czar of Russia might, no doubt, be induced to arbitrate upon the matter." See the issue of Aug. 24, p. 4.

5. Dalhousie to Couper, Oct. 19, 1849, in Baird, p. 96. In an earlier letter dated July 10, 1849, he had foreseen the result of the newsmongering rampant in England, and declared that "there is no more probability of a war with Gholab Singh than with Rajah of Bhurtpore [a tiny central Indian principality]" (Baird, p. 84).

6. Dalhousie to Couper, Nov. 2, 1849, in Baird, p. 103. Lee-Warner, *Dalhousie*, 1:271, believes that Dalhousie became convinced of the Dogra leader's innocuousness after conferring with his civil and military officials. He adds that the Governor-General "found a general agreement of opinion that the Maharaja was neither really intent upon mischief nor capable of causing it."

7. Charles to William, March 22, 1849, in Napier, *Life of Charles Napier*, 4:156.

8. Ibid.

9. Morison, p. 236.

10. Lee-Warner, *Dalhousie*, 1:319.

11. Dalhousie to Couper, Dec. 15, 1849, in Baird, pp. 104–5.

12. R. B. Smith, 1:345–46. John Lawrence, who accompanied Napier,

recorded that the General "was kind and courteous [and Gulab Singh] if possible, more civil and amiable than ever."

13. Charles Napier to Ellenborough, Feb. 26, 1850, in Napier, *Life of Charles Napier*, 4:236.

14. William W. Hunter, *The Marquess of Dalhousie* (Oxford, 1890), p. 216.

15. Napier's memorandum, Dec. 4, 1850, in William Napier, *Minutes on the Resignation of the late General Sir Charles Napier* (London, 1854), p. 49.

16. Charles to William, Aug. 9, 1850, in Napier, *Life of Charles Napier*, 4:288. Edwardes and Merivale, 2:160, write that Napier "contemplated with romantic delight a grand expedition in the style of Alexander the Great among the snowy summits of the Western Himalaya."

17. Charles to Lady Napier, Aug. 10, 1850, in Napier, *Life of Charles Napier*, 4:285.

18. Charles to Lady Napier, Aug. 26, 1850, in Napier, *Life of Charles Napier*, 4:286.

19. Lee-Warner, *Dalhousie*, 1:344.

20. Saif-ud-Din to Henry Lawrence, news from Nov. 17 to Dec. 8, 1850, "SDS," vol. 3, fol. 148/1.

21. Saif-ud-Din to Henry Lawrence, news from Dec. 23 to 28, 1850, "SDS," vol. 3, fol. 191/1.

22. Lee-Warner, *Dalhousie*, 1:366.

23. On Dec. 23 he complained to Couper: "I am driven hard just now by new barracks, a sore leg, the Maharajah, and a toothache. . . . The Maharajah and the barracks will be got rid of this week,—if the toothache does not accompany them I shall eject the offender, and the leg, I hope, will not lag behind." See Baird, p. 148.

24. *Dalhousie's Minute*, p. 112.

25. Lee-Warner, *Dalhousie*, 1:366–67.

26. According to Lee-Warner, *Dalhousie*, 1:367, "two incidents gave colour to this report. When the cavalry escorting His Highness arrived at the Governor-General's camp, they formed up across the street of canvas, and so shut out the view of the crowd. The

bazaar took up the false alarm, and the long duration of the interview lent weight to it. Then a fresh cause of anxiety occurred. Lady Dalhousie wished to see the proceedings, and to make this possible, Elliot had to clear an avenue through the people. On this the word went round that a piece of cannon was planted at the end of the space thus cleared, and that troops were in readiness to advance upon the Maharaja.".

27. Dalhousie to Couper, Jan. 6, 1851, in Baird, p. 150.

28. Word of Gulab Singh's offer ultimately reached Kabul and "caused the Amir and his court no little alarm." See Lee-Warner, *Dalhousie*, 1:367–69.

29. Dalhousie to Couper, Jan. 6, 1851, in Baird, p. 150.

30. Dalhousie to Couper, Feb. 18, 1851, in Baird, p. 154.

31. *Dalhousie's Minute*, p. 112.

32. Dalhousie to Couper, Oct. 21, 1851, in Baird, p. 179.

33. Baird, p. vii.

34. R. B. Smith, 1:337; Hunter, pp. 91–92.

35. Hunter, pp. 95, 98–99; Pearson, pp. 149–50.

36. Edwardes and Merivale, 2:127.

37. Morison, p. 236.

38. Ibid., letter dated Sept. 28, 1849.

39. Ibid., pp. 239–40. "Goolab Singh's territories," Dalhousie told him, "can't be said to be within your range." See Edwardes and Merivale, 2:158.

40. Dalhousie to Col. Mountain, March 11, 1852, *ASW*, p. 172.

41. Pearson, p. 150. For more on the clash between the two brothers over Gulab Singh, see Maud Diver, *Honoria Lawrence* (Boston, 1936), pp. 401–2.

42. Morison, p. 255.

43. Ibid. He was eventually allowed to donate a lakh of rupees toward the building of the Lawrence Military Asylum (p. 183). Earlier, Gulab Singh had contributed another lakh of rupees to the Lawrence Hill School at Sanawar. See Diver, p. 318.

44. Dalhousie to Couper, March 26, 1858, in Baird, p. 412.

45. Clerk expressed this view in a letter to Charles Napier during March, 1849. See Edwardes and Merivale, 2:61.

46. J. D. Cunningham, p. 332n.

47. Horace St. John, *History of the British Conquests in India* (London, 1852), 2:199–200.

48. R. W. Bingham, *General Gilbert's Raid To the Khyber* (1850), as quoted in *ASW*, p. [164].

49. Ganda Singh in *ASW*, pp. [164–65], provides this information but does not disclose its source. However, the incredible concept of an Anglicized Kashmir was probably first advanced by the British traveler G. T. Vigne. As early as 1842 he had recommended the acquisition of the area, and predicted: "Kashmir will become the focus of Asiatic civilization: a miniature England in the heart of Asia." He also recommended the conversion of Kashmiris to Christianity. See his *Travels*, 2:67–68.

50. Edwardes, *Year on the Punjab Frontier*, 1:200, wrote that the Maharaja "has the English papers read to him, and sees that he is an object of suspicion to all, and of ambitious hope to many."

51. Dalhousie to Couper, Aug. 11, 1850, in Baird, p. 137; Saif-ud-Din to John Lawrence, Oct. 6, 1855, "SDS," vol. 8, fol. 114/2.

52. Saif-ud-Din to John Lawrence, Jan. 4, 1855, "SDS," vol. 8, fol. 3/2.

53. Saif-ud-Din to John Lawrence, Sept. 15 and Dec. 19, 1856, "SDS," vol. 9, fols. 181/1, 271/2; Feb. 1, 1857, vol. 10, fol. 59/1.

54. Saif-ud-Din to John Lawrence, May 21 and May 30, 1857, "SDS," vol. 10, fols. 123/2, 137/2.

55. According to George Everard, ed., *The Starry Crown, A Sketch of the Life Work of Harriett E. H. Urmston* (London, 1898), p. 39, there "was a strong party at Court who had wished [Gulab Singh] to throw in his lot with the rebels."

56. He was distressed by the warnings of the astrologers that the Mutiny would escalate and even engulf Kashmir. See Saif-ud-Din to John Lawrence, June 16, 1857, "SDS," vol. 10, fol. 146/2.

57. J. Cave-Brown, *The Punjab and Delhi in 1857* (Edinburgh, 1861), 1:178. However, according to Saif-ud-Din's dispatch to John Lawrence, May 21, 1857, "SDS," vol. 10, fol. 119/1, "on hearing the news of the mutiny, the

Maharaja Sahib outwardly deplored it, but at heart seemed pleased."
58. R. B. Smith, 2:183.
59. Everard, pp. 36–39. There are references to the insubordination of Muslim servants, occasional sniper fire, and an attempt by a Kashmiri physician to poison Urmston.
60. Saif-ud-Din to John Lawrence, July 21, 1857, "SDS," vol. 10, fols. 186/2–187/1; Cave-Brown, 1:178; Everard, p. 39. Referring to the loan, H. D. Daly, then serving at Delhi, observed that "this is good, and shows how well the cunning old fox sees the game." He also characterized Gulab Singh as "the Talleyrand of the East." See H. Daly, Memoirs of General Sir Henry Dermot Daly (London, 1905), p. 77 and n.
61. PMP, p. 317.
62. Ibid., p. 379.
63. Gibbon, pp. 270–71.
64. PMP, p. 320.

65. Saif-ud-Din to John Lawrence, July 21, 1857, "SDS," vol. 10, fols. 186/2–187/1.
66. John Lawrence was particularly irked by the indecision of General Archdale Wilson, commander of the British forces at Delhi. In a letter to Edwardes, he referred to the ambiguous instructions from Wilson: "First it was said, 'Send the Jummoo troops;' then, 'We will not have them;' then, 'Send them, by all means; let them come quickly;' and now they begin to hedge. I feel rather sick of such vacillation." See R. B. Smith, 2:184.
67. A brief note on the Jammu and Kashmir State (Jammu, 1927), p. 2.
68. Gibbon, p. 299.
69. R. B. Smith, 2:184.
70. General Report on the Administration of the Punjab Territories for 1856–57 and 1857–58 (London, 1859), pp. 31–32.
71. Edwardes Memorials, 2:301.

11 Internal Administration: 1846–1857

1. William Moorcroft as quoted by Francis Younghusband, Kashmir (London, 1909; reprint ed., 1917), p. 160. According to Bamzai, p. 579, the Sikh rulers in 1822 obtained twenty-nine lakhs of rupees in land revenue. This policy of overassessment proved so disastrous that, although the Sikhs by 1838 "had reduced the demand to 18 lakhs . . . it was not possible to enforce even this collection."
2. Moorcroft as quoted by Younghusband, pp. 160–61.
3. Ibid., p. 161.
4. Ibid., p. 162. Younghusband himself adds: "The villages were fallen into decay. The rice-ground was uncultivated for want of labour and irrigation."
5. The Kashmiris detested him. Only a few months after he became the governor of Kashmir in 1841, the people petitioned Maharaja Sher Singh to remove him, contending "that were Sheikh Goolam Moheeoodeen to remain in charge of that valley, it would certainly be ruined." See "PI," Nov. 22, 1841, p. 261.

6. Younghusband, pp. 173–74.
7. Edwardes to Cowley Powles, a friend, Sept. 24, 1846, in Edwardes Memorials, 1:73.
8. Hardinge to SC, Dec. 4, 1846, PRAL, pp. 194–95.
9. Henry Lawrence to Elliot, Aug. 2, 1847, PRP, p. 68.
10. Charles to Walter, April 3, 1847, "PPHH," vol. 7.
11. Henry Lawrence to Jawala Sahai, June 4, 1847, Persian "Marasalajats," ref. 4382, p. 89.
12. However, Lawrence advised members of the Taylor mission "as much as possible, to act through the Maharajah, and to pay him all proper respect." See his letter to Elliot, Aug. 2, 1847, PRP, p. 68.
13. E. Gambier Parry, Reynell Taylor (London, 1888), pp. 84–85.
14. Lawrence to Hardinge, July 20, 1847, ASW, p. 39.
15. Khuihami, vol. 2, fol. 343.
16. Parry, p. 87.
17. Ibid.
18. See Elliot to Henry Lawrence, Oct. 13, 1847, PRP, p. 114.

19. Ibid.
20. Saif-ud-Din to Henry Lawrence, news of Sept. and Oct., 1849, "SDS," vol. 2, fol. 63/2.
21. Ibid., fols. 56/2, 58/1–62/1.
22. Morison, p. 236.
23. Saif-ud-Din to Henry Lawrence, news of Sept. and Oct., 1849, "SDS," vol. 2, fols. 68/1–87/2.
24. Saif-ud-Din to Henry Lawrence, news from Jan. to May, 1850, "SDS," vol. 3, fols. 59/1–73/1.
25. See Morison, p. 255.
26. Trotter, *Hodson*, p. 113.
27. Muhammad Khalil Mirjanpurı, "Tarikh-e-Kashmir," p. 331, Persian MS in RPD.
28. One *khirwar* approximates two maunds and three seers. A maund equals about 82 pounds.
29. Mirjanpuri, p. 331.
30. George H. Hodson, ed., *Hodson of Hodson's Horse* (London, 1883), p. 84.
31. Abdul Nabi, "Wajiz-ul-Tawarikh," fol. 59, Persian MS in RPD; Khuihami, vol. 2, fol. 343.
32. See Saif-ud-Din to Currie, Dec. 2, 1848, "SDS," vol. 1, fol. 98/1; Feb. 16, 1849, vol. 2, fols. 2–3; to John Lawrence, Mar. 12, April 5, and June 28, 1855, vol. 8, fols. 35, 39/2, 73.
33. Khuihami, vol. 2, fol. 343.
34. Nabi, f. 59, writes that the new rupee was devalued by twenty-five percent.
35. Ibid.
36. Mirjanpuri, p. 331.
37. Saif-ud-Din to Currie, Feb. 16, 1849, "SDS," vol. 2, fol. 28.
38. Khuihami, vol. 2, fol. 343. A news extract from the *Bombay Times* appearing in the *Times* of Oct. 4, 1849, pp. 4–5, confirms the increased assessment. It referred to the steep rise in prices of Kashmiri shawls "in consequence . . . of the Maharajah Gholab Singh having levied a treble tax on the poor people who make them." According to Hodson, the pashmina traders paid seventy-five percent of their income in taxes to Gulab Singh. See Trotter, *Hodson*, p. 114.
39. Saif-ud-Din to Currie, Dec. 2, 1848, "SDS," vol. 1, fols. 109–112/1.
40. Saif-ud-Din to Currie, Feb. 16, 1849, "SDS," vol. 2, fol. 4.
41. Saif-ud-Din to Henry Lawrence,

Feb. 14 and Sept. 1, 1851, "SDS," vol. 4, fols. 17/1, 78/1.
42. Gulab Singh used fifty begar laborers to carry his baggage from Kashmir to Jammu in 1850. See Saif-ud-Din to Henry Lawrence, news of Nov. and Dec., 1850, "SDS," vol. 3, fol. 150/1. See also his dispatches to Currie, July 17 and Aug. 22, 1848, "SDS," vol. 1, fols. 75, 83/1.
43. Mirjanpuri, p. 331. Saif-ud-Din, however, writes that the tax amounted to fifty rupees per marriage. See his dispatch to Henry Lawrence, Aug. 1, 1851, "SDS," vol. 4, fol. 73/2. It seems that the Maharaja also received a *nazarana* per marriage of four annas from the poor and a rupee from the wealthy. See Saif-ud-Din to Currie, Feb. 16, 1849, "SDS," vol. 2, fols. 5–6.
44. Saif-ud-Din to Henry Lawrence, Oct. 8, 1851, "SDS," vol. 4, fols. 102/2, 113/2.
45. Lionel J. Trotter, *The Life of Marquis of Dalhousie* (London, 1889), p. 133; Marshman, *History*, 3:358.
46. Saif-ud-Din to Currie, Feb. 16, 1849, "SDS," vol. 2, fols. 5, 7.
47. Saif-ud-Din to Henry Lawrence, May 1, 1851, "SDS," vol. 4, fol. 20/1.
48. Saif-ud-Din to Currie, Feb. 16, 1849, "SDS," vol. 2, fol. 8.
49. Saif-ud-Din to Currie, Dec. 2, 1848, "SDS," vol. 1, fol. 112/1.
50. Saif-ud-Din to Currie, Feb. 16, 1849, "SDS," vol. 2, fol. 5.
51. Ibid., fol. 6.
52. Saif-ud-Din to Currie, Oct. 6, 1848, "SDS," vol. 1, fol. 95.
53. Saif-ud-Din to Henry Lawrence, news from Jan. to May, 1850, "SDS," vol. 3, fols. 40–41.
54. Saif-ud-Din to John Lawrence, Nov. 16, 1853, "SDS," vol. 6, fol. 103; Jan. 18, 1855, vol. 8, fol. 11/2.
55. Saif-ud-Din to Henry Lawrence, July 16, 1847, "SDS," vol. 1, fol. 15/1.
56. Mazhar Ali quit the Dogra service over disagreements with official policies. In 1854 he was accused of conspiring with Jawahar Singh against the Maharaja and as a result was ejected from the state. See H. G. Kaul, p. 195; Saif-ud-Din to John Lawrence, Jan. 1, 1854, "SDS," vol. 6, fol. 178/1.
57. Saif-ud-Din to Henry Lawrence, Sept. 1 and Oct. 3, 1851, "SDS," vol. 4, fols. 78/1, 82/2, 107/1.

58. See Saif-ud-Din to Currie, Aug. 22, 1848, "SDS," vol. 1, fol. 82/1.
59. Ibid.
60. Saif-ud-Din to Currie, Dec. 2, 1848, "SDS," vol. 1, fol. 99/2.
61. Ibid., fol. 100/2.
62. Saif-ud-Din to Currie, Feb. 16, 1849, "SDS," vol. 2, fols. 21–22, 28.
63. See H. G. Kaul, p. 199.
64. Saif-ud-Din to Currie, Feb. 16, 1849, "SDS," vol. 2, fol. 27.
65. Saif-ud-Din to John Lawrence, Feb. 18, 21, 25, April 1, 15, 16, July 14, Dec. 26, 1855, "SDS," vol. 8, fols. 25/2, 26/2–28/2, 38, 39/2, 42/2, 78, 166/2; May 18, 1856, vol. 9, fol. 60/2.
66. See Honigberger, p. 181; Grey p. 239.
67. Saif-ud-Din to Currie, Feb. 16, 1849, "SDS," vol. 2, fol. 9; to Henry Lawrence, Dec. 1, 1851, vol. 4, fol. 124/2; Jan. 9, 1852, vol. 5, fol. 3/2.
68. Saif-ud-Din to John Lawrence, Feb. 7, 1856, "SDS," vol. 9, fol. 18/2.
69. Frederic Drew, The Northern Barrier of India (London, 1877), pp. 44–45.
70. Saif-ud-Din to Henry Lawrence, July 16, 1847, "SDS," vol. 1, fol. 3.
71. Saif-ud-Din to Henry Lawrence, Aug. 1, 1851, "SDS," vol. 4, fol. 55/2.
72. See Hardinge to SC, Dec. 4, 1846, PRAL, p. 194; Henry Lawrence to Jawala Sahai, May 24, 1847, Persian "Marasalajats," ref. 4382, p. 102; Henry Lawrence to Gulab Singh, July 9, 1847, Persian "Marasalajats," ref. 4382, p. 155; Henry Lawrence to Hardinge, July 20, 1847, ASW, p. 39.
73. Saif-ud-Din to John Lawrence, news of Feb., Mar., July, and Nov., 1854, "SDS," vol. 7, fols. 63/2, 78, 165, 300.
74. J. D. Cunningham, p. 301.
75. Currie to Henry Lawrence, Mar. 16, 1846, SD, "ESLI," vol. 103, enc. 8, letter 516; Trotter, Nicholson, p. 57.
76. Pearson, p. 82.
77. Hardinge to Currie, Dec. 10, 1846, ASW, p. 14.
78. Henry Lawrence to Gulab Singh, Jan. 16, 1847, Persian "Marasalajats," ref. 4382, pp. 13–14.
79. Edwardes, Year on the Punjab Frontier, 1:199.
80. Ibid., p. 198; Henry Lawrence to Gulab Singh, Jan. 19, 1847, Persian "Marasalajats," ref. 4382, pp. 15–16.

81. Saif-ud-Din to John Lawrence, June 10, 1855, "SDS," vol. 8, fol. 64.
82. Saif-ud-Din to John Lawrence, news of Sept. and Oct., 1854, "SDS," vol. 7, fol. 294/2.
83. Saif-ud-Din to John Lawrence, Jan. 13, 1856, "SDS," vol. 9, fol. 8/2.
84. He also noticed that Gulab Singh had "only 30 guns which might count in serious warfare." See Morison, p. 236.
85. Edwardes, Year on the Punjab Frontier, 1:199. It seems that the standard of the Kashmir army did not improve much under the Maharaja's immediate successors. Writing in 1887 Rajab Ali, Riyasat Jammu Kashmir ke Ta'alluqat Angrezi Government se (Amritsar), p. 50, observed that ten Kashmir regiments were equal to only one regiment of the British Indian army.
86. Saif-ud-Din to Henry Lawrence, May 31, July 1, Aug. 1, 1851, "SDS," vol. 4, fols. 45/1, 51/1, 55/2, 56/2, 61/2, 69/1.
87. Saif-ud-Din to Henry Lawrence, Aug. 1, 1851, "SDS," vol. 4, fol. 69/2.
88. See H. G. Kaul, p. 196.
89. Saif-ud-Din to Henry Lawrence, Oct. 1, 1851, "SDS," vol. 4, fol. 90/1.
90. Saif-ud-Din to Henry Lawrence, Oct. 8, 1851, "SDS," vol. 4, fol. 97/1.
91. Saif-ud-Din to Henry Lawrence, Oct. 1, 1851, "SDS, vol. 4, fol. 90/1.
92. Saif-ud-Din to Henry Lawrence, Oct. 8, 1851, "SDS," vol. 4, fols. 97–100.
93. Saif-ud-Din to Henry Lawrence, Jan. 9, 1852, "SDS," vol. 5, fol. 3/2; Pearson, p. 166; Morison, pp. 241–42.
94. Mir Saifullah, "Tarikh-Nama-e-Kashmir," Persian scroll in RPD.
95. Honiberger, p. 183.
96. Pearson, p. 166; Trotter, Nicholson, p. 190.
97. Morison, pp. 241–42.
98. Tucker, Lushington, and Wigram to Hardinge, Mar. 6, 1848, RD, "BDSL," vol. 20.
99. Saif-ud-Din to Henry Lawrence, Jan. 9 and May 1, 1852, "SDS," vol. 5, fols. 17/1, 52–56.
100. Trotter, Nicholson, pp. 190–91.
101. Edwardes and Merivale, 3rd ed., p. 388n.
102. See W. Napier, Life of Charles Napier, 4:287.

103. William Hodson witnessed this trade during 1851, and referred to Leh's reputation as "the 'Great Emporium' of trade between Yarkund and Kashgar, and Lhassa and Hindoostan." Although Hodson was disappointed by the shops, and called the merchants "pedlars," he was nonetheless impressed to meet caravans which had received "their goods from the yellow-haired Russians at the Nishni-Novogorod fair, and brought them across Asia to sell at Ladakh." See Hodson, p. 90.

104. Fisher, Rose, and Huttenback, pp. 61–63.

105. C. Hardinge, *Viscount Hardinge*, pp. 137–38.

106. They went, however, against the advice of Gulab Singh, who warned them of the unsettled conditions there because of Governor Mohiud-Din's death. See *Jammu Intelligence*, April 3, 4, 6, and 9, in SD, "ESLI," vol. 104, enc. 12.

107. For more on this visit, see *A Journey to Cashmeer*.

108. Henry Lawrence was one of the few exceptions. During his extended visit to Kashmir in 1849, he specifically forbade his staff to demand or accept gifts from Gulab Singh. See Saif-ud-Din's dispatch to Henry Lawrence, news of Sept. and Oct., 1849, "SDS," vol. 2, fol. 62/2.

109. But he seldom ate with his Christian guests, presumably because of religious taboos. See Honigberger, pp. 182–83.

110. C. Hardinge, *Viscount Hardinge*, p. 138.

111. Pearson, pp. 141–42.

112. Saif-ud-Din to Henry Lawrence, Dec. 16, 1851, "SDS," vol. 4, fol. 127/1; to John Lawrence, June 5, 1856, vol. 9, fol. 69/2.

113. Saif-ud-Din to Henry Lawrence, Jan. 9 and Mar. 14, 1852, "SDS," vol. 5, fols. 23/2, 32/1; to John Lawrence, Nov. 16, 1853, vol. 6, fols. 103, 108/1.

114. Saif-ud-Din to John Lawrence, Nov. 16, 1853, "SDS," vol. 6, fol. 103.

115. Saif-ud-Din to Henry Lawrence, Oct. 3, 1851, "SDS," vol. 4, fol. 107/1.

116. Saif-ud-Din to Henry Lawrence, Sept. 1, 1851, "SDS," vol. 4, fols.

76/1, 97/2; to John Lawrence, news of Sept. and Oct., 1854, vol. 7, fol. 212/2; Aug. 18, 1856, vol. 9, fol. 147/2.

117. Saif-ud-Din to John Lawrence, Nov. 21, 1855, "SDS," vol. 8, fol. 143; Aug. 3, 1856, vol. 9, fol. 131.

118. Saif-ud-Din to John Lawrence, news of Aug. and Sept., 1857, "SDS," vol. 10, fol. 206/1.

119. Saif-ud-Din to John Lawrence, Mar. 16 and 25, 1853, "SDS," vol. 6, fols. 20–22.

120. Saif-ud-Din to John Lawrence, April 24 and July 9, 1853, "SDS," vol. 6, fols. 28/1, 52/1.

121. Saif-ud-Din to John Lawrence, news of July and Aug., 1854, "SDS," vol. 7, fol. 181.

122. Saif-ud-Din to John Lawrence, June 27, 1855, "SDS," vol. 8, fol. 72/2.

123. See Saif-ud-Din to Henry Lawrence, Jan. 9, 1852, "SDS," vol. 5, fol. 5/1; to John Lawrence, Feb. 25 and 28, 1855, vol. 8, fols. 29, 30/2.

124. Saif-ud-Din to John Lawrence, news of April, 1857, "SDS," vol. 10, fol. 81/1.

125. Pearson, p. 84.

126. Saif-ud-Din to John Lawrence, June 19, 1855, "SDS," vol. 8, fol. 68; Mar. 4, 1856, vol. 9, fol. 31.

127. Saif-ud-Din to Henry Lawrence, news of Aug. and Sept., 1850, "SDS," vol. 3, fols. 82/1, 85/2–87/1.

128. Trotter, *Hodson*, p. 47.

129. Parry, p. 83.

130. C. Hardinge, *Viscount Hardinge*, p. 138.

131. Charles Hardinge, *Recollections of India* (London, 1847), pt. 2. This description is given opposite Gulab Singh's picture. There is no pagination.

132. Ibid.

133. Portraits of Gulab Singh which at present hang in some of the official buildings in the state of Kashmir are obviously of recent origin and were probably commissioned by the Maharaja's successors. These artists have tended to idealize the Dogra ruler and surround him with too regal an aura. Their productions bear little or no resemblance to the sketch made by Charles Hardinge.

134. *Dalhousie's Minute*, p. 117.

135. Saif-ud-Din to John Lawrence, May 1, 5, 7–9, 1857, "SDS," vol. 10, fols. 97/2, 99/2, 102/1, 109/1.

136. Some Englishmen persisted in their demands for Kashmir's annexation, and a rancorous debate over Gulab Singh's checkered life reappeared upon the publication of two pamphlets during his son's reign. See Robert Thorp, *Cashmere Misgovernment* (Calcutta, 1868), and *The Maharaja of Kashmeer and his Calumniators* (Tours, 1870). The continuing controversy may have been partly responsible for the temporary removal of his grandson, Pratap Singh, in 1889. For further details on this affair, see House of Commons, *Papers relating to Kashmir* (1890), 54:1–79; William Digby, *Condemned Unheard*, typescript (1890) in the Kashmir Government Archives, Srinagar; Bamzai, pp. 623–31.

137. See Dalhousie to Couper, Oct. 21, 1851, in Baird, p. 179. Saif-ud-Din also repeatedly records that the Maharaja suffered from diabetes. See his dispatches to Henry Lawrence, Aug. 1 and Oct. 1, 1851, "SDS," vol. 4, fols. 74/1, 66/1; to John Lawrence, Mar. 25, 1853, "SDS," vol. 6, fol. 82/2; Jan. 17, Aug. 9, Sept. 30, 1856, "SDS," vol. 9, fols. 10/1, 136/1, 199/2; Feb. 1, 1857, "SDS," vol. 10, fol. 16/1. However, Honigberger, p. 182, and Panikkar, p. 149, write that the Dogra ruler was ill with dropsy.

138. He was treated by several Hindu and Muslim medics. However,

while he accepted rubbing ointments from the Muslim physicians, he declined to take any medicine they prescribed for internal use. See Honigberger, p. 182; Saif-ud-Din to John Lawrence, Jan. 17, Aug. 9, Sept. 30, 1856, "SDS," vol. 9, fols. 10, 136, 199/2.

139. Saif-ud-Din to Henry Lawrence, Aug. 1 and Oct. 1, 1851, "SDS," vol. 4, fols. 74/1, 86/1; to John Lawrence, Mar. 25, 1853, "SDS," vol. 6, fol. 82/2.

140. Saif-ud-Din to John Lawrence, Feb. 1, 1857, "SDS," vol. 10, fols. 52/2, 59/1.

141. Saif-ud-Din to John Lawrence, news of Aug., 1857, "SDS," vol. 10, fol. 204.

142. Ibid., fols. 206–7.

143. Everard, p. 37.

144. Urmston and Jawala Sahai apparently played an important role in dissuading the widows. See Everard, pp. 36–38.

145. H. G. Kaul, p. 200, puts the total number of mourners at nearly one lakh.

146. Saif-ud-Din to John Lawrence, news of Aug., 1857, "SDS," vol. 10, fol. 207.

147. Everard, pp. 38–39.

148. According to H. G. Kaul, p. 200, Ranbir Singh arrived at Srinagar four days after his father's death.

149. Everard, p. 38.

12 Conclusion

1. See Edwardes to Powles, Sept. 24, 1846, in *Edwardes Memorials*, 1:71.

Appendix A
A Folk Song of the Poonch Warriors

1. This scholar is indebted to Principal Hassan Shah for providing the oral text of the ballad.

Appendix C
Did Gulab Singh Pay for Kashmir?

1. *Kashmir-ke-Halaat* (Qadian, 1931), p. 4.
2. See "EP," ref. 30/12/21, no. 7.

3. See his letter dated Sept. 3, 1846, *PRAL*, p. 180.
4. See "Dalhousie Papers," ref. GD

45/6/254, MSS in the Scottish Record Office, Edinburgh.

5. See A. N. Sapru, *The Building of the Jammu and Kashmir State—Being*

the Achievement of Maharaja Gulab Singh (Lahore, 1931), p. ix; Mahajan, p. 48n.

Appendix D
The Secret Dispatches of Saif-ud-Din

1. To the Resident, 1846–49; the President of the Board of Administration of Panjab, 1849–53; and the Chief Commissioner of Panjab, 1853–59.

2. A style of swift penmanship often used by Persian and Urdu writers.

3. However, no records of Abad Beg's correspondence have been found.

4. See Nabi, fol. 59. Private papers in Kemal-ud-Din's possession also include several communications from J. D. Cunningham to Abad Beg written in the late 1830's. Cunningham's letters, however, contain no reference to Gulab Singh.

5. This appellation is given to Saif-ud-Din by Nabi, fol. 59. However, C. A. Storey, *Persian Literature, A Bio-Bibliographical Survey* (London, 1936), section 2, p. 685, describes Saif-ud-Din as simply a "record writer in Kashmir."

6. Saif-ud-Din to Currie, Dec. 3, 1848, "SDS," vol. 1, fol. 118/2; to Henry Lawrence, news from Jan. to May, 1850, vol. 3, fol. 64/2; to John Lawrence, Feb. 1, 1857, vol. 10, fol. 26/1.

7. Saif-ud-Din to Currie, Dec. 3, 1848, "SDS," vol. 1, fol. 118/2.

8. Saif-ud-Din to John Lawrence, Dec. 16, 1853, "SDS," vol. 6, fol. 171/2.

9. Saif-ud-Din to John Lawrence, Feb. 1, 1857, "SDS," vol. 10, fol. 26/1.

10. Saif-ud-Din to Currie, Dec. 3, 1848, "SDS," vol. 1, fol. 116.

11. Saif-ud-Din to Henry Lawrence, July 16, 1847, "SDS," vol. 1, fol. 13/2.

12. His own partialities are discernible only on occasion. For instance, in his reports on the Jawala Sahai-Raj Dhar Kak controversies within Gulab Singh's administration (see my Chapter 11), his sympathies seem to lie with his fellow Kashmiri Kak. See his dispatches to Currie, Aug. 22 and Dec. 2, 1848, "SDS," vol. 1, fols. 82/1, 99/2, 100/2; Feb. 16, 1849, vol. 2, fols. 21–22, 28. And in an uncommon departure from objectivity he referred to the outcome of the Second Anglo-Sikh War as "the devastation, degradation, bewilderment and disgrace of the Sikhs who possessed the evil habits of beasts and compared well with them in their character." See his report to Henry Lawrence, May 31, 1849, "SDS," vol. 2, fol. 47/2. Whether such anti-Sikh remarks betrayed his own prejudice, or were meant merely to flatter the British, or were a combination of both, can only be conjectured.

13. It seems that some time after Saif-ud-Din's death the British employed his brother, Mirza Muhi-ud-Din to act as the *khufia navis*. See Storey, section 2, p. 685. But as in the case of Abad Beg, no trace of his correspondence has been found.

Glossary

Akhbar navis	News writer
Amir	Muslim chief or king
Atta	Wheat flour
Begar	Forced labor
Bhai	Saint; brother
Bulbul	A songbird
Chakwari	Royal boat
Crore, Krore	A hundred lakhs; ten million
Daftar	A book; register; volume
Darbar	Court
Deodhiwala	Keeper of the gate; Grand Chamberlain
Dewan	Steward; elder; financier
Doab	The land surrounded by two converging rivers
Dogirath	Two lakes
Gaddi	Cushion; throne
Ghor-charah	Cavalryman
Gulab	Rose; rose-water
Gurdwara	Sikh temple
Guru	Spiritual guide; religious teacher
Gyalpo	Ruler
Halal	Muslim-butchered meat
Halwa	A dessert; sweetmeat
Hookah	Tobacco water-pipe
Jagir	Fief
Jagirdar	Fiefholder
Jampan, Joupon	Portable sedan
Jhatka	Sikh-butchered meat
Kahlon	Prime minister
Kaniz	Maid servant
Kanwar	Prince
Khalsa	Sikh army
Khansama	Cook
Khilat	Robe of honor
Khirwar	A weight equivalent to one donkey's load
Khufia navis	Secret writer
Kos	About a mile and a half
Kotwal	Judge; sheriff
Lakh	One hundred thousand
Lama	Buddhist monk or saint
Maharaja	The great ruler; sovereign prince
Marasalajat	Communication; letter
Maund	About eighty-two pounds in weight

Mian	An appellation of respect; master
Mirza	Scholar; secretary
Misl	Military confederacy
Missar	A title given to Brahmans
Mohur	Seal
Mullah	Muslim priest
Nazar, Nazarana	Gift
Nazim	Governor; administrator
Nikah	Wedding
Panch, Panchayat	The executive council of Sikh regiments
Pandit	A title assumed by Hindus of the Brahman caste
Pargana	District; sub-division
Parwana	Communication; letter
Pashmina	Shawl wool
Peshkush	Gift; offering
Qanungo	Revenue officer
Raj	Government; rule
Raja	Ruler; chief
Raja-e-Rajgan	Raja of Rajas; ruler of rulers
Rani	Queen; princess
Rupee	The major denomination of Indian currency. At present about 19½ rupees equal a British pound; about 7½ rupees equal an American dollar
Sahib	Master; lord; a designation used for respectable Europeans and Indians
Salaam	A greeting
Sanad	Title; deed
Sanghara	Water chestnut
Sardar, Sirdar	Chief; commander
Sarkar, Sirkar	Maharaja; government
Sati	The self-immolation of a Hindu widow on her husband's funeral pyre
Seer	About two and a half pounds of weight
Shali	Unwinnowed rice
Sheikh	A title for saintly Muslims
Shikasta	Swiftly written Persian or Urdu
Singh	Lion; warrior
Sipahi	Sepoy; soldier
Taluka	District
Tarikh, Tawarikh	History
Thanadar	Police officer
Toshekhana	Treasury
Vakil	Agent; emissary
Wazarat	Ministry; office of wazir
Wazir	Minister
Zamindar	Landowner
Zanana	Ladies' quarters
Zilahdar	District officer

Bibliography

Unpublished Primary Sources

Abbott, Sir James. "A Letter to R. C. Taylor," dated Feb. 5, 1849. European MS in the India Office Library, London. Abbott, who was stationed at Hazara before and during the Second Anglo-Sikh War, describes in this letter Gulab Singh's attitude toward the conflict.

Badhrah, Ganesh Das. "Char Bagh-e-Panjab." Persian MS in the India Office Library, London. This is an extensive history of Panjab from antiquity to 1849. It includes valuable information on the Sikh-Dogra connection, and on Gulab Singh's part in the First Anglo-Sikh War. Badhrah once worked as a *qanungo* at Gujarat and after 1846 accepted service under Gulab Singh in the province of Jammu.

————. "Chiragh-e-Panjab." Persian MS in the India Office Library, London. This history is an abridged version of "Char Bagh-e-Panjab," and deals with Sikh history up to 1846. However, it contains lengthy references to events at Gujarat and Sialkot, and in Jammu and Kashmir. It was considered such a beautiful work of calligraphy that it was presented to Henry Lawrence and later displayed at the Imperial Exhibition in Paris.

————. "Raj-Darshani." Persian MSS in the British Museum, London. This is a voluminous three-volume history of the Rajas of Jammu from the earliest times to 1847. It sheds important light on the ancestors of Gulab Singh and also provides a broad narrative of the service of the three Jammu brothers under the Sikhs. A copy of this manuscript is also available at the India Office Library under the title "Tawarikh-e-Rajghan-e-Jammu."

"Board's Drafts of Secret Letters," vols. 13–33 (1840–49). MSS in the India Office Library, London. These volumes are comprised of letters from the Board of Directors of the East India Company to the Governor-General expressing its opinions on political developments in India.

Carter, Sgt. Major George. "Journal." European MS in the India Office Library, London. This work covers the period from 1839 to 1861, and gives long accounts of the two Anglo-Sikh wars.

"Chattar Singh Collection of Documents." Persian MSS in the Panjab State Archives, Patiala. This collection of eighty original documents is comprised of letters, title deeds, and compacts relating to jagirs, the proprietary rights, and the privileges of the Jammu family. These papers also throw light on the relations of Gulab Singh with the two surviving sons of Dhian Singh.

Cust, R. N. "Papers." European MS in the India Office Library, London. Cust was an assistant to the political agent on the Panjab frontier in 1845–46. His papers give interesting eye-witness accounts of the First Anglo-Sikh War, Gulab Singh, Charles Napier, and some other political figures of the period.

"Dalhousie Papers," vol. 1, section 6. MSS in the General Register House, Edinburgh. These important papers deal with the administration of Lord Dalhousie, Governor-General of India from 1848 to 1856. They include Dalhousie's correspondence with Gulab Singh, Henry Lawrence, Frederick Currie, and Charles Napier.

"Diary of an Expedition to Bunnoo." European MS in the India Office Library, London. This diary was written by an anonymous writer who accompanied a Sikh expedition, led by Sardar Shamsher Singh Sandhawalia and General Cortland, against rebels in Bannu in February, 1847. It contains interesting information about John Lawrence, Herbert Edwardes, and several prominent Sikh officials.

"Ellenborough Papers." (1842–1846). MSS in the Public Record Office, London. These papers contain correspondence of Lord Ellenborough, Governor-General of India from 1842 to 1844, with Queen Victoria, the Duke of Wellington, Henry Hardinge, and others.

"Enclosures to Secret Letters from India," vols. 87–137 (1841–49). MSS in the India Office Library, London. These confidential letters contain select passages from the reports of the Company's political agents and officials in the northwest to the Governor-General, and were usually sent to the East India Company's directors with a covering letter from the Governor-General evaluating the latest political developments in the Sikh kingdom.

Hardinge, Henry. "Private Papers of Henry Hardinge," vols. 4–8. MSS in the possession of Lady Helen Hardinge, Penshurst, Kent. This valuable, and hitherto inaccessible, collection of the private papers of Lord Henry Hardinge, Governor-General of India from 1844 to 1848, includes his correspondence with Prime Minister Sir Robert Peel (vols. 4 and 5), as well as his letters and those of his two sons to Lady Emily Hardinge and other relatives in England (vols. 6, 7, and 8). Letters to his family contain very candid and uninhibited accounts of events relating to the First Anglo-Sikh War, including some memorable observations on Gulab Singh.

"Home Miscellaneous Correspondence," vol. 836 (1841). MS in the India Office Library, London. It contains letters between the Chairman and the President of the Board of Control of the East India Company on various developments in India, including the Sikh kingdom.

"A Journey to Cashmeer." European MS in the India Office Library, London. The work lists no author but was apparently written by Ganeshi Lal (see below). "A Journey to Cashmeer" provides a comprehensive account of the visit to Jammu and Kashmir by various Englishmen led by Charles Hardinge during 1846. It gives a good description of the route followed through Gulab Singh's domain, and describes the meetings of the visitors with the Maharaja of Kashmir. It also contains a genealogy of the Dogra ruler's family.

Kachroo, Birbal. "Tarikh-e-Kashmir." Persian MS in the Research and Publication Department, Srinagar. This is a lengthy history of Kashmir from antiquity to 1846, based partly on the original Sanskrit text of Kalhana's *Rajatarangini*. However, the history tends to be rather sketchy at the end, and Kachroo closes his account quite abruptly with the intriguing observation: "One who is aloof wins a place of distinction."

Khuihami, Ghulam Hassan. "Tarikh-e-Hassan," vols. 1–3. Persian MSS in the Research and Publication Department, Srinagar. "Tarikh-e-Hassan" is a detailed political history of Kashmir from the earliest times to the reign of Maharaja Ranbir Singh. Khuihami pays special attention to the rule of Gulab Singh.

Lal, Ganeshi. "Siyahat-e-Kashmir." Persian MS in the Panjab State Archives, Patiala. Ganeshi Lal provides a highly informative record of a visit from Ludhiana to Srinagar and back by Charles and Arthur Hardinge and several other British officials of the East India Company in the spring of 1846. He also gives some information on the political, social, and economic conditions of the region. A few other versions of this work have also been discovered, including one in English entitled "A Journey to Cashmeer" which is available at the India Office Library, London. For information on others, see V. S. Suri, ed., *Siyahat-i-Kashmir* (Simla, 1955), pp. iii–iv.

Letters of J. D. Cunningham to Mirza Abad, an informer working for the Company in Kashmir during the late 1830s. MS in the private papers of Mirza Kemal-ud-Din, Srinagar.

"Marasalajats." Persian MS in the Kashmir Government Archives, Srinagar. These are communications between Gulab Singh and several British officials on Kashmir affairs after 1846. These marasalajats also include correspondence between Maharaja Gulab Singh and some of the hill chiefs under his jurisdiction.

"Marasalajats." Persian and Urdu MS in the Panjab State Archives, Patiala. Most of these marasalajats are copies of letters from British officials to prominent functionaries in the Sikh kingdom between 1838 and 1849. They also contain some letters to Gulab Singh.

Mirjanpuri, Muhammad Khalil. "Tarikh-e-Kashmir." Persian MS in the Research and Publication Department, Srinagar. A history of Kashmir from the earliest times to the reign of Maharaja Ranbir Singh. It was commissioned by Raj Dhar Kak, a high official in the Kashmir government.

Nabi, Abdul. "Wajiz-ul-Tawarikh." Persian MS in the Research and Publication Department, Srinagar. This is a short but enlightening history of Kashmir. The author makes numerous marginal notes on the manuscript and reveals interesting information about Mirza Saif-ud-Din, the Company's secret informer at Srinagar during the reign of Gulab Singh.

"Orders and Letters of Maharaja Gulab Singh." Persian MS in the John Rylands Library, Manchester. This volume contains several orders issued by Gulab Singh as Maharaja, and some letters he wrote to British officials before 1849.

Pearse, General George G. "Journal." European MS in the India Office Library, London. General Pearse commanded the British Horse Artillery during the Second Anglo-Sikh War and later served on the Afghan frontier. In this journal he refers to the role of many Sikh leaders prominent during the war and makes an estimate of the character of Gulab Singh.

Pester, Lt. H. L. "Papers." European MS in the India Office Library, London. Pester, who fought in the First Anglo-Sikh War, describes the part played by Gulab Singh's agents during the conflict.

"Political Correspondence." (1838–1846). Transcribed records in the Panjab State Archives, Patiala. This correspondence is comprised of extensive reports from Panjab sent to the Governor-General by his political agents at Ludhiana. The political agency at Ludhiana was the major source of news for the Company on events in the northwest up to 1846, and the British agents assiduously gathered intelligence from several informers in the Sikh kingdom, including some at the Sikh darbar. The "Political Correspondence" is perhaps the most detailed and reliable source of information for that period of Panjab history.

"Political Letters From India," vols. 13–17 (1845–49). MSS in the India Office Library, London. These letters from the Governor-General to the Company's directors are of a nonconfidential nature, but do contain some scattered information on Gulab Singh.

Ram, Kirpa. "Gulab Nama." Persian MS in the Panjab State Archives, Patiala. "Gulab Nama" is the official biography of Gulab Singh, written by a prime minister of Kashmir at the command of Maharaja Ranbir Singh. It is a very laudatory account of the Maharaja's career and achievements.

Saif-ud-Din, Mirza. "Khilasat-ut-Tawarikh." Persian MS in the private papers of Mirza Kemal-ud-Din, Srinagar. This is a short history of Kashmir up to 1859. The writer, being an eyewitness, throws valuable light on the events taking place in Srinagar.

——. "Secret Dispatches." Persian MSS in the Research and Publication Department, Srinagar. Saif-ud-Din compiled these extensive reports at Srinagar for the British government and sent them periodically to the British authorities at Lahore during the reigns of Gulab Singh and Ranbir Singh. These communications were discovered only recently and are now bound in twelve separate volumes. For more on Saif-ud-Din's dispatches, see Appendix D.

Saifullah, Mir. "Tarikh-Nama-e-Kashmir." Persian MS in the Research and Publication Department, Srinagar. This is a brief but interesting history of Kashmir written on a scroll.

"Secret Home Correspondence," vols. 14–22 (1845–49). MSS in the India Office Library, London. These papers include correspondence between the Governor-General and the officials of the Company in London. They also contain letters exchanged among the Company officials in London about Indian affairs, and are especially useful for the years between 1845 and 1849 when the two Anglo-Sikh Wars took place.

Singh, Mehtab. "Tawarikh-e-Mulk-e-Hazara." Persian MS in the India Office Library, London. This is a history of Hazara between the years 1819 and 1849. The author gives detailed information on Gulab Singh's brief rule over Hazara during 1846 and 1847, with special reference to the activities of Jawala Sahai in that province. He also provides an eyewitness account of the developments at Hazara before and during the Second Anglo-Sikh War.

Suri, Sohan Lal. "Umdat-ut-Tawarikh," vols. 1–5. Transcribed Persian chronicle in the Panjab State Archives, Patiala. This chronicle of events in Panjab is one of the most important sources of Sikh history from 1469 to 1849. Suri was the official *akhbar navis* (news writer) at the Sikh court from 1830 to 1849 and painstakingly described the day-to-day happenings in the kingdom. Although Vidya Sagar Suri completed the monumental task of translating these voluminous tracts into English many years ago, unfortunately only the third volume, covering the years from 1831 to 1839, has so far been published.

"Tarikh Nama." Persian MS in the Panjab State Archives, Patiala. A rare and, until recently, unnoticed history of Panjab up to its annexation by an anonymous author. It describes in detail the years immediately following the death of Ranjit Singh and Gulab Singh's role during that period.

Printed Sources

Ahluwalia, M. L., and Singh, Kirpal. *The Punjab's Pioneer Freedom Fighters*. Calcutta: Orient Longmans, 1963.

Ahmad, Zahiruddin. "Tibet and Ladakh: A History." In *Far Eastern Affairs: Number Three*. Edited by G. F. Hudson. Carbondale: Southern Illinois University Press, 1963.

Aitchison, C. U. *A Collection of Treaties, Engagements, and Sanads relating to India and Neighbouring Countries*. Vol. 11. Calcutta: Government Printing Press, 1909.

Ali, Rajab. *Riyasat Jammu Kashmir ke Ta'alluqat Angrezi Government se*. Amritsar: The Vakil-e-Hind Press, 1887.

Ali, Shahamat. *The Sikhs and Afghans*. London: John Murray, 1847.

Arnold, Edwin. *The Marquis of Dalhousie's Administration of British India*. 2 vols. London: Saunders, Oxley, and Co., 1862, 1865.

Atkinson, James. *The Expedition into Affghanistan*. London: Wm. H. Allen and Co., 1842.

Azeem, Muhammad. *Tarikh-e-Kashmir*. Translated from the Persian by Munshi Ashraf Ali. Delhi: Delhi Madrasa, 1846.

Baird, J. G. A., ed. *Private Letters of the Marquess of Dalhousie*. London: William Blackwood and Sons, 1910.

Bajwa, Fauja Singh. *Military System of the Sikhs*. Delhi: Motilal Banarsidass, 1964.

Bamzai, Prithivi Nath Kaul. *A History of Kashmir*. Delhi: Metropolitan Book Co., 1962.

Banerjee, Anil Chandra. *Anglo-Sikh Relations*. Calcutta: A. Mukherjee and Co., Ltd., 1949.

Barr, William. *Journal of a March from Delhi to Peshawar*. London: James Madden and Co., 1844.

Bazaz, Prem Nath. *The History of Struggle for Freedom in Kashmir*. New Delhi: Kashmir Publishing Company, 1954.

Beg, Aziz. *Captive Kashmir*. Lahore: Allied Business Corporation, 1957.

Bell, Evans. *The Annexation of the Punjaub, and the Maharajah Duleep Singh*. London: Trubner and Co., 1882.

Beveridge, Henry. *A Comprehensive History of India*. Vol. 3. London: Blackie and Son, 1862.

Bhavnani, Enakshi. "A Journey to 'Little Tibet.'" *National Geographic Magazine* 99 (1951), 603–34.

Birdwood, Lord. *India and Pakistan*. New York: Frederick A. Praeger, 1954.

Boulger, Demetrius C. *Lord William Bentinck*. Oxford: Clarendon Press, 1897.

Brecher, Michael. *The Struggle for Kashmir*. New York: Oxford University Press, 1953.

A brief note on the Jammu and Kashmir State. Jammu: Shree Ranbir Prakash Government Press, 1927.

Broadfoot, William. *The Career of Major George Broadfoot*. London: John Murray, 1888.

Bruce, George. *Six Battles For India*. London: Arthur Barker, Ltd., 1969.

Burnes, Alexander. *Travels into Bokhara*. 2nd ed. 3 vols. London: John Murray, 1839.

Butler, William F. *Sir Charles Napier*. London: Macmillan and Co., 1890.

Catalogue of Khalsa Darbar Records. Compiled by Sita Ram Kohli. 2 vols. Lahore: Government Printing Press, 1919, 1927.

Cave-Brown, J. *The Punjab and Delhi in 1857*. 2 vols. Edinburgh: William Blackwood and Sons, 1861.

Chopra, Gulshan Lall. *The Panjab as a Sovereign State (1799–1839)*. Lahore: Uttar Chand Kapur and Sons, 1928.

Colchester, Lord, ed. *History of the Indian Administration of Lord Ellenborough*. London: Richard Bentley and Son, 1874.

Conolly, Arthur. *Journey to the North of India*. 2 vols. London: Richard Bentley, 1834.

Cork, Barry Joyson. *Rider On A Grey Horse*. London: Cassell and Company, 1958.

Cotton, Julian James. *General Avitabile*. Calcutta: Edinburgh Press, 1906.

Cunningham, Alexander. *Ladak*. London: Wm. H. Allen and Co., 1854.

Cunningham, Joseph Davey. *A History of the Sikhs*. London: John Murray, 1849.

Daly, Major H. *Memoirs of General Sir Henry Dermot Daly*. London: John Murray, 1905.

Davies, Cuthbert Collin. *The Problem of the North-West Frontier*. Cambridge: University Press, 1932.

Dhillon, H. S. "Taxation System." In *Maharaja Ranjit Singh Centenary Volume*. Edited by Teja Singh and Ganda Singh. Amritsar: Khalsa College, 1939.

Diver, Maud. *Honoria Lawrence*. Boston: Houghton Mifflin Company, 1936.

Dodwell, H. H., ed. *The Cambridge History of India*. Vol. 5. New Delhi: S. Chand and Co., 1963.

Douie, James. *The Panjab, North-West Province and Kashmir*. Cambridge: University Press, 1916.

Drew, Frederic. *The Northern Barrier of India*. London: Edward Stanford, 1877.

Eden, Emily. *Up the Country*. 2 vols. London: Richard Bentley, 1866.

————. *Up the Country*. Edited by Edward Thompson. London: Oxford University Press, 1937.

Edwardes, Emma. *Memorials of the Life and Letters of Major-General*

246
Bibliography

Sir Herbert B. Edwardes. 2 vols. London: Kegan, Paul, Trench, and Company, 1886.

Edwardes, Herbert Benjamin. *A Year on the Punjab Frontier, in 1848–49.* London: Richard Bentley, 1851.

Edwardes, Herbert Benjamin, and Merivale, Herman. *Life of Sir Henry Lawrence.* 2 vols. London: Smith, Elder, and Co., 1872. [3rd edition published as a single volume in 1873.]

Edwards, William. *Reminiscences of a Bengal Civilian.* London: Smith, Elder, and Co., 1866.

Everard, George, ed. *The Starry Crown, A Sketch of the Life Work of Harriett E. H. Urmston.* London: Hodder Stoughton, 1898.

Fane, Henry Edward. *Five Years In India.* 2 vols. London: Henry Colburn, 1842.

Ferguson, James P. *Kashmir.* London: Centaur Press, 1961.

Fisher, Margaret W., Rose, Leo E., and Huttenback, Robert A. *Himalayan Battleground.* New York: Frederick A. Praeger, 1963.

Forrest, George. *The Life of Lord Roberts.* London: Cassell and Company, 1914.

Fortescue, John William. *A History of the British Army.* Vol. 12. London: Macmillan and Company, 1927.

Francke, A. H. *A History of Western Tibet.* London: S. W. Patridge and Co., 1907.

Garrett, W. E. "Mountaintop War In Remote Ladakh." *National Geographic Magazine* 123 (1963), 664–86.

Gibbon, Frederick P. *The Lawrences of the Punjab.* London: J. M. Dent and Co., 1908.

Gordon, J. D. *Work and Play In India and Kashmir.* London: Eden, Remington, and Co., 1893.

Gordon, John H. *The Sikhs.* London: William Blackwood and Sons, 1904.

Gough, Charles, and Innes, Arthur D. *The Sikhs and the Sikh Wars.* London: A. D. Innes & Co., 1897.

Grey, C. *European Adventurers of Northern India, 1785 to 1849.* Edited by H. L. O. Garrett. Lahore: Government Printing Press, 1929.

Griffin, Lepel Henry. *Our North-west Frontier.* Allahabad: Pioneer Press, 1881.

————. *Punjab Chiefs.* Lahore: C. F. Massey, 1890.

————. *Ranjit Singh.* Oxford: Clarendon Press, 1911.

Gupta, Anil Chandra Das, ed. *The Days of John Company, Selections from Calcutta Gazette, 1824–1832.* Calcutta: West Bengal Government Press, 1959.

Gupta, Hari Ram, ed. *Panjab on the Eve of First Sikh War.* Hoshiarpur: University of Panjab, 1956.

————. "The Yusafzais and the Sikhs." In *Sir Jadunath Sarkar Commemorative Volume.* Edited by Hari Ram Gupta. Hoshiarpur: Panjab University, 1958.

Gupta, Sisir. *Kashmir, A Study in India-Pakistan Relations.* Bombay: Asia Publishing House, 1966.

Hansard's Parliamentary Debates. Vol. 84. London: G. Woodfall and Son, 1846.

Hardinge, Charles. *Recollections of India.* London: Thomas M'Lean, 1847.

——. *Viscount Hardinge.* Oxford: Clarendon Press, 1891.

Harlan, J. *A Memoir of India and Avfghanistaun.* Philadelphia: J. Dobson, 1842.

Hasrat, Bikrama Jit. *Anglo-Sikh Relations: 1799–1849.* Hoshiarpur: V. V. Research Institute Press, 1968.

Herze, P. B. "The Strategic Significance of Recent Events in Tibet." *Royal Central Asian Journal,* April 1953, pp. 169–73.

History of the Campaign on the Sutlej and the War in the Punjaub. London: Charles Edmonds, 1846.

History of the Panjab. 2 vols. London: Wm. H. Allen and Co., 1846.

The History of the Sikhs. Calcutta: D'rozario and Co., 1846.

Hodson, George H., ed. *Hodson of Hodson's Horse.* London: Kegan, Paul, Trench, and Co., 1883.

Honigberger, John Martin. *Thirty-Five Years in the East.* London: H. Bailliere, 1852. Reprint. Calcutta: Bangabasi Office, 1905.

House of Commons. *Further Papers relating to the Late Hostilities on the North-Western Frontier of India.* 1846.

——. *General Report on the Administration of the Punjab Territories, for 1856–57 and 1857–58.* 1859.

——. *A Minute by the Marquis of Dalhousie, dated February 28, 1856, reviewing his Administration of India from January, 1848, to March, 1856.* May 1856.

——. *Papers relating to Kashmir.* 1890.

——. *Papers relating to Sheikh Imam-ud-Din's rebellion in Kashmir.* February 1847.

——. *Papers relating to the Articles of Agreement concluded between the British Government and the Lahore Durbar.* March 1847.

——. *Papers relating to the Articles of Agreement for the Administration of the State of Lahore.* February 1847.

——. *Papers relating to the Late Hostilities on the North-Western Frontier of India.* February 1846.

——. *Papers relating to the Mutiny in the Punjab, in 1857.* 1859.

——. *Papers relating to the Punjab, 1847–49.* May 1849.

——. *Papers relating to the treaties of 1834 and 1838 between Ranjit Singh and Shah Shujah.* 1839.

Hugel, Baron Charles. *Travels in Kashmir and the Panjab.* London: John Petheram, 1845.

Humbley, W. W. W. *Journal of a Cavalry Officer.* London: Longman, Brown, Green, and Longmans, 1854.

Hunter, William Wilson. *The Marquess of Dalhousie.* Oxford: Clarendon Press, 1890.

Huttenback, Robert A. "Gulab Singh and the Creation of the Dogra State of Jammu, Kashmir, and Ladakh." *Journal of Asian Studies* 20 (1961), 477–88.

————. "Kashmir As An Imperial Factor During the Reign of Gulab Singh." *Journal of Asian History* 1 (1968), 77–108.

Illustrated London News. 1846–1849.

Imlah, Albert H. *Lord Ellenborough.* Cambridge: Harvard University Press, 1939.

India Under Lord Ellenborough. London: John Murray, 1926.

Innes, J. J. McLeod. *Sir Henry Lawrence.* Oxford: University Press, 1898.

Jacquemont, Victor. *Letters From India.* 2 vols. London: Edward Churton, 1834.

————. *Letters From India.* Translated from the French with an introduction by Catherine Alison Phillips. London: Macmillan and Co., Ltd., 1936.

Kak, R. C. "Jammu and Kashmir, 1836–1890." *The Asiatic Review,* January–October, 1937, pp. 775–849.

Kashmir-ke-Halaat. Qadian: Allah Baksh Steam Press, 1931.

Kaul, Gwasha Lal. *Kashmir Through the Ages.* Srinagar: Chronicle Publishing House, 1960.

Kaul, Har Gopal. *Guldasta-e-Kashmir.* Lahore: Farsi Arya Press, 1883.

Kaye, John William. *History of the War in Afghanistan.* 2 vols. London: Richard Bentley, 1851.

————. *Lives of Indian Officers.* 2 vols. London: A Strahan and Co., 1867.

Keightley, Thomas. *A History of India.* London: Whittaker and Co., 1847.

Khan, Hashmat Ali. *Tarikh-e-Jammu.* Lucknow: H. M. Ibrahim and Sons, 1939.

Khan, M. M. Rahman. *The United Nations and Kashmir.* New York: J. B. Wolters, 1956.

Khanna, K. C. "Raja Gulab Singh's Aim After 1839." In *Sir Jadunath Sarkar Commemorative Volume.* Edited by Hari Ram Gupta. Hoshiarpur: Panjab University Press, 1958.

Khilnani, N. M. *The Punjab Under the Lawrences.* Simla: Punjab Government Record Office, 1951.

Knight, E. F. *Where Three Empires Meet.* London: Longmans, Green, and Co., 1905.

Knollys, H., ed. *Life of General Sir Hope Grant.* 2 vols. London: William Blackwood and Sons, 1894.

Kohli, Sita Ram. "The Organization Of The Khalsa Army." In *Maharaja Ranjit Singh Centenary Volume.* Edited by Teja Singh and Ganda Singh. Amritsar: Khalsa College, 1939.

————. *Sunset of the Sikh Empire.* New Delhi: Orient Longmans, 1967.

Koul, Salig Ram. *The Biography of Maharaja Gulab Singh.* Srinagar: Salig Ram Press, 1923.

Lal, Ganeshi. *Tohfa-e-Kashmir.* Lahore: Koh-e-Nur Press, 1852.

Lal, Kanihya. *Tarikh-e-Panjab.* Lahore: Victoria Press, 1877.

Lamb, Alastair. *The China-India Border.* London: Oxford University Press, 1964.

————. *Crisis in Kashmir.* London: Routledge and Kegan Paul, 1966.

————. "Tibet in Anglo-Chinese Relations: 1767–1842." *Journal of the Royal Asiatic Society of Great Britain and Ireland*, 1958, pt. 2, pp. 26–43.

Latif, Muhammad. *History of the Panjab*. Calcutta: Central Press, 1891. Reprint. New Delhi: Eurasia Publishing House, 1964.

————. *Lahore: Its History, Architectural Remains and Antiquities*. Lahore: The New Imperial Press, 1892.

Lawrence, H. M. L. *Adventures of An Officer in The Panjaub*. 2 vols. London: Henry Colburn, 1846. Reprint. Delhi: Panjab National Press, 1970.

Lee-Warner, Williams. *The Life of the Marquess of Dalhousie*. 2 vols. London: Macmillan and Co., 1904.

————. *The Protected Princes of India*. London: Macmillan and Co., 1894.

Login, Lady Lena. *Sir John Logan and Duleep Singh*. London: Wm. H. Allen and Co., 1890.

Low, Charles Rathbone. *The Life and Correspondence of Field-Marshal Sir George Pollock*. London: Wm. H. Allen and Co., 1873.

M'Gregor, William Lewis. *The History of the Sikhs*. 2 vols. London: James Madden, 1846.

Madhok, Balraj. *Kashmir: Centre of New Alignments*. New Delhi: Deepak Prakashan, 1963.

Mahajan, Jagmohan. *Circumstances Leading to the Annexation of the Punjab*. Allahabad: Kitabistan, 1949.

The Maharaja of Kashmeer and his Calumniators. Tours: J. Bonserez, 1870.

Majumdar, R. C., Raychaudhuri, H. C., and Datta, K. *An Advanced History of India*. 2nd ed. London: Macmillan & Co., Ltd., 1963.

Malleson, G. B. *The Decisive Battles of India*. London: Wm. H. Allen and Co., 1883.

Marshman, John Clark. *The History of India*. 3 vols. London: Longmans, Green, Reader, and Dyer, 1867.

————. *Memoirs of Major-General Sir Henry Havelock*. London: Longman, Green, Longman, and Roberts, 1860.

Masson, Charles. *Narrative of Various Journeys in Balochistan, Afghanistan, and the Panjab*. 3 vols. London: Richard Bentley, 1842.

Moorcroft, William, and Trebeck, George. *Travels in the Himalayan Provinces of Hindustan and the Panjab*. 2 vols. London: John Murray, 1841.

Morison, John L. *Lawrence of Lucknow*. London: G. Bell and Sons, Ltd., 1934.

Napier, William. *The Life and Opinions of General Sir Charles James Napier*. 4 vols. London: John Murray, 1857.

————. *Minutes on the Resignation of the late General Sir Charles Napier*. London: Charles Westerton, 1854.

Nargis, Narsingdas. *Zorawar Singh*. Jammu: Chand Publishing House, 1964.

Nath, Amar. *Zafarnama-e-Ranjit Singh*. Edited by Sita Ram Kohli. Lahore: Panjab University, 1928.

A note on the Jammu and Kashmir State. Jammu: Ranbir Printing Press, 1928.

Orlich, Leopold von. *Travels in India including Sinde and the Punjab*. Translated from the German by H. Evans Lloyd. 2 vols. London: Longman, Brown, Green, and Longmans, 1845.

Osborne, William Godolphin. *The Court And Camp of Runjeet Sing*. London: Henry Colburn, 1840.

Panikkar, K. M. *Gulab Singh*. London: Martin Hopkinson, 1930. [Reprinted by George Allen and Unwin in 1953 under the title *The Founding of the Kashmir State*.]

Parry, E. Gambier. *Reynell Taylor*. London: Kegan, Paul, Trench & Co., 1888.

Parshad, Debi. *Gulshan-e-Panjab*. Bareilly: Bareilly Press, 1850.

Payne, Charles Herbert. *A History of the Sikhs*. London: T. Nelson and Sons, 1915.

Pearse, Hugh, ed. *Memoirs of Alexander Gardner*. Edinburgh: William Blackwood and Sons, 1898.

Pearson, Hesketh. *The Hero of Delhi*. London: Collins, 1939.

Peshawari, Mohammad Naqi. "Sher Singh Nama." Translated from the Persian by Vidya Sagar Suri. *The Panjab University Historical Society Journal* 8 (1944).

Prinsep, Henry T. *Origin of the Sikh Power in the Punjab*. Calcutta: Military Orphan Press, 1834.

Rait, Robert S. *The Life and Campaigns of First Viscount Field-Marshal Gough*. 2 vols. London: Archibald Constable and Company, 1903.

—————. *The Life of Field-Marshal Sir Frederick Paul Haines*. London: Constable and Co., 1911.

Ram, Anant. *Report Majmuee Intzaam Mumalik Riyasat Jammu-va-Kashmir-va-Tibet-va-Ladakh*. Lahore: Koh-e-Nur Press, 1892.

Ram, Babu. *Mukhtsar-Sair-Gulshan-e-Hind*. Kanpur: Munshi Nawal Kishore, 1878.

Ram, Kirpa. *Gulzar-e-Kashmir*. Lahore: Koh-e-Nur Press, 1870.

Roberts, Field Marshal Frederick S. R. *Forty-one Years in India*. 2 vols. London: Richard Bentley and Sons, 1897.

Ross, David. *The Land of Five Rivers and Sindh*. London: Chapman and Hall, 1883.

St. John, Horace. *History of the British Conquests in India*. 2 vols. London: Colburn and Co., 1852.

Sapru, Arjun Nath. *The Building of the Jammu and Kashmir State— Being The Achievement of Maharaja Gulab Singh*. Lahore: Punjab Government Record Office, 1931.

Shadwell, General. *The Life of Colin Campbell, Lord Clyde*. 2 vols. Edinburgh: Blackwood and Sons, 1881.

Singh, Bawa Satinder. "Raja Gulab Singh's Role in the First Anglo-Sikh War." *Modern Asian Studies* 5 (1971), 35–59.

Singh, Ganda. *A brief account of the Sikh People*. Madras: G. S. Press, 1959.

—————., ed. *The Panjab In 1839–40*. Patiala: The New Age Press, 1952.

—————., ed. *Private Correspondence relating to the Anglo-Sikh Wars*. Madras: G. S. Press, 1955.

Singh, Kahan. *Tarikh-e-Rajgan Jammu-va-Kashmir*. Lahore: Dewan Printing Press, 1932.

Singh, Khushwant. *The Fall of the Kingdom of the Punjab*. Calcutta: Orient Longmans, 1962.

—————. *A History of the Sikhs*. 2 vols. Princeton: University Press, 1963, 1966.

—————. *Ranjit Singh*. London: George Allen and Unwin, Ltd., 1962.

Sinha, Narendra Krishna. *Ranjit Singh*. Calcutta: A Mukherjee and Co., 1951.

Smith, George. *Twelve Indian Statesmen*. London: John Murray, 1897.

Smith, Lt. General Sir Harry. *Autobiography*. Edited by G. C. Moore Smith. 2 vols. London: John Murray, 1901.

Smith, R. Bosworth. *Life of Lord Lawrence*. 2nd ed. 2 vols. London: Smith, Elder, and Company, 1883.

Smyth, G. Carmichael, ed. *A History of the Reigning Families of Lahore*. Calcutta: W. Thacker and Co., 1847.

Steinbach, Henry. *The Punjaub: being a brief account of the country of the Sikhs*. London: Smith, Elder, and Co., 1845.

Storey, C. A. *Persian Literature. A Bio-Bibliographical Survey*. London: Luzac and Co., 1936.

Strachey, H. "Physical Geography of Western Tibet." *The Journal of the Royal Geographical Society* 23 (1853), 1–69.

Suri, Vidya Sagar, ed. *Siyahat-i-Kashmir*. Simla: Controller of Printing and Stationery, Punjab, 1955.

Taylor, Lucy. *The Story of Sir Henry Lawrence*. London: T. Nelson and Sons, 1894.

Thackwell, Edward Joseph. *Narrative of the Second Sikh War, in 1848–49*. London: Richard Bentley, 1851.

Thomson, Thomas. *Western Himalaya and Tibet*. London: Reeve and Co., 1852.

Thornton, Edward. *A Gazetteer of the Countries Adjacent to India on the North-West*. 2 vols. London: Wm. H. Allen and Co., 1844.

Thorp, Robert. *Cashmere Misgovernment*. Calcutta: Wyman Brothers, 1868.

Thorburn, Septimus S. *The Punjab in Peace and War*. London: William Blackwood and Sons, 1904.

The *Times* (London). 1846–1849.

Trevaskis, Hugh Kennedy. *The Land of the Five Rivers*. London: Oxford University Press, 1928.

Trotter, Henry. "Account of the Pundit's Journey in Great Tibet from Leh in Ladakh to Lhasa, and of his Return to India via Assam." *Journal of the Royal Geographic Society* 47 (1877), 86–136.

Trotter, Lionel James. *The Earl of Auckland.* Oxford: Clarendon Press, 1893.

——. *History of India Under Queen Victoria from 1836 to 1880.* 2 vols. London: Wm. H. Allen and Co., 1886.

——. *Life of Hodson of Hodson's Horse.* London: William Blackwood and Sons, 1901.

——. *The Life of John Nicholson.* London: John Murray, 1897.

——. *The Life of Marquis of Dalhousie.* London: Wm. H. Allen and Co., 1889.

Vigne, Godfrey Thomas. *A Personal Narrative of a visit to Ghuzni, Kabul, and Afghanistan.* 2nd ed. London: George, Routledge, and Co., 1843.

——. *Travels In Kashmir, Ladak, Iskardo, etc.* 2 vols. London: Henry Colburn, 1842.

The War In India. London: John Ollivier, 1846.

"The War of the Punjab." *The Quarterly Review* 38 (1846), 175–215.

Younghusband, Francis. *Kashmir.* London: A. & C. Black, Ltd., 1909. Reprint 1917.

Unpublished Manuscripts

Digby, William. "Condemned Unheard." Typescript in the Kashmir Government Archives, Srinagar. 1890.

Singh, Bawa Satinder. "Gulab Singh of Jammu, Ladakh, and Kashmir, 1792–1846." Ph.D. dissertation, University of Wisconsin, 1966.

Index

092009